Taking action:
achieving gender equality and empowering women

Lead authors
Caren Grown
Geeta Rao Gupta, Coordinator
Aslihan Kes

UN Millennium Project
Task Force on Education and Gender Equality
2005

EARTHSCAN
London • Sterling, Va.

First published by Earthscan in the UK and USA in 2005

Reprinted 2005
Copyright © 2005
by the United Nations Development Programme
All rights reserved

ISBN: 1-84407-222-3 paperback

For a full list of publications please contact:

Earthscan
8–12 Camden High Street
London, NW1 0JH, UK
Tel: +44 (0)20 7387 8558
Fax: +44 (0)20 7387 8998
Email: earthinfo@earthscan.co.uk
Web: www.earthscan.co.uk
22883 Quicksilver Drive, Sterling, VA 20166-2012, USA

Earthscan is an imprint of James and James (Science Publishers) Ltd and publishes in association with the International Institute for Environment and Development

A catalogue record for this book is available from the British Library

Library of Congress Cataloging-in-Publication Data

A catalog record has been requested

This publication should be cited as: UN Millennium Project 2005. *Taking Action: Achieving Gender Equality and Empowering Women.* Task Force on Education and Gender Equality.

Photos: Front cover Giacomo Pirozzi/Panos Pictures; back cover, top to bottom, Christopher Dowswell, Pedro Cote/ UNDP, Giacomo Pirozzi/Panos Pictures, Liba Taylor/Panos Pictures, Jørgen Schytte/UNDP, UN Photo Library, Giacomo Pirozzi/UNICEF, Curt Carnemark/World Bank, Pedro Cote/UNDP, Franck Charton/UNICEF, Paul Chesley/Getty Images, Ray Witlin/World Bank, Pete Turner/Getty Images.

This book was edited, designed, and produced by Communications Development Incorporated, Washington, D.C., and its UK design partner, Grundy & Northedge.

The Millennium Project was commissioned by the UN Secretary-General and sponsored by the UN Development Group, which is chaired by the Administrator of the United Nations Development Programme. The report is an independent publication that reflects the views of the members of the Task Force on Education and Gender Equality, who contributed in their personal capacity. This publication does not necessarily reflect the views of the United Nations, the United Nations Development Programme, or their Member States.

Printed in Malta by Gutenberg Press on elemental chlorine-free paper

Foreword

The world has an unprecedented opportunity to improve the lives of billions of people by adopting practical approaches to meeting the Millennium Development Goals. At the request of the UN Secretary-General Kofi Annan, the UN Millennium Project has identified practical strategies to eradicate poverty by scaling up investments in infrastructure and human capital while promoting gender equality and environmental sustainability. These strategies are described in the UN Millennium Project's report *Investing in Development: A Practical Plan to Achieve the Millennium Development Goals,* which was coauthored by the coordinators of the UN Millennium Project task forces.

The task forces have identified the interventions and policy measures needed to achieve each of the Goals. In *Taking Action: Achieving Gender Equality and Empowerment of Women,* the Task Force on Education and Gender Equality underscores the need to place women's empowerment at the center of development plans—an emphasis that is shared by *Investing in Development.* There can be no development, and no lasting peace on the planet, if women continue to be relegated to subservient and often dangerous and back-breaking roles in society. This report explains why gender equality is vital for achieving all of the Millennium Development Goals. Women carry the brunt of poverty. They support and care for their families. They sustain life by collecting food, fuel, and water.

It is time for development practice not only to honor those life-sustaining roles, but to promote women's rights, empowerment, and leadership actively at the center of economic development. This report shows how to do this in practical terms. It argues persuasively for policies and actions to guarantee universal access to sexual and reproductive health and rights, invest in infrastructure to reduce women's time and work burdens, guarantee women's and girls' property and inheritance rights, reduce gender gaps in employment and wages, increase women's political participation, and combat violence against women. *Taking Action* presents compelling evidence and sound analysis to show that these priorities are essential and achievable.

This report was prepared by a group of leading experts who contributed in their personal capacity and generously volunteered their time to this important task. I am very grateful for their thorough and skilled efforts, and I am sure that the practical options for action in this report will make an important contribution to achieving the Millennium Development Goals. I strongly recommend this remarkable report to all and look forward to the implementation of its wise and valuable recommendations.

Jeffrey D. Sachs
New York
January 17, 2005

Contents

Boxes

Figures

Tables

Task force members

Task force coordinators

Nancy Birdsall, President, Center for Global Development, United States

Amina Ibrahim, National Coordinator, Education for All, Federal Ministry of Education, Nigeria

Geeta Rao Gupta, President, International Center for Research on Women, United States

Task force members

Charles Abani, Country Director, ActionAid International, Nigeria

Carmen Barroso, Regional Director, Western Hemisphere Region, International Planned Parenthood Federation, United States

Barbara Bruns, Lead Economist, Human Development Network, World Bank, United States

Mayra Buvinic, Chief, Social Development Division, Sustainable Development Department, Inter-American Development Bank, United States

Winnie Byanyima, Director, Women, Gender and Development, African Union, Ethiopia

Jennifer Chiwela, Executive Director, People's Action Forum, Zambia

Christopher Colclough, Professor, Economics of Education, Director, Centre for Commonwealth Education, University of Cambridge, United Kingdom

Diane Elson, Professor, Global Social Change and Human Rights, University of Essex, United Kingdom; Senior Scholar and Director, Gender Equality and the Economy, Levy Economics Institute, Bard College, United States

Tamara Fox, Program Officer, Population Program, William and Flora Hewlett Foundation, United States

Carolyn Hannan, Director, Division for the Advancement of Women, United Nations Department of Economic and Social Affairs, United States

Noeleen Heyzer, Executive Director, United Nations Development Fund for Women, United States

Ruth Kagia, Director, Education Network, World Bank, United States

Lin Lean Lim, Deputy Regional Director, Regional Office for Asia and the Pacific, International Labour Organization, Thailand

Nora Lustig, President, Universidad de las Américas, México

Karen Mason, Director, Gender and Development, World Bank, United States

Arlene Mitchell, Chief, School Feeding Service, Policy, Strategy and Program Support Division, World Food Programme, Italy

Penina Mlama, Executive Director, Forum for African Women Educationalists, Kenya

Mary Joy Pigozzi, Director, Division for the Promotion of Quality Education, United Nations Educational, Scientific and Cultural Organization, France

Magaly Pineda, Founder and Coordinator, Centro de Investigación para la Acción Femenina, Dominican Republic

Anastasia Posadskaya-Vanderbeck, Director, Network Women's Program, Open Society Institute, United States

Paulo Renato Souza, President and Founder, Paulo Renato Souza Consultants, Brazil

Richard Sabot, Professor Emeritus, Economics, Williams College; Chairman of the Board and Cofounder, Eziba.com, United States

Gita Sen, Sir Ratan Tata Chair Professor, Indian Institute of Management, India; Founding Member, Development Alternatives with Women for a New Era

Gorgui Sow, Coordinator, Education Specialist, Africa Network Campaign for Education for All, Senegal

Gene Sperling, Director, Center for Universal Education, Council on Foreign Relations, United States

Albert Tuijnman, Senior Economist, Human Capital, European Investment Bank, Luxembourg

Cream Wright, Chief, Education Section, United Nations Children's Fund, United States

Senior task force associates

Caren Grown, Director, Poverty Reduction and Economic Governance Team, International Center for Research on Women, United States

Ruth Levine, Director of Programs and Senior Fellow, Center for Global Development, United States

Preface

At the Millennium Summit in 2000 the 189 member states of the United Nations made a commitment in the Millennium Declaration to achieve eight goals, now referred to as the Millennium Development Goals (see Goals on p. xviii). Goal 3 is to promote gender equality and empower women. In setting this goal, the UN member states recognized the contributions that women make to economic development and the costs to societies of the multiple disadvantages that women face in nearly every country.

To accelerate progress toward achievement of the Millennium Development Goals, UN Secretary-General Kofi Annan and United Nations Development Programme (UNDP) Administrator Mark Malloch Brown launched the UN Millennium Project, a three-year effort to identify the best strategies for meeting the Millennium Development Goals, including identification of priorities, strategies, organizational means, and costs of meeting the Goals. The project's ultimate objective is to help ensure that all developing countries meet the Goals.

Most of the project's analytical work has been carried out by 10 task forces whose members represent the UN system, academia, civil society organizations, and other private and public sector groups. Membership of the Task Force on Education and Gender Equality, which produced this report (and the companion report on Goal 2 for primary education), is diverse and includes presidents and directors of nongovernmental organizations in India, Nigeria, Kenya, the United States, and Zambia; leaders of activist groups in the Dominican Republic and Kenya; academic scholars in Luxembourg, the United Kingdom, and the United States; parliamentary and government officials in Brazil, Nigeria, and Uganda; and directors at the UNDP, United Nations Children's Fund, United Nations Development Fund for Women, United Nations Educational, Scientific and Cultural Organization, Inter-American Development

Bank, International Labour Organization, UN Division for the Advancement of Women, World Bank, and World Food Programme; and sectoral experts from other agencies.

Because the task force members recognize the importance of giving adequate attention to both the gender and education goals, the work was divided into those two areas, with members focusing on one or both of the goals, depending on their backgrounds and interests. The result is two reports—this one on gender equality and women's empowerment, and a companion report on universal primary education (UN Millennium Project 2005c). Although distinct in focus, the reports are complementary in perspective and recommendations.

The main audience for this report is the United Nations system and donor development agencies, policymakers at the national level, and women's advocacy organizations.

Acknowledgments

The authors would like to express thanks to the following individuals. Kavita Sethuraman (International Center for Research on Women), Ruth Levine (Center for Global Development), Chandrika Bahadur (UN Millennium Project), Mayra Buvinic (Inter-American Development Bank), Karen Mason (World Bank), Diane Elson (University of Essex), Christopher Colclough (University of Cambridge), Joanne Sandler (United Nations Development Fund for Women), Carolyn Hannan (United Nations Department of Economic and Social Affairs), and Akanksha Marphatia (ActionAid International) prepared analysis and material used in several chapters. In addition, the report has adapted material, as indicated, from papers by Carmen Barroso and Francoise Girard, Mala Htun, Vijay Modi, Joann Vanck, and Caroline Moser and Annalise Moser. The task force gratefully acknowledges the assistance of Suzan Atwood and Elizabeth Nicoletti in the production of the background paper, interim report, and final report. Nata Duvvury and Hema Swaminathan, and members of the Task Force on Education and Gender Equality provided valuable input into and comments on various drafts. The report was edited and produced by Meta de Coquereaumont, Bruce Ross-Larson, Mary Goundrey, Thomas Roncoli, Christopher Trott, and Elaine Wilson of Communications Development Incorporated.

The task force gratefully acknowledges constructive comments from participants in an online consultation facilitated by ActionAid International (appendix 6) and feedback from participants at numerous conferences and workshops at which earlier drafts of this report were presented. The UN Commission on the Status of Women, the United Nations Development Fund for Women, the United Nations Development Programme, the Asian Development Bank, the World Bank, the Inter-American Development Bank, the Economic Commission for Latin American and the Caribbean, the Commonwealth Secretariat, the Organisation for Economic Co-operation and Development/Development Assistance Committee, Interaction, the University of Utah, American University, and the International Association for Feminist Economics all generously provided opportunities for task force members to present and discuss the ideas in this report with a broader audience.

Abbreviations

AGI	Alan Guttmacher Institute
CEDAW	Convention on the Elimination of All Forms of Discrimination against Women
CRC	Convention on the Rights of the Child
DALY	disability-adjusted life years
DDS	Deccan Development Society
GNP	gross national product
IDB	Inter-American Development Bank
OECD	Organisation for Economic Co-operation and Development
NGO	nongovernmental organization
PEM	Minimum Employment Program
POJH	Employment Program for Household Heads
SEWA	Self-Employed Women's Association
UNAIDS	Joint United Nations Programme on HIV/AIDS
UNIFEM	United Nations Development Fund for Women
UIS	UNESCO Institute for Statistics

goals

Millennium Development Goals

Goal 1

Eradicate extreme poverty and hunger

Target 1.
Halve, between 1990 and 2015, the proportion of people whose income is less than $1 a day

Target 2.
Halve, between 1990 and 2015, the proportion of people who suffer from hunger

Goal 2

Achieve universal primary education

Target 3.
Ensure that, by 2015, children everywhere, boys and girls alike, will be able to complete a full course of primary schooling

Goal 3

Promote gender equality and empower women

Target 4.
Eliminate gender disparity in primary and secondary education, preferably by 2005, and in all levels of education no later than 2015

Goal 4

Reduce child mortality

Target 5.
Reduce by two-thirds, between 1990 and 2015, the under-five mortality rate

Goal 5

Improve maternal health

Target 6.
Reduce by three-quarters, between 1990 and 2015, the maternal mortality ratio

Goal 6

Combat HIV/AIDS, malaria, and other diseases

Target 7.
Have halted by 2015 and begun to reverse the spread of HIV/AIDS

Target 8.
Have halted by 2015 and begun to reverse the incidence of malaria and other major diseases

Goal 7	

Ensure environmental sustainability

Target 9.
Integrate the principles of sustainable development into country policies and programs and reverse the loss of environmental resources

Target 10.
Halve, by 2015, the proportion of people without sustainable access to safe drinking water and basic sanitation

Target 11.
Have achieved by 2020 a significant improvement in the lives of at least 100 million slum dwellers

Goal 8	

Develop a global partnership for development

Target 12.
Develop further an open, rule-based, predictable, nondiscriminatory trading and financial system (includes a commitment to good governance, development, and poverty reduction—both nationally and internationally)

Target 13.
Address the special needs of the Least Developed Countries (includes tariff- and quota-free access for Least Developed Countries' exports, enhanced program of debt relief for heavily indebted poor countries [HIPCs] and cancellation of official bilateral debt, and more generous official development assistance for countries committed to poverty reduction)

Target 14.
Address the special needs of landlocked developing countries and small island developing states (through the Program of Action for the Sustainable Development of Small Island Developing States and 22nd General Assembly provisions)

Target 15.
Deal comprehensively with the debt problems of developing countries through national and international measures in order to make debt sustainable in the long term

Some of the indicators listed below are monitored separately for the least developed countries, Africa, landlocked developing countries, and small island developing states

Target 16.
In cooperation with developing countries, develop and implement strategies for decent and productive work for youth

Target 17.
In cooperation with pharmaceutical companies, provide access to affordable essential drugs in developing countries

Target 18.
In cooperation with the private sector, make available the benefits of new technologies, especially information and communications technologies

Executive summary

How can the global community achieve the goal of gender equality and the empowerment of women? This question is the focus of Goal 3 of the Millennium Development Goals endorsed by world leaders at the UN Millennium Summit in 2000 and of this report, prepared by the UN Millennium Project Task Force on Education and Gender Equality.

The report argues that there are many practical steps that can reduce inequalities based on gender, inequalities that constrain the potential to reduce poverty and achieve high levels of well-being in societies around the world. There are also many positive actions that can be taken to empower women. Without leadership and political will, however, the world will fall short of taking these practical steps—and meeting the goal. Because gender inequality is deeply rooted in entrenched attitudes, societal institutions, and market forces, political commitment at the highest international and national levels is essential to institute the policies that can trigger social change and to allocate the resources necessary to achieve gender equality and women's empowerment.

Many decades of organizing and advocacy by women's organizations and networks across the world have resulted in global recognition of the contributions that women make to economic development and of the costs to societies of persistent inequalities between women and men. The success of those efforts is evident in the promises countries have made over the past two decades through international forums. The inclusion of gender equality and women's empowerment as the third Millennium Development Goal is a reminder that many of those promises have not been kept, while simultaneously offering yet another international policy opportunity to implement them.

The task force perspective

The task force affirms that gender equality and women's empowerment are central to the achievement of all the Millennium Development Goals. Development

Achieving Goal 3
depends on the
extent to which
the priorities
suggested here
are addressed
and the extent
to which actions
taken to achieve
the other Goals
are designed
to promote
equality

policies and actions that fail to take gender inequality into account or that fail to enable women to be actors in those policies and actions will have limited effectiveness and serious costs to societies. The reverse is also true: the achievement of Goal 3 depends on the extent to which each of the other goals addresses gender-based constraints and issues.

This task force believes that ultimate success in achieving Goal 3 depends both on the extent to which the priorities suggested here are addressed and the extent to which the actions taken to achieve the other Goals are designed to promote equality of men and women and boys and girls. While this interdependence among the Goals is important, the task force wishes to underscore that Goal 3 has intrinsic value in itself. That is why the report focuses on priorities and actions to achieve Goal 3.

Like race and ethnicity, gender is a social construct. It defines and differentiates the roles, rights, responsibilities, and obligations of women and men. The innate biological differences between females and males form the basis of social norms that define appropriate behaviors for women and men and that determine women's and men's differential social, economic, and political power.

The task force has adopted an operational framework of gender equality with three dimensions:

- The *capabilities domain*, which refers to basic human abilities as measured by education, health, and nutrition. These capabilities are fundamental to individual well-being and are the means through which individuals access other forms of well-being.
- The *access to resources and opportunities domain*, which refers primarily to equality in the opportunity to use or apply basic capabilities through access to economic assets (such as land or housing) and resources (such as income and employment), as well as political opportunity (such as representation in parliaments and other political bodies). Without access to resources and opportunities, both political and economic, women will be unable to employ their capabilities for their well-being and that of their families, communities, and societies.
- The *security domain*, which is defined to mean reduced vulnerability to violence and conflict. Violence and conflict result in physical and psychological harm and lessen the ability of individuals, households, and communities to fulfill their potential. Violence directed specifically at women and girls often aims at keeping them in "their place" through fear.

These three domains are interrelated. Change in all three is critical to achieving Goal 3. The attainment of capabilities increases the likelihood that women can access opportunities for employment or participate in political and legislative bodies but does not guarantee it. Similarly, access to opportunity decreases the likelihood that women will experience violence (although in certain circumstances, it may temporarily increase that likelihood). Progress in

Seven interdependent priorities are the minimum necessary to empower women and alter the historical legacy of female disadvantage

any one domain to the exclusion of the others will be insufficient to meet the goal of gender equality.

The concept of empowerment is related to gender equality but distinct from it. The core of empowerment lies in the ability of a woman to control her own destiny (Malhotra, Schuler, and Boender 2002; Kabeer 1999). This implies that to be empowered women must not only have equal capabilities (such as education and health) and equal access to resources and opportunities (such as land and employment), they must also have the agency to use those rights, capabilities, resources, and opportunities to make strategic choices and decisions (such as are provided through leadership opportunities and participation in political institutions). And to exercise agency, women must live without the fear of coercion and violence.

The seven strategic priorities

To ensure that Goal 3 is met by 2015, the task force has identified seven strategic priorities. These seven interdependent priorities are the minimum necessary to empower women and alter the historical legacy of female disadvantage that remains in most societies of the world:

1. Strengthen opportunities for postprimary education for girls while simultaneously meeting commitments to universal primary education.
2. Guarantee sexual and reproductive health and rights.
3. Invest in infrastructure to reduce women's and girls' time burdens.
4. Guarantee women's and girls' property and inheritance rights.
5. Eliminate gender inequality in employment by decreasing women's reliance on informal employment, closing gender gaps in earnings, and reducing occupational segregation.
6. Increase women's share of seats in national parliaments and local governmental bodies.
7. Combat violence against girls and women.

These seven priorities are a subset of the priorities outlined in previous international agreements, including the Cairo Programme of Action and the Beijing Declaration and Platform for Action. The recommendations made in these international agreements remain important for achieving gender equality and women's empowerment, but the task force sees the seven priorities as areas needing immediate action if Goal 3 is to be met by 2015. Although empowerment and equality should be enjoyed by all women and men, the task force believes that action on the seven priorities is particularly important for three subpopulations of women:

- Poor women in the poorest countries and in countries that have achieved increases in national income, but where poverty remains significant.
- Adolescents, who constitute two-thirds of the population in the poorest countries and the largest cohort of adolescents in the world's history.
- Women and girls in conflict and postconflict settings.

**Gender
inequalities
exist among
the rich and
the poor, but
they tend to be
greater among
the poor**

A focus on poor women is justified for several reasons. Gender inequalities exist among the rich and the poor, but they tend to be greater among the poor, especially for inequalities in capabilities and opportunities. Moreover, the well-being and survival of poor households depend on the productive and reproductive contributions of their female members. Also, an increasing number of poor households are headed or maintained by women. A focus on poor women is therefore central to reducing poverty.

Investing in the health, education, safety, and economic well-being of adolescents, especially adolescent girls, must also be a priority. Adolescence is a formative period between childhood and adulthood. It is a time when interventions can dramatically alter subsequent life outcomes. Additionally, the sheer size of the current adolescent cohort in poor countries means that interventions to improve their lives will affect national outcomes. The task force has given priority to the needs of adolescent girls because in most countries they experience greater social, economic, and health disadvantages than boys do. Therefore, investments to help girls complete good quality secondary schooling, support their transition from education to work, develop healthy sexuality, and guarantee their physical safety are urgently needed and can simultaneously accelerate progress toward several of the Millennium Development Goals.

Responding to these strategic priorities is particularly urgent for women in conflict and postconflict situations. Situations of conflict have disproportionate impacts on women and children, who are typically the majority of displaced persons in refugee camps and conflict zones. Postconflict periods present a window of opportunity for reducing gender barriers and creating a gender-equitable society, which is more likely to occur if the reconstruction process fosters the full participation of women.

Strategic priority 1: strengthen opportunities for postprimary education for girls while simultaneously meeting commitments to universal primary education

Gender parity in access to schooling is the first step toward gender equality in education. However, the world is still far from achieving gender parity in enrollment and completion rates, particularly at the secondary school level. A review of trends shows that gender parity ratios remain below 0.90 in Sub-Saharan African and South Asia even though girls' primary school enrollment rates rose steadily over the 1990s and are now relatively high. While the trends at the primary level are positive, a number of countries are likely to miss both the 2005 and 2015 Millennium Development Targets. Projections are for 19 of 133 countries to have girls' to boys' primary enrollment ratios in the 0.70–0.89 range in 2005 and for 21 countries to have ratios below 0.9 in 2015. Twelve countries in this second group are in Sub-Saharan Africa, which should be viewed as a "priority" region for interventions.

The achievement of Goal 3 requires strengthening postprimary education opportunities for girls

The picture is less hopeful if primary school completion is used as the indicator. In 1990 boys completed primary school at a higher rate than girls in all regions of the world except Latin America and the Caribbean. In South Asia the difference was almost 14 percentage points in favor of boys, while in the Middle East and North Africa and Europe and Central Asia, boys' completion rates were about 11 percentage points ahead of girls'. Despite these gender gaps, there have been improvements in girls completion in all regions since 1990, and narrowing of the gender gap has been due mostly to increases in girls' completion rates.

Less encouraging is progress at the secondary school level. Across the world there is greater variation in enrollment rates at the secondary than at the primary level. Once again, South Asia and Sub-Saharan Africa fare poorly, with gender parity ratios below 0.90. East Asia and the Pacific, Europe and Central Asia, and the Middle East and North Africa have a gender parity ratio above 0.90. Latin America and the Caribbean and developed countries have reverse gender gaps (girls' to boys' enrollment ratios higher than 1).

A closer look at the numbers, however, shows that girls' enrollment rates are still low in most regions. Although 78 of 149 countries for which there are data have girls' to boys' secondary enrollment ratios of 1.0 or greater in 2000, only 33 of the 78 countries have female enrollment rates above 90 percent. In South Asia the female secondary enrollment rate is 47.1 percent and in Sub Saharan Africa it is only 29.7 percent.

Country projections for gender parity in secondary education show that 24 of 118 countries are expected to have gender parity ratios below 0.90 in 2005. That number rises to 27 in 2015. These results suggest that achieving gender parity at high levels of enrollment will take concerted national and international action.

Global commitments to girls' education have focused in the main on primary education. While this focus must continue, and international commitments to universal primary education must be met, the task force notes that the achievement of Goal 3 requires strengthening postprimary education opportunities for girls. This focus is justified for several reasons.

First, the 2005 target for Goal 3 will be missed for both primary and secondary education but by a larger number of countries for secondary education. Second, evidence suggests that among all levels of education, secondary and higher levels of education have the greatest payoff for women's empowerment. These empowering effects are manifested in a variety of ways, including increased income-earning potential, ability to bargain for resources within the household, decisionmaking autonomy, control over their own fertility, and participation in public life. Third, focusing on secondary education can strengthen the pipeline that channels students through the education system and give parents an incentive to send their children to primary school. Primary, secondary, and tertiary education are not separate components but are an integral part of an education system.

Sexual and reproductive health and rights are central to women's ability to build their capabilities

For all these reasons the task force believes that achieving Goal 3 requires strengthening postprimary education opportunities for girls and that this can be achieved without wavering from the global commitments to universal primary education.

A number of interventions that have proven effective for increasing girls' participation in primary school may also apply to postprimary education. These include making schooling more affordable by reducing costs and offering targeted scholarships, building secondary schools close to girls' homes, and making schools girl-friendly. Additionally, the content, quality, and relevance of education must be improved through curriculum reform, teacher training, and other actions. Education must serve as the vehicle for transforming attitudes, beliefs, and entrenched social norms that perpetuate discrimination and inequality. All interventions taken to promote gender equality in education must, therefore, be transformational in nature.

Strategic priority 2: guarantee sexual and reproductive health and rights

Goal 3 cannot be achieved without the guarantee of sexual and reproductive health and rights for girls and women. A large body of evidence shows that sexual and reproductive health and rights are central to women's ability to build their capabilities, take advantage of economic and political opportunities, and control their destinies. Conversely, gender inequality that restricts women's access to economic resources compromises their sexual and reproductive autonomy. For this reason, the task force has identified guaranteeing sexual and reproductive health and rights as a strategic priority for achieving gender equality and empowering women.

Maternal mortality rates are high, particularly in developing countries where women's chances of dying from pregnancy-related complications are almost 50 times greater than in developed countries. Women's unmet need for contraception is also high. One-fifth of married women in the Middle East and North Africa and one-quarter of married women in Sub-Saharan Africa are unable to access the contraception they need. Iron-deficiency anemia is also widespread, affecting 50–70 percent of pregnant women in developing countries. Severe anemia has been shown to be associated with postpartum hemorrhage and is thought to be an underlying factor in maternal mortality. Women are also more vulnerable than men to sexually transmitted infections, particularly HIV/AIDS. Today, almost 50 percent of the HIV-infected adults worldwide are women, and in Sub-Saharan Africa, that proportion is 57 percent.

Adolescent girls are particularly vulnerable to a range of sexual and reproductive health problems. In Sub-Saharan Africa about 75 percent of those ages 15–24 who are infected with HIV are women. Many sexually active adolescents do not use contraception. Of the roughly 260 million women ages 15–19 worldwide, both married and unmarried, about 11 percent (29 million) are sexually active and do not want to become pregnant but are not using a modern method

Women's and girls' ability to participate in educational, productive, and civic activities is limited by a household division of labor that assigns them the bulk of responsibility for every day maintenance tasks

of birth control. Underdeveloped physiology, combined with a lack of power, information, and access to services, means that young women experience much higher levels of maternal illness and death than do women who bear children when they are older. Their limited negotiating power exposes them to greater risk of sexually transmitted infection, especially in the common instance of having partners who are much older and more sexually experienced.

According to the World Health Organization's 2001 estimates, sexual and reproductive health problems account for 18 percent of the global burden of disease and 32 percent of the burden among women ages 15–44. By comparison, neuropsychiatric conditions account for 13 percent of all disability adjusted life years lost, respiratory illnesses for 11 percent, and cardiovascular diseases for 10 percent. Moreover, investing in reproductive and sexual health services is cost effective. An early study in Mexico found that every peso the Mexican social security system spent on family planning services during 1972–1984 saved nine pesos for treating complications of unsafe abortion and providing maternal and infant care. Beyond such savings, reproductive and sexual health services deliver other medical, social, and economic benefits, including prevention of illness and death, improvements in women's social position, and increases in macroeconomic investment and growth.

Interventions to improve sexual and reproductive health and rights must therefore be a priority and should occur both within and outside the health system. At a minimum, national public health systems must provide quality family planning services, emergency obstetric care, safe abortion (where legal), postabortion care, prevention and treatment of sexually transmitted infections (including HIV), and interventions to reduce malnutrition and anemia. Outside the health system sexuality education programs are needed to lay the foundation for improved sexual and reproductive health outcomes. Ultimately, these interventions must be supported by an enabling policy and political environment that guarantees women's and girls' sexual and reproductive rights.

Strategic priority 3: invest in infrastructure to reduce women's and girls' time burdens

Women's and girls' ability to participate in educational, productive, and civic activities and thus to empower themselves economically and politically is often limited by a household division of labor that assigns to women and girls the bulk of the responsibility for everyday household maintenance tasks. For poor women and girls this responsibility is made more onerous by the underinvestment in public infrastructure that characterizes most low-income countries. Three types of infrastructure are particularly critical to reduce women's time burden: transport, water and sanitation, and energy.

In most rural communities around the world women are the primary collectors of fuel wood and water. One study comparing women's time use in Sub-Saharan Africa found that women spent more than 800 hours a year in

**The time spent
by women
and girls on
routine tasks
can be reduced
dramatically by
the provision
of accessible
and affordable
transport,
energy, and
water and
sanitation**

Zambia and about 300 hours a year in Ghana and Tanzania collecting fuel-wood. Studies in various countries show that women also spend long hours in water collection and management. Women's time burdens are exacerbated by inadequate transport systems. For instance, 87 percent of trips in rural Africa take place on foot, and women account for more than 65 percent of the house-hold time and effort spent on transport (Malmberg Calvo 1996).

The time spent by women and girls on routine tasks can be reduced dra-matically by the provision of accessible and affordable sources of transport systems, energy, and water and sanitation systems. Feeder and main roads can greatly expand women's opportunities, especially when combined with accessible and affordable modes of transportation. They can increase women's chances of finding employment or training, boosting sales of goods outside the village, thereby increasing income, expanding their social networks, accessing health care, and approaching town and district government headquarters to seek redress for their problems. The probability that girls will attend school also increases. To increase the likelihood that these benefits will accrue to women and girls, the design of transport projects must also address safety and security needs. Providing adequate street lighting and ensuring that the loca-tion of bus stops and terminals are not remote or secluded are examples of ways to address these needs.

Improving women's access to alternative sources of energy other than tra-ditional biofuels can reduce women's time burdens, their exposure to indoor air pollution, and the risks of other health problems. Cooking fuels such as kerosene and LPG are recognized as good substitutes for traditional biofuels because of their higher thermal efficiency and relative lack of pollutants. Other interventions that can bring about the same benefits include the promotion of improved cook-stoves.

Rural electrification is probably the most desirable alternative to biofuels. However, the high cost and limited availability of electricity in developing countries restricts its use by households for some tasks, including cooking. One option is to strengthen transitional, low-cost solutions that the poor are already using. An example is diesel-powered mini-grids for charging batteries that can be carried to households. Another example is a multifunctional platform pow-ered by a diesel engine for low-cost rural motive power. Such an intervention, implemented in Mali, has been particularly successful in reducing women's time and effort burdens.

Even when infrastructure is made available, access for poor women and men may be constrained by other factors such as cost. With respect to alterna-tive sources of energy such as LPG and kerosene, a combination of interven-tions can assist in lowering transport and distribution costs: improved road and port infrastructure, improved handling and storage facilities at ports, bulk purchases of fuels, and impetus from the government through regulatory reform. Giving the poor direct subsidies or lease/finance mechanisms to cover

Ensuring female property and inheritance rights would help empower women both economically and socially and rectify a fundamental injustice

the upfront costs of these fuel sources (such as the cost of an LPG stove or cylinder) will also reduce costs.

Increasing women's participation in the design and implementation of infrastructure projects can help to overcome obstacles to access and affordability. This is best illustrated in the sanitation and water sector, where women play key roles as users and managers. As primary collectors of water, women have key information about such issues as seasonal availability from various sources, water quality, and individual and communal rights to those sources. If incorporated in project design, this information could also improve project outcomes. There is strong evidence from community water and sanitation projects that projects designed and run with the full participation of women are more sustainable and effective than those that ignore women.

Adapting modern science and technology to meet the infrastructure needs of poor people in a way that builds on the knowledge and experience of women and is accessible and affordable to all is therefore a development priority.

Strategic priority 4: guarantee women's and girls' property and inheritance rights

Ownership and control over assets such as land and housing provide economic security, incentives for taking economic risks that lead to growth, and important economic returns, including income. Yet, women in many countries around the globe are far less likely than men to own or control these important assets. Ensuring female property and inheritance rights would help empower women both economically and socially and rectify a fundamental injustice. Rectifying this injustice will also have other positive outcomes because women's lack of property has been increasingly linked to development-related problems, including poverty, HIV/AIDS, and violence.

Secure tenure to land and home improves women's welfare. Land and home ownership confer such direct benefits as use of crops and rights to the proceeds thereof and having a secure place to live. Indirect advantages include the ability to use land or houses as collateral for credit or as mortgageable assets during a crisis.

Beyond the direct economic impact, assets in the hands of women have other welfare impacts. Land ownership can act as a protective factor for women against domestic violence. Research in Kerala, India, found that 49 percent of women with no property reported physical violence, whereas only 7 percent of women with property reported physical violence, controlling for a wide range of factors. Some studies found that in societies where husbands control most household resources, as in Bangladesh, expenditures on children's clothing and education were higher and the rate of illness among girls was lower in households where women owned assets than in households where women did not.

In addition to welfare gains, gender-equal land rights can enhance productive efficiency. Land title can serve as collateral, improving women's access to

Several types of changes are necessary within countries to ensure women's property rights, including reforming laws and promoting legal literacy

credit, which in turn can increase output. This can be especially crucial in situations where women are the principal farmers, such as where male outmigration is high, where widows (or wives) cultivate separate plots owned by others, or where women farm independently of men, as in much of Sub-Saharan Africa.

Relatively little data exist on the magnitude of gender asset gaps within and across countries, but these gaps are thought to be substantial. Deere and Leon (2003) compiled a rough approximation of the distribution of land by sex in five Latin American countries and found that land ownership is extremely unequal, with women representing one-third or less of landowners in the five countries. There are similar gender disparities in rights to land in Sub-Saharan Africa, South Asia, and Central Asia.

There are myriad channels through which men and women may acquire land: inheritance, purchase in the market, or transfers from the state through land reform programs, resettlement schemes for those displaced by large dams and other projects, or antipoverty programs. The literature shows that each channel has a gender bias: male preference in inheritance, male privilege in marriage, gender inequality in the land market, and male bias in state programs of land distribution.

Since 1995 there has been growing awareness and policy attention to women's property and inheritance rights drawing on evolving human rights-based frameworks. There is no one global blueprint for increasing women's access to and control over land; rather, approaches and interventions must be context-specific. Nonetheless, several types of changes are necessary within countries to ensure women's property rights: amending and harmonizing statutory and customary laws, promoting legal literacy, supporting women's organizations that can help women make land claims, and recording women's share of land or property. These reforms need to be implemented in tandem to have maximum impact. In areas that are moving toward formal land registration systems, joint titling can enhance women's access to land. It can help guard against capricious decisionmaking by a spouse; protect against the dispossession of women due to abandonment, separation, or divorce; and increase women's bargaining power in household and farm decisionmaking. Joint titling can be mandatory or voluntary for legally married couples, although mandatory joint titling provides the most secure land rights for women.

International efforts to improve women's property rights have gained momentum in recent years. The Convention on the Elimination of All Forms of Discrimination against Women has focused on equality in property as one of its important directives. The United Nations Conference on Human Settlements (UN-HABITAT) focuses centrally on women and land. A number of international nongovernmental organizations (NGOs) and UN agencies are working to enhance women's access to land and property; these efforts deserve greater support.

Paid employment is critical to women's empowerment

Strategic priority 5: eliminate gender inequality in employment
Women's work, both paid and unpaid, is critical to the survival and security of poor households and an important route through which households escape poverty. Moreover, paid employment is critical to women's empowerment. In settings where women's mobility is restricted, increased employment opportunities can improve women's mobility and enable women to seek and access reproductive health care. It can also expose them to new ideas and knowledge and broaden the community with which they engage.

In the 1980s and 1990s women's overall economic activity rates increased everywhere, except in Sub-Saharan Africa, parts of Europe and Central Asia, and Oceania. Yet, despite these increasing economic activity rates, women's status in the labor market remains significantly inferior to that of men's worldwide.

Gender inequalities exist in entry to work, conditions at work, and in exit from the labor market. Early marriage, early childbearing, and low education constitute barriers to women's and girls' labor market entry. These barriers are beginning to crumble with the creation of new employment opportunities in many countries and as women's education levels rise. To further reduce barriers to entering employment, important strategies are increasing women's access to postprimary and vocational and technical education and improving the quality of education. Of particular importance for adolescent girls' participation and achievement in postprimary education is their enrollment and achievement in math, science, and other technical courses.

One barrier to entry that has remained the most resistant to change is women's responsibility for providing care for children, the elderly, and the sick. Studies from around the world indicate that the presence of young children and a lack of childcare options constrain women's entry into paid employment and their job opportunities. Increased migration, the breakdown of extended families, and changing social arrangements in some parts of the world have made extended families a less reliable source of childcare than formerly, which necessitates other types of care services.

Expansion of national policies and programs to provide support for care—of children, people with disabilities, and the elderly—is an important intervention to enable women to participate in paid employment. The governments of most industrialized countries accept some public responsibility for sharing the cost of rearing their nations' children, and many governments have developed comprehensive family policies. Recognizing the value of early education, especially targeted to poor children, governments in many developing countries, including China and India, also support childcare and early education services. Yet, no single country provides the investment in care services that is required to fully meet the needs of women and their children. Filling this gap is essential for meeting Goal 3.

With regard to the conditions at work, women's status in the labor market is inferior to men's in most countries of the world, according to key indicators

Employment-enhancing economic growth is a prerequisite for low-income countries, coupled with social policy that eliminates discriminatory employment barriers

such as occupational distribution, earnings, the nature and terms of employment, and unemployment. In the labor force women and men typically perform different tasks and are located in different industries and occupational sectors. Occupational segregation by sex is extensive in both developed and developing countries. Approximately half of all workers in the world are in occupations where at least 80 percent of workers are of the same sex. In many countries, occupational segregation is significantly higher for the least educated workers than for those with higher education.

Gender gaps in earnings are among the most persistent forms of inequality in the labor market. In all countries men earn more than women, and this is true across different groups of workers (agricultural, services) and different types of earnings (monthly, hourly, salaried).

Employment—both formal and informal—has become increasingly flexible in the past two decades with globalization. Numerous studies show women's increased participation in temporary, casual, contract, and part-time labor in manufacturing. Although men are also affected by these trends, the percentage of women in "flexible" jobs greatly exceeds that of men.

Gender differences are also apparent in unemployment, with women more likely to be unemployed than men in recent years. Studies from the Caribbean economies and transition economies show that women have experienced declines in access to jobs relative to men.

To improve the nature and conditions of work, employment-enhancing economic growth is a prerequisite for low-income countries, coupled with social policy that eliminates discriminatory employment barriers. For poor women, especially those in rural areas, public employment guarantee schemes can be an important intervention for providing work and increasing income, although evaluations of country programs reveal a mixed track record. Public employment guarantee schemes can also be gender-biased. In many programs, women earn less than men, partly because they are excluded from higher wage and physically difficult tasks. Women are also more susceptible to cheating and exploitation.

For countries with large informal economies, one of the highest priorities to improve the conditions of work is social protection for workers in that sector. Social protection and safety net programs all too often exclude women by failing to account for gender differences in labor market participation, access to information, unpaid care responsibilities, and property rights. When programs do not account for these gender differences, women are more vulnerable to poverty and the risks associated with economic and other shocks to household livelihoods.

Another avenue for increasing income for poor women is through micro-enterprise development. Microfinance programs have been a popular economic strategy over the past two decades to assist poor and landless women to enter self-employment or start their own business. In order to have greater impact,

Having access to paid work is critical to family survival, but it is not sufficient for reducing poverty or empowering women. Decent, productive work for all should be the goal

however, microfinance programs need to be coupled with other types of products and services, including training, technology transfer, business development services, and marketing assistance, among others. More attention also needs to be given to innovative savings and insurance instruments for low-income women.

In both developed and developing countries, a common intervention to improve pay and working conditions is the passage and implementation of equal opportunity or antidiscrimination legislation. This includes family leave policies, equal pay and equal opportunity laws and policies, and legislation guaranteeing rights at work. Empirical evidence of the impact of each of these on women's employment and on relative wages comes mostly from industrial countries and suggests that there have been some improvements, but these are conditional on the degree of enforcement and other factors.

In light of current demographic trends, female vulnerability in old age has gained increasing importance. Women live longer than men and in most regions are more likely to spend time as widows, when they are more vulnerable to poverty than men. Because pension entitlements are predominantly through work, women's responsibilities for unpaid care work, as well as their predominance in informal employment and seasonal and part-time jobs, restrict their access to the private pension-covered sector. In many countries, jobs in the public sector have historically been a major source of pensions; as the public sector has contracted (due to structural adjustment, privatization, and cuts in government spending), women have lost pension coverage.

Many countries, especially in Latin America and in Eastern and Central Europe, are reforming their pension and social security programs. Gender equality has not been a high priority in these reform efforts. To protect retired women, it is important that the design of old age security systems take account of gender differences in earnings, labor force experience, and longevity. The specifics of pension reform vary across countries, and there are too few studies to draw clear conclusions about the effect of different types of pension programs on women. Nonetheless, it is clear that programs that have a redistributive component and that require fewer years of contributions are better able to protect women in old age.

While opportunities for paid employment for women have increased in countries around the world, the nature, terms, and quality of women's employment have not improved commensurately. Having access to paid work is critical to family survival, but it is not sufficient for reducing poverty or empowering women. Decent, productive work for all should be the goal.

At the international level, a framework exists for promoting equal access to and treatment in employment—the International Labour Organization (ILO) Decent Work Initiative. This initiative has four interrelated objectives: fostering rights at work and providing employment, social protection, and social dialogue. The primary goal is "to promote opportunities for women and men to

**Gender quotas
and reservations
are an effective
policy tool
to increase
women's
representation**

obtain decent and productive work, in conditions of freedom, equity, security, and human dignity." The gender sensitivity of the decent work framework, and the sex-disaggregated indicators it proposes for monitoring country performance, make it suitable for tracking a country's progress toward eliminating gender inequalities in labor markets. The task force recommends that the ILO be given the resources and authority to take the leadership in providing data and monitoring progress for this initiative.

Strategic priority 6: increase women's share of seats in national parliaments and local governmental bodies

Increasing women's representation in political office is now a widely held development goal and one of the four Millennium Development Indicators for tracking progress toward Goal 3. Indeed, the Beijing Platform for Action recommended that governments set a target of 30 percent of seats for women in national parliaments.

There are three reasons why the task force has selected political participation as a strategic priority. Countries where women's share of seats in political bodies is less than 30 percent are less inclusive, less egalitarian, and less democratic. Equality of opportunity in politics is a human right. Evidence also suggests that women's interests often differ from men's and that women who participate directly in decisionmaking bodies press for different priorities than those emphasized by men. Finally, women's participation in political decisionmaking bodies improves the quality of governance.

Yet, around the world women are largely absent from decisionmaking bodies. Only 14 countries have met the proposed target of 30 percent of seats held by women. In another 27 countries women held 20–29 percent of seats in 2004. Despite these low levels, women have made notable progress in political life since 1990. Of the 129 countries that have longitudinal data, in 96 women have increased their share of seats in parliament while in 29 countries women's representation declined over the decade and in 4 it remained unchanged.

Gender quotas and reservations are an effective policy tool to increase women's representation in political bodies. Experience suggests four lessons about the conditions under which quotas effectively enhance women's voice in political bodies. The first lesson is that the impact of quotas varies significantly according to a country's electoral system. Quotas work best in closed-list, proportional representation systems with placement mandates and with large electoral districts (that is, where many candidates are elected from each electoral conscription, and parties can expect several candidates running in the district to gain a seat). Second, placement mandates are critical to the success of quotas in closed-list proportional representation electoral systems. Because candidates are elected from party lists according to the order in which they appear, placement on the list affects the chances of being elected. Placement mandates require parties to place women in high positions on party lists. Without these

Violence against women has serious health and development impacts and is a gross violation of women's rights

mandates, political parties tend to comply with quotas in the most "minimalist" manner permitted by law, that is, with the lowest possible places on the list. Third, quota laws must be specific and stipulate details of implementation. When quota laws are vague, they leave considerable discretion to political parties to apply—or fail to apply—quotas as they see fit. Finally, for quota laws to be effective, parties must face sanctions for noncompliance. The strongest sanction is to have a party's list of candidates declared invalid and to forbid the party from contesting the election. These sanctions require that judges be willing and able to monitor party compliance and that groups be willing and able to challenge noncompliant lists in court.

Even without quotas and reservations, countries have several ways to catalyze women's political representation. A country's political culture plays an important role in affecting women's political participation. A recent cross-country study of women's presence in parliaments in 190 countries found that governments that make the provision of welfare (or "care work" for children, the sick, and the elderly) an "affirmative duty of the state" tend to elect around 5 percent more women to national legislatures than countries without these policies (holding all other factors constant). The same study found an interactive effect between constitutionalized care-work policies, policies upholding democratic civil rights, and women's political representation. Countries with both sets of policies could be expected to have 7 percent more women in their national legislatures than other countries. The presence of a strong women's political movement can also make a difference in increasing women's political representation. Women's organizations can mobilize a political constituency and pressure governments to implement specific measures to ensure that women are well represented in political parties and national decisionmaking bodies.

Strategic priority 7: combat violence against girls and women

Violence against women has serious health and development impacts and is a gross violation of women's rights. Its continued existence is thus fundamentally inconsistent with Goal 3. However, violence against women is prevalent in epidemic proportions in many countries around the world. This report focuses on two important types of violence: intimate partner violence and sexual violence or abuse by nonrelatives or strangers within the wider community.

Violence against women has many health consequences. Worldwide, it is estimated that violence against women is as serious a cause of death and incapacity among reproductive-age women as is cancer, and it is a more common cause of ill-health among women than traffic accidents and malaria combined. Physical and sexual abuse lie behind unwanted pregnancies, sexually transmitted infections, including HIV/AIDS, and complications of pregnancy. Studies around the world have found that one woman in four is physically or sexually abused during pregnancy. Some studies indicate that women battered during

Infrastructure,

legal, judicial,

enforcement,

education,

health, and

other service-

related actions

can significantly

reduce violence

against women

pregnancy run twice the risk of miscarriage and four times the risk of having a low birthweight baby as women who are not battered. Violence may also be linked to a sizable portion of maternal deaths.

In the past decade evidence has shown that violence against women is an important development constraint. National governments, women's organizations, and the United Nations now recognize violence against women as a basic human rights abuse; atrocities such as rape committed against women during armed conflict are acknowledged as a "weapon of war" and a gender-based crime; and social violence in the home is correlated with economic crime outside the home, as well as with political and institutional violence at the local and national levels.

Accurate statistical data on the prevalence of gender-based violence are difficult to come by because of underreporting by victims and underrecording by the police. Few national statistical bodies collect data on the topic, and few of the available studies yield information that is comparable across countries or regions. Where population-based surveys are available, they typically find that violence against women cuts across socioeconomic, religious, and ethnic groups and across geographical areas. Evidence from diverse contexts reveals that women living in poverty are often especially vulnerable to gender-based violence, as are adolescent girls. Women are at risk of violence when carrying out essential daily activities—walking or taking public transport to work, collecting water or firewood—especially when these activities are undertaken early in the morning or late at night.

Although no single intervention will eliminate violence against women, a combination of infrastructure, legal, judicial, enforcement, education, health, and other service-related actions can significantly reduce such violence and ameliorate its negative consequences. Throughout the 1990s countries around the world adopted new legislation on intimate partner violence and reformed laws on rape. To date, 45 nations (28 in Latin America and the Caribbean) have adopted legislation against domestic violence, 21 more are drafting new laws, and many countries have amended criminal assault laws to include domestic violence.

The health system is often the first entry point for victims of abuse. Most female victims of partner or sexual violence visit healthcare service providers but often resist contact with the police or other services. A range of interventions can be identified in the health sector to provide victim support and to deter additional violence. Education provides another important entry point for combating or preventing gender-based violence. Educational interventions include both school-based programs and broader communications campaigns aimed at raising community awareness about the damaging effects of violence. Communications media such as pamphlets, radio, television, and theater serve to educate and promote change, as they can reach large audiences. Because violence often occurs in unsafe public spaces,

The task force suggests 12 indicators for countries and international organizations to use in monitoring the progress toward Goal 3

interventions to improve public infrastructure can contribute to reducing violence against women.

Although international agencies and the global community have rallied to address other epidemics (such as HIV and tuberculosis), they have not responded in the same way to the epidemic of violence against women. For instance, while the UN General Assembly resolution 50/166 established the Trust Fund to End Violence against Women at the United Nations Development Fund for Women, country needs and requests far outstrip the fund's current resources. The task force seeks to complement national, regional, and global efforts by calling for a global campaign to end violence against women, spearheaded by the UN secretary-general and endorsed by the General Assembly. The goal of the global campaign would be to mobilize leadership at all levels—local, national, and international—to generate action to make violence against women unacceptable.

Data and indicators

The task force suggests several indicators for monitoring progress on the seven strategic priorities at both the country and international levels. These indicators are intended to supplement, or in some cases substitute for, the indicators chosen by the UN expert group to assess progress during 1990–2015, when the Millennium Development Targets are expected to be met.

Although the task force has not recommended the adoption of new international or country-level targets for the seven strategic priorities, countries may wish to set their own quantifiable, time-bound targets for establishing progress on each of the seven strategic priorities. Examples of such targets to be achieved by the year 2015 are, for strategic priority 2, "universal access to sexual and reproductive health services through the primary health care system, ensuring the same rate of progress or faster among the poor and other marginalized groups," and for strategic priority 6, "a 30 percent share of seats for women in national parliaments."

Millennium Development Goal 3 includes four indicators for tracking progress:

- The ratio of girls to boys enrolled in primary and secondary education.
- The ratio of literate females to males among 15- to 24-year-olds.
- The share of women in wage employment in the nonagricultural sector.
- The proportion of seats held by women in national parliaments.

The indicators proposed for tracking Goal 3 are insufficient to track all seven strategic priorities and suffer from several technical shortcomings. To address these limitations, the task force suggests 12 indicators for countries and international organizations to use in monitoring the progress toward Goal 3 (box 1).

None of these indicators measure the *quality* of equality, the process that brings it about, or the nature of the outcomes. Achieving numerical balance—parity—is clearly important in a world where even this goal has yet to be

Box 1

Proposed indicators for tracking progress on strategic priorities for Goal 3

Education
- The ratio of female to male gross enrollment rates in primary, secondary, and tertiary education.
- The ratio of female to male completion rates in primary, secondary, and tertiary education.

Sexual and reproductive health and rights
- Proportion of contraceptive demand satisfied.
- Adolescent fertility rate.

Infrastructure
- Hours per day (or year) women and men spend fetching water and collecting fuel.

Property rights
- Land ownership by male, female, or jointly held.
- Housing title, disaggregated by male, female, or jointly held.

Employment
- Share of women in employment, both wage and self-employment, by type.
- Gender gaps in earnings in wage and self-employment.

Participation in national parliaments and local government bodies
- Percentage of seats held by women in national parliament.
- Percentage of seats held by women in local government bodies.

Violence against women
- Prevalence of domestic violence.

attained. However necessary, parity by itself is not a sufficient condition for achieving the greater goal of gender equality. Unless indicators are also developed for measuring the quality of change, we run the risk of placing too much weight on mere parity of outcomes as opposed to the quality of these outcomes and the way in which they are achieved.

Work to prepare several of the indicators proposed by the task force on gender equality and women's empowerment is well under way. Improving countries' capacity to enhance the coverage, quality, and frequency of collection of sex-disaggregated data remains a priority, however. Country statistical agencies need an infusion of resources to strengthen their capacity and efforts to do all that is necessary to collect and prepare sex-disaggregated data. Work at the country level also requires technical support from key international statistical agencies to develop methodological guidelines and undertake new data collection efforts. Concurrently, substantial funding is required to coordinate these activities within the appropriate international and regional organizations.

At the international level, the task force recognizes the importance of a focal point in the UN statistical system to bring together the various gender indicators and recommends the continuation of the Women's Indicators and Statistics Database (WISTAT) series, which served this purpose. The *Trends in the World's Women*, which was based on WISTAT, should also continue to be published on a quinquennial basis.

**An accurate
cost analysis
is the first
step in efforts
to mobilize
the financial
resources
needed to
implement
the various
interventions
and policy
measures**

The financial costs

As the above discussion demonstrates, eliminating gender inequality is a multidimensional and a multisectoral effort. For this reason, the financial costs of these efforts are difficult to calculate. An accurate cost analysis is the first step in efforts to mobilize the financial resources needed to implement the various interventions and policy measures that have been proposed.

In collaboration with the UN Millennium Project Secretariat, the Task Force on Education and Gender Equality adapted the general needs assessment methodology developed by the UN Millennium Project for estimating the financing requirements of the gender-related interventions. There are several caveats concerning this methodology. First, the needs assessment comprises only some of the actions and strategies necessary to meet the goal of gender equality. Adequate resources alone will not achieve gender equality. Second, a gender needs assessment is possible only at the country level and meaningful only as part of a Goals-based national poverty reduction strategy in which all stakeholders participate. The estimated costs that such assessment yield depend on the interventions to be included, and these need to be locally identified based on nationally determined targets. Third, gender needs assessments should be carried out in conjunction with similar exercises in such other Goals-related areas as education, health, transport and energy infrastructure, water and sanitation, agriculture, nutrition, urban development, and environment. This simultaneous estimation of needs is important to ensure that the total resources capture all gender-related interventions and strategies.

The UN Millennium Project approach to assessing the needs for gender-related interventions follows two tracks. The first track covers gender interventions to meet all other Millennium Development Goals affecting gender equality and empowerment of women, and the second track covers the additional specific interventions to meet Goal 3.

The first track includes gender-specific interventions in agriculture, education, health, nutrition, rural development, urban development, water and sanitation, environment, trade, and science and technology. In each area there are interventions that empower women and reduce gender inequality. Three of the seven strategic priorities have been partially included in the needs assessment for specific sectors: postprimary education for girls has been costed as part of the education needs assessment methodology, the provision of sexual and reproductive health services has been costed within the health sector needs assessment methodology, and infrastructure to reduce women's time burdens has been costed as part of the infrastructure needs assessment methodology.

The second track involves estimating the resources for additional specific interventions to meet Goal 3. Examples of specific interventions for Goal 3 that are not costed in any other Goals needs assessment include:

- Providing comprehensive sexuality education within schools and community programs.

A transformation

is needed in the

way societies

conceive of

and organize

men's and

women's roles,

responsibilities,

and control

over resources

- Providing care services (for children, the elderly, the sick, and people with disabilities) to allow women to work.
- Providing training to female candidates in elections at the local, regional, and national level.
- Preventing violence against women through awareness campaigns and education, hotlines, and neighborhood support groups.
- Strengthening national women's machineries through increased budgetary allocations and staffing of ministries of women's affairs and gender focal points in other ministries.
- Undertaking institutional reform through sensitization programs to train judges, bureaucrats, land registration officers, and police officers.
- Investing in data collection and monitoring activities to track gender outcomes.

This needs assessment methodology is now being applied in several countries. The results from Tajikistan, although preliminary, are illustrative. They suggest that the costs of universal primary and expanded secondary education in Tajikistan would be roughly $20 per capita on average annually for 2005–15; the costs of setting up a primary health care system (for child health and maternal health, major infectious diseases, and sexual and reproductive health) would average roughly $29 per capita annually; and the costs of water and sanitation provision would average roughly $9.50 per capita.

The preliminary estimates suggest that the additional cost of gender-specific interventions to meet Goal 3 (such as training and awareness campaigns, interventions to reduce violence against women, and systematic interventions to improve ministry capacities) will average approximately $1.30 per capita annually for 2005–15, with costs peaking at $2.00 in 2015. Most of these costs will be for programs to end violence against women. In absolute numbers, the cost of additional specific interventions to meet Goal 3 in Tajikistan is $10.56 million each year, totaling $112 million for 2005–15, or about 0.003 percent of GDP over this period. To put this amount into context, debt-servicing payments alone accounted for about 4 percent of GDP in Tajikistan in 2001.

Making it happen

This report describes practical actions that can be taken within each strategic priority to bring about gender equality and empower women. Within and across sectors, within institutions, and in different country and community contexts, different combinations of these actions have been implemented and shown positive results. The problem is not a lack of practical ways to address gender inequality but rather a lack of change on a large and deep enough scale to bring about a transformation in the way societies conceive of and organize men's and women's roles, responsibilities, and control over resources. Essential for that kind of transformation are:

The first ingredient of transformation requires a critical mass of change agents committed to the vision of a gender equitable society

- Political commitment by and mobilization of a large group of change agents at different levels within countries and in international institutions who seek to implement the vision of the world.
- Technical capacity to implement change.
- Institutional structures and processes to support the transformation, including structures that enable women to successfully claim their rights.
- Adequate financial resources.
- Accountability and monitoring systems.

Commitment and mobilization of change agents

The first ingredient of transformation requires a critical mass of change agents committed to the vision of a gender equitable society. These change agents include leaders at all levels of government who control critical levers for change—financial and technical resources—and set the priorities for actions affecting the lives of many. To be effective, government leaders must work in partnership with civil society institutions, especially organizations that represent women's interests. Simultaneously, there must be a critical mass of change agents at the international level in the institutions that provide support to national governments and civil society organizations in implementing changes necessary for a gender-equitable society.

Technical capacity

Achieving gender equality and bringing about women's empowerment also requires technical expertise and knowledge of how to mainstream gender into development policies and programs. At the 1995 Fourth World Conference on Women the world community endorsed gender mainstreaming as a key institutional response for promoting gender equality and empowering women. Gender mainstreaming is not an end in itself but a means to the goal of gender equality. It is both a technical and a political process, requiring shifts in organizational culture and ways of thinking, as well as in the structures of organizations and in their resource allocations. As a technical tool, mainstreaming can be effective only if supported by a strong political or legal mandate.

Gender mainstreaming is often compromised by a lack of conceptual clarity about the meaning of gender and by the assumption that certain policy areas, such as infrastructure development or macroeconomic measures, are in principle gender neutral. Such conceptual confusion can be clarified through gender analysis and gender training. Gender analysis involves gathering and examining information on what women and men do and how they relate to each other. Gender training builds capacity to use the information from gender analysis in policy and program development and implementation.

An unfortunate consequence of training a broad range of professionals is the elimination or downgrading of specialized gender units and professionals.

**Women's
organizations
are key agents
in bringing about
institutional
transformation
at the
national and
international
level**

Because mainstreaming requires a shift of responsibility for promoting gender equality to all personnel, especially managers, gender specialists are perceived as being no longer needed. In fact, the reverse is true: gender mainstreaming can increase the need for specialist support.

Institutional structure and processes

Institutional transformation—fundamental change in the rules that specify how resources are allocated and how tasks, responsibilities, and values are assigned in society—is the third ingredient essential for achieving gender equality and women's empowerment on a large scale. Women's organizations are key agents in bringing about institutional transformation at the national and international level because they articulate women's priorities and organize and advocate for change. At the international level regional and global women's movements mobilized throughout the 1990s to put gender equality and women's empowerment on the agendas of major UN conferences, thereby transforming international norms on women's roles and rights.

Government agencies also play key roles in institutional transformation because they create an enabling national environment for gender equality. Through legislation, regulatory reform, and the expansion and strengthening of public services, governments can rectify the deep-seated gender biases that are inherent in their own institutions, as well as put in place structures and processes such as women-friendly law enforcement systems that enable women to claim their rights. To make such institutional changes happen, a central unit or ministry needs a mandate to ensure that gender equality and the empowerment of women are addressed across all ministries and departments. At the 1995 Fourth World Conference on Women in Beijing governments agreed that national women's machineries should be the institutional entity within government to support and build capacity to mainstream gender equality across all development planning and implementation processes.

Bringing about institutional transformation at the international level requires changes within international agencies similar to those within national government, including the creation of a gender unit that is structurally and functionally placed so that it can influence decisions on policy and program development and resource allocation. This is particularly important because of the interdependency between donors and low-income country governments and because international institutions often set the parameters for the resource envelope and policy changes that are possible at the country level.

Adequate financial resources

The fourth essential ingredient for large-scale reductions in gender inequality is the allocation of adequate financial resources for direct interventions by both governmental and nongovernmental organizations in building capacity, collecting data, and evaluating outcomes. Too often, insufficient funds are allocated

The Convention on the Elimination of All Forms of Discrimination against Women provides a powerful legal mechanism for holding governments accountable for meeting Goal 3

for these purposes. Even if all the other ingredients described here are in place, they cannot be effective without adequate resources.

In part, efforts to promote gender equality are underfunded because isolating the costs of gender interventions from the overall costs of a sectoral intervention is challenging. However, methodologies for estimating such costs have been developed and can now be applied. Another reason why gender equality efforts are typically underfunded is that the costs associated with them are incorrectly perceived as additional to the core investment yielding only a marginal return rather than more accurately as an essential expenditure for maximizing the return on the core investment. A third reason is that gender equality is viewed as a cross-cutting issue, which typically receives lower priority in budgetary allocations than sector-specific issues. Because cross-cutting issues are supposed to be everyone's business, they tend to become no one's responsibility.

The question is how to ensure that the required resources will be available and committed. Changes are needed in the international system, including debt cancellation for heavily indebted poor countries, dramatically scaled up and better quality official development assistance, and trade reform that levels the playing field for developing countries, in order to increase the availability of resources. Domestic resource mobilization is also important for generating the resources to achieve gender equality.

Accountability and monitoring mechanisms

Accountability and monitoring systems need to be in place within countries and international agencies to ensure that fundamental change is broad-based and lasting. At the country level, the needed systems include a strong legal framework along with the mechanisms to enforce it within and outside government, and a strong women's movement along with the processes that enable women's groups to inform and influence government policies and resource allocations.

The Convention on the Elimination of All Forms of Discrimination against Women provides a powerful legal mechanism enabling stakeholders at the country level to hold their governments accountable for meeting Goal 3. The reporting obligation established in the convention, and the work of the Committee on the Elimination of Discrimination against Women, provide a context in which discrimination against women can be eliminated and in which women can de facto fully enjoy their rights. Frequently, the reporting process has created partnerships between government, NGOs, and United Nations entities that work together to achieve the goals of the convention. The convention has had a positive impact on legal and other developments in countries throughout the world. It has led many countries to strengthen provisions in their constitutions guaranteeing equality between women and men and providing a constitutional basis for protecting women's human rights.

The international system needs to support a well functioning country-level accountability and monitoring system

NGOs such as women's organizations and other civil society organizations have taken the lead in holding governments and international agencies accountable for implementing their commitments to gender equality and women's empowerment. Indeed, much of the progress made to date has been due to the political efforts and the mobilization of such organizations.

In its interaction with countries the international system needs to support these components of a well functioning country-level accountability and monitoring system. Simultaneously, the United Nations and the Bretton Woods institutions must ensure that mechanisms are in place to hold themselves accountable for implementing international mandates and commitments to gender equality, and that watchdog agencies external to the international UN and Bretton Woods system, particularly international women's organizations, have sufficient input into policy formulation and implementation and resource allocation.

Country case studies

The efforts of Cambodia, Chile, Rwanda, and South Africa to improve women's status and reduce gender inequality illustrate the complicated processes involved in promoting gender equality and women's empowerment. These countries are attempting significant institutional reform, catalyzed by strong and dynamic advocacy by women's organizations and other actors (such as other civil society movements or donors). Some of these countries also made progress on a majority of the seven strategic priorities described above, although it is difficult to attribute changes to specific government actions.

Each of the four countries has been affected in its recent past by significant internal turmoil and conflict. In each case powerful change agents in women's organizations and government have seized the opportunity to rectify societal inequalities. Although periods of peace-building and postconflict by definition provide space for societal restructuring of the status quo existing before the conflict, such restructuring can also occur in nonconflict settings if some combination of the five elements described above (change agents with a vision, institutional structures and processes, technical capacity, financial resources, and accountability mechanisms) are in place.

Cambodia, Rwanda, and South Africa have all made significant progress in the last decade in closing gender gaps in primary and secondary education and in improving key aspects of women's sexual and reproductive rights and health. However, despite gains in lowering maternal mortality ratios and the unmet need for contraception, women in Cambodia, Rwanda, and South Africa have been hit hard by the HIV/AIDS epidemic. Of the four case study countries Chile stands alone in opposing women's reproductive rights. On women's political participation, Rwanda and South Africa have achieved high levels of representation of women at both the national and local level. Chile and Rwanda have taken strong legal measures to address violence against women, and Cambodia has added the elimination of violence against women as one of

Cambodia, Rwanda, and South Africa all made commitments to gender equality a key component of their constitutions

its additional Millennium Development Targets. No country has adequately addressed women's poverty and economic opportunity—either in terms of their participation in labor markets or of asset ownership and control.

In each of the four countries the conditions have been created for fostering large-scale societal transformation. Each country has a critical mass of change agents, within government and civil society, with a vision of gender equality and women's empowerment. In some instances, such as in Rwanda and South Africa, leaders in governments have worked in alliance with leaders in civil society, while in others, as in Chile, the pressure of an independent women's movement forced change within government. Institutional structures and processes are all being transformed through constitutional change, legal reform, and the formation of new government organizations. Cambodia, Rwanda, and South Africa all made commitments to gender equality a key component of their constitutions, and all three, as well as Chile, have implemented major legal and legislative reforms to advance equality between women and men. And, in each country a national women's machinery has been put in place, supported by political leaders, with strong mandates for achieving gender equality.

It is difficult to establish whether adequate technical resources exist in each of these countries for implementing the country's commitments to gender equality. However, the multilayered responses (legislative, policy, and project) to gender inequality in each country suggest that technical capacity is not lacking.

Moreover, based on the evidence available, it is not possible to comment explicitly on whether the gender equality machinery in each country has adequate financial resources to do its work. Yet, the advent of gender budget initiatives, especially in Chile, Rwanda, and South Africa, holds the promise of such information becoming available and useful to gender equality advocates within and outside government.

Finally, each country has women's movements that can hold governments to their promises. Gender budget initiatives are an important monitoring and accountability mechanism. Each country is also a signatory to the Convention on the Elimination of All Forms of Discrimination against Women, but it is not clear whether the associated monitoring mechanism truly serves to hold governments accountable for bringing about the changes required to meet the convention's provisions.

Gender mainstreaming in Millennium Development Goals-based country policy processes

Poverty reduction strategies within low-income countries are the mechanisms for influencing development policies and plans and ensuring that actions to address the Millennium Development Goals are implemented. Thus, a critical entry point for promoting gender equality and women's empowerment at the country level is the poverty reduction strategy process.

The next 10 years provide a new window of opportunity to take action on a global scale

A core recommendation of the UN Millennium Project is that every developing country restructure its short-term poverty reduction strategy in the context of a 10-year Millennium Development Goals framework. This offers a new opportunity to apply the lessons from past poverty reduction strategy processes so that the new Goals-based poverty reduction strategies succeed in fully mainstreaming gender and empowering women. The UN Millennium Project suggests a five-step approach to designing an MDG-based poverty reduction strategy.

Gender considerations should be an integral component of each step. First, the data that countries use to diagnose the nature and dynamics of poverty must be sex-disaggregated. Second, in undertaking a systematic needs assessment to evaluate policies, governance structures, and public investments, countries should use the tools and methodologies described throughout this report, including gender analysis, gender training, and gender needs assessment, in a consultative process that allows for the full participation of women's organizations.

Third, in converting the needs assessment into a financing strategy, both the plan for public spending and services and the financing strategy should be based on a gender analysis of public expenditure and revenue. A gender-aware public spending plan must include sex-disaggregated, gender-sensitive measures for inputs, outputs, and outcomes; must make gender equality an explicit indicator of performance; and must incorporate into the budget framework dimensions of costs and expenditures that are not typically included, such as the unpaid care of children, the elderly, and sick, provided by women (Sharp 2003).

Finally, the public sector management strategy, with its focus on transparency, accountability, and results-based management, should include processes that allow stakeholders committed to gender equality to participate in meaningful ways. For example, women's organizations and other civil society groups that promote gender equality must be given full information and be able to participate in formal feedback mechanisms through which accountability can be exercised.

Conclusion

Much of what is said in this report has been known for several decades, but it has been difficult to translate that knowledge into development policy and practice at the scale required to bring about fundamental transformation in the distribution of power, opportunity, and outcomes for both women and men. The next 10 years provide a new window of opportunity to take action on a global scale to achieve gender equality and empower women, which are critical for meeting all the Millennium Development Goals. Governments and international organizations can provide an enabling environment to make this possible. Women's organizations need the space and resources to bring about the societal transformations that remove the constraints, fulfill the potential, and guarantee the rights of women in all countries. The recommendations made in this report can pave the way toward that future.

Chapter 1

A problem with a solution

How can the global community achieve the goal of gender equality and the empowerment of women? This question is the focus of Goal 3 of the Millennium Development Goals endorsed by world leaders at the UN Millennium Summit in 2000. It is also the focus of this report.

Gender inequality is a problem that has a solution. Two decades of innovation, experience, and activism have shown that achieving the goal of greater gender equality and women's empowerment is possible. There are many practical steps that can reduce inequalities based on gender—inequalities that restrict the potential to reduce poverty and achieve high levels of well-being in societies around the world. There are also many positive actions that can empower women. Without leadership and political will, however, the world will fall short of taking these practical steps—and meeting the Goal. Because gender inequality is deeply rooted in entrenched attitudes, societal institutions, and market forces, political commitment at the highest international and national levels is essential to institute the policies that can trigger social change and to allocate the resources necessary for gender equality and women's empowerment.

Before the UN Millennium Summit in 2000 nearly every country had made a commitment to equal rights for women and girls by ratifying the Convention on the Elimination of All Forms of Discrimination against Women (CEDAW) and the Convention on the Rights of the Child (CRC).[1] Signatories are legally obligated to meet the commitments they specify. Often described as the international bill of rights for women, CEDAW provides for women's equal enjoyment with men of civil, cultural, economic, political, and social rights. It is unique in establishing legal obligations for state parties to ensure that discrimination against women does not occur in the public sphere or the private sphere.

UN member states also made important commitments to promoting gender equality and women's empowerment at the 1994 International Conference

Genuine equality means more than parity in numbers, which can sometimes be achieved by lowering the bar for all—it means equality is achieved at high levels of well-being

on Population and Development in Cairo and the 1995 Fourth World Conference on Women in Beijing.[2] The inclusion of gender equality and women's empowerment as Millennium Development Goal 3 is a reminder that many of those promises have yet to be kept. It also offers a critical opportunity to implement those promises.

National and international women's movements have worked to hold governments accountable for the legal and political commitments they have made through CEDAW, the Beijing Platform for Action, and other international agreements. It is women's activism and social mobilization, combined with innovative responses from some governments and civil society organizations, that have led to significant improvements in women's and girls' status since the first UN Conference on Women in 1975 in Mexico City. Investing in women's advocacy organizations is key to holding the international community and national governments accountable for achieving Millennium Development Goal 3.

In the past three decades women have made gains, particularly in health and education, as evidenced in lower mortality rates, higher life expectancy, and reduced gender gaps in primary school education. Despite these gains, it is clear that many countries will miss the first deadline for the Goal 3 target: eliminate gender disparity in primary and secondary education preferably by 2005 and in all levels of education no later than 2015. This will be the first visible Millennium Development Goal failure. That failure should spur the global community to reenergize and take action so that the 2015 target deadline is met. In doing so, countries should strive to achieve more than numerical parity.

The spirit of the Goal—gender equality and the empowerment of women—requires fundamental transformation in the distribution of power, opportunities, and outcomes for both men and women. Genuine equality means more than parity in numbers, which can sometimes be achieved by lowering the bar for all—men and women. It means justice, greater opportunity, and better quality of life so that equality is achieved at high levels of well-being.

To ensure that Millennium Development Goal 3 is met by 2015, the task force has identified seven strategic priorities (box 1.1). These interdependent priorities are the minimum necessary to empower women and alter the historical legacy of female disadvantage that remains in most societies of the world.

These seven priorities are much broader than the Goal 3 target. That target is restricted to education, a focus justified by the strong evidence that investing in girls' education yields high returns for girls themselves and high returns for development (Schultz 2001).[3] By setting an ambitious target for eliminating gender disparities in primary and secondary education—in less than a decade—Goal 3 sends a clear message that gender inequality in education in the twenty-first century is unconscionable and must be rectified.

Important as it is for women's well-being and the development of societies, education alone is insufficient to eliminate the wide range of gender inequalities

Box 1.1

Seven strategic priorities for action on Millennium Development Goal 3

1. Strengthen opportunities for postprimary education for girls while meeting commitments to universal primary education.
2. Guarantee sexual and reproductive health and rights.
3. Invest in infrastructure to reduce women's and girls' time burdens.
4. Guarantee women's and girls' property and inheritance rights.
5. Eliminate gender inequality in employment by decreasing women's reliance on informal employment, closing gender gaps in earnings, and reducing occupational segregation.
6. Increase women's share of seats in national parliaments and local government bodies.
7. Combat violence against girls and women

found in many societies. Education may be an important precondition to women's empowerment, but it does not guarantee that empowerment. For this to occur, women must also enjoy equal rights with men, equal economic opportunities, use of productive assets, freedom from drudgery, equal representation in decisionmaking bodies, and freedom from the threat of violence and coercion.

Achieving true gender equality and women's empowerment requires a different vision for the world, not just piecemeal rectification of different aspects of inequality.[4] The task force's vision is of a world in which men and women work together as equal partners to secure better lives for themselves and their families. In this world women and men share equally in the enjoyment of basic capabilities, economic assets, voice, and freedom from fear and violence. They share the care of children, the elderly, and the sick; the responsibility for paid employment; and the joys of leisure. In this world the resources now used for war and destruction are invested in human development and well-being, institutions and decisionmaking processes are open and democratic, and all human beings treat each other with respect and dignity.

It is our vision of such a world, together with our analysis of why women and men today rarely enjoy equality, that underlies the recommendations in this report.

Chapter 2

Task force perspective on gender equality and empowerment

The task force affirms that gender equality and women's empowerment are central to the achievement of all the Millennium Development Goals (box 2.1). Development policies and actions that fail to take gender inequality into account and that fail to enable women to be actors in those policies and interventions will have limited effectiveness and serious costs to societies (World Bank 2003c). The reverse is also true: achievement of Goal 3 depends on how well each of the other goals addresses gender-based constraints and issues (box 2.2). Thus, this task force believes that achieving Goal 3 depends both on the extent to which the priorities suggested here are addressed and the extent to which the actions taken to achieve the other Goals promote equality of boys and girls and men and women. While this interdependence among the Goals is important, the task force wishes to underscore that Goal 3 has intrinsic value in and of itself. That is why this report focuses on priorities and actions to achieve Goal 3.

Defining gender equality and empowerment

Like race and ethnicity, gender is a social construct. It defines and differentiates the roles, rights, responsibilities, and obligations of women and men. The innate biological differences between females and males form the basis of social norms that define appropriate behaviors for women and men and determine the differential social, economic, and political power between the sexes. Although the specific nature and degree of these differing norms vary across societies and across time, at the beginning of the twenty-first century they still typically favor men and boys, giving them more access than women and girls to the capabilities, resources, and opportunities that are important for the enjoyment of social, economic, and political power and well-being.

In addressing Goal 3, the task force has focused on the historical disadvantage experienced by women and on how gender norms and the policies based on those

Box 2.1	Millennium Development Goal	Importance of gender equality for achieving the goal
Gender equality is critical to achieving all the Goals	**Goal 1** Eradicate extreme poverty and hunger	• Gender equality in capabilities and access to opportunities can accelerate economic growth. • Equal access for women to basic transport and energy infrastructure (such as clean cooking fuels) can lead to greater economic activity. • Gender equality in farm inputs helps increase agricultural production and reduce poverty because women farmers form a significant proportion of the rural poor. • Equal investment in women's health and nutritional status reduces chronic hunger and malnourishment, which increases productivity and well-being.
	Goal 2 Achieve universal primary education	• Educated girls and women have greater control over their fertility and participate more in public life. • A mother's education is a strong and consistent determinant of her children's school enrollment and attainment and their health and nutrition outcomes.
	Goal 4 Reduce child mortality **Goal 5** Improve maternal health	• A mother's education, income, and empowerment have a significant impact on lowering child and maternal mortality.
	Goal 6 Combat HIV/AIDS, malaria, and other diseases	• Greater economic independence for women, increased ability to negotiate safe sex, greater awareness of the need to alter traditional norms about sexual relations, better access to treatment, and support for the care function that women perform are essential for halting and reversing the spread of HIV/AIDS and other epidemics.
	Goal 7 Ensure environmental sustainability	• Gender-equitable property and resource ownership policies enable women (often as primary users of these resources) to manage them in a more sustainable manner.
	Goal 8 Develop a global partnership for development	• Greater gender equality in the political sphere may lead to higher investments in development cooperation.

norms have perpetuated that disadvantage. This report notes the ways in which gender norms and policies also negatively affect boys and men, but the primary focus is to rectify the most common gender-based disadvantages—those faced by women and girls. The report recognizes, however, that men's engagement in meeting Goal 3 is vital. They can work as partners with women to bring about changes in gender roles and norms that can benefit both women and men. The report, therefore, suggests ways in which policies and interventions can engage men as equal partners in achieving gender equality and the empowerment of women.

Identifying the dimensions of gender equality

Based on past analyses of gender in society, the task force has adopted an operational framework for understanding gender equality that has three main dimensions:

- The *capabilities domain*, which refers to basic human abilities as measured by education, health, and nutrition. These capabilities are fundamental to individual well-being and are the means through which individuals access other forms of well-being.

	Millennium Development Goal	**Importance of Goal for gender equality**
Box 2.2 **Achieving the Millennium Development Goals is critical for gender equality**	**Goal 1** Eradicate extreme poverty and hunger	• Failure to design actions that reduce poverty equally for women and men will leave significant pockets of female poverty in many countries.
	Goal 2 Achieve universal primary education	• Failure to achieve universal primary education has significant consequences for girls' enrollment and completion of higher levels of education and hence their ability to access resources and opportunities to the same extent as boys.
	Goal 4 Reduce child mortality	• Child mortality is one reason fertility remains high in some parts of the world. High fertility is associated with greater unpaid work burdens for women, and multiple pregnancies are associated with elevated risks of disability or death. In some countries child mortality partly reflects discrimination against girls in nutrition and medical care. Reducing child mortality in these countries will mean ending such discrimination.
	Goal 5 Improve maternal health	• Women cannot enjoy equal rights, opportunities, and voice with men if they continue to suffer the ill-health, disability, and risks of dying associated with pregnancy and childbirth. The ability to have the number of children they desire when they desire is also critical if women are to take control of their lives and contribute productively to their families, communities, and societies.
	Goal 6 Combat HIV/AIDS, malaria, and other diseases	• Because the HIV/AIDS pandemic is rapidly being feminized, both in risk of becoming infected and in the burden of care, failure to control this epidemic is likely to leave girls and women increasingly vulnerable.
	Goal 7 Ensure environmental sustainability	• Because women are the major food producers in the developing world, failure to ensure environmental sustainability is likely to damage their ability to feed themselves and their families. Failure to limit certain types of pollutants, such as indoor smoke from cooking fires, will also have particularly deleterious effects on the health of women and children.

- The *access to resources and opportunities domain*, which refers primarily to equality in the opportunity to use or apply basic capabilities through access to economic assets (such as land, property, or infrastructure) and resources (such as income and employment), as well as political opportunity (such as representation in parliaments and other political bodies). Without access to resources and opportunities, both political and economic, women will be unable to employ their capabilities for their well-being and that of their families, communities, and societies.

- The *security domain*, which is defined here to mean reduced vulnerability to violence and conflict. Violence and conflict result in physical and psychological harm and lessen the ability of individuals, households, and communities to fulfill their potential. Violence directed specifically at women and girls often aims at keeping them in "their place" through fear.

These three domains are interrelated, and change in all three is critical to achieving Goal 3. The attainment of capabilities increases the likelihood that women can access opportunities for employment or participate in political and legislative bodies but does not guarantee it. Similarly, access to opportunity decreases the likelihood that women will experience violence (although in certain circumstances, it may temporarily increase that likelihood).

The seven strategic priorities represent first-generation development problems that have not yet been addressed systematically

Progress in any one domain to the exclusion of the others will be insufficient to meet the Goal of gender equality. For example, in many countries in Latin America girls enroll in primary school at the same rate as boys and even outnumber them in secondary school. However, many studies in Latin America show that women are disadvantaged in the labor market relative to men with similar education and experience. Thus, investments need to be directed to interventions across all three domains in order to achieve the Goal.

The strategic priorities listed in box 1.1 are based on this conceptual framework. The first two—strengthening opportunities for postprimary education for girls while meeting commitments to universal primary education and guaranteeing universal access to a broad range of sexual and reproductive health information and services—represent the priority for strengthening women's capabilities. The next four (investing in infrastructure to reduce women's time burdens, guaranteeing girls' and women's property and inheritance rights, eliminating gender inequality in employment, and increasing women's share of seats in national parliaments and local governmental bodies) reflect priorities for economic and political opportunity. And the final strategic priority—combating violence against girls and women—addresses the security domain.

Understanding the importance of female empowerment

The concept of empowerment is related to gender equality but distinct from it. The core of empowerment lies in the ability of a woman to control her own destiny (Malhotra, Schuler, and Boender 2002; Kabeer 1999). This implies that to be empowered women must not only have equal capabilities (such as education and health) and equal access to resources and opportunities (such as land and employment), but they must also have the agency to use those rights, capabilities, resources, and opportunities to make strategic choices and decisions (such as is provided through leadership opportunities and participation in political institutions). And for them to exercise agency, they must live without the fear of coercion and violence.

Because of the historical legacy of disadvantage women have faced, they are still all too often referred to as a vulnerable minority. In most countries, however, women are a majority, with the potential to catalyze enormous power and progress. While this report identifies the constraints that women face, it also emphasizes their resilience and the contributions they make to their families, communities, and economies despite those constraints—contributions that could be multiplied if those constraints were removed.

The case for the seven strategic priorities

The seven strategic priorities selected by the task force for action on the international and national level represent first-generation development problems that have not yet been addressed systematically within and across countries.

The task force believes that three subpopulations of women must receive preference in implementing the strategic priorities and allocating resources

They are interrelated: empowering women and promoting gender equality entail action on all of them. The task force considered selecting a smaller set of priorities but decided that dropping any one of the seven priorities would compromise achieving Goal 3 because gender inequality results from an inter-locking, self-reinforcing set of conditions. Some of the priorities are already present in the Millennium Development Goal framework (as indicators for Goal 3 and the target of Goal 4), but the task force wishes to highlight their importance for achieving Goal 3.

These seven priorities are a subset of the priorities outlined in previous international agreements, including the Beijing Declaration and Platform for Action and the Cairo Programme of Action. The recommendations in these international agreements remain important for achieving gender equality and women's empowerment, but the task force sees the seven priorities as needing immediate action if the Goal is to be met by 2015.

Although empowerment and equality should be enjoyed by all women and men, the task force believes that three subpopulations of women must receive preference in implementing the strategic priorities and allocating resources if poverty is to be reduced:

- Poor women in the poorest countries and in countries that have achieved increases in national income but where poverty remains significant.
- Adolescents, who constitute two-thirds of the population in the poorest countries and the largest cohort of adolescents in the world's history.
- Women and girls in conflict and postconflict settings.

Prioritizing these groups is not intended to minimize the vulnerability and needs of other groups of women, but to emphasize that investments in these subpopulations are a priority for achieving immediate and long-term results in reducing poverty.

A focus on poor women is justified for several reasons. Poor women have the greatest needs. Investments in them will produce the greatest benefits. It is often suggested that women outnumber men among the poor. Although precise estimates of the relative proportion of males and females living in pov-erty are not available, recent research suggests that women are overrepresented among the poor (Quisumbing, Haddad, and Peña 2001). Gender inequalities tend to be greater among the poor than the rich, especially for inequalities in capabilities and opportunities (World Bank 2001a; Filmer 1999). Moreover, the well-being and survival of poor households depends disproportionately on the productive and reproductive contributions of their female members. Also, an increasing number of poor households are headed or maintained by women (Bruce, Lloyd, and Leonard 1995).

Investing in the health, education, safety, and economic well-being of ado-lescents, especially adolescent girls, must also be a priority. Adolescence is a for-mative period, one of transition between childhood and adulthood. It is a time when interventions can dramatically alter subsequent life outcomes. The sheer

Investments are needed to help girls complete secondary schooling, support their transition from education to work, develop healthy sexuality, and guarantee their physical safety

size of the current adolescent cohort in poor countries means that interventions to improve their lives will affect national outcomes. One example illustrates this point well. If the mean age of childbearing in Bangladesh were to rise by five years, the country's population growth would fall by 40 percent—and the well-being of young women would almost certainly improve (Mensch, Bruce, and Greene 1998, p. 3). Within the adolescent cohort the task force has given priority to the needs of adolescent girls because they experience greater overall social, economic, and health disadvantages in most countries than do boys.[1] Therefore, investments to help girls complete good quality secondary schooling, support their transition from education to work, develop healthy sexuality, and guarantee their physical safety are urgently needed and can accelerate progress toward several of the Millennium Development Goals.

Finally, responding to these strategic priorities is particularly urgent for women in conflict and postconflict situations. Situations of conflict have disproportionate impacts on women and children, who typically are the majority of displaced persons in refugee camps and conflict zones (Landsberg-Lewis 2002). In times of conflict women and children are also more likely to be heads of households, underscoring the need for special assistance in overcoming the gender barriers that restrict their access to resources and threaten the survival of their households. Postconflict periods present a window of opportunity to reduce gender barriers and create a gender-equitable society, which is more likely to occur if reconstruction fosters the full participation of women. For example, in Rwanda the postconflict period was used as an opportunity to right previous gender inequalities in access to resources and political participation. One result was that Rwanda now has one of the largest proportions of national parliamentary seats held by women anywhere in the world.

Chapter 3

Strengthen opportunities for postprimary education for girls

Global commitments to girls' education have focused in the main on primary education. As a result, over the past decade, girls' primary school enrollment rates have increased in most regions. While this focus must continue, and international commitments to universal primary education must be met, the task force notes achieving Goal 3 requires strengthening postprimary education opportunities for girls. The evidence suggests that among all levels of education, secondary and higher levels of education have the greatest payoff for women's empowerment.

Moreover, focusing on secondary education can strengthen the pipeline that channels students through the education system and give parents an incentive to send their children to primary school. It is obvious that for girls (and boys) to reach secondary education, investments must be made in primary education. Thus it is important not to separate primary, secondary, and tertiary education into discrete components but to see them as an integral part of an education system in which each component has knock-on effects on the others.[1]

A number of interventions that have proven their effectiveness for increasing girls' participation in primary school may also apply to postprimary education. These include making schooling more affordable by reducing costs and offering targeted scholarships, building secondary schools close to girls' homes, and making schools safe and girl-friendly. Additionally, the content, quality, and relevance of education must be improved through curriculum reform, teacher training, and other actions (DeJaeghere 2004). Most important, education must serve as the vehicle for transforming attitudes, beliefs, and entrenched social norms that perpetuate discrimination and inequality. All interventions taken to promote gender equality in education must, therefore, be transformational in nature.

Investments must be made simultaneously in secondary education while meeting global commitments for universal primary education

Why strengthening girls' opportunities for postprimary education is a strategic priority

Education is a life-long process and can occur at different ages. Deficits in education can also be rectified at different ages and through different mechanisms, both formal and nonformal. Adult literacy, nonformal programs for dropouts, and other efforts are a valuable complement to the formal education system. However, because the target for Goal 3 focuses entirely on the formal education system, this chapter primarily discusses how that system can be transformed to eliminate gender gaps.[2]

Within formal education the task force has chosen to highlight postprimary education for several reasons. First, the 2005 target for Goal 3 will be missed for both primary and secondary education but by a much larger number of countries for secondary education. Concerted effort will have to be made today if gender disparities in both primary and secondary education are to be eliminated at least by the 2015 deadline. Investments in postprimary education cannot wait until universal primary education has been achieved.

Second, the research evidence shows that postprimary education has far stronger positive effects on women's own outcomes than primary education does—their health and well-being, position in family and society, economic opportunities and returns, and political participation. Therefore, investments must be made simultaneously in secondary education while meeting global commitments for universal primary education. The task force's companion report on universal primary education discusses in detail policies and interventions to achieve that goal and the target of gender parity in primary education, while the evidence presented here focuses on how postprimary education leads to or leverages changes and impacts in the other domains of gender equality and in empowerment (UN Millennium Project 2005c).

Education and women's empowerment

Data from around the world show that increased education is associated with the empowerment of women (Malhotra, Pande, and Grown 2003). Educated women are more effective at improving their own well-being and that of their family. They are better equipped to extract the most benefit from existing services and opportunities and to generate alternative opportunities, roles, and support structures. These empowering effects of women's education are manifested in a variety of ways, including increased income-earning potential, ability to bargain for resources within the household, decisionmaking autonomy, control over their own fertility, and participation in public life.

Any such impacts, however, are highly dependent on the context. They are strongly conditioned by such factors as level of economic development, depth of the labor market, and degree of gender stratification. The impact of women's education is greater in settings that are already relatively egalitarian. Under such conditions even modestly educated women are more likely to participate

**Higher levels
of education
increase
the gains
from formal
labor force
participation
more for women
than for men**

in important family decisions, to work in nonfarm occupations, and to control economic resources.[3] Education alone may not be transformative in the absence of other normative shifts and changed power relations. In such settings, it takes more than education to reach thresholds of change.

Labor market benefits to educated women

Studies in Latin America, Asia, and Africa show that higher levels of education increase the probability that women will engage in formal paid employment (Birdsall and Behrman 1991; Cameron, Dowling, and Worsick 2001). Higher levels of education increase the gains from formal labor force participation more for women than for men (Deolalikar 1994; Aromolaran 2002; Birdsall and Fox 1985). A review of the literature on returns to investment in education finds that, overall, women receive only slightly higher returns to their schooling investments (10 percent) than men (9 percent; Psacharopoulos and Patrinos 2002). Returns vary, however, by level of schooling. Women experience higher returns to secondary education (18 percent) than do men (14 percent), but lower returns (13 percent) to primary education than do men (20 percent).

The impact of education on fertility and mortality

Female secondary education is a critical influence on fertility and mortality. Subbarao and Rainey (1995) conducted a cross-country study of fertility and secondary school attainment among women in 65 low- and middle-income countries in 1985 that covered 93 percent of the population of the developing world. In countries where few women had a secondary education, families averaged more than five children, of whom one or two died in infancy. In countries where half the girls were educated at the secondary level, the fertility rate fell to just over three children and child deaths were rare. Subbarao and Rainey calculate that in these 65 countries, doubling the proportion of girls educated at the secondary level from 19 percent to 38 percent, holding constant all other variables (including access to family planning and healthcare) would have cut the fertility rate from 5.3 children per woman to 3.9 and the infant mortality rate from 81 deaths per 1,000 births to 38.

Another study summarizing sample surveys across the developing world found that the higher the level of female education, the lower is desired family size and the greater the success in achieving it (Schultz 1993). Further, each additional year of a mother's schooling cuts the expected infant mortality rate by 5–10 percent (table 3.1).

The impact of education on women's health and bodily integrity

Higher levels of education play an important role in promoting health. Studies have found that only at secondary or higher levels of schooling does education have a significant beneficial effect on women's own health outcomes, for risks of disease, and their attitudes toward female genital cutting (Malhotra, Pande,

Table 3.1	Years of schooling	Total fertility rate	Desired family size
Total fertility rate and desired family size by years of schooling, by region: averages for countries with World Fertility Surveys in the 1970s	*Africa (8 countries)*		
	7 or more	5.0	5.0
	4–6	6.2	5.9
	1–3	7.2	6.4
	0	7.0	6.9
Source: Schultz 1993.	*Latin America (13 countries)*		
	7 or more	3.2	3.7
	4–6	4.8	4.2
	1–3	6.2	4.7
	0	6.8	4.8
	Asia and Oceania (13 countries)		
	7 or more	3.9	4.0
	4–6	5.8	4.2
	1 3	6.4	4.3
	0	7.0	5.4

and Grown 2003). Higher levels of education—six years or more—always have a positive effect on a woman's use of prenatal and delivery services and postnatal care, and the effect is always much larger than the effect of lower levels of schooling (Elo 1992; Bhatia and Cleland 1995; Govindasamy 2000).[4]

Profiles of nine African countries found that the traditional practice of female genital cutting was more prevalent among uneducated than among educated women (Population Reference Bureau 2001). Women with primary or no education are more likely to have been cut than those who have received secondary instruction. In the Central African Republic, for example, 48 percent of women with no education and 45 percent with primary education have been cut, while only 23 percent of women with secondary education have been subjected to the practice. Another study by the World Health Organization (WHO 1998a) reports that in Côte d'Ivoire, 55 percent of uneducated women had been cut, compared with 24 percent of women with a primary or higher level of education.

Women's education also affects their attitude toward the genital cutting of their daughters. A study in Egypt found that women who had some secondary education were four times more likely to oppose female genital cutting in general and for their daughters and granddaughters than were women who had never completed primary school (El-Gibaly and others 1999). In Burkina Faso a study found that 78 percent of girls whose mothers had not graduated from primary school had been cut compared with 48 percent of girls whose mothers had received some secondary education (WHO 1998a).

Education is also strongly related to women's age at marriage. Girls with fewer than seven years of schooling are more likely to be married by age 18 than those with higher levels of schooling (Population Reference Bureau 2000).

Female education can reduce violence against girls and women and enhance their control over their own bodies

Enrollment of young women in secondary school is inversely related to the proportion of girls married before the age of 18 (figure 3.1). Other multicountry studies confirm that girls who drop out of school and marry in their early teens typically begin childbearing before their bodies are mature and continue with closely spaced births. The result is high mortality among both children and mothers. Evidence also consistently shows that women with less than primary schooling tend to marry earlier, bear children earlier, and have more children than women who have completed primary schooling (Herz and Measham 1987; Ainsworth, Beegle, and Nyamete 1996). Early marriage is also associated with women's lack of bargaining power and decisionmaking in the household.

There is a similar relationship between higher levels of education and the incidence of violence against women. Female education can reduce violence against girls and women and enhance their control over their own bodies (although it does not eliminate violence). A recent analysis of Demographic and Health Survey (ORC-Macro 2004) data from Cambodia, Colombia, India, and Nicaragua finds that women with more education are less likely to report ever having experienced violence (Kishor and Johnson 2004).[5] In the Dominican Republic, Egypt, Peru, and Zambia the highest rates of violence were found among women with primary education and the lowest rates among women with secondary or higher education (Kishor and Johnson 2004).

The impact of education on women's vulnerability to HIV/AIDS

The HIV infection rate in many developing countries is growing fastest among teenage girls and young adult women. Education for girls may be critical for breaking that pattern, by increasing their understanding of risks and their capacity to avoid them. Primary education has a significant positive impact on knowledge of HIV prevention and condom use, but secondary education has an even greater impact (Global Campaign for Education 2004). As Herz and Sperling (2004, p. 35) explain, "Girls who attend school are far more likely to

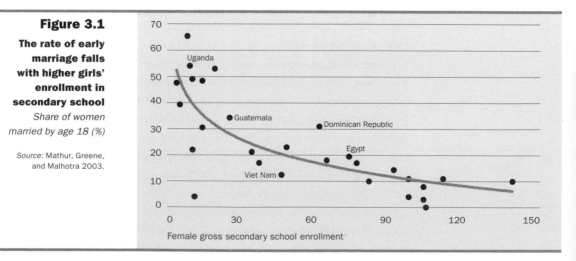

Figure 3.1

The rate of early marriage falls with higher girls' enrollment in secondary school

Share of women married by age 18 (%)

Source: Mathur, Greene, and Malhotra 2003.

Female gross secondary school enrollment

Improving educational opportunities for girls is essential to improving the next generation's educational outcomes

understand the risks involved in risky behavior, not believe the myths associated with sex, and (in the case of good school programs) even know effective refusal tactics in difficult sexual situations."

A 32-country study found that women with postprimary education are five times more likely than illiterate women to know facts about HIV/AIDS. For example, literate women are three times less likely than illiterate women to think that a healthy-looking person cannot be HIV-positive and four times less likely to believe that there is no way to avoid AIDS (Vandemoortele and Delmonica 2000). Another study in rural Uganda found that during the 1990s people who finished secondary education were seven times less likely to contract HIV—and those who finished primary education half as likely—as those who received little or no schooling (De Walque 2002).

It must be noted, however, that because sexual assaults of adolescent girls also occur at secondary schools, schools need to be made safer so that these education benefits can accrue.

Intergenerational effects of girls' education

Education of girls and mothers leads to sustained increases in educational attainment from one generation to the next. Multiple studies find that a mother's level of education has a strong positive effect on her daughters' enrollment—more than on sons and significantly more than the effect of fathers' education on daughters (Lavy 1996; Ridker 1997; King and Bellew 1991; Lillard and Willis 1994; Alderman and King 1998; Kambhapati and Pal 2001; Parker and Pederzini 2000; Bhalla, Saigal, and Basu 2003). Further, the more educated a mother is, the stronger the effects. A study by the Inter-American Development Bank (1998) finds that in Latin America 15-year-old children whose mothers have some secondary schooling will remain in school for two to three more years than the children of mothers with less than four years of education.

Improving educational opportunities for girls, therefore, is essential to improving the next generation's educational outcomes. But to what extent does providing educational opportunities to uneducated or illiterate mothers of young children today facilitate better education outcomes in the current generation? Although limited, information on this question suggests that adult literacy programs for women are beneficial to themselves and their children.

A longitudinal study in Nepal concluded that women's literacy programs contributed to women's overall empowerment through improvements in their reproductive health and participation in income-generating and community and political activities (Burchfield 1997). They also positively affected children's education and family health. The women in the sample who did not participate in adult literacy programs were poorer, less active in community activities, less knowledgeable about several health and political related issues, and less likely to send their children to school.[6] Another longitudinal study in

**All regions
except South
Asia and Sub-
Saharan Africa
had primary
enrollment
ratios close to
parity in 2000**

Bolivia found that NGO literacy programs had a significant positive impact on women's social and economic development (Burchfield and others 2002). Taking into account factors such as education level, marital status, locality, and home material possessions, the study found that participants in literacy programs showed greater gains in reading skills than individuals in the control group and were better able to help their children with homework. At the same time, few women were reading to their young children, and the program had little impact on women's involvement in their children's school.

Progress toward gender equality in education, 1990–2000

Gender parity in access to schooling is the first step toward gender equality in education. However, the world is still far from achieving gender parity in enrollment and completion rates, particularly in secondary school. Worldwide, it is estimated that 54–57 percent of all out-of-school children are girls.[7] In South Asia girls constitute two-thirds of all out of school children (UNESCO 2004).

There are two indicators for tracking progress toward gender parity in education: the ratio of girls to boys in primary, secondary, and tertiary education and the ratio of literate females to males ages 15–24. Although enrollment rates are important indicators of educational inputs, school completion rates are a better proxy for outcomes (Bruns, Mingat, and Rakotomala 2003). For this reason, this section reports on both enrollment and completion rates. The literacy indicator, which was chosen to reflect the performance of the national education system and the quality of the human resources, is problematic because countries differ in their definition of literacy and in how they collect data on this indicator. Thus the literacy indicator is not included in the analysis of progress described here, although it is shown in appendix table A1.10 to assess progress toward the target for Goal 3.

Primary school enrollment and completion

All regions except South Asia and Sub-Saharan Africa had enrollment ratios close to parity in 2000 (table 3.2). While the gender gap has not closed in these two regions, both experienced a 10 percent or more increase in girls' gross enrollment rates over the past decade, from 79.5 percent to 96.6 percent in South Asia and from 68.1 percent to 87.1 percent in Sub-Saharan Africa (table 3.3). It is encouraging to see that the convergence toward parity in primary school has occurred mainly through increases in girls' gross enrollment rates.[8] At this rate of progress, the task force believes that gender parity in primary enrollment is attainable with appropriate public policy and investments.

While the trends are positive, several countries are likely to miss both the 2005 and 2015 targets. Projections are that 19 of 133 countries will still have primary enrollment ratios in the 0.70–0.89 range in 2005. By 2015, 21 countries are expected to have girls' to boys' primary enrollment ratios below 0.9. Of these,

Table 3.2

Gender parity in primary school gross enrollment rates, 1990 and 2000

Gender parity index

Source: UNESCO 2004.

Region	1990	2000
Developed countries	0.99	0.99
East Asia and Pacific	0.95	0.97
Europe and Central Asia	0.98	0.98
Latin America and the Caribbean	0.98	0.97
Middle East and North Africa	0.86	0.92
South Asia	0.77	0.89
Sub-Saharan Africa	0.80	0.86

Table 3.3

Primary school gross enrollment rates by sex, 1990 and 2000

Percent

Source: UNESCO 2004.

Region	1990		2000	
	Male	Female	Male	Female
Developed countries	102.2	102.2	104.4	104.1
East Asia and Pacific	105.5	101.1	107.2	104
Europe and Central Asia	95.4	94.3	99.8	98
Latin America and the Caribbean	100.0	98.9	113.0	111.0
Middle East and North Africa	93.9	82.4	97.6	91.3
South Asia	100.0	79.5	107.0	96.6
Sub-Saharan Africa	81.4	68.1	99.3	87.1

12 are in Sub-Saharan Africa, which should be viewed as a "priority" region for interventions.[9] (Projection results are reported in detail in appendix table A1.7.)

The picture is less hopeful for primary school completion.[10] In 1990, with the exception of Latin America and the Caribbean, boys completed primary school at a higher rate than girls in all regions (table 3.4). Overall, boys' primary completion rates were more than 7 percentage points ahead of girls', although this varied by region. In South Asia the difference was almost 14 percentage points in favor of boys, while in the Middle East and North Africa and Europe and Central Asia, boys' completion rates were about 11 percentage points ahead of girls'.

Despite these gender gaps, there have been improvements in girls' completion rates in all regions. The biggest improvement has been in Europe and Central Asia, where the difference between girls' and boys' completion rates declined from 11 percentage points to 2 percentage points.[11] This narrowing of the gender gap was due mostly to increases in girls' completion rates, except in South Asia and the Middle East and North Africa, where slight drops in boys' completion rates have contributed to improved parity.

In absolute levels, completion rates for both boys and girls are still low, particularly in the Middle East and North Africa, South Asia, and Sub-Saharan Africa. School dropout is a major problem (discussed below).

Secondary school enrollment and completion
Across the world there is greater variation in enrollment rates at the secondary level than at the primary level (table 3.5). Once again, South Asia and

Table 3.4		1990		2000	
Primary school completion rates by sex, 1990 and 2000	Region	Male	Female	Male	Female
Percent	East Asia and Pacific	88.8	85.4	91.2	90.9
	Europe and Central Asia	96.0	85.7	95.6	93.9
Source: World Bank 2004f.	Latin America and the Caribbean	83.4	86.7	85.7	88.6
	Middle East and North Africa	82.6	71.7	80.5	72.3
	South Asia	94.9	81.0	87.8	81.3
	Sub-Saharan Africa	56.2	46.2	56.9	51.9

Sub-Saharan Africa fare poorly, with girls' to boys' gross enrollment ratios below 0.90. East Asia and Pacific, Europe and Central Asia, and the Middle East and North Africa have a gender parity ratio above 0.90. Latin America and the Caribbean and developed countries have reverse gender gaps.

A closer look at the numbers, however, shows that girls' enrollment rates are still fairly low in most regions (table 3.6). Although 78 of 149 countries for which there are data have girls' to boys' secondary enrollment ratios of 1.0 or greater in 2000, only 33 of the 78 countries have female enrollment rates above 90 percent. The female secondary enrollment rate is 47.1 percent in South Asia and only 29.7 percent in Sub-Saharan Africa.

Projections show that 24 of 118 countries are expected to have gender parity ratios in secondary education below 0.90 in 2005 (appendix table A1.8). Projections for 2015 show that the number of countries with ratios below 0.90 will rise to 27.[12] These results suggest that achieving gender parity at high levels of enrollment will take concerted national and international action.

Data on secondary school completion rates are scarce. The World Education Indicators program, a collaboration between the UNESCO Institute for Statistics and the Organisation for Economic Co-operation and Development (OECD), gathers data on upper secondary graduation rates from 26 OECD countries and 19 middle-income countries. With such a highly constrained sample, the inferences that can be drawn for developing countries are fairly limited, but it is noteworthy that female completion rates and total completion rates are below 50 percent for all 19 middle-income countries in the sample.

Differences within countries

The regional averages reported above often mask variations within countries arising from differences in geography, ethnicity, or wealth. Recent studies point to a high correlation between household income and education demand (table 3.7). Filmer and Pritchett (1999), for instance, find that in Senegal enrollment of 6- to 14-year-olds is 52 percent lower for the poorest households than for the richest households. The difference is 48.8 percent in Benin and 36 percent in Zambia.

In many countries gender and wealth effects interact, and the outcome is almost always to the disadvantage of the girls. This trend is particularly visible

Table 3.5

Gender parity in secondary school gross enrollment rates, 1990 and 2000

Gender parity index

Source: UNESCO 2004.

Region	1990	2000
Developed countries	1.02	1.03
East Asia and Pacific	0.88	0.95
Europe and Central Asia	0.99	0.99
Latin America and the Caribbean	1.14	1.07
Middle East and North Africa	0.87	0.96
South Asia	0.64	0.86
Sub-Saharan Africa	0.68	0.77

Table 3.6

Secondary school gross enrollment rates, by sex, 1990 and 2000

Percent

Source: UNESCO 2004.

Region	1990		2000	
	Male	Female	Male	Female
Developed countries	95.9	97.9	112.3	117.0
East Asia and Pacific	46.4	43.2	64.3	63.7
Europe and Central Asia	83.2	83.0	85.8	85.2
Latin America and the Caribbean	49.2	54.5	77.5	82.5
Middle East and North Africa	58.2	52.7	69.1	68.7
South Asia	50.1	35.3	53.7	47.1
Sub-Saharan Africa	24.9	19.4	35.6	29.7

in Egypt, India, Morocco, and Niger (Filmer 1999). In India, for example, there is a 2.5 percentage point difference in enrollment between girls and boys for the richest households, but a 24 percentage point difference for the poorest households (table 3.7).

In the majority of 41 countries with appropriate data, gender parity deteriorates with declining household income.[13] In 13 countries, however, the girls' to boys' enrollment ratio is higher in poorer households than richer households (Ghana, Bangladesh, Kenya, Madagascar, Namibia, Dominican Republic, Haiti, Nicaragua, Indonesia, Philippines, Brazil, Kazakhstan, and Colombia).[14]

Education and gender in countries in conflict

UNESCO (2004) reports that half of the 104 million out-of-school children, two-thirds of them girls, live in countries in the midst of or recovering from armed conflict. Of the 17 Sub-Saharan African countries in which enrollment declined in the 1990s, 6 are countries affected by or recovering from conflict (Angola, Burundi, Democratic Republic of the Congo, Liberia, Sierra Leone, and Somalia). Of the 14 Sub-Saharan African countries with very low girls' to boys' enrollment ratios, 3 are currently in conflict (Burundi, Côte d'Ivoire, and Liberia) and 2 are recovering from it (Ethiopia and Mozambique; UNESCO 2004). Armed conflict particularly disrupts the education of girls, who may be forced to care for younger siblings as mothers become more engaged in survival and livelihood activities, or who are not allowed to go to school because of fear of rape, abduction, and sexual exploitation.

Table 3.7			Male		Female		Parity ratio	
Enrollment rates and	Country	Year	Rich	Poor	Rich	Poor	Rich	Poor
ratios of 6- to 14-year-	Benin	1996	84.7	33.2	60.3	14.2	0.71	0.43
olds by wealth and sex	Burkina Faso	1992–93	70.2	18.7	56.2	9.9	0.80	0.53
Percent	Cameroon	1991	93.6	55.9	90.6	42.5	0.97	0.76
Note: For countries in bold type,	Central African Republic	1994–95	83.3	50.8	78.0	28.7	0.94	0.56
the girls' to boys' enrollment	Chad	1998	64.2	30.4	50.2	14.2	0.78	0.47
ratio is higher in poorer than	Côte d'Ivoire	1994	84.6	38.6	64.2	24.9	0.76	0.65
in richer households.	**Ghana**	**1993**	**93.6**	**70.3**	**88.1**	**68.2**	**0.94**	**0.97**
	Mali	1995–96	68.1	14.4	56.1	7.9	0.82	0.55
Source: Filmer 1999.	Niger	1997	58.7	14.9	51.2	8.1	0.87	0.54
	Senegal	1992–93	71.0	17.8	60.3	10.0	0.85	0.56
	Togo	1998	94.7	67.6	80.3	50.0	0.85	0.74
	Egypt	1995–96	95.2	77.9	95.7	56.5	1.01	0.73
	Morocco	1992	94.4	38.5	84.5	14.4	0.90	0.37
	Bangladesh	**1996–97**	**86.0**	**65.6**	**80.9**	**68.0**	**0.94**	**1.04**
	India	1992–93	95.4	61.4	92.9	37.5	0.97	0.61
	Nepal	1996	90.1	73.3	81.5	49.8	0.90	0.68
	Pakistan	1990–91	85.8	50.0	85.4	21.3	1.00	0.43
	Comoros	1996	78.8	45.5	68.4	32.7	0.87	0.72
	Kenya	**1998**	**94.0**	**86.2**	**90.2**	**87.6**	**0.96**	**1.02**
	Madagascar	**1997**	**90.5**	**46.5**	**89.5**	**47.1**	**0.99**	**1.01**
	Malawi	1996	93.0	88.7	93.6	85.4	1.01	0.96
	Mozambique	1997	77.6	51.2	77.8	36.4	1.00	0.71
	Namibia	**1992**	**93.0**	**81.9**	**90.8**	**86.0**	**0.98**	**1.05**
	Rwanda	1992	65.0	46.5	65.0	45.3	1.00	0.97
	Tanzania	1996	62.8	40.0	64.0	39.6	1.02	0.99
	Uganda	1995	83.5	64.1	81.9	53.8	0.98	0.84
	Zambia	1996–97	85.3	49.7	84.4	48.0	0.99	0.97
	Zimbabwe	1994	92.6	82.2	92.9	80.0	1.00	0.97
	Dominican Republic	**1996**	**98.3**	**87.7**	**97.3**	**89.9**	**0.99**	**1.03**
	Guatemala	1995	91.2	51.3	90.5	41.7	0.99	0.81
	Haiti	**1994–95**	**93.6**	**55.5**	**86.8**	**54.9**	**0.93**	**0.99**
	Nicaragua	**1998**	**90.8**	**61.4**	**94.9**	**66.4**	**1.05**	**1.08**
	Indonesia	**1997**	**95.1**	**79.4**	**94.9**	**81.5**	**1.00**	**1.03**
	Philippines	**1998**	**95.0**	**75.5**	**94.6**	**82.5**	**1.00**	**1.09**
	Bolivia	1997	99.1	89.7	96.5	85.8	0.97	0.96
	Brazil	**1996**	**99.4**	**87.7**	**96.4**	**89.4**	**0.97**	**1.02**
	Colombia	**1995**	**98.7**	**79.1**	**96.5**	**82.7**	**0.98**	**1.05**
	Peru	1996	94.7	87.0	94.4	84.5	1.00	0.97
	Kazakhstan	**1995**	**84.0**	**85.5**	**83.6**	**86.0**	**1.00**	**1.01**
	Turkey	1993	83.7	68.0	76.6	53.6	0.92	0.79
	Uzbekistan	1996	78.4	79.6	83.8	80.8	1.07	1.02

There is ample understanding of how to remedy the problem of girls' low enrollments

Learning differentials

Despite problems with international literacy data (described more fully in chapter 10), it is apparent that large gender gaps exist in adult literacy in many countries. In 2000 the adult literacy rate in developing countries was 66 percent for women and 81 percent for men (UNESCO 2004). Less than half of all adult women were literate in the Middle East and North Africa (48 percent) and South Asia (44 percent). And in Sub-Saharan Africa the female adult literacy rate was 52 percent. In 2000, the gender parity ratio in the three regions ranged from below 0.7 to 0.75.

The costs of gender inequality in education to productivity and economic growth

Research on education and economic growth has shown that failing to invest in girls' education lowers gross national product (GNP) (Knowles, Lorgelly, and Owen 2002; Klasen 2001). Hill and King (1995) estimate that, everything else being equal, countries in which the ratio of girls' to boys' enrollment in primary or secondary education is less than 0.75 can expect levels of GNP that are roughly 25 percent lower than countries in which there is less gender disparity in enrollments.

More recently, Abu-Ghaida and Klasen (2002) report that countries that fail to meet the goal of gender parity in education will face considerable costs, both in forgone economic growth and in reductions in fertility, child mortality, and malnutrition. And without appropriate action, these costs will increase over time. They estimate that countries that are off-track in female primary and secondary school enrollment might lose 0.1–0.3 percentage point in annual economic growth between 1995 and 2005 and an average of 0.4 percentage point between 2005 and 2015.

Interventions to increase gender parity in primary and secondary education

Current efforts must be scaled up in order to meet the target date for Goal 3 of eliminating gender disparities in primary and secondary education, preferably by 2005 and at all levels no later than 2015. The insights and lessons learned in the past two decades of experimenting with a range of interventions (Subrahmanian 2002) must be applied and the interventions brought to scale in the next 12 years.

There are few rigorous evaluations of which interventions have the greatest impact on increasing girls' participation in secondary education, and more research is needed to fill gaps in current knowledge. But there is ample understanding of how to remedy the problem of girls' low enrollments. Herz and Sperling (2004) identify four approaches that increase girls' participation in primary school that can also be applied to secondary school. These strategies have all been effective in a variety of countries:

**Scholarship
programs have
been effective
in boosting
adolescent girls'
enrollment and
retention rates**

- Making girls' schooling more affordable by reducing fees and offering targeted scholarships.
- Building schools close to girls' homes, involving the community in school management, and allowing flexible scheduling.
- Making schools girl-friendly by improving the safety of schools, the design of facilities (such as latrines for girls), and instituting policies that promote girls' attendance (such as permitting married adolescents to attend).
- Improving the quality of education by training more female teachers for the secondary level, providing gender-sensitive textbooks, and developing a curriculum for girls that is strong in math and sciences and that projects gender equality.

Within countries these interventions must give highest priority to marginalized and excluded populations of girls, such as those who belong to ethnic minority groups or who live in poor communities. Many of the national averages on girls' enrollment and completion rates mask the disadvantage that excluded groups continue to face. In Latin American countries, for example, it is particularly important to invest in the education of girls from poor households and indigenous populations, where participation remains low.

Making schools affordable

There are two ways to make school affordable for poor families: by eliminating user fees and other school fees to reduce direct costs and by providing incentives to families to send their girls to school, for instance, through scholarships, take-home rations programs, or other means. Eliminating or substantially reducing school fees has resulted in increases in primary enrollment, particularly for girls. When free schooling was introduced in Uganda in 1997, primary school enrollment nearly doubled from 3.4 million to 5.7 million children, rising to 6.5 million by 1999. Total girls' enrollment increased from 63 percent to 83 percent, while enrollment among the poorest fifth of girls rose from 46 percent to 82 percent (World Bank 2002c). In Tanzania the elimination of primary school fees in 2002 resulted in additional enrollment of 1.5 million students (Coalition for Health and Education Rights 2002). Abolishing user, uniform, and other fees is important for ensuring that girls' attend and complete school.[15]

Scholarship programs have also been effective in boosting adolescent girls' enrollment and retention rates. Bangladesh launched a nationwide stipend program in 1994 for girls in secondary schools, including all *madrasas* (religious schools). The program has had a substantial impact on girls' enrollment, particularly in rural areas (box 3.1; UNESCO 2004; World Bank 2001a). In Tanzania a scholarship program for girls significantly increased their enrollment in secondary school. The program was subsequently extended to boys.

Cambodia established a national program of scholarships for girls and ethnic minorities to encourage the transition from primary to secondary school

Box 3.1

The Bangladesh Female Secondary School Assistance Program increases girls' enrollment

Source: Herz and Sperling 2004; Orlando 2004; Filmer, Prouty, and Winter 2002; UNESCO 2004.

Bangladesh's Female Secondary School Assistance Program began in 1994, building on earlier NGO efforts begun in 1982. Its purpose was to increase rural girls' enrollment and retention in secondary school, assist them in passing their Senior School Certificate examination, and enhance their employment opportunities. The program:

- Provides scholarships to girls in grades 6–12 living outside the metropolitan areas of Bangladesh covering full tuition, exam costs, text books, school supplies, uniforms, and transport.
- Increases the number of female teachers in secondary schools.
- Educates communities on the importance of girls' education and encourages parents to get involved through parent education committees.
- Improves school infrastructure.
- Reforms curricula and adds occupational skills training to have immediate application in labor markets.

In 1991/92 only 27 percent of girls enrolled and only 5 percent of those completed secondary school. In 2002 girls accounted for 54 percent of all secondary school enrollments in the program areas. Their attendance and achievement also improved, surpassing those of boys: in 2002, attendance was 91 percent for girls and 86 percent for boys, and 89 percent of girls obtained passing marks in year-end exams compared with 81 percent of boys.

The program has steadily extended its coverage, and by 2002 it was supporting 5,000 schools in the 118 poorest rural districts. The number of girls receiving scholarships increased from 197,000 in 1994 to 875,858 in 1999. The requirements for eligibility and continuation of the scholarship are regular attendance (at least 75 percent of total school days), maintaining a minimum 45 percent in the yearly and half-yearly exams, and being unmarried. The annual stipend ranges from $12 for grade 6 to $36 for grade 10 and is awarded directly to the girls through their own banking account. This feature aims to teach girls about banking practices and to give them saving habits.

The program also sought to recruit more female teachers, setting a target of 40 percent of new teachers. By 2002 this target was almost achieved. The program also upgraded school infrastructure, to make it more friendly to girls. By 2002, 3,667 latrines and 3,652 tubewells had been built. Between 1994 and 2002, 3,080 girls received occupational skills training that prepared them to enter the labor market. The program had one other significant impact: between 1994 and 2000 the proportion of married girls dropped from 29 percent to 14 percent among girls ages 13–15 and from 72 percent to 64 percent among girls ages 16–19.

and from secondary to postsecondary education. The scholarship is not only for newly enrolled girls but also girls who are at risk of dropping out because of high costs. It covers tuition, board, and lodging for those who need it most. Though the program has not yet been systematically evaluated, a pilot girls' scholarship program in four districts of Kompon Cham province had a 90–95 percent success rate for enrollment and retention (UNESCO 2004).

Some programs provide cash grants to poor households with school-age children. Grants are conditional on regular school attendance. The programs aim to increase enrollment and attendance by compensating households for the direct and opportunity costs of sending children to school. Such programs

Decreasing
the distance
to school
encourages
girls' enrollment
and attendance

simultaneously raise the immediate incomes of impoverished families and help to educate poor children. Conditional cash transfer programs are well established in Mexico (Progresa, now called Oportunidades), Brazil (Bolsa Escola), and Bangladesh (Food for Education). Mexico's Progresa provides cash transfers to poor households in marginal rural areas conditional on children attending school regularly (box 3.2). It has increased enrollment rates at the primary level and even more at the secondary level, especially for girls. Such programs are also in place or under development in Argentina, Chile, Colombia, Ecuador, Honduras, Jamaica, Nicaragua, and Turkey (Morley and Cody 2003). School-feeding and take-home rations programs also provide incentives for school enrollment and retention. These programs have demonstrated effects in boosting girls' enrollments at the primary level, but they are not widely implemented at the secondary level (IFPRI 2001).

Reducing the distance to school

Decreasing the distance to school encourages girls' enrollment and attendance, by alleviating concerns for safety and reputation. Research in such diverse countries as Ghana, India, Malaysia, Peru, and the Philippines indicates that distance matters for all children, but especially for girls (Sipahimanlani 1999; Lavy 1996; Gertler and Glewwe 1992; King and Lillard 1987). Providing schools within local communities has been shown to substantially increase enrollments for girls in Egypt, Indonesia, and several Sub-Saharan African countries. In Egypt, following a campaign to construct rural primary schools, girls' enrollment grew 23 percent, while boys' enrollments grew 18 percent (Duflo 2001; Rugh 2000; Filmer 1999).

Improving safety and infrastructure

Schools also need to be safe places for girls. This includes freedom from harassment from male peers and from the predatory behavior of male teachers (Lloyd and Mensch 1999). In Rajasthan, India, community initiatives led to the formation of the Shikshakarmi Project, which appoints a female helper to escort

---

Box 3.2

Cash for education programs— Mexico's Progresa

Source: ILO/UNCTAD Advisory Group 2001; Morley and Coady 2003; Skoufias and McClafferty 2003.

Progresa, the largest cash for education program in Latin America, reaches 2.6 million households, or 40 percent of rural families. The Mexican government, concerned by evidence showing that girls tend to drop out at very high rates after primary school, initiated the program in 1997. Progresa's grant schedule awards increasingly higher payments for girls to attend secondary school. In grade 7 boys receive 240 pesos a month, while girls receive 250 pesos a month; in grade 8 boys receive 250 pesos a month, while girls receive 285 pesos a month, and so forth. The program increased girls' primary school enrollment by 0.96–1.45 percentage points from an initial level of about 93 percent. At the secondary level, where girls' enrollment rates before the program were 67 percent, girls' enrollment rose by 3.5–5.8 percentage points.

Opportunity costs for girls' education that arise from their large burden of household chores can be addressed in a variety of ways

girls to and from school and provide care during school hours. According to Jain (2003), this has increased girls' attendance rates. In countries where parents are apprehensive about sending girls (especially postpuberty) to school if it involves contact with male teachers or students, girls-only secondary school might be an option (Jha and Subrahmanian 2004).

Although ministries of education have been slow to address gender-based violence systematically throughout their school systems, NGO efforts have emerged in countries around the world to counter gender-based violence in schools. They offer workshops, theater, and a range of other program activities for students on destructive gender norms and violence and attempt to shape positive, nonviolent masculine and feminine identities. These efforts, which have mostly been limited to individual schools, are gaining popularity. They need to be rigorously evaluated and, if proven effective, expanded throughout school systems.

Another minimal but essential step toward making schools hospitable environments for girls is providing private latrine facilities. Experience across 30 African countries, for example, indicates that a majority of young women do not attend school when they are menstruating if there are no private latrine facilities to enable them to care for personal hygiene (Forum for African Women Educationalists 2001; World Bank 1996, 2001b).

Opportunity costs for girls' education that arise from their large burden of household chores can be addressed in a variety of ways. Some measures reduce the need for girls' work: providing day-care centers and preschools for younger siblings or for students' children, or improving the supply of accessible water and fuel. Changing policies to permit married and pregnant adolescents to attend school can also promote girls' attendance, as in Botswana, Guinea, Kenya, Malawi, and Zamiba (UNESCO 2004). Other measures—such as flexible school schedules—enable girls to pursue an education while meeting household responsibilities. Take-home food rations for the families of school-attending girls can offset the loss to the household of the girls' labor. Flexible schedules, double sessions, and evening school hours have been introduced in Bangladesh, China, India, Morocco, and Pakistan (Herz and others 1995). There do not appear to be any programs designed to transfer some of the domestic burden to boys, although countries should consider this as another option.

Improving the quality of education

Girls and their families may find little reason to attend school if the curriculum or their teachers or counselors convey the message that girls are less important than boys or if the school tracks girls into fields of study or training for low-paid occupations considered appropriate for females. Analyses of textbooks in the Middle East, Asia, and Africa consistently find heavily stereotyped material, with women portrayed as subordinate and passive and men as intelligent, leaders, and dominant (Lloyd and Mensch 1999; Herz and Sperling 2004).

**Support
to literacy
programs for
adult women can
be an important
complement to
interventions to
increase access
and retention
rates of children
in school**

Many developing countries also practice gender tracking in secondary school, directing girls away from math and science (Herz and others 1995). Teaching practices—such as giving boys more opportunities than girls to ask and answer questions, to use learning material, and to lead groups—may further discourage girls (UNICEF 2002). Several countries in Africa and Asia are beginning to use gender sensitivity training for teachers and administrators to encourage girls' participation (UNICEF 2001).

Providing female teachers for girls may address some security concerns as well as provide useful role models. International cross-section data suggest a positive correlation between gender parity in enrollment and the proportion of female teachers (Herz and others 1995). Qualified female teachers are in short supply, however. Young women are now being recruited, particularly in rural areas. Their lack of educational qualification may be compensated for by their knowledge of and commitment to local communities (Herz and Sperling 2004).

Educating illiterate women
A large body of evidence shows that providing education for uneducated or illiterate mothers of young children can facilitate better education outcomes for their children. Support to literacy programs for adult women can be an important complement to interventions to increase access and retention rates of children in school. Adult literacy programs, especially when combined with the acquisition of other skills relevant to the learner, may be particularly useful where there are pockets of undereducated women, such as among ethnic minorities and indigenous communities.

Chapter 4

Guarantee sexual and reproductive health and rights

Achieving Goal 3 requires guaranteeing women's and girls' sexual and reproductive health and rights.[1] Currently, their reproductive health status is poor, and their sexual and reproductive rights are not fully realized in many countries. Maternal mortality rates are high, and women's chances of dying of pregnancy-related complications are almost 50 times higher in developing countries than in developed countries. Women's unmet need for contraception is also high. One-fifth of married women in the Middle East and North Africa and one-quarter in Sub-Saharan Africa are unable to access the contraception they need. Women are also more vulnerable to sexually transmitted infections, particularly HIV/AIDS. Today, women and girls make up almost half the infected population ages 15–49 worldwide, and in Sub-Saharan Africa the rate is close to 60 percent. Adolescent girls are particularly disadvantaged in all of these aspects of sexual and reproductive health. Adolescent fertility rates remain high, and young women have higher chances of suffering from complications at birth. They also have a higher unmet need for contraception and higher HIV infection rates, particularly in Sub-Saharan Africa.

Necessary actions to address these problems are ensuring universal access to sexual and reproductive health services through the primary healthcare system, providing women and girls with full access to sexual and reproductive health information, and fulfilling all the commitments in the Cairo Programme of Action of the UN International Conference on Population and Development of 1994. Interventions are needed within and outside the health system. At a minimum national public health systems must provide quality family planning, emergency obstetric services, safe abortions (where legal), postabortion care, interventions to reduce malnutrition and anemia, and programs to prevent and treat sexually transmitted infections, including

Sexual and reproductive health and rights are important for gender equality in education and access to economic resources, as well as for women's empowerment

HIV. Outside the health system sexuality education programs are needed to lay the foundation for improved sexual and reproductive health outcomes. Ultimately, these interventions must be supported by an enabling policy and political environment that guarantees women's and girls' sexual and reproductive rights. Current threats to those rights must be opposed if Goal 3 is to be achieved.

Why guaranteeing sexual and reproductive health and rights is a strategic priority

Goal 4 on child mortality, Goal 5 on maternal mortality, and Goal 6 on HIV/AIDS cover only limited aspects of sexual and reproductive health and rights. Yet, a large body of evidence shows that sexual and reproductive health and rights are central to women's ability to build their capabilities, take advantage of economic and political opportunities, and control their destinies.[2] For this reason, the task force has identified guaranteeing sexual and reproductive health and rights as a strategic priority for achieving gender equality and the empowerment of women.

Today, these rights are threatened by actions to limit and withdraw funding from effective reproductive health programs, censor or distort information and research on comprehensive health interventions and issues, and renege on previous international agreements on sexual and reproductive health and rights. Such actions threaten the progress of the last 10 years in improving women's reproductive health and may worsen the reproductive health status of poor women around the world.

Links between reproductive health and other domains of gender equality

Sexual and reproductive health and rights are important for gender equality in education and access to economic resources, as well as for women's empowerment.

Education. The links between secondary education and reproductive health are discussed in chapter 3. Note, too, that early marriage reduces girls' access to education and that anticipation of an early marriage often precludes secondary education for girls (Huq and Amin 2001).

Economic resources. Access to reproductive health is often a precondition for access to economic assets and resources and opportunities to employ them productively. For example, access to family planning allows women to balance the size of their family and timing of their children with their need and desire to earn income, as many studies have shown. The ability to control their fertility also allows women to seek additional education or training, prepares them for better employment, and permits them to take part in other desirable activities such as community affairs (Family Health International 1998). For

Each year half a million women die of preventable complications of pregnancy and childbirth and another 18 million are left disabled or chronically ill

example, research has shown that women who begin childbearing before age 20 complete less schooling than women who delay having children until their 20s (Johns Hopkins School of Public Health 1999a).

Women's economic status can in turn affect reproductive health outcomes. Women's economic dependency makes them more vulnerable to HIV and other sexually transmitted infections. Research from around the world has shown that when women are economically vulnerable, they are less able to negotiate the use of condoms or other forms of safer sex, less likely to be able to leave a relationship that they perceive to be risky, and more likely to increase their risk by exchanging sex with multiple partners for money or goods (Rao Gupta and Weiss 1994).

Empowerment. Having the ability to make strategic life choices is central to empowerment. Whether to have children, when to have them, how many to have, and which sexual partners to have are central choices in everyone's life, but particularly in women's lives because they bear the responsibility for biological and social reproduction. Providing women the opportunity to make those decisions is one pathway to empowerment. This is why the human rights conventions guarantee women the right to control their fertility and sexuality (UN 1994). Without this right women cannot realize their other rights—whether to obtain an education, work outside the home, run for office, or participate in the cultural life of their community.

Status of women's sexual and reproductive health and rights

Maternal health and sexually transmitted infections. Each year half a million women die of preventable complications of pregnancy and childbirth and another 18 million are left disabled or chronically ill. Women have a 1 in 2,800 chance of dying from pregnancy-related causes in developed countries, a 1 in 61 chance in developing countries, and a 1 in 15 chance in Sub-Saharan Africa (WHO/UNICEF/UNFPA 2003).

Although married women's contraceptive use has risen globally from 14 percent in 1965 to more than 50 percent today, the number of women who wish to space or limit further childbearing but are not using contraception (mainly because of a lack of access to information and family planning services) remains very large. In the mid-1990s the World Health Organization estimated that some 120 million women had an unmet need for contraception (WHO 1998b).[3] Among countries with data for both 1990 and 2000 there has been a slight drop in the share of women with unmet need, but the level of unmet need remains high, especially in Sub-Saharan Africa and in the Middle East and North Africa (appendix table A2.1). Except in the Middle East and North Africa and Sub-Saharan Africa unmet need is higher among adolescents than among adult women of reproductive age and is highest in Latin America and the Caribbean.

At the end of 2004 about 40 million people were estimated to be living with HIV/AIDS—most are in developing countries and about half of those 15–49 years old are women

One result of high levels of unmet need in some regions of the world is a high incidence of unsafe abortions. Of the 20 million unsafe abortions that WHO (1998b) estimates occur annually, worldwide, an estimated 70,000 result in death, accounting for 13 percent of the overall maternal mortality rate. Evidence suggests that reducing the unmet need for contraception would reduce the need to resort to abortion, thereby improving maternal health and female longevity.

Sexually transmitted infections are another global reproductive health problem. WHO (2003) estimates that 340 million new sexually transmitted infections occur annually, and there is clear evidence that the presence of a sexually transmitted infection increases the risk of HIV infection. HIV/AIDS is itself a devastating global health problem. In 2004 an estimated 4.9 million people were newly infected with HIV, higher than ever. At the end of 2004 about 40 million people were estimated to be living with HIV/AIDS, most (95 percent) in developing countries and about half of those 15–49 years old are women. In Sub-Saharan Africa women constitute 57 percent of all adults living with HIV/AIDS. About three-quarters of young people (15–24 years old) infected with HIV/AIDS on that continent are women and girls. Prevalence rates for women are nearing those of men in the Caribbean and in North Africa and the Middle East (table 4.1; UNAIDS/WHO 2004).

Yet, worldwide, fewer than one in five people at risk of HIV infection today have access to prevention programs (UNAIDS 2003a). Fewer than four percent of people in need of antiretroviral treatment in low- and middle-income countries were receiving the drugs at the end of 2001. And less than 10 percent of people with HIV/AIDS have access to palliative care or treatment for opportunistic infections (UNAIDS/WHO 2004).

Nutrition and reproductive health. The nutritional status of women and adolescent girls is often overlooked when examining issues related to reproductive health. Malnutrition significantly increases the risk of poor reproductive

Table 4.1

HIV prevalence rate among population ages 15–49, 2004

Percent

Source: UNAIDS/WHO 2004.

Region	Women	Men
Sub-Saharan Africa	8.4	6.4
Caribbean	2.3	2.4
Eastern Europe and Central Asia	0.6	1.0
Latin America	0.4	0.8
South and South East Asia	0.4	0.9
Middle East and North Africa	0.3	0.3
North America	0.3	0.9
East Asia	0.1	0.2
Oceania	0.1	0.3
Western and Central Europe	0.1	0.4
Global	1.1	1.2

**Reproductive
health problems
are particularly
acute for
adolescent girls**

health outcomes, and multiple pregnancies at short intervals may aggravate women's nutritional status, resulting in poor maternal health overall (Christian 2003; King 2003). Because malnutrition weakens the immune function, malnourished women are less resistant to infection (Reed and others 2000). Chronic malnutrition in childhood leads to stunting, which can increase the risk of obstructed labor (Konje and Ladipo 2000). Data on low body mass index (<18.5 kg/m^2), a measure of chronic malnutrition in adults, show that 34 percent of women in South Asia and 18 percent in Sub-Saharan Africa are malnourished.[4] By comparison the prevalence is 4 percent in developed countries (Christian 2003; ACC/SCN 2000). Low body mass index is a known risk factor for adverse pregnancy outcomes, including low birthweight infants and infant and maternal death and illness (Allen and Gillespie 2001).

Iron-deficiency anemia affects 50–70 percent of pregnant women in developing countries (ACC/SCN 2000). Severe anemia has been shown to be associated with postpartum hemorrhage and is thought to be an underlying factor in maternal deaths, though more studies are needed to substantiate this (Christian 2003; Reed and others 2000). Similarly, other nutritional deficiencies with adverse effects on reproductive outcomes are thought to be widely prevalent (Christian 2003). Improving the nutritional status of women and girls is therefore a prerequisite for them to achieve health and well-being.

Adolescent reproductive health. Reproductive health problems are particularly acute for adolescent girls, because they have the highest levels of unmet need for contraception and are the most vulnerable to unwanted pregnancy and sexually transmitted infections, including HIV. Many sexually active adolescents do not use contraception. Of the roughly 260 million women ages 15–19 worldwide, both married and unmarried, about 11 percent (29 million) are sexually active and do not want to become pregnant but are not using a modern method of birth control. Every year some 14 million young women become mothers (AGI 1998) and an estimated 1–4 million young women ages 15–19 have induced abortions, many of them unsafe (Family Care International and the Safe Motherhood Inter-Agency Group 1998).

An estimated 17 million adolescent girls are married before the age of 20 (AGI 1998). Rates of early marriage are highest in Western Africa, South Asia, and Sub-Saharan Africa, where 30 percent or more of girls ages 15–19 are married (figure 4.1). Early marriage contributes to a series of negative consequences for young women and the societies in which they live. Early marriage usually leads to early childbearing. In Guatemala, India, Mali, and Yemen, among others, 24–45 percent of women ages 20–24 had given birth by age 18. That compares with 2 percent in France and 1 percent in Germany (figure 4.2).

Worldwide an estimated 15 million girls ages 15–19—both married and unmarried—give birth each year. The rates are particularly high in developing countries. It is estimated that between one-quarter and one-half of all

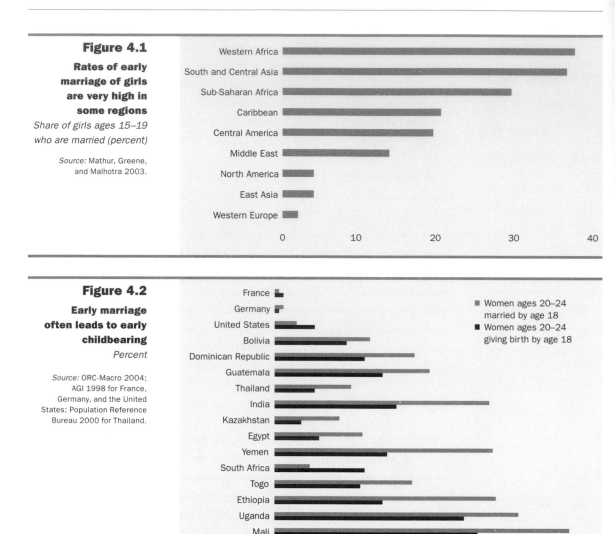

Figure 4.1

Rates of early marriage of girls are very high in some regions

Share of girls ages 15–19 who are married (percent)

Source: Mathur, Greene, and Malhotra 2003.

Figure 4.2

Early marriage often leads to early childbearing

Percent

Source: ORC-Macro 2004; AGI 1998 for France, Germany, and the United States; Population Reference Bureau 2000 for Thailand.

young women in the developing world give birth before they turn 18 (UNFPA 2003b). In Bangladesh, for example, more than half of all women have their first child by age 19.

Adolescent fertility rates and progress during the past decade in reducing these rates vary significantly across regions (table 4.2). Developed countries have the lowest adolescent fertility rates, at 16 live births per 1,000 adolescents, down from 19 live births per 1,000 in 1990. Adolescent fertility rates are highest in South Asia and Sub-Saharan Africa—and those rates increased between 1990 and 2000.

Underdeveloped physiology, combined with a lack of power, information, and access to services, means that young married women who bear children experience much higher levels of maternal illness and death than do women who bear children when they are older (figure 4.3). Severe complications, such

Region	1990	2000
Developed countries	19	16
East Asia and the Pacific	44	38
Europe and Central Asia	45	41
Latin America and the Caribbean	87	76
Middle East and North Africa[a]	60	25
South and West Asia	71	84
Sub-Saharan Africa	128	133

Table 4.2

Adolescent fertility rates by region, 1990–2000

Live births in one year per 1,000 women ages 15–19

a. Few countries have data for 2000.

Source: WISTAT 1999.

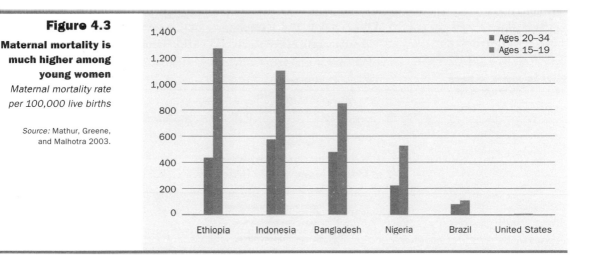

Figure 4.3

Maternal mortality is much higher among young women

Maternal mortality rate per 100,000 live births

Source: Mathur, Greene, and Malhotra 2003.

as obstructed labor and the fistula that may result, occur most commonly among young women (UNFPA and EngenderHealth 2003; Jarret 1994; *The Lancet* 2004).

Women who marry young have little negotiating power and are exposed to greater risk of sexually transmitted infections, especially in the common instance of having partners who are much older and more sexually experienced. In Kenya and Zambia, for example, young married women are more likely to be HIV-positive than their unmarried peers because they have sex more often, use condoms less often, are unable to refuse sex, and have partners who are more likely to be HIV-positive (Bruce and Clark 2003; Luke and Kurz 2002).

The costs of poor reproductive health

A recent report by the Alan Guttmacher Institute (AGI) and the United Nations Population Fund (UNFPA) synthesizes current evidence on the costs and benefits of sexual and reproductive healthcare (AGI/UNFPA 2004). The health costs are expressed in disability-adjusted life years (DALYs).[5] According

Interventions to
improve girls'
and women's
sexual and
reproductive
health and
rights are
needed in the
health system,
education, and
the legal system

to the WHO's 2001 estimates, sexual and reproductive health problems account for 18 percent of the global burden of disease and 32 percent of the burden among women ages 15–44 worldwide (AGI/UNFPA 2004). More specifically:

- Pregnancy and delivery-related complications—hemorrhage, sepsis, obstructed labor, pregnancy-related hypertensive disorder, and unsafe abortion—account for 2 percent of all DALYs lost and 13 percent of all DALYs lost among reproductive-age women.
- Perinatal conditions (low birth weight, birth asphyxia, and birth trauma) account for 7 percent of all DALYs lost.
- HIV/AIDS accounts for 5 percent of all DALYs lost and 14 percent among women ages 15–44.
- Other sexual and reproductive health conditions—sexually transmitted infections other than HIV/AIDS, iron-deficiency anemia among women, genitourinary diseases, and breast, ovarian, cervical, and uterine cancer—account for 3 percent of all DALYs lost and 5 percent among women ages 15–44.

By comparison, respiratory illnesses account for 11 percent of all DALYs lost, cardiovascular diseases for 10 percent, and neuropsychiatric conditions for 13 percent.

The report also notes that investing in reproductive and sexual health services is cost effective. An early study in Mexico found that for every peso the Mexican social security system spent on family planning services during 1972–84, it saved nine pesos for treating complications of unsafe abortion and providing maternal and infant care. Every $1 invested in Thailand's family planning program saved the government more than $16. An analysis in Egypt found that every $1 invested in family planning saved the government $31 (AGI/UNFPA 2004). Beyond these savings, reproductive and sexual health services deliver other medical, social, and economic benefits, including prevention of illness and death, improvements in women's social position, and increases in macroeconomic investment and growth.

Interventions for sexual and reproductive health and rights

Interventions to improve girls' and women's sexual and reproductive health and rights are needed both in the health system and in other sectors, such as education and the legal system. Important health sector interventions include policies that promote universal access to reproductive health services, including family planning, safe abortion (where legal), postabortion care, prevention and treatment of sexually transmitted infections, and nutrition interventions. Ensuring that all deliveries are attended by appropriately skilled health personnel and that all women have access to health facilities providing emergency obstetric care in the event of life-threatening obstetric complications will reduce maternal mortality (UN Millennium Project 2005b).

Counseling, prevention, and treatment services for sexually transmitted infections and HIV should be integrated with other reproductive health services

Interventions for family planning and safe abortion services

Access to quality family planning services that provide women with a range of contraceptive options and informed choice helps reduce high-risk pregnancies associated with multiple pregnancies and helps women avoid unwanted and unsafe abortions (Lule and others 2003). In developing countries family planning programs were responsible for an estimated 43 percent of the decline in fertility between 1960 and 1980 (Bongaarts and Bruce 1995). If the unmet need for contraception were met so that women could have only the pregnancies they wanted, maternal mortality would drop by an estimated 20–35 percent (Doulaire 2002; Maine 1991).

The WHO estimates that safe abortion services could prevent at least 13 percent of maternal deaths worldwide (WHO 1998b). In almost all countries abortion to save a woman's life is legal. In more than three-fifths of countries abortion is also permitted to preserve women's physical and mental health, and in 40 percent of countries, abortion is allowed in cases of rape, incest, or fetal malformation. One-third of countries allow abortion on socioeconomic grounds, and one-quarter allow abortion on request (Barroso and Girard 2003). But in many cases where abortion is legal, safe services are unavailable (WHO 2003).

Interventions for prevention and treatment of sexually transmitted infections and HIV/AIDS

Counseling, prevention, and treatment services for sexually transmitted infections and HIV should be integrated with other reproductive health services and made available through the primary healthcare system, which is most likely to reach populations in greatest need, such as adolescents and the poor. Single-purpose programs for preventing and treating sexually transmitted infections almost always fail to reach women because many women are asymptomatic, and seeking treatment is socially stigmatized.

Women urgently need a female-controlled method of prevention for sexually transmitted infections, and programs need to target men as well as women for prevention and treatment of such infections. The female condom, now available in industrialized countries and in some countries in the developing world, needs to be made more accessible and affordable. The male condom, the only widely available method of prevention, requires the cooperation of the male partner. Women worldwide report that male opposition is a significant hurdle to using a condom.

Simultaneously, investment is needed in research and development to produce a safe and effective microbicide that women can use to protect themselves against a wide range of sexually transmitted pathogens, including HIV. There are some 60 different compounds in the pipeline with potential microbicidal properties, but substantial funding is required to test them for efficacy and bring the effective compounds rapidly to market. The benefits to low-income countries could be enormous. For example, researchers at the London School

A critical priority

is access to

emergency

obstetric care

of Hygiene and Tropical Medicine have estimated that if microbicides were used by 20 percent of the women in low-income countries reachable through existing services, 2.5 million new HIV infections in women, men, and children could be avoided over a period of three years (Public Health Working Group 2002).

Also important is tracking the use of antiretroviral treatment by sex to ensure that women are being reached. Experience with antiretroviral treatment for the prevention of mother-to-child transmission has shown that even when the drugs are available, women choose not to use them because of the stigma that is associated with AIDS. Research in Ethiopia, Tanzania, and Zambia has revealed that the consequences of stigma are often more severe for women than for men (Nyblade and others 2003). Combining treatment with community education and interventions for stigma reduction is therefore important for ensuring that antiretroviral treatments reach the women who constitute an increasingly large share of the world's HIV-positive population.

Interventions to prevent maternal illness and death

Because nearly half of maternal deaths in the developing world occur during labor, delivery, or the immediate postpartum period, access to skilled care and emergency obstetric services during these periods is critical. About two-thirds of births worldwide occur outside health facilities (WHO 1997a). Hence, a critical priority is access to emergency obstetric care (UN Millennium Project 2005b). Also needed are skilled birth attendants trained in the use of safe and hygienic birthing techniques and necessary drugs and equipment. Maternal mortality rates have been reduced through the availability of trained but nonspecialist medical personnel, such as medical assistants in Tanzania, assistant anesthetists in Burkina Faso and Malawi, and nurses in the Democratic Republic of Congo (Lule and others 2003). For maximum impact on reproductive health skilled birth attendants and emergency obstetric services must be closely linked within a strong health system. Strong health systems, in turn, depend on adequate infrastructure, including good roads and transportation networks, electricity, and clean water.

In addition to improving the supply of emergency obstetric care, increased efforts are needed to ensure that women seek such care. Life-threatening delays can occur during a difficult labor if women or other family members do not understand the signs of a difficult labor or the serious consequences of not seeking more expert care. Teaching women and other family members the signs of a difficult labor should be a priority for reducing maternal mortality.

Nutrition interventions

Historically, nutrition programs to improve reproductive health outcomes have focused mainly on pregnancy and the postpartum period, for example, by providing women with iron-folate supplements.[6] This emphasis has had only a

Programs for adolescents need to be scaled up to provide full services to the entire adolescent population

limited impact on the prevalence of malnutrition in women and children. Current research suggests that interventions may be more important before conception, because the risks of a poor outcome are as great from being underweight before pregnancy as from being underweight during pregnancy (Allen and Gillespie 2001). Programs therefore need to target nonpregnant women and adolescents. One approach is to decrease nutrient depletion by reducing early and unwanted fertility, which can improve both reproductive health outcomes and nutritional status. Family planning services and programs to encourage later marriage can both be important here. So can improving women's diet and nutritional intake through food security measures, diet diversity, and reducing infections such as intestinal worms.

Interventions for adolescents

All the health services and interventions mentioned above should be designed for married and unmarried adolescents as well as for adults. Young married and unmarried girls are among the most underserved groups, yet their needs may be the most pressing. Many service providers—including doctors, nurses, midwives, and traditional birth attendants—do not recognize the need among this age group, particularly among unmarried adolescent girls, for reproductive health advice, information, and services. Programs for adolescents are small, with limited coverage. They need to be scaled up to provide full services to the entire adolescent population.

Interventions to involve men as partners in reproductive health

Men influence their partner's reproductive health, in part through decisions about contraceptive use and desired family size. That makes them important allies in efforts to improve women's health (Greene, Rasekh, and Amen 2004). Two types of program models have been developed recently to engage men. One involves men as partners. This type of program works within traditional reproductive health arenas such as family planning and maternal health services and seeks to increase men's involvement in women's reproductive health. Such programs are based on the principle that couples, not individual women or men, are responsible for reproductive health outcomes. Thus men must collaborate with their female partners and be accountable to them, to ensure positive reproductive health outcomes.

A second model supports men as agents of change by motivating them to actively address gender inequalities. Such programs recognize that gender norms and the unequal balance of power between women and men have negative consequences for the health of both women and men (UNDAW 2003). They seek to change gender roles and norms by challenging attitudes and behaviors that compromise both men's and women's health and safety. Evaluations of these programs have not yet been conducted so their impacts are not known.

**Schools can
provide life
skills education**

Financing interventions for sexual and reproductive health and rights

Governments have generated funds to finance reproductive health services in many ways. Each involves tradeoffs between equity and efficiency (see table 4.2 in the report of the Task Force on Child Health and Maternal Health; UN Millennium Project 2005b). Most health services are financed by general tax revenue, but user fees have become a complementary source of financing in many countries in recent decades. User fees have many problems. They tend to be highly regressive and to curtail the use of services by poor people. User fees also reduce women's use of reproductive health services (Nanda 2002), and they do not generate adequate revenue to support the provision of basic services. Abolishing user fees for basic sexual and reproductive health services, such as family planning and maternal health services, is therefore an important recommendation of the task force.

Interventions outside the health sector

Improvements in reproductive and sexual health also require interventions outside the health sector. Girls' education is important. Schools can provide life skills education, including information on health, nutrition, and family planning. Ideally, such curricula would be introduced in primary schools and continue through the secondary level.

Sexuality education remains a divisive topic in most parts of the world (Kirby and others 1997). In many developing countries schools do not offer sexuality education and in others it is offered too late to influence behavior. And while the typical school-based curriculum may contain useful information about the differences between male and female reproductive systems, it does not usually provide an opportunity for young people to learn relationship skills or discuss norms and peer pressure (Raju and Leonard 2000; Laack 1995; Laack and others 1997).

Yet, there are many good programs. Evaluations of comprehensive sexuality education programs in the United States found the programs to be associated with delayed sexual initiation and reduced abortion and birthrates among the participants (Jorgensen, Potts, and Camp 1993; Kirby and others 1997). Evaluations of other programs worldwide indicate that they increase knowledge among youth about HIV/AIDS prevention and increase the confidence of young people to practice safe behaviors such as refusing sexual intercourse or using condoms. Program impact is usually greatest among girls and younger youth (Grunseit 1997; Kirby and others 1997).

Interventions to build political consensus

Finally, both health and nonhealth sector interventions to improve sexual and reproductive health require an enabling policy and political environment. To this end, stronger and more visible efforts to advance the Cairo Programme of Action must continue. Policymakers should base decisionmaking on scientific evidence rather than ideological principle (*The Lancet* 2004). Technical agencies like the World Health Organization and the U.S. Centers for Disease Control and Prevention should document the costs of misrepresentation of scientific evidence and actively disseminate accurate evidence. Women's organizations working to promote reproductive rights for women should be given greater financial support, and donor funding should target the real needs of recipients, with political strings kept to a minimum (*The Lancet* 2004). Finally, the number of bilateral donors supporting sexual and reproductive health and rights should be increased so that if a leading donor country restricts its funding, alternative sources of support can step in to fill the gap.

Chapter 5

Invest in infrastructure to reduce women's and girls' time burdens

Women's and girls' ability to empower themselves economically and politically by going to school and engaging in productive and civic activities is often limited by their responsibility for everyday maintenance tasks in the household division of labor. For poor women and girls this burden is even greater because of the underinvestment in public infrastructure in most low-income countries. The time women and girls spend on routine tasks can be reduced dramatically if the appropriate infrastructure is in place: efficient sources of energy (especially new forms of fuel for cooking and heating), transport systems, and water and sanitation systems. Investments in such infrastructure to relieve women's time burdens are essential to maximize the impact of the strategic priorities discussed in this report and to reduce poverty.

Why reducing women's and girls' time burdens is a strategic priority
Providing infrastructure in both rural and urban areas benefits poor men and women. But lack of adequate physical facilities (such as roads, utility supply systems, communication systems, water and waste disposal systems) and the underprovision of services flowing from those facilities typically results in a far greater time burden on women than on men because of a gender-based household division of labor. As Modi (2004, p.16) says, "It would be hard to imagine in the developed world today a family spending one or more hours every day gathering biomass such as wood, agricultural residues, and dung when one could instead buy cooking fuel for the same purpose at a price that reflects a mere two or five minutes of income from work. Yet this is the burden of women in the developing world."

Three types of infrastructure are particularly important: energy, transport, and water and sanitation. This section reviews the limited evidence on gender-differentiated access to and use of such infrastructure.

**Access to
electricity
dramatically
reduces the
time women
spend collecting
fuel or fetching
water**

Heavier time burdens

In most rural communities around the world women are the primary collectors of fuelwood. One study found that women spent more than 800 hours a year in Zambia and about 300 hours a year in Ghana and Tanzania collecting fuelwood (figure 5.1; Malmberg Calvo 1994).

Collection times have risen with the increasing scarcity of locally available biofuels (Barnes and Sen 2003). Studies on firewood collection in India found that women traveled between 4 and 10 kilometers in search of firewood, depending on the ecological environment. In forested areas women might collect wood twice a week, while in depleted areas they have to collect it every day.

Women also spend many hours fetching water. Rosen and Vincent (1999) report that households (primarily women) spend an average of 134 minutes a day collecting water. The study of three Sub-Saharan African countries cited above found that women spent more than 700 hours a year on water provision in Ghana, 500 hours in Tanzania, and 200 hours in Zambia (figure 5.2; Malmberg Calvo 1994). They also collected a higher volume of water than men did.

Access to electricity dramatically reduces the time women spend collecting fuel or fetching water. For instance, in India women in households with electricity spend less time collecting fuels, fetching water, and cooking and more time earning an income, reading, and watching television than do women in households with no electricity (Barnes and Sen 2003; table 5.1 and figure 5.3).[1] By enabling women to spend more time reading, electricity may help to address gender gaps in capability.

Women's time burdens are also affected by inadequate transport systems (Bryceson and Howe 1993). A World Bank study found that 87 percent of trips in rural Africa take place on foot, and women's time accounts for more than 65 percent of the household's time and effort spent on transport (Malmberg Calvo 1996). The daily transport burden of a typical adult woman was equivalent to

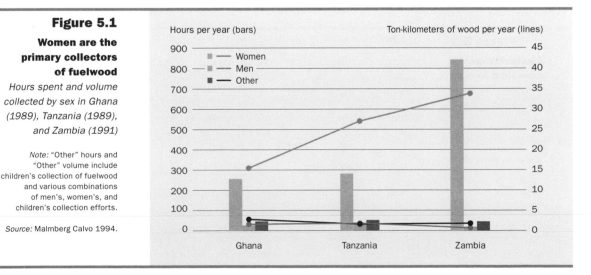

Figure 5.1

**Women are the
primary collectors
of fuelwood**

*Hours spent and volume
collected by sex in Ghana
(1989), Tanzania (1989),
and Zambia (1991)*

Note: "Other" hours and
"Other" volume include
children's collection of fuelwood
and various combinations
of men's, women's, and
children's collection efforts.

Source: Malmberg Calvo 1994.

Figure 5.2

Women are the primary collectors of water

Hours spent and volume collected by sex in Ghana (1989), Tanzania (1989), and Zambia (1991)

Note: "Other" hours and "Other" volume include children's collection of water and various combinations of men's, women's, and children's collection efforts.

Source: Malmberg Calvo 1994.

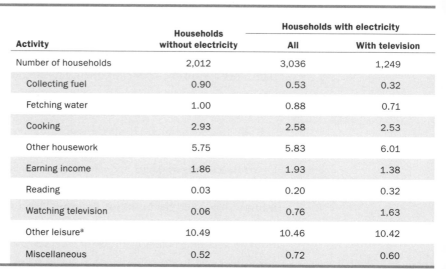

Table 5.1

Women's time allocation in households with and without electricity, 1996

Mean hours spent

a. Includes taking meals, bathing, leisure, sleeping, and so forth.

Source: Barnes and Sen 2003, based on Operations Research Group (ORG) Household Survey 1996.

Activity	Households without electricity	Households with electricity	
		All	With television
Number of households	2,012	3,036	1,249
Collecting fuel	0.90	0.53	0.32
Fetching water	1.00	0.88	0.71
Cooking	2.93	2.58	2.53
Other housework	5.75	5.83	6.01
Earning income	1.86	1.93	1.38
Reading	0.03	0.20	0.32
Watching television	0.06	0.76	1.63
Other leisure[a]	10.49	10.46	10.42
Miscellaneous	0.52	0.72	0.60

Figure 5.3

Electricity means more time to read

Hours per day spent reading, 1996

Source: Barnes and Sen 2003, based on Energy Sector Management Assistance Programme survey 1996.

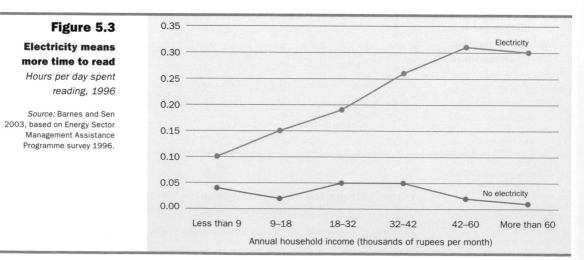

Countries need
to analyze
infrastructure
needs and
constraints by
gender, income
group, and
geographic
location

carrying a load of 20 kilograms for 1.4–5.3 kilometers. Barwell (1998) finds that women make frequent trips to agricultural plots for cultivation and harvesting and that women carry more than three times the ton-kilometers (a measure of weight and distance) per year than do men. In many parts of Africa women are required to transport their husband's produce as well as their own.

Access to roads also affects women's level of income. Booth, Hammer, and Lovell (2000) report that women in a village on a main road in Cameroon made more than twice the income earned by women in a village 90 minutes away from the road, because they had more time available to produce food to sell. Even when transportation is available, however, women typically have less ability to pay for it and so are less able to take advantage of it than men. This has significant implications for women in rural Sub-Saharan Africa, where rural transport charges are higher than in any other region in the world (Ellis and Hine 1998).[2]

Harmful effects on health

Inadequate infrastructure has significant negative consequences for women's health. The heavy water containers that women typically carry injure their heads, necks, and backs. In addition, almost half of the population in developing countries suffers from one or more of the main diseases associated with inadequate provision of water and sanitation services (UN Millennium Project 2005b). Poorly planned sanitation projects can also increase women's vulnerability to violence. An evaluation of communal sanitation block projects in Egypt, India, Nigeria, Sudan, and Zambia revealed a high incidence of attacks on women using the facilities (Allély and Drevet-Dabbou 2002). Inadequate transportation and the high cost associated with it also discourage women's use of health services (Mwaniki, Kabiru, and Mbugua 2002).

The declining availability and quality of fuelwood in many countries also harms women's health. Women must walk further to find fuelwood and often respond by gathering larger loads. The increased energy expenditure can have long-term health consequences (Barnes and Sen 2003). Traditional biofuels have other negative health impacts. Recent studies of traditional stoves using biomass fuels have found that prolonged exposure to the smoke severely damages the lungs and eyes of anyone close to the stoves—usually women and girls. Women who cook on indoor open fires using biofuels also suffer from chronic obstructive pulmonary diseases (Ostro and others 1995; Parikh and Laxmi 2000; Smith 1987, 1998; Smith and Mehta 2000; International Institute of Population Sciences 1995, all cited in Barnes and Sen 2003).

Interventions for gender-responsive infrastructure

To meet women's infrastructure needs and overcome the special constraints they face, countries need to analyze infrastructure needs and constraints by gender, income group, and geographic location. Studies need to explore how

**Taking women's
perceptions and
opinions into
consideration
is critical**

women's economic and domestic activities are affected by infrastructure or its absence and to identify the kinds of infrastructure they require to enhance their productivity and civic participation and their daughters' school attendance. Increasing women's participation in finding answers to some of these questions can help to improve infrastructure access and affordability for women.

Improving women's participation in planning and implementation of infrastructure projects

Taking women's perceptions and opinions into consideration is critical when developing infrastructure projects. This is best illustrated for water and sanitation since women play key roles as users and managers of sanitation and water facilities (ADB 2000; AusAID 2000). Men and women have different preferences for sanitation facilities derived from their different roles in household hygiene management (Masika and Baden 1997). Women tend to be more concerned with privacy and safety and may prefer enclosed latrines in or near the house (IRC 1994). Women and men have different priorities in water issues as well (Regmi and Fawcett 1999). A study of *panchayats* (local governing councils) in India found that female *panchayat* heads tend to emphasize drinking water provision while male heads tend to emphasize irrigation systems (Chattopadhyay and Duflo 2004). These findings underscore the need to include women in decisionmaking in order to meet their needs.

Yet research shows that women are seldom involved in planning. Studies of water management in Sub-Saharan Africa and South Asia find that men play a greater role in community decisionmaking, finance, and infrastructure construction than women do, even though women are heavy users of water for domestic and productive purposes. As the primary collectors of water, women have important information about seasonal availability, water quality, and individual and communal rights to various sources (Fong, Wakeman, and Bhushan 1996; van Koppen 1990)[3]—information that could also improve project outcomes (box 5.1).

A study of community water and sanitation projects in 88 communities in 15 countries finds strong evidence that projects designed and run with the full participation of women are more sustainable and effective than those that ignore women (Gross, van Wijk, and Mukherjee 2001). This finding corroborates an earlier World Bank study that found that women's participation was strongly associated with water and sanitation project effectiveness (Fong, Wakeman, and Bhushan 1996).

Increasingly, international and regional water supply and sanitation networks such as the Global Water Partnership, the International Water Management Institute, the International Water and Sanitation Center, and the Water and Sanitation Collaborative Council are promoting women's roles in planning, designing, implementing, and managing water projects (IRC 2003). Donors such as the World Bank and the regional development banks have also

Box 5.1

The Ghana Community Water and Sanitation Project gains from women's participation

Source: World Bank 2003e; McCann 1998.

During the 1990s the government of Ghana began to decentralize the country's infrastructure services. As part of this decentralization effort Ghana launched the Community Water and Sanitation Project in 1994 to provide water and sanitation services to communities in 26 of 110 districts. Communities, represented by water boards and water and sanitation committees, decided whether to participate in the project. They also decided what level of service they wanted, depending on their willingness to pay for capital costs (5–10 percent of household income) and maintenance and repair of the facilities. Communities established their own policies on user fees. Some communities did not require them, while in others fees varied from a flat rate to a per unit charge. Some communities exempted certain population groups, such as the elderly, from the payment of fees.

In the first phase of the project, 1,288 water points, 29 pipe schemes, and 6,000 household latrines were constructed. The new water points provided access to improved water sources for 32,000 rural inhabitants (World Bank 2003e).

The project viewed women's involvement as integral to ensuring sustainability and emphasized gender balance in the community water committees, with women representing at least 30–40 percent of the committees. In 2000, 44 percent of members were women. A World Bank (2003e) study also found several gender-differentiated impacts:

- Slightly more poor male-headed households (91 percent) than poor female-headed households (87 percent) contributed to capital costs, while the reverse was true for operation and maintenance costs (92 percent of poor female-headed households and 84 percent of poor male-headed households). Yet 29 percent of women and 26 percent of men still accessed unimproved water.
- There was little difference between men and women in satisfaction with the location of improved water sources (92 percent of men and 90 percent of women) or with the quantity of water available (90 percent of men and 88 percent of women). But fewer women than men were satisfied with water-fetching arrangements (82 percent compared with 92 percent) and water quality (81 percent compared with 90 percent).
- Women (73 percent) were more informed than men (61 percent) about the project's latrine program.

come to recognize the welfare and efficiency gains of addressing gender issues in water and sanitation projects, and their efforts need to be sustained.

While the importance of women's participation has been recognized in the water and sanitation sector, change has been slow in other infrastructure sectors. A review of transport projects supported by the World Bank found that in 2002 just 4 percent of projects included a gender component or gender actions, compared with 15 percent of water supply projects and 35 percent of agriculture projects (World Bank 1999).

Increasing access and affordability of infrastructure services for poor women
Improved roads and transportation services are needed to increase women's access to all resources and services. Feeder and main roads can greatly reduce the burden on women's time and expand their opportunities, especially when combined with accessible and affordable modes of transportation. They can

Cost is often a
constraint to
women's access
to infrastructure

increase women's chances of finding employment or training, selling their goods and increasing their income, expanding their social networks, accessing health care, and visiting local government headquarters for redress for their problems (Whitehead and Kabeer 2001). The probability that girls will attend school also increases. A rural transport project in a remote area of Morocco led to the tripling of girls' school enrollments (World Bank 1996).[4] Transport projects must also address the safety and security needs of women and girls, such as by providing adequate street lighting and ensuring that bus stops and terminals are not located in remote or secluded areas.

Improving women's access to alternative sources of energy other than traditional biofuels can reduce their time burdens, exposure to indoor air pollution, and other risks to their health. Cooking fuels such as kerosene and liquefied petroleum gas (LPG) are good substitutes for traditional biofuels because of their higher thermal efficiency and relative lack of pollutants. The use of such fuels also saves women time for more productive or empowering activities by eliminating the need to walk long distances to gather fuel and reducing cooking time. Time saved can be used for income-earning pursuits, attention to children, civic participation, or leisure (Barnes and Sen 2003).

The use of improved stoves can result in similar benefits. In India the government is promoting cooking stoves with greater thermal efficiency and lower indoor air pollution emissions than traditional stoves (Barnes and Sen 2003). In the short term, because charcoal is a more convenient cooking fuel than wood and is already accepted in many parts of the world, investing in efficient charcoal production and improved charcoal stoves can make an important contribution by requiring less fuelwood and reducing harmful emissions (Modi 2004).

Rural electrification is probably the most desirable alternative to biofuels. But the high cost and limited availability of electricity in developing countries restricts household use for some tasks, including cooking. One option is to strengthen transitional, low-cost solutions that are already being used by the poor (Modi 2004). These include diesel-powered mini-grids for charging batteries that can be carried to households and multifunctional platforms powered by a diesel engine for low-cost rural motive power. Such an intervention, implemented in Mali, has been particularly successful in reducing women's time and effort burdens (box 5.2).

Cost is often a constraint to women's access to infrastructure. Sometimes a combination of interventions can assist in lowering costs. Improved road and port infrastructure, improved handling and storage facilities at ports, bulk purchases of fuels, and regulatory reform can all help to reduce the cost of alternative fuels, for example (Modi 2004). Direct subsidies or lease-finance mechanisms to cover the upfront costs of these fuel sources (such as the cost of an LPG stove or cylinder) is another intervention to reduce costs that is widely supported. An unresolved issue is whether and how to subsidize recurring costs. To address concerns about the possibility of subsidies leaking to the

Box 5.2

Diesel-powered multifunctional platforms reduce the burdens on women in Mali

Source: Modi 2004.

By many measures Mali is one of the poorest and least developed countries in the world. Nearly three-quarters of its roughly 12 million people live in semi-arid rural areas, where poverty is most severe. Electrification is virtually nonexistent, and most of the country's energy supply, particularly in rural areas, comes from biomass. Women and girls are responsible for the time-consuming and labor-intensive work of fuel collection.

Beginning in 1993 the UN Industrial Development Organization (UNIDO) and the International Fund for Agricultural Development (IFAD) initiated a program to decrease the burden of fuel collection by supplying labor-saving energy services and multifunctional platforms to rural villages and promoting the empowerment of women by involving them in design, management, and implementation of the project. The multifunctional platform is a 10-horsepower diesel engine with modular components that can supply motive power for time- and labor-intensive work such as agricultural processing (milling, de-husking) and electricity for lighting (approximately 200–250 small bulbs), welding, or pumping water. Between 1999 and 2004, 400 platforms were installed, reaching about 8,000 women in villages across the country.

Although the benefits are shared by many in the villages, women's organizations own, manage, and control the platform. Capacity building and institutional support by UNIDO and IFAD, strong in the early phases, taper off, leaving the women's groups in charge of platform operation, relying on a network of private suppliers, technicians, and partners. The women's groups cover 40–60 percent of initial cost. The remaining costs are covered by international donors and local partners (nongovernmental organizations, social clubs, and other donors).

A study of 12 villages found several beneficial impacts:

- The platforms reduced the time required for labor-intensive tasks from many hours to a matter of minutes. The time and labor women saved was shifted to income-generating activities, leading to an average daily increase in women's income of $0.47. Rice production and consumption also increased, an indirect benefit arising from time saved.
- The ratios of girls to boys in schools and the proportion of children reaching grade 5 improved, as young girls were needed less for time-consuming chores.
- Increases in mothers' socioeconomic status and time accompanying the introduction of the platforms correlate with improvements in women's health and increases in the frequency of women's visits to local clinics for prenatal care.

Overall, the program in Mali offers compelling evidence that time saved in the lives of women and children, combined with the added socioeconomic benefits to women's groups of controlling and managing the platform as a resource, can yield substantial benefits to health and welfare.

nonpoor, appropriate exit strategies from subsidies can be designed for those who consume and earn more, and bill collection schemes can be implemented that minimize the cost of collection.

Local governments have come to rely increasingly on user fees to cover the investment and operating costs of public utilities (Kessler 2002). In some cases user fees have reduced poor women's and girls' access to those services (Vandemoortele 2001). Because women often have less access than men to financial resources, their inability to pay for water-related resources is a barrier (Cleaver and Elson 1995). If user fees are imposed, some form of cross-subsidies should be given to poor women to avoid shutting out those who cannot afford to pay for services (Bardhan and Mookherjee 2003). And there are other, more efficient ways than user fees (such as general tax revenues) to finance key public goods infrastructure like water and sanitation.

Conclusion

Lack of investment in basic infrastructure facilities for the poor is a significant barrier to development as well as to meeting Millennium Development Goal 3. Without investments in energy, roads and transportation, and water and sanitation systems, the women and girls who live in poor communities will continue to be burdened by the everyday tasks of survival, making it difficult for them to climb out of poverty. Adapting modern science and technology to meet the infrastructure needs of the poor in a way that is accessible and affordable is therefore a development priority.

Chapter 6

Guarantee women's property and inheritance rights

It is now widely recognized that ownership and control over assets such as land and housing provide economic security, incentives for taking economic risks that lead to growth, and important economic returns including income. Yet, women in many countries are far less likely than men to enjoy ownership or control of these important assets. Ensuring female property and inheritance rights would help to empower women and rectify a fundamental injustice. Although lack of data on the gender asset gap makes it difficult to determine the precise magnitude of the problem, the available information suggests that the problem is serious in most countries of the world. The task force calls on UN member countries to collect systematic data on women's share of land and housing. Meeting Goal 3 will also require institutional arrangements that enhance the extent and security of women's rights to land, houses, and other productive assets.

Why guaranteeing women's property rights is a strategic priority

Throughout the developing world women control land and other productive assets far less frequently than men do.[1] This inequality results from a variety of factors, including unequal inheritance practices, the practice of registering land and houses in the name of the head of household (usually defined as a man), unequal access to land markets due to custom, tradition, and unequal economic assets, and gender-biased land reforms. Inequality in property rights contributes to women's generally low status and vulnerability to poverty compared with men. Women's lack of property has been increasingly linked to development-related problems across the globe, including poverty, HIV/AIDS, urbanization, migration, and violence.

An important distinction is between access to productive assets and ownership of those assets. While women's access to land and property may derive

Effective land rights for women and equal access to credit, technical information, and other inputs are important for improving women's welfare and their bargaining power

from informal arrangements or traditional methods of household and communal decisionmaking, women's ownership or rights of use (usufruct) can be guaranteed only through land and property rights that relate to an enforceable claim and ensure women's freedom to rent, bequeath, or sell the property (Strickland 2004). Secure tenure means being protected against involuntary removal from one's land or residence, except in exceptional circumstances, and then only through a known and agreed legal procedure that is objective, equally applicable, contestable, and independent (UN-HABITAT 2004). For women tenure security is increasingly linked to the establishment and enforcement of land, housing, and property rights, particularly as land tenure systems evolve and local ownership patterns shift in response to profound economic and demographic changes.

Effective land rights for women, coupled with equal access to credit, technical information, and other inputs, are important for improving women's welfare and their bargaining power within the household, as well as for broader economic efficiency.

Property rights and women's welfare and empowerment

Secure tenure to land and home improves women's welfare. Land and home ownership confer such direct benefits as having the right to the use of land and the proceeds from crops and having a secure place to live (Agarwal 2002). Indirect advantages include the ability to use land or a house as collateral for credit or as mortgageable assets during a crisis. Ownership or control of land also increases self-employment income. For example, Chadha (1992) found that individuals who owned land generated much higher rural nonfarm earnings from self-employment than did those without land. Assets can also give women greater bargaining power within households (box 6.1).

Beyond the direct economic impact, property ownership can protect women against the risk of domestic violence. Research in Kerala, India, found that 49 percent of women with no property reported physical violence, whereas 7 percent of women with property did, controlling for a wide range of other factors such as household economic status, education, employment, and other variables (Panda 2002).

Box 6.1

How land rights can empower women

Source: Agarwal 2002; Manimala 1983; Alaka and Chetna 1987.

In the Gaya district of Bihar, India, a local temple-monastery complex held land in violation of land ceiling laws. In the late 1970s women and men of landless households jointly agitated for ownership rights on the land they had cultivated for decades. In 1981 the government redistributed about 1,000 acres of the land to the farmers. Women demanded independent land rights and, in two villages, they received them. In the villages where men alone received titles, women's insecurity grew, as did the frequency with which men threatened their wives with eviction in situations of domestic conflict. In the villages where women were given titles of their own, the women had greater bargaining power.

Gender equality in land rights can enhance productive efficiency

Having assets in the hands of women has other welfare impacts. Some studies have found that it increases the share that households spend on children's well-being. In Bangladesh and South Africa, for instance, a study found that the assets that women bring into a marriage, though fewer than those that men bring, play a significant role in household decisionmaking (Quisumbing and Maluccio 2003). Even in societies such as in Bangladesh where husbands control most household resources, expenditures on children's clothing and education were higher and the rate of illness among girls was lower in households where women owned assets (Quisumbing and de la Briere 2000; Hallman 2000).

Women's lack of property ownership has particularly grave consequences in areas where HIV/AIDS is prevalent. By making women less secure economically and more dependent on the men who control property and assets, lack of ownership may increase women's vulnerability to infection. It may also undermine their ability to cope with the disease and its impacts if they or their family members become infected (Drimie 2002; FAO 2003). The consequences are especially severe in some countries in Sub-Saharan Africa where women farm independently of men but normally gain access to land through their husband. A husband's death often means the loss of land, house, and tools to the husband's relatives, leaving the wife and her children without assets and other coping mechanisms just when they are most in need of support.

Property rights and economic efficiency

In addition to welfare gains, gender equality in land rights can enhance productive efficiency. Property ownership may confer incentives to work harder or take greater economic risk. Studies in countries as diverse as China, Ghana, Pakistan, Thailand, and Viet Nam have found a clear association between secure land tenure and increased outputs or improvements to land (Mason and Carlsson 2004). Land ownership, while not guaranteeing access to credit (often, income is also needed; Giovarelli and Lastarria 2004), can serve as collateral, improving women's access to credit, which in turn can increase output. This can be especially crucial where women are the principal farmers, whether because male out-migration is high, women traditionally farm independently of men, as in much of Sub-Saharan Africa, or other reasons.

Women's importance in food production underscores the need to provide them with security of tenure for the land they cultivate, as well as access to credit and other inputs necessary to increase agricultural productivity. Rural women are responsible for half the world's food production, and in developing countries they produce 60–80 percent of the food. In Sub-Saharan Africa and in the Caribbean women produce about 80 percent of household food, and in Asia women do 50–90 percent of the work in rice fields. Security of tenure can improve agricultural production by enabling long-term investment in land. Granting formal title to women may also improve their

Gathering

systematic

evidence on

the gender

asset gap must

be a priority

access to information that can enhance agricultural productivity. In many developing countries agricultural extension agents target owners of the land, who are usually men, rather than the actual users of the land, who are often women.

The status of women's property rights: the gender asset gap

Relatively little data exist on the magnitude of gender asset gaps within and across countries, but the gaps are thought to be substantial. Deere and Leon (2003) compiled an approximation of the distribution of land by gender in five Latin American countries, finding it to be extremely unequal, with women representing one third or less of land owners (table 6.1). Such disparities are especially noteworthy in light of the relatively small gender disparities in human development indicators in this region and the existence of relatively equal inheritance laws.

Gender disparities in land ownership exist in other regions as well. In Cameroon, where women do more than 75 percent of the agricultural work, it is estimated that women hold fewer than 10 percent of land certificates (Mason and Carlsson 2004). There are similar gender disparities in rights to land in Kenya, Nigeria, Tanzania, and elsewhere in Sub-Saharan Africa. A 2001 household survey in Pakistan found that women owned less than 3 percent of the plots, even though 67 percent of the sampled villages reported that women had a right to inherit land (Mason and Carlsson 2004).[2]

The lack of data seriously hampers efforts to track the progress that countries are making on this strategic priority. Gathering systematic evidence on the gender asset gap must be a priority if the goal of gender equality and empowerment of women is to be met. This is discussed further in chapter 10.

Table 6.1

Distribution of landowners by sex in five Latin American countries, various years

Percent

— Not available.
a. For farms larger than 50 hectares.
b. Ejido sector only (ejidatarios, posesionarios, and avecindados).
c. Excludes members of production cooperatives.
d. Based on households with land titles.
e. Based on ownership of titled land parcels; excludes nonhousehold members.

Source: Deere and Leon 2003, based on sources cited therein.

Country, year	Women	Men	Couple	Total	Sample size
Brazil[a], 2000	11.0	89.0	—	100	39,904
Mexico[b], 2002	22.4	77.6	—	100	2.9 million
Nicaragua[c], 1995	15.5	80.9	3.6	100	839
Paraguay[d], 2001	27.0	69.6	3.2	100	1,694
Peru[e], 2000	12.7	74.4	12.8	100	1,923

Channels of land acquisition

Men and women acquire land in many ways, through inheritance, purchase, or transfers from the state (land reform programs, resettlement schemes for people displaced by large dams and other projects, antipoverty programs). Research shows that each channel of land ownership has a gender bias: male preference in inheritance, male privilege in marriage, gender inequality in the land market, and male bias in state programs of land distribution (Deere and Leon 2001).

Inheritance. In Latin America women become landowners mainly through inheritance while men do so through purchases in land markets (Deere and Leon 2003; table 6.2). Latin America has the most favorable legal traditions and egalitarian gender inheritance norms of all developing regions. Nonetheless, inheritance has historically been skewed toward men, in part because agriculture is defined as a male activity and in part because legal headship status confers male privilege in marriage (Deere and Leon 2003). That is changing,

Table 6.2

Form of acquisition of land ownership, by sex in six Latin American countries

Percent

— Not available.

Note: Distribution by sex is statistically significant at the 99 percent level of confidence.

a. In areas of community ownership, distribution by the communal authority is one channel through which women access or acquire land.
b. "Other" includes donations by private parties.
c. For farms larger than 5,000 square meters only. "Other" includes imperfect donations by private parties and other responses.
d. Based on total parcels acquired by 1,586 individuals assuming principal agriculturalist is the owner. "Other" includes land held in usufruct, which is treated as private property.
e. From a nationally representative sample of ejidatarios and posesionarios; based on total parcels titled to 1,576 individuals. "Other" includes adjudications based on judicial actions.
f. For individual landowners only.
g. "Other" includes parcels held in co-ownership with family and nonfamily members of unspecified sex.

Source: Deere and Leon 2003, based on data cited therein.

	Inheritance	Community[a]	State	Market	Other	Total	Sample size
Brazil [b]							
Women	54.2	—	0.6	37.4	7.8	100	4,345
Men	22.0	—	1.0	73.1	3.9	100	34,593
Chile [c]							
Women	84.1	—	1.9	8.1	5.9	100	271
Men	65.4	—	2.7	25.1	6.8	100	411
Ecuador [d]							
Women	42.5	—	5.0	44.9	7.6	100	497
Men	34.5	—	6.5	43.3	15.6	100	1,593
Mexico [e]							
Women	81.1	1.8	5.3	8.1	3.7	100	512
Men	44.7	14.8	19.6	12.0	8.9	100	2,547
Nicaragua [f]							
Women	57.0	—	10.0	33.0	—	100	125
Men	32.0	—	16.0	52.0	—	100	656
Peru [g]							
Women	75.2	1.9	5.2	16.4	1.3	100	310
Men	48.7	6.3	12.4	26.6	6.0	100	1,512
Couples	37.3	1.6	7.7	52.6	0.8	100	247

In Sub-Saharan Africa women have historically enjoyed access rights to land and related resources through a male relative

however, with higher levels of legal literacy among women, smaller family size, migration of children, and growing land scarcity, and wives are increasingly inheriting their husband's property.

In South Asia land is acquired through inheritance, which in most places is passed through the male line (although there are areas where ancestral property is passed through the female line) (Agarwal 2002).[3] During the twentieth century women's organizations teamed up with lawyers and social reformers to advocate for more gender-equitable inheritance laws, but women are still disadvantaged.[4] In India Hindu women's inheritance in tenancy land depends on state-level tenure laws, which in most northwestern states specify an order of inheritance that strongly favors men, and these inequalities cannot be challenged on constitutional grounds. Muslim women continue to be disadvantaged in the share of family property they inherit. Sri Lanka has the most favorable laws toward women in the region. The General Law, applicable to the entire population unless covered by one of three personal laws, offers equal inheritance of parental property to women and men, allows for widows to inherit all of the deceased husband's property in the absence of descendants, and gives married women complete rights to acquire and dispose of their individually owned property.

Inheritance laws and practices throughout the Middle East and North Africa are based largely on *Sharia* law, which defines the shares that go to each member of the family: the woman's share is half that of a man when there are both male and female heirs. However, there is a difference between Sunni and Shi'a inheritance rules; in Shi'a tradition, the wife (or wives) and daughters share the inheritance when there are no male heirs (Hijab and El-Solh 2003). Religious law does not prevent women from owning assets, which may be given to them by a father or brother during their lifetimes. However, in some areas women who are widowed or abandoned by their husbands may cede their one-third share of family land to their brothers in exchange for economic support. Thus both laws and the economic realities faced by women in many parts of the Muslim world reduce the likelihood that women own real property.

In Sub-Saharan Africa women have historically enjoyed access rights to land and related resources through a male relative (father, brother, or husband), depending on the lineage system in particular communities. In Kenya, for instance, women obtain property through their relationships with husbands, fathers, brothers, or sons. When a relationship ends through death, divorce, or other estrangement, women often lose their land, homes, and other property. Some widows are forced to undergo customary "wife inheritance" or "cleansing" rituals to continue to enjoy access to their husband's property. Kenya's land law system is being overhauled, presenting an opportunity for incorporating women's equal property and inheritance rights.

In Ghana, where matrilineal inheritance has traditionally been practiced (the property of a deceased man is transferred to his sister's sons), women own nearly 30 percent of cocoa land.[5] But parental discrimination against daughters still exists. Fathers tend to transfer smaller areas of land to their daughters than to their sons (Quisumbing, Estudillo, and Otsuka 2004).

Many Sub-Saharan African countries (Kenya, South Africa, Tanzania, Uganda) have recently enacted legislation guaranteeing women the right to own and inherit property in their own names and prohibiting sex-based discrimination (table 6.3). Although statutory reform has been applauded by many women's rights activists, the reforms have been mixed. For instance, Uganda's 1998 Land Action and Condominium Law provides the basis for women's equal right to buy and own land and housing. However, inheritance laws have yet to be adequately reformed. Widows have no right to sell land, but can only farm or till it until their death. They also lose occupancy rights upon remarriage. No such restrictions apply to widowers (Benschop 2002). In other countries, such as Tanzania, the reforms are not being adequately enforced.

Part of the problem in the application of property and inheritance rights is that statutory and customary laws have not been harmonized in many countries in Sub-Saharan Africa.[6] Customary law is embedded in traditional attitudes and practices, and although customary laws vary across countries, women generally cannot own or inherit land, housing, or property in their

Table 6.3

Status of legislation on women's rights to land, housing, and property in five Sub-Saharan African countries, as of 2004

Sources: Adapted from Benschop 2002; COHRE 2004.

Legislation	Uganda	Kenya	Tanzania	South Africa	Rwanda
Gender-based discrimination prohibited	Yes	Yes	Partly; discrimination still allowed in application of personal law and customs	Yes	Yes
Application of customary laws that discriminate against women prohibited	Yes	Partly; only if it denies women lawful access to ownership, occupancy, or use of land	No	Yes	Yes
Women's equal right to acquire land and housing	Yes; implicitly recognized in Article 26 of the Constitution	Yes; implicitly recognized in the Married Women's Property Act and Registered Land Act	Yes; explicitly recognized in Section 3(2) of the Land Act and the Village Land Act	Yes	Yes; private property rights guaranteed for every "person" by Article 29 of the Constitution
Spousal co-ownership presumed	No	No	Yes (Section 161 of the Land Act)	No	No
Women's equal inheritance rights					
For widows	No	No	No	Yes	Yes
For daughters	Partly	Partly; only for Christians	Yes	Yes	Yes

Land markets have been a weaker means of transferring property to women than inheritance

own name. However, there have been cases where local customary courts and authority systems have not been hostile to women (Walker 2003). Customary law is dynamic and has evolved over time in response to social, cultural, and demographic changes. Whether this evolution bodes well for women's rights or not depends on the nature of the changes.[7] It is important to capitalize on aspects of customary law that are consistent with basic principles of equality and nondiscrimination and to harmonize them with provisions of statutory law.

Rwanda provides a picture of promising change. Serious gender inequalities in land rights were rectified during post-conflict reconstruction. The Law of Matrimonial Regimes, Succession, and Liberalities now enshrines the principle that women may own and inherit property on an equal basis with their brothers. It also requires couples registering for marriage to make a joint commitment to a choice of options for the shared ownership and disposition of marital property.

Land markets. Evidence from many parts of the world shows that land markets have been a weaker means of transferring property to women than inheritance. In Latin America, for instance, Deere and Leon (2003) note that land markets are not gender-neutral; men are more likely than women to participate successfully as buyers. Evidence from their ethnographic work suggests that discrimination against women is prevalent. Deere (1990) found that in hacienda land sales in Peru in the 1950s and 1960s, women tended to buy smaller parcels and to pay higher prices than men for land of similar size and quality, reflecting women's lower bargaining power. Some landowners refused outright to sell to women. Moreover, inequalities in labor and credit markets produce gender-biased disparities in land markets. The case studies profiled in Deere and Leon (2001) demonstrate that explicit, well enforced public policies are needed to help women participate in land markets.

Women potentially could gain from land sales through the market. Agarwal (2002) describes how in parts of South Asia groups of landless women have used subsidized credit provided by the government to lease or purchase land in groups and cultivate it jointly. Through such collective ventures, and with external financial support, land markets could become an important supplementary channel through which women acquire land, even if not the primary one. However, this has not yet happened on a large scale.

Land markets also exist in most rural areas of Sub-Saharan Africa.[8] Lastarria-Cornhiel (1997) has found that privatization of land in many countries has resulted in titles being transferred to male "heads" of households, to powerful groups, or to corporate or other entities and that women have lost rights they once had. Women suffer systematic disadvantages in the market because their opportunities to buy land are limited. In some places, however, small elite groups of professional or wealthy women have gained secure freehold ownership rights in land (Walker 2003).

Attention needs to focus on identifying and eliminating the points at which discriminatory practices come into play

Government-initiated land reforms and resettlement schemes. Although government land redistribution programs provide an opportunity to equalize property rights between men and women, this happens infrequently. In India, Agarwal (2002, p. 8) concludes that, "irrespective of the program under which the transfers occur, typically the land is allotted almost exclusively to males, even in communities which traditionally practiced matrilineal inheritance, such as the Garos of northeast India."

In Uzbekistan international agencies have been heavily involved in setting the land reform agenda, favoring establishing secure and tradable property rights and eliminating price distortions and production quotas. As a consequence, the private sector share in agricultural production has increased substantially. This has led to the emergence of a new category of private holdings in which management is almost exclusively in male hands while the unpaid family labor that keeps the private holdings viable is predominantly female (Razavi 2004).

In some Latin American countries, such as Colombia and Costa Rica, the experience has been somewhat better. And Viet Nam has recently piloted a program to retitle land jointly in the names of both husband and wife (Mason and Carlsson 2004). But in other countries—such as Bolivia and Ecuador—land reform has failed to address women's land rights. Although most agrarian reform laws were gender neutral, the legal beneficiaries were household heads, defined culturally as the male (Deere and Leon 2003).

Interventions for property rights

Since 1995 there has been growing awareness and policy attention to women's property and inheritance rights, drawing on evolving human rights-based frameworks. Within countries attention needs to focus on identifying and eliminating the points at which discriminatory practices come into play, including complex or archaic legal systems, deep-rooted social and cultural norms, and persistent lack of awareness about individual rights and legal protections. A common problem is how to approach property and inheritance where informal or traditional practices might offer more security to women than newer market-oriented practices that formalize ownership and establish title to land and other property. Countries need to understand how privatization of property (whether through purchase, inheritance, or other means) affects men and women differently, especially where legal regimes discriminate by sex. Interventions for increasing women's access to land and housing must be context-specific: there is no single global blueprint.

Reforming laws and supporting women's claims to property

Several changes are necessary within countries to ensure women's property rights: amending and harmonizing statutory and customary laws, promoting legal literacy, supporting organizations that can help women make land claims, and recording women's share of land or property. These reforms need to be implemented together to have maximum impact.

Government efforts to reform relevant laws (including constitutional, marital, property, and family law) are an important first step. Reform includes applying provisions of the Convention on the Elimination of All Forms of Discrimination against Women to national law, clarifying interpretations of relevant laws, and changing legal practices concerning land and property titling. Several countries have established paralegal services to help women pursue and defend their property and inheritance rights. Many countries have instituted community- and national-level human rights and legal training of advocates, judges, registrars, police, elders, and others. Box 6.2 highlights an effort in Kyrgyzstan to enhance women's land rights.

Many of these efforts appear to be successful, but there is widespread concern about their sustainability and ensuring consistent standards of service provision (legal aid, for example) within countries. Such activities deserve greater support because they have the potential to transform gender-biased social and cultural norms. They need to receive adequate budget support. Local government land authorities should be provided with gender training, and their administrative and institutional capacity to implement and enforce equal property and inheritance laws need to be strengthened.

Box 6.2

Land reform changes focus on women's land rights in Kyrgyzstan

Source: UNIFEM 2003c.

Kyrgyzstan was the first country in the former Soviet Union to introduce land reform. Shortly after independence in the early 1990s, the transition government introduced legislation that privatized collective farms and other state property, established legal guarantees for private land entitlements, and created legal and administrative land market mechanisms.

Despite the fact that women make up a sizeable portion of the agricultural workforce in Kyrgyzstan, and rural women are one of the poorest segments of society, a land distribution survey in 2002 revealed that only 450 of 38,724 farms belonged to women. Women's land ownership is still constrained by a combination of legal, procedural, and cultural factors. Prominent among them are the precedence of customary over statutory law in determining property and inheritance issues and limited awareness by rural women of their land rights and entitlements.

Following up on this survey, women's groups, supported by UNIFEM, carried out a public awareness campaign to bring attention to this situation and to advocate for changes in legislation guaranteeing women's access to land and inheritance rights. In 2003 an amendment was drafted to the Land Code guaranteeing women's equal rights to land ownership; it is currently before the parliament. Meanwhile, women worked with government officials at the municipal and local levels to strengthen the capacity to better protect women's rights to land as well as to strengthen women's entrepreneurship and sustainable agricultural skills. In addition, a media competition for programs on women's land possession resulted in a series on women's land rights broadcasted by 10 of the publicly owned TV and radio companies in the country. This series has raised awareness in rural areas.

Joint titling

Land titling is often suggested as a solution to gender disparities in land rights.[9] While titling and formal registration are not the only way to provide women with access to land, where it exists, men and women should both be able to acquire title, individually or jointly.[10]

Joint titling helps to guard against capricious actions by one spouse; protects against the dispossession of women through abandonment, separation, or divorce; and increases women's bargaining power in household and farm decisionmaking. Joint titling can be mandatory or voluntary for legally married couples. Mandatory joint titling provides the most secure land rights for women. Rights are established in civil law, through co-ownership rules. In practice, proof of marriage and sometimes proof of commingling of household resources may be required.[11] Voluntary joint titling is less secure and requires significant education of women, registration personnel, legal services, and other actions.

In Latin American and the Caribbean a major advance has been joint adjudication and titling of land to couples (Deere and Leon 2003). During 1988–95 five countries (Brazil, Colombia, Costa Rica, Honduras, and Nicaragua) passed agrarian legislation for joint adjudication or titling of land to couples. In countries where mechanisms of inclusion have been adopted and implemented, women have benefited to a greater extent than they have from previous agrarian reforms (Deere and Leon 2003). This was also the case in Viet Nam, which revised its marriage and family law in 2001 to require joint titling for land and other family assets (box 6.3).

Box 6.3 **Joint titling improves women's access to land in Viet Nam** *Source:* Prosterman and Hanstad 2003; Ravallion and van de Walle 2004; World Bank 2002d.	As part of the transition to a market-oriented economy, Viet Nam has instituted a series of land reforms. Although the government remains the sole owner of land, under a 1993 law granting use rights for up to 20 years individuals can transfer, exchange, mortgage, and bequest their use rights. Initially, the land tenure certificates issued to households had space for only one signature. As a result, the certificates typically bore the signature of the male head of the household. Women could claim their rights only in the presence of their husbands or male relatives and could lose their rights in case of divorce or death. In 2001 the marriage and family law was revised so that both spouses' signatures are required on any documents registering family assets and land use rights. The government aims to achieve universal joint titling by 2005. In cooperation with the World Bank the Vietnamese government selected two communes for a pilot project to reissue land title certificates with joint signatures. The project organized village meetings and distributed leaflets about the new law. As a result of the pilot, some 2,600 households now have joint titles. A 2002 evaluation by the World Bank concluded that the project also: • Enabled the establishment of a gender-responsive land administration system. • Improved the ability of local governments to implement land reform. • Enabled local practices to comply with national law. • Disseminated knowledge on national law in remote communities.

At the international level, the scale and energy of efforts focused on women's property and inheritance rights have grown in recent years

In India, however, joint titling has had mixed effects (Agarwal 2002). Joint titles are usually favored in the limited cases where women's claims to land are recognized by courts or informal tribunals. Although having some claim to land is better than no claim, joint titles can create problems, making it difficult for women to control the produce of the land, to exercise their priorities in land use if those differ from the priorities of their husbands, to bequeath a portion of the land as they want, or to claim their shares in case of marital conflict. Individual titles may give women greater flexibility and control over the land than joint titles, enabling them to explore alternative institutional arrangements for cultivation and management. Even then, women often lack funds for equipment or inputs. Where holdings are very small, individual investment in equipment can prove uneconomical. Women may also face considerable pressure from male relatives who want to acquire or control the land.

Collective approaches to support women's access to land

Agarwal (2002) identifies five types of institutional solutions to these problems. One is to help women who own individual holdings to invest in capital inputs jointly with other women, while managing production individually. A second type of arrangement involves women purchasing land jointly while owning it individually and farming it collectively.[12] A third possibility is for women to lease land and cultivate it as a group.[13] A fourth type of institutional arrangement is for women's groups to manage and oversee cultivation on land owned by men. A fifth type of arrangement is for poor rural women to hold group rights over land distributed by the government or otherwise acquired by them (Agarwal 2002).[14]

More generally, women's land rights must be complemented by other changes that enhance women's access to credit and to important inputs such as seeds, fertilizers, and new technologies. Credit programs that provide loans for land and housing purchases can promote joint titling and titling in women's names. Improving access to markets for women's products, through improved infrastructure and transportation as noted in chapter 5, is also complementary to the legal changes discussed in this chapter.

International actions

At the international level, the scale and energy of efforts focused on women's property and inheritance rights have grown in recent years, spurred by expansion of the Internet even to remote areas and the continuous efforts by women's and rights-oriented networks. The Convention on the Elimination of All Forms of Discrimination against Women has focused on equality in property as one of its important directives. The UN Conference on Human Settlements at its Istanbul meeting in 1996 also focused centrally on women and land.

Since then the Huairou Commission, a network of women's organizations, in conjunction with the United Nations Development Programme,

UN Human Settlements Program (UN-HABITAT), the Women's Environmental and Development Organization, and the Women's Caucus of the UN Commission on Sustainable Development has held discussions with women's groups worldwide to examine regional progress in enhancing women's access to land and property (Agarwal 2002). The Huairou Commission, the UN Center for Human Settlements, the Centre on Housing Rights and Evictions, and the Food and Agriculture Organization have begun a joint initiative in Sub-Saharan Africa to strengthen advocacy for law and policy reform and implementation and for dissemination of tools and strategies used by women's organizations in the region. The UN Special Rapporteur on the Right to Adequate Housing has given content to specific human rights such as the right to adequate housing. And the United Nations has passed several increasingly specific resolutions over the past decade concerning women's right to ownership of, access to, and control over land, housing, and other property (OHCHR 2003; CESCR 1991). All these efforts deserve greater support.

Chapter 7

Reduce gender inequality in employment

During the 1980s and 1990s women's economic activity rates increased everywhere except in Sub-Saharan Africa, parts of Europe and Central Asia, and Oceania (UN 2000). Between 1990 and 2002, women's share of nonagricultural employment increased in 93 of 131 countries, driven in part by changes in the international economic environment. Yet women's status in the labor market remains significantly inferior to men's according to several key indicators. Occupational segregation by sex is widespread and leads to allocational inefficiencies and gender wage gaps. Gender inequality in employment contravenes women's right to decent work and is costly for women, their households, and their communities.

Women's employment status and low earnings are associated with poverty in many countries around the world. Women tend to be concentrated in informal employment, where pay and conditions of work are worse than in public and formal jobs. Unless improving women's earnings is seen as central to increasing the incomes of poor households, it will be difficult to meet the Millennium Development Goals of halving poverty, reducing gender inequality, and empowering women.

Why reducing gender inequality in employment is a strategic priority

Women's work, both paid and unpaid, is critical to the survival and security of poor households and an important route by which households escape poverty. Paid employment is critical to women's empowerment. Yet, a range of gender inequalities pervade labor markets around the world and must be addressed if the Millennium Development Goals are to be met.

Despite the low pay that women receive, their income has important welfare consequences for children and families. An extensive literature reports

Women's access to jobs empowers them by improving their self-esteem and bargaining power

that women are more likely than men to spend their incomes on food, education, and healthcare that enhance the welfare of their children as well as their own (Guyer 1988; Thomas 1992; Haddad, Hoddinott, and Alderman 1997). Dependency on women's income is even greater in households where they are the sole breadwinners. Female-headed and -maintained households constitute one-fifth to one-third of households in many countries (Quisumbing, Haddad, and Peña 2001).

Beyond the income that women bring into the household, their unpaid work has economic value because it saves expenditures and, in times of economic crisis, replaces income.[1] In rural economies the proportion of labor time allocated to nonmarket production tends to be high—as much as three times the amount spent in market production—because households serve as economic units providing most of their own subsistence needs (Floro 1995). Although important to household survival and reproduction, this unpaid work is not counted in most systems of national accounts.

Few countries collect national time use data, and even fewer take repeated measurements to produce trend data, but available evidence indicates that women often work more hours in paid and unpaid activities than men do (UN 2000). Some studies suggest that women's paid and unpaid labor time has increased in recent decades (Floro 1995) as women compensate for reduced household income and declining public services. Men's performance of unpaid household labor does not appear to have increased enough to compensate for the increase in women's paid employment, suggesting a decline in female leisure.

There is also convincing evidence from such disparate countries as Bangladesh and the Dominican Republic that women's access to jobs empowers them by improving their self-esteem and bargaining power within the household (Safa 1995; Kabeer 2000). In settings where women's mobility is restricted, increased employment opportunities can release constraints on mobility and enable women to seek and access reproductive healthcare (Amin and others 1995). Access to employment can also expose them to new ideas and knowledge and broaden the community with which they engage. As Kabeer (2000) notes, however, the extent to which paid employment expands women's range of choices and their influence within the household is related to the type of job, level and security of pay, and other factors.

Changing patterns in women's employment, 1990–2000

Compared with indicators on health and education, there are far fewer indicators available on women's status in the labor force. Where information is available, it is often not up to date, especially for countries in Sub-Saharan Africa and North Africa. There are also serious problems of data quality, since women's employment is undercounted, especially in agriculture and in informal manufacturing and service activities. Nonetheless, the data reviewed below suggest that although women's participation in nonagricultural wage employment has

In only 17 of 110

countries with

data in 2002

was women's

share of

nonagricultural

wage

employment

50 percent

or greater

increased over the past decade, women tend to be concentrated in informal employment and to experience higher unemployment than men.

In only 17 of 110 countries with data in 2002 was women's share of nonagricultural wage employment 50 percent or greater (table 7.1). In another 76 countries the share was 25–49 percent. The Middle East and North Africa region had a high proportion of countries in the "low" share of employment category—11 of 13 countries had shares below 25 percent.

Of 111 countries with data for both 1990 and 2002, women's share of nonagricultural employment rose in 81 and declined in 29. Most of the declines were in Europe and Central Asia and the Middle East and North Africa.

In developing and transition economies informal jobs constitute one-half to three-quarters of nonagricultural employment—and the share is growing rapidly (ILO 2004a). Informal employment includes all remunerative work—both self-employment and wage employment—that is not recognized, regulated, or protected by legal or regulatory frameworks and all nonremunerative work undertaken in income-producing enterprises.[2] In Sub-Saharan Africa, Latin America, and India the share of informal employment in total nonagricultural employment is higher for women than for men (table 7.2). In several countries—Benin, Chad, Guinea, and Kenya—most of the female nonagricultural labor force is in informal employment.

Agricultural employment. Agriculture remains an important, if declining, source of employment for poor women in many developing countries. Economic trends such as trade expansion and the internationalization of production processes have reduced women's share of agricultural employment over the last decade (Mehra and Gammage 1999). Female agricultural employment fell from 34.6 percent of total agricultural employment in 1990 to 29.7 percent in 2000. The largest drop was in Sub-Saharan Africa, followed by East Asia and the Pacific (table 7.3). Only in Latin America and the Caribbean did women's share of agricultural employment rise during this period.

Table 7.1

Share of women in nonagricultural wage employment, by region, 1990 and 2002

Number of countries

Source: UN 2004a.

Region	High (more than 50%)		Medium (25%–49.9%)		Low (less than 24.9%)	
	1990	2002	1990	2002	1990	2002
Developed countries	3	5	20	18	0	0
East Asia and Pacific	1	1	17	10	1	0
Europe and Central Asia	8	9	18	15	1	1
Latin America and the Caribbean	1	1	26	23	0	0
Middle East and North Africa	0	0	4	3	15	11
South Asia	0	0	1	3	8	2
Sub-Saharan Africa	3	1	23	4	14	4
Total	16	17	109	76	39	18

Table 7.2	**Region and country**	**Women**	**Men**

Table 7.2

Informal employment in nonagricultural employment, by sex and region, 1994 and 2000

Percent

Source: ILO 2002b.

Region and country	Women	Men
North Africa	43	49
Algeria	41	43
Morocco	47	44
Tunisia	39	53
Egypt	46	57
Sub-Saharan Africa	84	63
Benin	97	87
Chad	95	60
Guinea	87	66
Kenya	83	59
South Africa	58	44
Latin America	58	48
Bolivia	74	55
Brazil	67	55
Chile	44	31
Colombia	44	34
Costa Rica	48	42
Dominican Republic	84	63
El Salvador	69	46
Guatemala	69	47
Honduras	65	74
Mexico	55	54
Venezuela	47	47
Asia	65	65
India	86	83
Indonesia	77	78
Philippines	73	71
Thailand	54	49
Middle East and North Africa		
Syria	35	43

Adolescent employment. In Sub-Saharan Africa, South Asia, and large parts of Latin America most young people who work are employed in informal activities, such as shop assistants, farm hands, clerical assistants, typists, stewards and cooks in hotels and restaurants, street traders, and casual labor (ILO 2002b). Adolescent girls often work as hairdressers, dressmakers, petty traders, and domestic servants. They are more vulnerable to unfair treatment, in part because gender socialization tends to teach girls docility and obedience from an early age (Population Council and ICRW 2000).

Youth unemployment rates rose everywhere between 1990 and 2000 (table A3.1 in appendix 3): male rates rose from 12.0 percent to 14.2 percent and female rates rose from 14.6 percent to 16.9 percent (ILO 2004b). The relative disadvantage of youth in the labor market is more pronounced in developing

	Region	1990–95	1996–2001
Table 7.3	Developed countries	29.44	29.89
Female share in agricultural employment by region, 1990–95 to 1996–2001	East Asia and Pacific	42.01	32.75
	Europe and Central Asia	45.82	40.05
Percent	Latin America and the Caribbean	16.35	18.59
	Middle East and North Africa	24.31	22.27
Source: ILO 2003a.	South Asia	37.18	30.47
	Sub-Saharan Africa	46.72	33.82

countries, where they make up a higher proportion of the labor force, than in developed countries (ILO 2004b). Youth unemployment rates were higher for females than for males in 23 of the 41 countries with data in 2000, and the difference was especially stark in Latin America and the Caribbean.

Gender inequalities in employment

Gender inequalities persist in entry to work, conditions at work, and exit from the labor market.

Barriers to entry into the labor market

Early marriage and early childbearing, low education, and women's care responsibilities (for children, the sick, and the elderly) present barriers to women's and girls' employment. Early marriage and early childbearing have historically limited young women's access to education and thereby to employment opportunities. In some parts of the world young women's employment is seen as a threat to culturally accepted gender roles, and many families fear for the safety of girls in the workplace and traveling to and from work. Even when young married girls want to work or need to support their families, they have few marketable skills that can be translated into decent work. Thus most young married girls who are employed work in home-based or other types of informal employment (Population Council and ICRW 2000). Some studies suggest that early marriage and childbearing may be lessening as a barrier to employment in those parts of the world where wage employment has become rapidly available, such as in garment factories in Bangladesh and Morocco (Amin and Lloyd 1998; Amin 1997; Cairoli 1999).

Low education has traditionally been another barrier to entry into formal employment. Generally, the greater a woman's education, the greater the probability that she will enter the labor market. Cameron, Dowling, and Worsick's (2001) study of women's labor market participation decisions in Indonesia, the Republic of Korea, the Philippines, Sri Lanka, and Thailand finds that primary education affects the probability of labor market participation only in Indonesia but that secondary education increases the probability in Indonesia and Thailand and tertiary education increases the probability in all countries. Similarly, Mammen and Paxson (2000) find that postsecondary schooling has large positive effects on women's probability of working in India and Thailand.[3]

Achieving gender equality in labor markets requires the extension and upgrading of childcare

The level of education also affects the type of employment that women are likely to enter. More education is found to increase women's likelihood of working in formal wage employment and in the public sector rather than being self-employed or doing informal work, but this is conditioned by the types of jobs that are available.[4] Some studies have found that the type of education (general schooling, vocational education) also influences women's labor force participation. Tansel (1994) finds that young women in Turkey who are graduates of vocational high schools are more likely to enter the labor force than women who graduate from regular high schools.

These barriers to entry have been crumbling over the past decade as new employment opportunities arise in many countries and women's education levels rise. As a result, these barriers are no longer the key problem in most parts of the world, except perhaps in South Asia and some countries in the Middle East and North Africa and Sub-Saharan Africa.

One barrier to employment that has not crumbled, however, is women's responsibility for caring for children, the elderly, and the sick. Studies from around the world indicate that young children and a lack of childcare options constrain women's entry into paid employment and type of job. Increased migration, the breakdown of extended families, and changing social arrangements in some parts of the world have made extended families a less reliable source of childcare than formerly, necessitating other types of care services.

The availability of childcare often enables women to take permanent, full-time jobs rather than seasonal, part-time, or temporary work (Alva 1999; Chang and Kim 1999; North-South Institute 1999; Connelly, DeGraff, and Levison 1996; Folbre 1994; Kula and Lambert 1994; Doan and Popkin 1993). Yet in most developing countries and some developed countries the reach of both formal and informal childcare programs is inadequate. They often cover only certain age groups, operate at specific times of day that may be incompatible with women's working hours, and are located in inconvenient locations underserved by safe and affordable transportation services. Achieving gender equality in labor markets requires the extension and upgrading of childcare services and making them affordable for poor women who do not have viable care options.

Inferior conditions of employment

Women's status in the labor market is inferior to men's in most countries of the world, according to key indicators such as occupational distribution, earnings, the nature and terms of employment, and unemployment.

Occupational segregation. Women and men typically perform different tasks and are located in different industries and occupational sectors. About half of workers worldwide work in occupations in which at least 80 percent of workers are of the same sex (Anker 1998). Occupational segregation by sex is extensive

Gender gaps in earnings remain among the most persistent forms of inequality in the labor market

in both developed and developing countries but is greatest in Latin America and the Caribbean, followed by North Africa and the Middle East, the Organisation for Economic Co-operation and Development countries, Eastern Europe, Sub-Saharan Africa, and East Asia (Deutsch and others 2002). In many countries occupational segregation is highest among the least educated workers (Anker 1998; Deutsch and others 2002).

On the supply side, occupational segregation may partly reflect women's tendency to select "traditional" occupations, such as teaching and nursing. But those choices are influenced by such factors as education and social expectations. Thus, women are more likely to graduate from programs in education, arts, humanities, social sciences, and law while men are more likely to graduate from programs in natural resources, mathematics, and engineering (Bradley 2000). Women may also "adapt" their preferences to occupations that are socially acceptable, and there is evidence that women are inclined to pursue careers that are more conducive to combining work and reproductive responsibilities, which leads to their concentration in certain sectors (Chang 2004).[5] On the demand side, employer practices also contribute to occupational segregation. Many studies have found that garment factory owners in most countries prefer to hire women as sewing machine operators (Paul-Majumder and Begum 2000; Cairoli 1999; Anker and Hein 1985). In some countries in Eastern Europe and the former Soviet Union job advertisements specify vacancies by sex (UNICEF 1999).[6]

Occupational segregation has significant costs, including rigidities in the labor market, larger male-female wage gaps, underutilization of women's labor (allocative inefficiency), and lower levels of output and future growth rates because of lower than optimal investments in girls' education (Anker 1998; Deutsch and others 2002). There is also increasing evidence that feminization of an occupation negatively affects the overall wage rate in that occupation (Goldin 2002).

Gender gaps in earnings. The principle of equal pay for work of equal value has gained wide acceptance and is reflected in several International Labour Organization conventions. Yet, gender gaps in earnings remain among the most persistent forms of inequality in the labor market.[7] In all countries around the world men earn more than women, and this is true across different groups of workers (agricultural, manufacturing, production, supervisory) and different types of earnings (monthly, hourly, salaried).

Studies of the gender wage gap show conflicting results. There is some evidence that the gender wage gap has narrowed slightly in some occupations in some countries in the 1990s (Tzannatos 1999; Artecona and Cunningham 2002; Oostendorp 2002). Elsewhere, gender wage gaps have widened (Standing 1999; Mehra and Gammage 1999). In the East Asian countries that have grown rapidly, in large part because of exports produced with female labor, gender wage gaps remain large and have worsened in some cases (Seguino 2000).

Although most at risk and therefore most in need, informal workers—the majority of them women—have little or no social protection and receive little or no social security

While wages tend to be lower for both men and women in informal employment, the gender gap in earnings appears to be higher than in formal employment (ILO 2002b). Within informal employment earnings tend to decline from self-employed workers (dominated by men) to casual wage workers to subcontracted workers (dominated by women; Chen, Vanek, and Carr 2004).

Nature and terms of employment: informalization and flexibilization of work. With globalization (Standing 1989, 1999) and the growth of nonregular and nonwage employment (Bettio 1996) employment has become increasingly flexible. Numerous studies show the increased use of women as temporary, casual, contract, and part-time workers in manufacturing (Standing 1989, 1999; Carr, Chen, and Tate 2000; and Balakrishnan 2002). The agricultural sector has also been affected as seasonal employment in agricultural exports has expanded (UNDAW 1999). Women are the preferred source of temporary workers in the Chilean and South African export grape industries but hold only a small share of permanent jobs (Barrientos 2001). Men are increasingly affected by informalization and flexibilization as well, as the jobs they hold take on the character of women's jobs (temporary or casual status, limited job mobility, few or no benefits), but the share of women in flexible jobs greatly exceeds that of men (UNDAW 1999; Standing 1999).

Informal employment is often characterized by undefined workplaces, unsafe and unhealthy working conditions, low levels of skills and productivity, low or irregular incomes, long working hours, and a lack of access to information, markets, finance, training, and technology. Although most at risk and therefore most in need, informal workers—the majority of them women—have little or no social protection and receive little or no social security, either from their employer or from the government (ILO 2002a).

Unemployment. Gender differences are also apparent in unemployment, with women more likely than men to be unemployed in recent years. Unemployment data often are of questionable quality because of measurement problems and limited population coverage in low-income economies, where the majority of the population engages in informal or self-employment. In the Caribbean economies, for which more reliable data are available because of the way unemployment is measured (Seguino 2003), women's unemployment rates are almost double those of men. Similarly, in transition economies, women have experienced declines in access to jobs relative to men (Bridger, Kay, and Pinnick 1996).

Inequalities in pensions and retirement
Women live longer than men, and in most regions they are more likely to spend time as widows, when they are more vulnerable to poverty than are men. Many older women, especially widows, have little income security in old age. Women's responsibilities for unpaid care work and their predominance in informal

An important strategy in addressing barriers to employment is increasing women's access to postprimary and vocational and technical education

employment and seasonal and part-time jobs restrict their access to jobs with pension coverage. Private pension coverage is more extensive in larger firms and in industries requiring a skilled, stable, and full-time labor force—just the kind of jobs in which women are likely to be underrepresented. In many countries jobs in the public sector have historically been a major source of pensions; as the public sector has contracted (due to structural adjustment, privatization, and cuts in government spending), women have lost pension coverage.

Because the statutory retirement age is lower for women than for men in many countries, women retire earlier and receive smaller annuities since they have fewer years of contributions and more years of expected longevity (World Bank 2001a). If pensions are not indexed properly to inflation, women's living standards fall disproportionately with age because women live longer than men.

Interventions to decrease gender inequality in employment

Interventions to improve women's access to employment take many forms. Those discussed here are interventions to address barriers to entry, improve the conditions of employment, and provide support to women who need social protection when they leave the labor market.

Interventions to reduce barriers to entry

An important strategy in addressing barriers to employment is increasing women's access to postprimary and vocational and technical education and improving the quality of education. Secondary school should prepare adolescents for employment as well as for postsecondary education. Especially important for adolescent girls' participation and achievement in postprimary education is their enrollment and achievement in math, science, and other technical courses. Parents may be more willing to send girls to secondary school if there is a strong curriculum, particularly for girls in science (Herz and Sperling 2004).

The Forum of African Women Educators, through its Female Education in Mathematics and Science in Africa program, aims to increase girls' participation and achievement in math, sciences, and technical subjects through multiple interventions. One way is through a gender-sensitive curriculum and pedagogy that relates these subjects to girls' daily experiences and to the uses of science and math in the local community. The material should be presented in ways that engage girls, such as through problem solving and collaborative learning (Harding 1996). These types of programs need to be scaled up.

Policy changes are also needed in vocational and technical education. Current policies and resource allocations in many countries restrict access and limit fields of technical study for girls (Hoffmann-Barthes, Nair, and Malpede 1999; UNESCO 1999). More emphasis is needed on encouraging girls to go into nontraditional vocational and technical programs, such as engineering and computer technology (UNESCO 2004). Botswana, for instance,

National policies that support caregiving and programs that provide care services are important to enable women to participate in paid employment

has established a Technical and Vocational Gender Reference Group to advise the Ministry of Education on guidelines for addressing gender inequities (UNESCO 2004).

National policies that support caregiving and programs that provide care services—for children, the disabled or ill, and the elderly—are important to enable women to participate in paid employment. Childcare services, especially important, can be provided in private homes, at community centers, or at work sites. Care can range from custodial to a full range of services that support children's health, growth, and development and respond to women's needs, such as for flexible hours (Connelly, DeGraff, and Levison 1996; Evans 1995; Chatterjee and Macwan 1992; Himes, Landers, and Leslie 1992; Leonard and Landers 1991; Myers and Indriso 1986; Evans and Myers 1995; OEF 1979).[8]

Public policy debates focus on whether governments should guarantee universal availability of services, what form government subsidies should take (direct subsidies to parents or public provision of services), the degree of public regulation of service quality, and the need for public support of training and quality improvements. The governments of most developed countries accept some responsibility for sharing the cost of rearing their nations' children, and many have comprehensive family policies (Helburn 1999). European countries provide publicly supported childcare and other programs that absorb the costs of raising children and make it easier for women to juggle employment and care for children. Nordic countries have made the greatest commitment to supporting working parents by providing good quality, inexpensive care for children over one year old and parental leave benefits that compensate parents for loss of income and guarantee their job.

Recognizing the value of early education, especially for poor children, governments in many developing countries also support childcare and early education services. In India as early as 1944 a government commission recommended that the states establish free preschools. Today, there are a variety of federal, private, and voluntary programs (although coverage is far from universal). Institutionalized childcare is provided in China, where more than 90 percent of young mothers are employed. Yet, not one country provides the investment in care services that is required to fully meet the needs of women and their children. Filling this gap is essential for meeting Goal 3.

Interventions to improve the nature and conditions of employment

Employment-enhancing economic growth is a prerequisite for low-income countries, coupled with social policy that eliminates discriminatory employment barriers. It is easier to improve wages and working conditions in a growing economy. Equity in earnings is also needed, with both women and men able to earn wages high enough to permit them to provide for their families. Relatively secure income sources are also crucial, particularly for women who head households but also for married women, to achieve a more equitable

For poor women, public employment guarantees can provide an important source of work and income

distribution of household resources and unpaid labor and to improve women's bargaining power (Seguino and Grown 2003).

Public employment guarantee schemes. For poor women, especially in rural areas, public employment guarantees can provide an important source of work and income, although evaluations of country programs reveal a mixed track record. Perhaps the most well known and best studied scheme in developing countries is the Maharashtra Employment Guarantee Scheme, introduced in Maharashtra, India, in 1972. The scheme guarantees employment to unemployed rural adults on a defined piece-rate basis. The objectives are to sustain household welfare in the short run and contribute to development of the rural economy in the long run by improving rural infrastructure and assets. Women's participation in the scheme increased gradually, rising from 41 percent in 1979 to 53 percent in 1987, and has remained fairly stable since.[9] The localized nature of the employment offered and the systematic provision of childcare reduce the costs of women's participation, and there is no overt gender discrimination in wages. Women's earnings from the scheme constitute as much as 30 percent of household income (Engkvist 1995).

However, public employment guarantee schemes can also be gender biased. In many programs women earn less than men, partly because they are excluded from higher wage or physically difficult tasks. Women are more susceptible to exploitation, and village studies in India show higher rates of female participation than official registers, suggesting that women work as unpaid labor on behalf of men (Engkvist 1995).

Baden (1995) notes that other public works schemes have a varied record on female participation. Phase one of the Rural Employment Sector Program in Bangladesh achieved more than 40 percent participation of women. Women attended meetings and saved more regularly than men, but they were allocated fewer days of work at lower daily rates. Few women's groups participated in project planning, compared with men's groups.

There has been little attempt to draw women into more lucrative economic development programs. In Chile's Minimum Employment Program (PEM), set up in 1975, 73 percent of participants were women by 1987. To counter the "feminization" of PEM, the government set up the Employment Program for Household Heads (POJH), paying the minimum wage to heads of household, twice the rate under PEM. POJH attracted mainly men and discouraged the wives of poor men from working outside the home.

Social protection. For countries with large informal workforces, providing social protection for them is one of the highest priorities.[10] Too often social protection and safety net programs exclude women by failing to account for gender differences in labor market participation, access to information, and unpaid care responsibilities. That makes women more vulnerable to poverty

and the risks associated with economic and other shocks to household livelihoods (Lund and Nicholson 2003).

Increasingly, NGOs are providing social protection to informally employed
workers to fill gaps in public provision of health insurance, child care, and
disability. The Self-Employed Women's Association in India is one example
of an NGO effort, alone and in partnership with the Indian government, to
deliver innovative services to address the needs of informal workers (box 7.1).
Although NGO efforts are essential, maintaining an adequate level of social

Box 7.1

**The Self-Employed
Women's
Association of
India addresses
the needs of
the informally
employed**

Source: Blaxall 2004.

The Self-Employed Women's Association (SEWA) was started in 1972 in Gujarat, India,
as a membership organization for women who work in the informal sector. Membership
growth since the mid-1980s has been rapid, averaging 25–35 percent a year. In 2003, with
700,000 members, SEWA had branches in rural and urban areas in seven Indian states.

SEWA's flexible organizational structure incorporates a range of activities to address
the needs of informally employed women:

- A trade union that helps women organize, negotiate better working conditions, and
  gain fair access to markets. In 2003 the urban branch of the union had 166,000
  members in more than 70 occupations or trades, including home-based workers,
  producers, manual laborers, and service providers. In rural areas the union focuses
  on creating alternative employment opportunities for its 370,000 members.
- SEWA cooperatives help their members produce and market their goods and services. The cooperatives ensure quality control and provide pricing and marketing
  services. In 2003 there were more than 100 SEWA cooperatives. Gram Mahila
  Haat, one of the more successful cooperatives, had arranged sales of products
  valued at more than $3.5 million by 2002, for its 23,000 members in 1,000 pro-
  ducer groups.
- SEWA Bank, launched in 1974 and with more than 300,000 member shareholders,
  is a pioneer of micro-credit. In 2003 it had deposits of $13.9 million in 200,000
  accounts and 50,000 outstanding loans totaling $3 million. The average loan size
  is $60 at an interest rate of 20 percent. The loan repayment rate is 96 percent.
- SEWA provides basic healthcare services, usually organized around midwives and
  healthcare worker cooperatives. SEWA also encourages its members to use govern-
  ment-run clinics and government-sponsored health and immunization campaigns.
  In 2002 nearly 300,000 people obtained healthcare services through SEWA teams,
  and SEWA provided low-cost medicines worth $250,000 through medical shops in
  Ahmedabad hospitals.
- In 2002 SEWA had 128 childcare centers serving 6,300 children.
- SEWA provides insurance through SEWA Bank and government insurance companies, covering more than 100,000 members in 2002. It covers maternity benefits,
  illness, death, and loss of property.
- SEWA provides training to members who want to upgrade their homes. SEWA
  helped members rebuild homes after the 2001 earthquake. In 2002 a total of
  2,600 homes were built with ownership registered in the woman's name.
- SEWA also works to improve infrastructure services. An electrification initiative,
  initially started with 150 households, provided legalized electricity and cheaper
  and better service to the community and is now expanding.

Many developed and developing countries try to influence pay and working conditions through equal opportunity or anti-discrimination legislation

protection is ultimately a critical government function that needs sufficient budget support.

Microfinance. Microfinance programs have been the most popular economic strategy over the past two decades to assist poor and landless women in entering self-employment or starting their own business. According to the State of the Microcredit Summit Campaign 2001 Report, 14.2 million of the world's poorest women now have access to financial services through specialized microfinance institutions, banks, NGOs, and other nonbank financial institutions (Druschel, Quigley, and Sanchez 2001). Many microfinance programs, which incorporate savings components, have enabled women to build assets to use as collateral, reduce volatility in consumption, and self-finance investments rather than turning to creditors (Morduch 1999). According to Pitt and Khandker (1998), non-land assets increase substantially more when women borrow than when men do.

Perhaps the most important impact of microfinance programs is to stabilize household income (Kevane and Wydick 2001).[11] Studies find some employment growth among family members of borrowers, but because the employment impact outside the family has been small (Dawson and Jeans 1997), microfinance programs should not be depended on to accelerate economic growth or large-scale poverty reduction. Donors should continue to support microfinance programs, but to boost their impact, microfinance programs need to be coupled with other types of products and services, including training, technology transfer, business development services, and marketing assistance. More attention also needs to be given to innovative savings and insurance instruments for low-income women (box 7.1).

Legislation. Many developed and developing countries try to influence pay and working conditions through equal opportunity or antidiscrimination legislation (Rodgers 1999).[12] Such legislation typically includes family leave policies; equal pay and equal opportunity issues; and standards for and rights at work. (See table A3.2 in appendix 3 for the status of maternity leave benefits by country, an example of such legislation.) Empirical evidence of the impact of such legislation on women's employment and relative wages is mixed for developed countries and scant for developing countries.

In Costa Rica, for instance, evidence suggests that legislation to lengthen maternity leave had little impact on wages and employment until a new enforcement mechanism was created in 1990 (Gindling and Crummet 1977). With improved enforcement and stricter penalties for firms that violated the law, women's wages fell significantly while their labor force participation did not increase. The evidence on equal pay and equal opportunity policies suggests that they have improved women's relative wages in economies where collective bargaining is common (Australia, Canada, and United Kingdom) but have

**Countries
need better
resourced labor
inspectorates
and assistance
for women
in bringing
legal cases**

been less successful in countries with decentralized wage-setting practices such as the United States.[13] Enforcement is a big obstacle, especially in developing countries with neither the resources nor the institutional infrastructure to monitor employment practices (Rodgers 1999). Countries need better resourced labor inspectorates and assistance for women in bringing legal cases.

Although important, equal pay laws do not address lower earnings that result from occupational segregation by sex. Some countries have laws stipulating equal pay for work of comparable value. Some have tackled occupational segregation through legislation that improves women's access to occupations that have traditionally been dominated by men. Closely related measures that prevent discrimination on the basis of marital status or family responsibilities have similar objectives, but their impact has not been rigorously evaluated.

Policies to protect migrant women workers—a particularly vulnerable group—are being implemented in some countries. As a result of a United Nations Development Fund for Women regional program on migration, Jordan and the Philippines have agreed to a minimum set of standards embodied in a special working contract for migrant domestic workers. The contract provides migrant women workers with benefits including life insurance, medical care, rest days, and workplace protections. Whether this contract is being enforced is not known, and the results of such policies have yet to be evaluated.

Interventions to reduce inequalities in pensions and retirement

Many countries, especially in Latin America and in Eastern and Central Europe, are reforming their pension and social security programs. Gender equality has not been a high priority in these reform efforts (Fultz, Ruck, and Steinhilber 2003). To protect retired women, such programs need to take account of gender differences in earnings, labor force experience, and longevity.

Because the specifics of pension reform vary across countries and there have been few studies of their effects, it is difficult to draw clear conclusions about the effects of different types of pension programs on women. Nonetheless, it is clear that programs that have a redistributive component and that do not require many years of contributions are better able to protect women in old age. Redistributive components may be based on residence or prorated by years of employment. Both are superior to an all or nothing benefit requiring a lifetime of formal market employment (World Bank 2001a). Since women's earnings tend to be lower than men's, minimum pension guarantees, survivor benefits, and joint annuities can ensure that women receive a minimum threshold level of benefits (World Bank 2001a).

South Africa's pension scheme has reduced poverty among elderly women. It is a noncontributory, means-tested public pension that is payable to women after age 60 and men after age 65 (Burns, Keswell, and Leibbrandt forthcoming).[14] A little more than three-fifths of people 60 and older are women. And because women qualify earlier and live longer, the social pension reaches almost

Decent, productive work for all should be the goal

three times as many women as men, giving it a strong gender dimension (Case and Deaton 1998; South African Department of Social Development 2002a, 2002b). It has been estimated that more than 80 percent of the elderly in South Africa have access to no other income apart from the social pension and that the pension reduces the poverty gap for the elderly by 94 percent (South African Department of Social Development 2002a, 2002b).

Further research is necessary to determine whether women are better or worse off in non-public pension schemes (occupational pensions, mandatory private pensions, or voluntary private pensions). Pension reforms of the past decade in Latin America and Eastern Europe have eliminated many of the redistributive elements of public pensions. In some cases (Chile) the rules are more favorable to women, but in other cases (Czech Republic, Hungary, and Poland) the risks have increased. A detailed analysis of Chile's efforts to implement a defined contribution plan model found that it increased women's incentives to participate in the labor market, to save, and to use the social security system as a channel for their savings (Duryea, Cox Edwards, and Ureta 2001). The study also found that three characteristics raised the marginal benefit of own contributions for working women relative to the old system: there is no minimum contribution level, early contributions have a greater weight because of compound interest, and widows can keep their own pension in addition to their former husband's pension.[15] In the Czech Republic, Hungary, and Poland, by contrast, where reforms aimed at linking individual pension benefits more closely to workers' earnings and work history, lower-income workers, especially women, have been hurt (Fultz, Ruck, and Steinhilber 2003).

In countries moving to private pension schemes, public pension schemes are an important supplement because they provide insurance and redistribution on a wider scale than private pensions. Public pensions are also a better alternative for women in low-income countries, where informal employment and widespread poverty coexist.

Conclusion

While opportunities for women to earn an income have increased, the nature, terms, and quality of women's employment have not improved commensurately. Having access to paid work is critical to family survival, but it is not sufficient for reducing poverty or empowering women. Decent, productive work for all should be the goal.

The International Labour Organization's Decent Work initiative provides a framework at the international level for promoting equal access to employment and equal treatment. The initiative seeks to foster rights at work, provide employment and social protection, and encourage social dialogue. Its goal is "to promote opportunities for women and men to obtain decent and productive work, in conditions of freedom, equity, security, and human dignity" (Anker and others 2002, p. 1). The gender sensitivity of the decent work framework and the sex-disaggregated indicators it proposes for monitoring country performance make it suitable for tracking a country's progress toward eliminating gender inequalities in labor markets. The task force recommends that the International Labour Organization be given the resources and authority to take the leadership in collecting and disseminating data and monitoring progress for this initiative.

Chapter 8

Increase women's representation in political bodies

Ensuring that women can participate in decisionmaking in all political arenas on equal footing with men is crucial for meeting Goal 3. Some countries have made noticeable progress on women's representation in political bodies since 1991. Their experience suggests that gender quotas and reservations are effective for increasing women's representation in national and local legislatures. Strong women's movements and government policies that reduce women's multiple burdens can also facilitate women's political participation.

Why women's increased political representation is a priority

Increasing women's representation in political office is now a widely held development goal and one of the four indicators for tracking progress toward Goal 3.[1] The Beijing Platform for Action recommended that governments set a target reserving 30 percent of seats in national parliaments for women. A target of 30 percent is only a first step toward gender equality in political participation, because true gender equality and empowerment requires 50 percent representation by women and the agency to shape decisions and outcomes.

There are three reasons why the task force selected political participation as a strategic priority. First, equality of opportunity in politics is a human right. Moreover, countries where women's share of seats in political bodies is less than 30 percent are less inclusive, less egalitarian, and less democratic.

Second, equality of political participation is important to ensure that women's interests are fairly represented in decisionmaking. Evidence suggests that women who participate directly in decisionmaking bodies press for different priorities than those emphasized by men. Women are often more active in supporting laws benefiting women, children, and families. The likelihood that women will promote such laws rises when there is a critical mass of women leaders and when there are mechanisms to institutionalize collective action

Some countries have introduced provisions for women's representation at local levels

such as women's caucuses or multiparty women's alliances. Research in the United States has shown that female and male legislators have different policy priorities (Thomas 1991; Carroll 2001). A study of local government bodies in India found that female and male heads emphasized different policies (Chattopadhyay and Duflo 2004).

Third, evidence suggests that women's participation in political decision-making bodies improves the quality of governance. Three studies find a positive correlation between increased women's participation in public life and a reduction in the level of corruption.[2] And a poll conducted by Gallup and the Inter-American Dialogue in five Latin American countries in 2000 found that most of those surveyed believed that having more women in power improves government and that women are better able than men to handle a wide range of policy issues.

In general, women's opportunities to exercise power tend to be greater at the local than at the national level. The greater the number of local governing bodies, the more opportunities there may be for aspiring women leaders. In federal systems where power is devolved to the local level and local bodies are popularly elected, women have greater opportunities to gain access to political office (table 8.1). Brazil, France, and India have policies to increase women's political participation in local legislative bodies. In France and India these policies have produced massive growth in women's presence in local office.

Some countries have introduced provisions for women's representation at local levels as part of recent decentralization initiatives. In Pakistan the Devolution of Power Plan of March 2000 reserves 33 percent of legislative seats for women at the union, municipality (*tehsil*), and district levels. India's 73rd and 74th constitutional amendments of 1993, intended to decentralize power to states and strengthen systems of local governance, requiring that 33 percent of seats in *panchayats* (local governing councils) be reserved for women.

In India studies of women in *panchayats* attest to the myriad ways women's presence has changed local politics (Vyasulu and Vyasulu 2000). There are

Table 8.1

Women's political representation in selected federal countries, late 1990s

Percent

— Not available.
a. Cities over 3,500 inhabitants.
b. Average across 22 states.
c. Percentage of local seats reserved for women.
d. Percentage in California in 1995.

Source: Htun 2003b.

Country	National congress	State legislatures	City councils
Brazil	9	13	12
France	12	—	48[a]
India	9	9[b]	33[c]
Mexico	16	4.5	12

Only 14 countries have met the Beijing Platform for Action target of 30 percent of seats held by women

reports that women have made the *panchayats* more responsive to community demands for infrastructure, housing, schools, and health. Women officials have improved implementation of various government programs, and their presence has made women citizens more likely to take advantage of state services and demand their rights. When women are the heads of *panchayats*, there is a greater likelihood that policies that are sensitive to women's needs will be implemented (Chattopadhyay and Duflo 2004). Such effects take time to register, however. In the early stages of women's reservations, many women councilors seem merely to act as surrogates of their male relatives, but over time, they acquire the confidence and skills to act independently (Kudva 2003).

Slow progress in women's political participation, 1990–2000

Around the world women are still largely absent from national parliaments.[3] Only 14 countries have met the Beijing Platform for Action target of 30 percent of seats held by women: Argentina, Bahamas, Belgium, Costa Rica, Cuba, Denmark, Finland, Iceland, Mozambique, Netherlands, Norway, Rwanda, South Africa, and Sweden. In another 27 countries women held between 20 and 29 percent of seats in 2004.[4] Yet, women have made notable progress in political life since 1990. Of the 129 countries that have longitudinal data, women have increased their share of seats in parliament in 96 countries. In 29 countries women's representation declined over the decade, and in four it remained unchanged.[5]

Latin America and the Caribbean made the most noticeable progress (table 8.2) of any region in the world. In just one decade the number of countries with very poor representation of women dropped from 20 to 7. Rwanda has also made rapid progress, with women now holding almost 50 percent of seats in the national parliament, up from 17 percent in 1990. Several other countries have also taken advantage of postconflict reconstruction to increase women's parliamentary representation, including Timor-Leste (box 8.1).

Table 8.2

Share of women-held seats in national parliaments, 1990 and 2004

Number of countries

Source: IPU 2004.

Region	Countries with high shares (more than 30%)		Countries with medium shares (20%–29.9%)		Countries with low shares (10%–19.9%)		Countries with very low shares (less than 10%)	
	1990	2004	1990	2004	1990	2004	1990	2004
Developed countries	4	7	2	7	8	7	9	1
East Asia and Pacific	0	0	3	3	2	4	14	15
Europe and Central Asia	2	0	4	5	1	11	2	12
Latin America and the Caribbean	2	4	0	6	8	16	20	7
Middle East and North Africa	0	0	0	0	1	5	11	10
South Asia	0	0	0	0	2	1	7	6
Sub-Saharan Africa	0	3	1	6	13	15	18	17
Total	8	14	10	27	35	59	81	68

Box 8.1

A strong women's political movement increases women's parliamentary representation in Timor-Leste

Source: Prepared by Karen Mason, World Bank 2004.

In some settings political mobilization by women's movements and groups can be an effective alternative to quota systems for ensuring women's political representation.

In the run-up to the first post-independence parliamentary election in Timor-Leste (the former Indonesian province of East Timor), women's organizations and their UN advisers discussed establishing a quota for women's parliamentary representation. The Timor-Leste Women's Network (REDE), a network of 14 women's organizations, campaigned for mandatory quotas of 30 percent of women candidates with every third candidate on the list being a woman. The campaign was opposed by the United Nations on the grounds that winning parliamentary seats in an openly contested election would, in the long run, provide more sustainable and effective representation of women's interests in national decisionmaking.

But REDE's campaign led the UN to make funds and training available to women candidates. In addition, parties with at least 30 percent of candidates who were women received extra television airtime. So even without an official quota some 27 percent of parliamentary seats went to women candidates.

Interventions to increase women's political representation

Gender quotas and reservations have demonstrated their effectiveness at increasing women's representation in political bodies. Statutory gender quotas require that political parties field a minimum number or percentage of female candidates in legislative elections. Argentina's 1991 Quota Law (la Ley de Cupos), for example, requires that each party list contain a minimum of 30 percent women. Political parties often adopt quotas on a voluntary basis rather than by legal statute. Reservations or reserved seats are mechanisms to set aside a percentage of legislative seats for women. These seats may be filled through competitive election or by appointment. In Taiwan Province of China, the seats go to women who receive the most votes in general elections. In Tanzania each party appoints women to fill the reserved seats in proportion to the votes it receives (Htun 2003b).

In 2004, 37 countries had gender quotas or reservations (table A4.2 in appendix 4). Of these 37 countries 23 had statutory gender quotas and 14 reserved seats in national legislatures or local councils. In an additional 33 countries political parties applied gender quotas on a voluntary basis. Quotas have been used in both rich and poor countries and in both old and new democracies.

Every region includes countries with statutory quotas or reservations, but two regional patterns stand out. In Latin America and the Caribbean 11 countries adopted national gender quota legislation in the 1990s and a 12th (Colombia) introduced quotas for senior posts in the executive branch. This experience suggests the influence of regional diffusion of quota policies. In the Balkans during the 1990s gender quotas were introduced in every new electoral regime in the former Yugoslavia (Bosnia and Herzegovina, Kosovo, Macedonia, Serbia and Montenegro, and Slovenia), except for Croatia. The Balkan experience shows that in the period following civil war or the founding

Experience offers four lessons about the conditions under which quotas effectively enhance women's voice in political bodies

of a new state the crafting of new electoral institutions opens a window of opportunity for increasing women's representation. In some cases the international community has influenced adoption of such policies. In others women's groups within the country have been the most important actors.

Although many countries have introduced quotas, there is tremendous variation in women's legislative representation in these countries (table A4.3 in appendix 4). Thus, quotas do not automatically ensure women's equal representation in legislative bodies (Tinker 2002).

Making quotas more effective

Experience offers four lessons about the conditions under which quotas effectively enhance women's voice in political bodies. The first lesson is that a country's electoral system strongly influences the impact of quotas (Htun 2003b). Quotas work best in closed-list, proportional representation systems with placement mandates and where electoral districts are large—where many candidates are elected from each electoral district and parties can expect several candidates running in the district to gain a seat. In such systems voters vote for a party list, not for individual candidates, and party leaders control the placement of candidates on the list. The number of votes received by the party determines how many candidates from the rank-ordered list are elected.

Second, placement mandates are critical to the success of quotas in closed-list proportional representation electoral systems. Because candidates are elected from party lists in the order in which they appear, placement on the list determines the chances of being elected. Placement mandates require parties to place women in high or "electable" positions on party lists (for example, by alternations of women's positions with men's on the party list). This system sets up a reasonably direct relationship between the number of women candidates and the number of women elected. Without these mandates political parties tend to comply with quotas in the most "minimalist" manner permitted by law, assigning women the lowest places on the list (Jones 1998). For example, the Costa Rican quota law contained no placement mandate for the first two elections in which it was applied, and parties placed many women near the bottom of party lists, where they stood no realistic chance of getting elected. Following the Costa Rican Supreme Court ruling requiring parties to adopt placement mandates, women's representation in the national parliament jumped from 19 percent to 35 percent.

Third, quota laws must specify details of implementation. Vague laws leave too much discretion to political parties to apply—or fail to apply—quotas as they see fit. For example, the first Mexican quota law of 1996 failed to specify whether the quotas applied to regular candidates, alternates, or both. As a result political parties complied with the gender quota by including women as alternate candidates. In the national elections of 2000, 70 percent of alternate candidates were women. Mexico's law, revised substantially in 2002, also fails

Women's organizations can pressure governments to implement measures to ensure that women are well represented in political parties and national decisionmaking bodies

to specify how the quota is supposed to be applied in the 300 single-member districts that elect three-fifths of the Mexican Chamber of Deputies.[6]

Finally, for quota laws to be effective, there must be sanctions for noncompliance. The strongest sanction is to have a party's list of candidates declared invalid and for the party to be forbidden from contesting the election. For these sanctions to work, judges must be able to monitor party compliance and groups must be able to challenge noncompliant lists in court. When a quota law was first applied in Argentina in 1993, for example, very few party lists complied (Aggio 2001). Networks of women politicians and feminist activists, spearheaded by the National Women's Council of the executive branch, appeared in court to challenge party lists. In most cases electoral judges refused to validate the lists and sent them back to the political parties (Durrieu 1999).

Other ways to increase women's political representation

Even without quotas and reservations, there are ways to catalyze women's increased political representation. A country's political culture plays an important role. For instance, social welfare states such as the Nordic countries tend to be more conducive to women's leadership. By offering generous provisions for childcare and other family support, welfare states make women's gender roles less of an obstacle to participation in public life. A recent study of women's representation in parliaments in 190 countries found that governments that consider the provision of welfare (or "care work" for children, the sick, and the elderly) an "affirmative duty of the state" tend to elect some 5 percent more women to national legislatures than countries without these policies (holding all other factors constant; McDonagh 2002). The same study found an interactive effect between constitutionalized care work policies, policies upholding democratic civil rights, and women's political representation. Countries with both sets of policies could be expected to have 7 percent more women in their national legislatures than other countries.

The presence of a strong women's political movement can also make a difference, as Timor-Leste shows (box 8.1). Women's organizations can mobilize a political constituency and pressure governments to implement specific measures to ensure that women are well represented in political parties and national decisionmaking bodies.

In the final analysis women's political representation can be increased through several mechanisms. The most direct are party quotas, statutory quotas, and reservations. Women's participation in political bodies can also be facilitated by state policies that institutionalize care responsibilities, and a strong women's movement. The presence of women in power serves as an indicator of a society's fairness and has the potential to trigger more fundamental changes in gender relations and beliefs about appropriate gender roles.

Chapter 9

Combat violence against women

Violence against women occurs in epidemic proportions in many countries around the world. In surveys conducted in various countries between 10 and 69 percent of women report having experienced domestic violence (which is only one form of violence against women; see Heise, Ellsberg, and Gotte-moeller 1999).

Violence against women has serious health and development impacts and is a gross violation of women's rights. Its continued existence is fundamentally inconsistent with Goal 3. Although no single intervention will eliminate violence against women, a combination of infrastructural, legal, judicial, enforcement, educational, health, and other service-related actions can significantly reduce it and its consequences. For that to happen, however, violence against women must first be viewed as unacceptable. A global campaign to establish this norm, combined with a scaling-up of community-based interventions and analyses that document the costs of violence against women, is needed if violence against women is to become a rare occurrence rather than a global epidemic.

Why combating violence against women is a strategic priority

Gender inequality perpetuates violence against women, and violence against women restricts women's ability to use their capabilities and take advantage of opportunities, thereby reinforcing gender inequality.[1] Worldwide, it is estimated that violence against women is as serious a cause of death and incapacity among reproductive-age women as is cancer, and it is a more common cause of ill-health among women than traffic accidents and malaria combined.

Violence against women exists on a continuum, from domestic violence to violence as a weapon of war. It is widely recognized as an important development constraint that retards economic growth and poverty reduction (Moser

Violence against women is an important development constraint

and Moser 2003; Fajnzylber, Lederman, and Loayza 1998). Gender-based violence is the most widespread manifestation of the many interrelated categories of daily violence. Yet this type of violence is still relatively invisible because it typically occurs within the private sphere and is often viewed as a routine and accepted feature of male-female relationships (Kelly and Radford 1998).

Violence against women has many health consequences (Heise, Pitanguy, and Germaine 1994; World Bank 1993). Physical and sexual abuse lie behind unwanted pregnancies, sexually transmitted infections, including HIV/AIDS, and complications of pregnancy (Johns Hopkins School of Public Health 1999b). A large survey of married men in Uttar Pradesh, India, for example, showed that men who admitted to forcing their wives to have sex were 2.6 times more likely than other men to have caused an unplanned pregnancy. Abusive men were also more likely to expose their wives to sexually transmitted infections because they were also more likely than other men to have engaged in extramarital sex (Martin and others 1999). Across 13 Demographic and Health Surveys an average of 9 percent of married women with an unmet need for contraception cited their husbands' disapproval as the main reason for not using contraception (Bongaarts and Bruce 1995).

In some cases the experience of violence can be a strong predictor of HIV. In a study in Tanzania of women who sought services at a voluntary counseling and testing service center, women who were HIV positive were 2.6 times more likely to have experienced violence in an intimate relationship than women who were HIV negative (Maman and others 2000). Moreover, violence appears to increase women's risk of gynecological disorders, including chronic pelvic pain, irregular vaginal bleeding, vaginal discharge, pelvic inflammatory disease, and sexual dysfunction (Johns Hopkins School of Public Health 1999b).

Around the world studies have found that one woman in four is physically or sexually abused during pregnancy (Johns Hopkins School of Public Health 1999b). Violence before and during pregnancy can have serious health consequences for women and their children. Some studies indicate that women who are battered during pregnancy run twice the risk of miscarriage and four times the risk of having a low birth-weight baby compared with women who are not battered (Stark and others 1981; Bullock and McFarlane 1989). Violence may also be linked to a sizable portion of maternal deaths. A recent study of maternal deaths in more than 400 villages in three districts in Maharashtra, India, revealed that 16 percent of deaths during pregnancy were caused by domestic violence (Ganatra 1996).

Over and above this, evidence collected in the past decade shows that violence against women is an important development constraint.[2] National governments, women's organizations, and the United Nations now recognize that violence against women is an abuse of basic human rights and that atrocities such as rape committed against women during armed conflict are a weapon of war and a gender-based crime. Social violence in the home has been found to

Surveys often find that violence against women cuts across socioeconomic, religious, and ethnic groups and across geographical areas

be correlated with economic crime outside of the home, as well as with political and institutional violence at the local and national level (Moser 2001).

This chapter focuses on two important types of violence: domestic or intimate partner violence and sexual violence by strangers or nonfamily members. Domestic or intimate partner violence occurs in the home, at the hands of intimate partners or relatives, and its manifestations include rape and other forms of sexual violence, physical violence, and psychological abuse. Sexual violence occurs within the wider community, and its manifestations include rape and sexual assault or intimidation in public spaces. Women are at increased risk of this type of violence in conflict situations. In both conflict and nonconflict settings women are primarily the victims of sexual violence and men are primarily the perpetrators.

Prevalence of violence against women

Accurate statistical data on the prevalence of gender-based violence are difficult to come by because of underreporting by victims and underrecording by police, which also mean that existing evidence most likely underestimates prevalence.[3] Few national statistical bodies collect data on the topic, and few of the available studies yield information that is comparable across countries or regions.[4]

The population-based surveys that are available often find that violence against women cuts across socioeconomic, religious, and ethnic groups and across geographical areas.[5] Evidence from diverse contexts reveals that women living in poverty are especially vulnerable to gender-based violence (WHO 2002b; KfW and City of Cape Town 2002; Bid, Nanavaty, and Patel 2002; Omorodion and Olusanya 1998), as are adolescent girls. In some countries, however, it is better-off women who are at greater risk (Kishor and Johnson 2004).

Women are at risk of violence when carrying out essential daily activities—walking or taking public transport to work, collecting water or firewood—especially early in the morning or late at night. Using public transport can make women especially vulnerable to rape, as reported in India (Bid, Nanavaty, and Patel 2002), Papua New Guinea (Sen 1998), and Zambia, where girls are at risk of sexual abuse by school bus drivers (Human Rights Watch 2002). Secluded or unlit areas, such as isolated bus stops, public latrines, or dark places are also frequent locations of rape (KfW and City of Cape Town 2002; Louw and Shaw 1997; Human Rights Watch 1995). A study in metropolitan South Africa found that 15.5 percent of incidents of sexual abuse occurred in outdoor public places (Bollen and others 1999).

Adolescent girls are also at risk of violence, sometimes experiencing sexual violence in schools. This problem is particularly acute in Africa. An Africa Rights report identified cases of teachers gaining "sexual favors" in return for good grades in the Democratic Republic of Congo, Ghana, Nigeria, Somalia, South Africa, Sudan, Zambia, and Zimbabwe (Omaar and de Waal 1994).

Some 10–35 percent of women in Latin America and 13–45 percent in Sub-Saharan Africa have experienced physical violence by intimate partners at some time in their lives

Studies also estimate that a third of schoolgirls in Johannesburg have been subjected to sexual violence at school (Hayward 2000).[6]

In 48 surveys from around the world 10–69 percent of women report having been assaulted by an intimate male partner at some time in their lives (Heise, Ellsberg, and Gottemoeller 1999). In a geographically diverse group of countries in Latin America, North Africa, Sub-Saharan Africa, and South and East Asia, Demographic and Health Survey interviewers asked women whether they had ever been subject to intimate partner violence or violence from any member of their community. The reported rates of violence by intimate partners or strangers are high for all countries (table 9.1). In Zambia more than half of the women surveyed and in Colombia, Haiti, and Peru more than a third reported that they had been attacked.

Some 10–35 percent of women in Latin America and 13–45 percent in Sub-Saharan Africa have experienced physical violence by intimate partners at some time in their lives (Buvinic, Morrison, and Shifter as cited in Morrison and Biehl 1999; Heise, Ellsberg, and Gottemoeller 1999). Smaller scale studies find similar levels of violence against women, with 67 percent in rural Papua New Guinea, reporting having been physically abused by an intimate partner, 66 percent of women in rural Bangladesh, 59 percent in Japan, 52 percent in Nicaragua, 41 percent in Uganda, 40 percent in India, and 35 percent in Egypt (Schuler, Hashemi, and Badal 1998; Sancho-Liao 1993; UNICEF 2000; ICRW 2000).

Intimate partner rape is also common. In national surveys 10–15 percent of women report having been forced to have sex with their intimate partner (Heise, Pitanguy, and Germaine 1994). Local level data reinforce this finding. A study in Guadalajara, Mexico, found that 23 percent of women reported having been the victim of a rape by a partner in their lifetime. Similar figures have been reported for Georgia, United States (42 percent); Midlands, Zimbabwe (25 percent); Lima, Peru (23 percent); and North London, England (23 percent) (WHO 2002b; Kalichan and others 1998).

Global prevalence is also high for nonfamily or stranger sexual violence, with at least one in five women suffering rape or attempted rape (WHO

Table 9.1
Percentage of women ages 15–49 who have experienced any violence since age 15, latest available data

a. Sample includes only women who are or have been married.
b. Includes only women who have ever experienced violence since first marriage.

Source: Kishor and Johnson 2004 based on Demographic and Health Surveys.

Country	Women ever beaten by anyone	Women ever beaten by a spouse or partner
Cambodia[a]	23.4 (n = 2,403)	17.5 (n = 2,403)
Colombia	41.0 (n = 11,536)	44.1 (n = 7,602)
Dominican Republic	23.9 (n = 8,746)	22.3 (n = 6,807)
Egypt[a, b]	35.0 (n = 7,123)	34.4 (n = 7,123)
Haiti	35.2 (n = 3,389)	28.8 (n = 2,347)
India[a]	21.0 (n = 90,303)	18.9 (n = 90,303)
Nicaragua[a]	32.6 (n = 8,507)	30.2 (n = 8,507)
Peru	47.4 (n = 27,259)	42.4 (n = 17,369)
Zambia	58.7 (n = 5,029)	48.4 (n = 3,792)

The economic, social, and health-related costs of violence against women are thought to be substantial

1997b).[7] South Africa has the highest reported rape rate, with a woman raped every 90 seconds (Coomaraswamy 1994). In Papua New Guinea one study found that 55 percent of women had been raped (IRNVAW 1998). Crime victim surveys reveal that 8 percent of women in Rio de Janeiro, Brazil report having been sexually assaulted in the previous five years, 6 percent in Tirana, Albania, and 1.6 percent in Beijing, China, (WHO 2002b). Studies also show that many young women experience forced sexual initiation, with figures at 48 percent in Caribbean countries (WHO 2002b), 21 percent in the Central African Republic (Heise, Ellsberg, and Gottemoeller 1999), and 32 percent of pregnant adolescents in an antenatal clinic in Cape Town, South Africa (Jewkes and others 2001).

An International Rescue Committee study suggests that sexual violence has been a strategy of armed conflict in virtually all recent armed conflicts (Ward 2002). Documentary evidence of this phenomenon comes from Afghanistan, Algeria, Angola, Argentina, Bangladesh, El Salvador, Guatemala, Indonesia, Kuwait, South Africa, and Sudan.[8] While wartime rape may be an end in itself, it can also be used as a means of subverting community bonds, both as "war booty" and "asset stripping" as in Mozambique (Turshen 2001), or as a tool of ethnic cleansing as in Bosnia and Herzegovina (Cockburn 1998), Rwanda (WHO 2002b), and Sudan (Amnesty International 2004). In postconflict contexts women are also extremely vulnerable to rape in refugee camps. One study found that 26 percent of Burundi women in a Tanzanian camp had experienced sexual violence since becoming a refugee (Nduna and Goodyear 1997). In the Rwandan camps in 1994 it was reported that virtually every woman and girl past puberty had been sexually assaulted (Coomaraswamy 1998).

The costs of violence against women

The economic, social, and health-related costs of violence against women—for women, their families, and social and economic development—are thought by many researchers to be substantial. Most of the data on the costs of violence refer to the experiences of Western industrialized countries such as Australia, Canada, Finland, New Zealand, and the United Kingdom, where systems of information and services are well developed. A few recent studies, however, have estimated the costs of violence against women in countries in Latin America.

Estimates distinguish four types of costs: monetary, nonmonetary, economic multiplier effects, and social multiplier effects.[9] Monetary costs refer to the monetary value of goods and services used in preventing violence, treating victims, and apprehending and prosecuting perpetrators (Buvinic and Morrison 1997). For example, the annual monetary cost of violence against women in Canada has been estimated at Can$684 million in the criminal justice system and Can$187 million for police. Counseling and training in response to violence is estimated at Can$294 million, for a total of more than Can$1 billion a year (Korf and others 1997). Table 9.2 summarizes some of the estimates of other studies.

	Region	Total estimated cost (US$ million)	Year	Type of violence	Costs included in estimate
Table 9.2 **Estimated cost of violence against women, selected countries and regions** *Source:* New South Wales 1991 for Australia; Greaves, Hankivsky, and Kingston-Riechers 1995 for Canada; and Korf and others 1997 for the Netherlands, as cited in Buvinic and Morrison 2000.	New South Wales, Australia	1,000	1991	Domestic violence	Individual, government, employer and third party—health care, legal, criminal justice, social welfare, employment, child care, and housing
	Canada	2,750	1995	Physical violence, sexual assault, rape, incest, child sexual abuse	Individual, government, and third party—social services and education, criminal justice, labor and work, health and medical
	Netherlands	80	1997	Physical and sexual domestic violence against women	Police and justice, medical, psychosocial care, labor and social security

Nonmonetary costs include increased suffering, illness, and death; abuse of alcohol and drugs; and depression. A World Bank (1993) study estimated that annual rates of rape and domestic violence translated into 9 million years of disability-adjusted life years lost, including premature mortality as well as disability and illness. A study in Mexico City found violence to be the third most important cause of death among women (Lozano as cited in Morrison and Biehl 1999).

The broader economic effects of violence against women—the economic multiplier effects—include increased absenteeism; decreased labor market participation; reduced productivity; lower earnings, investment, and savings; and lower intergenerational productivity. In Chile domestic violence reduced women's earnings by $1.56 billion in 1996, or more than 2 percent of GDP; in Nicaragua earnings were reduced by $29.5 million, or 1.6 percent of GDP (Morrison and Orlando in Morrison and Biehl 1999). In both countries abused women earned far less than other women, controlling for a number of factors likely to affect earnings. Research conducted in India estimated that women lost an average of 7 working days after an incident of violence (ICRW 2000).

Violence against women also affects their children's schooling. A study in Nicaragua found that 63 percent of children of female victims of violence had to repeat a school year and left school an average of four years earlier than other children (Larraín, Vega, and Delgado 1997).

Social multiplier effects include the impact of violence on interpersonal relations and quality of life, such as the effect on children of witnessing violence, a reduced quality of life, and reduced participation in democratic processes. Children who witness abuse, or who are victims themselves, tend to imitate and perpetuate that behavior (Larraín, Vega, and Delgado 1997). Women who have been abused by intimate partners are socially isolated, often at the partner's insistence. This prevents a woman from participating in community and income-earning activities, but perhaps most important, it robs her of the social interaction that might help her end the abuse (Buvinic, Morrison, and Shifter as cited in Morrison and Biehl 1999).

Interventions for combating violence against women

The scale and complexity of gender-based violence means there are no uniform global solutions to this problem. Needed are multisectoral strategies that deal with the complex and intersecting dynamics that perpetuate violence against women. Great progress has been made in the last 10 years in addressing this issue. Documentary evidence reveals an extensive rage of interventions designed to prevent gender-based violence, to support survivors of abuse, and to punish perpetrators. The effectiveness of particular interventions is, however, less well documented.

Moser and Moser (2003) classify current solutions by their objectives, level, and main type of intervention (table 9.3). Interventions may be separate gender-based violence initiatives or components of other sectoral programs. As with any categorization, these are ideal types. In reality, policymakers and practitioners are shifting toward more integrated approaches and are mainstreaming gender-based violence interventions into cross-sectoral violence reduction strategies.

Human rights instruments

In the past decade several international treaties have defined violence against women as a human rights violation. In an interpretative statement in 1992 the monitoring body of the Convention on the Elimination of All Forms of Discrimination against Women clarified that gender-based violence constituted discrimination and thus was covered under the convention (UN 1979), obliging signatories to report on measures to reduce gender-based violence.

Table 9.3

Sector-level interventions to address gender-based violence

Source: Moser and Moser 2003.

Sector policy or program	Objective in addressing gender-based violence	Level of intervention	Type of intervention
Human rights	Legal enforcement by states and other social actors	International	Global human rights documents and policies
Criminal justice	Deterrence and control	National laws	Gender-based violence laws
		National and municipal programs	Legal reform Conciliatory mechanisms Training of police and judiciary Women's police stations
Health	Prevention and victim support	State and municipal programs	Training and procedures Crisis services for victims Programs for perpetrators
Education	Prevention and reduction	National, municipal, and nongovernmental organizations	School-based education programs Communication campaigns
Community-driven development	Victim support and empowerment	Community, through municipal and national programs	Shelters and hotlines Peer partnerships Community-based protection
Conflict prevention and reconstruction	Deterrence and reduction through reconstruction activities	International, national, and municipal	UN guidelines Services for refugees
Urban upgrading and infrastructure	Deterrence and reduction through environmental improvements	Municipal	Land use planning Transport Water and sanitation

Throughout the 1990s countries adopted new legislation on intimate partner violence and reformed laws relating to rape

In June 1993 the Vienna Declaration and Program of Action incorporated a special emphasis on gender-based violence. In December 1993 the UN General Assembly adopted the Declaration on the Elimination of Violence against Women, addressing abuse of women at home, in the community, and by the state. It recognized the state's duty to prevent, investigate, and punish acts of violence against women (UN 1993). These advances were reinforced by the Beijing Declaration and Platform for Action (UN 1995).

These treaties and policy instruments represent important achievements, and several countries have attempted to reform national laws and judicial systems to make them congruent with the international treaties. Many Latin American countries have taken steps to modify laws and policies in accordance with a regional convention, the Inter-American Convention on the Prevention, Punishment, and Eradication of Violence against Women (Belem do Para 1994), which provided a framework for national action.

National, sectoral, and local interventions

Throughout the 1990s countries around the world adopted new legislation on intimate partner violence and reformed laws relating to rape. By 2003, 45 nations (28 in Latin America and the Caribbean) had adopted legislation against domestic violence, 21 more were drafting new laws, and many countries had amended criminal assault laws to include domestic violence (UNIFEM 2003a). This legislation broadens the definition of rape to include acts by intimate partners, reforms sentencing rules for rapists, facilitates the granting of restraining orders, and removes requirements to corroborate a victim's account or prove her lack of consent, among others. Despite significant advances, considerable challenges remain for consistent and effective implementation and enforcement of the legislation.

Complementing national initiatives are an extensive range of interventions that target gender-based violence in specific areas.[10] Criminal justice, with its emphasis on deterrence and control, is an accepted institutional approach to combating gender-based violence. Legislation criminalizing and deterring such violence—complementing national legislation—forms the top tier of criminal justice interventions. Other innovations include alternative conciliatory mechanisms, judicial and police training, and all-women police stations.

The health system is often the first entry point for victims of abuse. Most women victims of partner or sexual violence visit health care service providers but often resist contact with the police or other services (Heise, Pitanguy, and Germaine 1994). A range of interventions can provide victim support and deter additional violence, from training protocols for health care providers, integrated victim service centers, and referral systems that link health care settings with legal and law enforcement services to programs for perpetrators.

Education provides another important entry point for combating or preventing gender-based violence. Interventions include school-based programs

Communities play an important role in defining solutions to violence and providing support to victims

and broader communications campaigns aimed at raising community awareness about the damaging effects of violence. Pamphlets, radio, television, theatre, and other public awareness media can educate and promote change by reaching large audiences. Posters can also be effective in linking those in need with service providers. After a poster campaign to combat domestic violence was launched in New York's subways and buses, calls to the advertised hotline increased by 14 percent (UNIFEM 2001).

Communities play an important role in defining solutions to violence and providing support to victims of abuse. Crisis shelters, telephone hotlines, community-based networks, and locally devised and implemented dispute resolution processes are examples of local-level interventions.

Infrastructure-related interventions

Because violence often occurs in unsafe public spaces, interventions to improve public infrastructure can reduce violence against women. To address the problem of violence on unsafe streets and public transport, the City of Montreal introduced the Between Two Stops bus service, allowing women to get off the bus at night between bus stops if that is closer to their destination. The Bangkok Mass Transit Authority implemented The Lady Bus service in 2000 in response to women's complaints of sexual harassment and violence while commuting. The Lady Bus accepts only women passengers, and male bus drivers and conductors are directed to protect the women passengers in case of emergency. On salary payment days (the most risky period for women using public transport), every third bus is a Lady Bus—a service that will be increased if the project proves successful (UN-HABITAT 2001a). In Mumbai, India, commuter trains include women-only cars.

Women's security while using public latrines is another important concern, not always well addressed. For instance, the sanitation component of an Oxfam urban development program in Addis Ababa, Ethiopia, designed latrines with inadequate doors and no electric light. Local women did not consider them safe and so did not use them (Tadele 1996). In India, by contrast, the National Slum Dwellers Federation and the women's organization Mahila Milan built a new community toilet managed by local women on a pay-and-use system. The facilities have improved safety and cleanliness (UN-HABITAT 2001a).

Urban upgrading has been identified as an important entry point for addressing violence, including sexual abuse. In Cape Town, South Africa, the recent Violence Prevention through Urban Upgrading project responds to extreme violence levels in the Khayelitsha township through an interlinked triangle of urban renewal strategies for better physical arrangements (to reduce opportunities for violence), criminal justice measures (to discourage potential violators), and public health and conflict resolution interventions (to support victims of violence; KfW and City of Cape Town 2002). The project feasibility study had demonstrated a strong relationship between levels of violence and

The task force calls for a new global campaign to end violence against women, spearheaded by the UN Secretary-General and endorsed by the General Assembly

crime and inadequate infrastructure provision. Narrow paths, open fields, distant communal latrines, unsafe transport hubs, poor lighting, empty shacks, and proximity to *shebeens* (bars or pubs) were found to exacerbate already high levels of rape.

Regional and global initiatives

Although the international community has rallied to address other epidemics (such as HIV and tuberculosis), it has not responded in the same way to the epidemic of violence against women. For instance, while UN General Assembly resolution 50/166 established a Trust Fund to End Violence against Women at the United Nations Development Fund for Women (UNIFEM), country needs and requests far outstrip the fund's current resources: the trust fund receives about $15 million in requests annually but has only $1 million to disburse. With its visibility and track record, the trust fund could serve as an important mechanism for a strong global response.

Other global initiatives have sought to change the norms that support violence against women. Two visible examples are The 16 Days of Activism to End Violence against Women, celebrated each year from November 25 through December 10 (International Human Rights Day), which engages tens of thousands of (mostly) women's NGOs in nearly every country, and the V-Day Campaign, which uses Valentine's Day (February 14) to raise awareness of intimate partner violence against women.[11]

At the regional level the Inter-American Development Bank's efforts to mainstream the objective of reducing violence against women in its lending operations for citizen security is a promising approach that should be replicated by other regional and international financial institutions (box 9.1). Because violence against women has high economic and social development costs, incorporating a focus on violence against women is well within the mandate of these institutions.

The task force seeks to complement the global, national, and regional efforts by calling for a new global campaign to end violence against women, spearheaded by the UN Secretary-General and endorsed by the General Assembly. The task force recommends that the campaign draw links between violence against women and women's vulnerability in the HIV/AIDS epidemic, highlighting yet another reason to bring about the changes in attitudes and practices required to end violence against women and building on the leadership that the United Nations and the Secretary-General have already provided in the fight against the global HIV/AIDS epidemic.

The global campaign to end violence against women would mobilize leadership at all levels—local, national, and international—to generate action to make violence against women unacceptable. Important components would be mass media campaigns, support for collecting and analyzing country-level data on violence against women, and an infusion of resources to the UNIFEM

Box 9.1

**Mainstreaming
attention to
domestic violence
in lending
operations: six
elements of
Inter-American
Development
Bank success**

Source: Prepared by Mayra
Buvinic, Inter-American
Development Bank 2004.

The Inter-American Development Bank (IDB) has mainstreamed the objective of reducing domestic violence against women in its lending operations for citizen security. Since 1998 the IDB has approved more than $123 million in lending for the control and prevention of violence in five countries (Chile, Colombia, Honduras, Jamaica, and Uruguay). These loans have raised substantial domestic counterpart funds in all five countries to fight violence.

Some loans integrate gender concerns in most project components, for instance, making sure that indicators for gender and domestic violence are collected in national information systems on crime and violence and that the police are trained to handle domestic violence cases (Colombia); that the court system trains judges and probation officers on intrafamily violence (Jamaica); or that the multisector models from crime prevention that are piloted on specific topics include abuse against women and children (Chile). The projects in Honduras and Uruguay include a specific component to prevent domestic violence and treat its victims. In most loans some funding goes to women's NGOs with expertise in research, advocacy, and treatment of domestic violence against women.

How did this happen, and how can it be replicated? Six elements have contributed to the IDB's success.

- *Relevance.* Latin America and the Caribbean is the second most violent region in the world (after Sub-Saharan Africa). Along with high rates of homicide, there are high rates of victimization of women and rising violence since the mid-1980s. As a result, reducing violence is a priority for citizens in the region, and there is growing awareness of violence against women, especially in the NGO sector.

- *Leadership.* Listening and responding to these citizen concerns, IDB President Enrique V. Iglesias, in a bold move for a development bank, launched work on violence reduction in 1996 and assigned resources to it. The IDB organized high-visibility seminars to catalyze interest in the region and undertook badly needed research. The region's response and interest were immediate.

- *Grant financing.* Modest but critical grant financing was made available to undertake the work (IDB and Nordic Trust Fund monies to the IDB).

- *Availability of expertise.* The IDB was able to tap into local expertise in the region on domestic violence, facilitating research and project interventions.

- *Research.* Research showed the intrinsic as well as the instrumental value of mainstreaming attention to domestic violence in lending for violence reduction operations. It made the case that violence is mostly a learned behavior and that one of the earliest opportunities for learning violence is in the home. Thus, domestic violence is deserving of attention in its own right and as a key to preventing the transmission of violence. The research also provided a sound economic rationale for investing in domestic violence reduction operations (Morrison and Orlando as cited in Morrison and Biehl 1999).

- *Openness to innovation.* A new generation of IDB operations, citizen security lending, was launched in parallel with the mainstreaming efforts to emphasize violence prevention in all IDB loans. These new designs provided a unique opportunity for mainstreaming a gender perspective from the start, increasing the likelihood that this perspective would be incorporated in future designs. This last element is perhaps the most difficult to replicate because the very nature of the mainstreaming task calls for integrating new thinking into established practice.

trust fund. The trust fund could award numerous grants for evaluating and expanding local interventions, increasing the visibility of interventions that reduce the levels of violence against women, and disseminating best practices. The campaign would also call on communities and leaders to address this gross violation of women's rights. Plans for such a campaign are already under way through the Global Coalition for Women and AIDS, established by the Joint United Nations Programme on HIV/AIDS (UNAIDS) and its sponsoring agencies.

Chapter 10

Data and indicators for monitoring progress

The previous chapters have discussed the seven strategic priorities that need to be addressed to accelerate progress toward Millennium Development Goal 3. This chapter suggests indicators to use in monitoring progress on these strategic priorities at country and international levels. These indicators are intended to supplement, or in some cases to substitute for, the indicators chosen by the UN expert group to assess progress during 1990–2015, the period when the Millennium Development Targets are expected to be met.[1]

The task force has not recommended adoption of new international or country-level targets for the seven strategic priorities. However, countries may wish to set their own quantifiable, time-bound targets for establishing national or subnational progress on each of the seven strategic priorities. Examples of such targets to be achieved by 2015 are universal access to sexual and reproductive health services through the primary healthcare system, ensuring the same rate of progress or faster among the poor and other marginalized groups (strategic priority 2) and a 30 percent share of seats for women in national parliaments (strategic priority 6).

For the indicators discussed below to become operational, national governments and the international system need to improve the quality and frequency with which sex-disaggregated data are collected. Considerable improvements have been made in gender statistics over the last decade. Data users know much more today about differences in women's and men's situations. Furthermore, users of data are asking more questions and demanding high-quality statistics. Yet, cross-country data are still lacking on many topics that are important for assessing inequalities between women and men within and across countries. The conclusion to this chapter suggests key areas for improving current data gathering efforts.

The task force suggests 12 indicators for monitoring progress toward Goal 3

Indicators for the seven strategic priorities

The Millennium Development Goals include four indicators for tracking progress toward Goal 3:

- Ratio of girls to boys enrolled in primary, secondary, and tertiary education.
- Ratio of literate females to males among 15- to 24-year-olds.
- Share of women in wage employment in the nonagricultural sector.
- Proportion of seats held by women in national parliaments.

These indicators are inadequate for tracking all seven strategic priorities for Goal 3. They also suffer from several technical shortcomings.[2] The ratio of girls to boys in school does not provide information on what proportion of boys or girls of school age are enrolled, or any insights into student learning outcomes. Literacy is not a simple concept with a single universally accepted meaning, and different countries measure it differently. Additionally, the quality of the literacy data is suspect. The female share of paid, nonagricultural employment measures only the share of women relative to that of men in this category of work but not the differential barriers to entry into paid employment or the terms of work itself, such as workplace conditions, benefits or job security, and earnings. It also ignores the agricultural sector, which employs a high proportion of poor women. Finally, the proportion of seats held by women in national parliaments does not measure women's decisionmaking power within these bodies, and it ignores women's participation at the local and regional level altogether.

To address these limitations, the task force suggests 12 indicators for countries and international organizations to use in monitoring progress toward Goal 3 (box 10.1). In choosing these indicators, the task force considered several criteria—simplicity, reliability, comparability, sustainability, timeliness, policy relevance, and affordability (Braveman 1998).

None of the proposed indicators measures the quality of equality, the process that brings it about, or the nature of the outcomes. Achieving numerical balance (parity) is clearly important in a world where even this goal has yet to be attained. However necessary, by itself parity is not a sufficient condition for achieving the greater goal of gender equality. Unless indicators are also developed for measuring the quality of change, too much weight may be placed on mere parity of outcomes as opposed to the quality of these outcomes and how they are achieved.[3]

Strategic priority 1: strengthen opportunities for postprimary education for girls

Because of limitations with the two indicators for measuring progress toward gender equality in education, the task force recommends two changes. First, the enrollment indicator should be changed from the ratio of girls to boys in primary, secondary, or tertiary education to the ratio of either gross or net

Box 10.1

Proposed indicators for tracking progress toward strategic priorities for Goal 3

Education
- The ratio of female to male gross enrollment rates in primary, secondary, and tertiary education.
- The ratio of female to male completion rates in primary, secondary, and tertiary education.

Sexual and reproductive health and rights
- Proportion of contraceptive demand satisfied.
- Adolescent fertility rate.

Infrastructure
- Hours per day (or year) women and men spend fetching water and collecting fuel.

Property rights
- Land ownership by male, female, or jointly held.
- Housing title, disaggregated by male, female, or jointly held.

Employment
- Share of women in employment, both wage and self-employment, by type.
- Gender gaps in earnings in wage and self-employment.

Participation in national parliaments and local government bodies
- Percentage of seats held by women in national parliament.
- Percentage of seats held by women in local government bodies.

Violence against women
- Prevalence of domestic violence.

female enrollment rates to gross or net male enrollment rates in primary, secondary, and tertiary education.[4] Sex-specific enrollment rates give the number of girls and boys enrolled in a given level of education relative to the population of the age group that should be enrolled at that level. This ratio of the sex-specific enrollment rates permits tracking whether shrinking gender gaps are being achieved through increases in girls' enrollment rates or through decreases in boys' enrollment rates.

The second recommended change is to replace the literacy ratio with the ratio of girls' to boys' completion rates at the primary, secondary, and tertiary levels. The completion rate captures the total number of students successfully completing, or graduating from, the last year of a given education cycle in a given year, expressed as a proportion of the total number of children of graduation age in the population (UNESCO 2004). The United Nations Educational, Scientific and Cultural Organization (UNESCO) and the World Bank's Human Development Network have data on sex-disaggregated completion rates in primary school.[5] However, secondary completion rates are not being tracked or reported regularly by countries, so there are no comprehensive cross-country data for this indicator. The data that are available for secondary completion rates come primarily from developed countries and a few middle-income developing countries.[6] The task force recommends the collection of data on secondary school completion in developing countries, using UNESCO's International Standard Classification of Education 1997 (ISCED–97) for education cycles.

The task force recommends two additional sexual and reproductive health and rights indicators

The task force does not recommend the use of literacy data until the quality of the data can be improved. The UNESCO Institute for Statistics (UIS) has already developed an alternative literacy assessment method, the Literacy Assessment and Monitoring Programme (LAMP), which uses assessments of individuals' skills to measure literacy across a range of levels. LAMP is now being piloted in several countries. The task force recommends that additional resources be made available to UIS to consolidate improvements in the LAMP survey and implement it in 50 more countries by 2010 and in all developing countries by 2015.

Strategic priority 2: guarantee sexual and reproductive health and rights

Several indicators for Goals 5 and 6 measure aspects of women's reproductive health: the maternal mortality ratio, the proportion of births attended by skilled health personnel, HIV prevalence among 15- to 24-year-old pregnant women, and the contraceptive prevalence rate. These are useful indicators, but they do not assess women's and adolescents' ability to act on their reproductive preferences. The task force therefore recommends two additional sexual and reproductive health and rights indicators. One, the proportion of contraceptive demand satisfied, captures the central connection between women's control over their reproductive preferences and their decisionmaking ability.

The proportion of contraceptive demand satisfied is the contraceptive prevalence rate as a proportion of the sum of the contraceptive prevalence rate and the unmet need for family planning (Bernstein 2004).[7] It thus measures the proportion of all women of reproductive age whose demand for contraception is actually satisfied (which the more common unmet need measures does not). The United Nations Population Division (UNPD) and ORC-Macro's Demographic and Health Surveys include the data needed to compute this indicator for 75 developing countries and for two time periods, 1990–95 and 1996–2002. The usefulness of this indicator has been established by Bernstein (2004). However, further work is needed to synchronize UNPD and ORC-Macro surveys to produce data for a larger sample of countries and to popularize the use of this indicator. The task force recommends supporting such an effort.

The second indicator, the adolescent fertility rate, gives insight into the reproductive behavior of an important target population for meeting the sexual and reproductive health and rights strategic priority. Childbearing among girls ages 15–19 is of special concern because births to teenagers are more likely to be unintended and premature and are associated with greater risks of complications during delivery and higher levels of maternal and child mortality. This indicator refers to births per 1,000 women ages 15–19.[8] Most countries now report fertility statistics by age. In 2000 the UN Database had adolescent fertility statistics for 107 countries.[9] This enables regular monitoring of this indicator for a large number of countries.

The task force recommends expanding the collection of time-use data

Strategic priority 3: invest in infrastructure to reduce women's and girls' time burdens

Chapter 5 recommends investments in infrastructure to reduce women's and girls' time burdens. The indicator proposed by the task force to measure women's and girls' time burdens as a result of the lack of infrastructure is hours per day (or year) women (girls) and men (boys) spend fetching water and collecting fuel. Unlike the other indicators recommended in this chapter, this indicator is intended only for country-level monitoring, not as a global indicator because of the geographic specificity of infrastructure deficits.

There is not enough systematic collection of time-use data within countries to permit the development of an indicator to track progress across countries. To do tracking, new questions on time use would have to be incorporated into regularly repeated household surveys or small area surveys. Several countries and institutions such as the World Bank sponsor national or subnational surveys that include time-use modules to capture the division of labor within households. For instance, the World Bank's Living Standards Measurement Study surveys include time-use and infrastructure questions in selected country surveys. The task force recommends expanding the collection of time-use data, with periodic updates, in a representative sample of developing countries where infrastructure deficits are large.

Strategic priority 4: guarantee women's and girls' property and inheritance rights

As noted in chapter 6, sex-disaggregated data on the distribution of land and housing ownership are patchy. Very few agricultural censuses ask for the legal landowner in the household or keep records on ownership of land by sex. In Africa and Asia most of the information on the distribution of land ownership by sex comes from scattered household surveys. Some of the Living Standards Measurement Study surveys have included questions on land ownership, but the frequency is low and the questions have been included in surveys for only a few countries in Sub-Saharan Africa. National agricultural surveys in some Latin American countries also collect information that can be used to calculate the distribution of landowners by sex (Deere and Leon 2003). The task force recommends that a lead agency from among the UN statistical agencies be designated to develop and lead a global effort to standardize data collection and indicator development on this issue.

Data on housing titles are also scarce. UN-HABITAT has a Global Campaign for Secure Tenure, which emphasizes the importance of women's rights to tenure security. It recommends collecting data on the percentage of female- and male-headed households in different tenure categories (owned, rental, communal property, government-owned). Within countries a coordinated effort is needed to gather such data from government and private agencies that register sales and

The task force recommends two additional indicators reflecting women's status in employment

transfers of land and housing. The task force recommends that UN-HABITAT be given the resources and authority to lead such an effort.

Strategic priority 5: eliminate gender inequality in employment

In place of the female share of paid nonagricultural employment, the task force recommends two additional indicators reflecting women's status in employment: the share of women in wage employment and self-employment by type (which subsumes the current indicator), and gender gaps in earnings in wage employment and self-employment.

The share of women in wage employment and self-employment by type combines several indicators into a composite indicator. It shows women employed in different types of employment (agricultural employment, nonagricultural formal and informal wage employment, and nonagricultural formal and informal self-employment) as a percentage of total female employment (appendix 5).

Some of the data required for this indicator are available in International Labour Organization (ILO) databases, and the remainder can be obtained as part of regular ILO data collection exercises. In addition, some special data collection will be necessary to consolidate data that are currently available at the national level but not at the international level. These data collection and consolidation activities will require additional resources. For instance, the ILO has laid the groundwork for a comprehensive program to develop sex-disaggregated data on informal employment. It has assisted a number of countries, including India, Mexico, and South Africa, in collecting these data and has developed guidelines for defining informal employment, compiling available data, and developing methodological materials. The International Conference of Labour Statisticians has endorsed these guidelines (Chen, Sebstad, and O'Connell 1999). International donors should now support the ILO Bureau of Statistics in working with a critical mass of countries to implement these guidelines.

The development of data for the second indicator on sex differentials in earnings from employment is at an earlier stage.[10] Work is required to develop and test questions in countries and prepare methodological guidelines before any large-scale data collection effort can be undertaken. The task force recommends that donors support the ILO in working with countries to collect and standardize statistics on sex differences in earnings from employment.

Strategic priority 6: increase women's representation in political bodies

The United Nations recommends tracking women's share of seats in national parliaments. Data for this indicator are collected for 182 countries by the Inter-Parliamentary Union. Recently, United Cities and Local Governments, an organization supported by the Ministry of Foreign Affairs of the Netherlands, has begun to collect data on the proportions of female local elected representatives, councilors, and mayors in 54 countries. They plan to construct a global data-

Improving
countries'
capacity to
enhance the
coverage,
quality, and
frequency
of collection
of sex-
disaggregated
data remains
a priority

base on women in local government. As this data collection effort is scaled up, the task force recommends that countries and the international system use the information to complement the data on women's parliamentary representation.

Strategic priority 7: combat violence against women

The task force recommends that the prevalence of domestic violence be used to track progress toward ending violence against women. The prevalence rate is expressed as a percentage of women ages 15–49 who report experiencing physical violence in the past year at the hands of an intimate partner.

Several international agencies have undertaken substantial work to collect data for this indicator. The Demographic and Health Survey now includes a module on intimate partner violence that has been used in 12 nationally representative household surveys. The WHO has worked with partners in eight countries to collect data on the dimensions, health consequences, and the risk and protective factors of violence against women.[11] It is currently collaborating with the Economic Commission of Latin America and the Caribbean, the European Women's Lobby, and the U.S. Centers for Disease Control to strengthen data collection on this issue. The task force recommends providing additional resources to the WHO to consolidate the methodological lessons from these efforts.

Recommendations for data gathering and strengthening statistical systems

Data are a critical tool for accountability. A lack of sex-disaggregated data impedes efforts to address the seven strategic priorities and to monitor progress in implementing them. Work to prepare new indicators on gender equality and women's empowerment is well under way. Such efforts are supported by key recommendations of international conferences on women, as well as by other international mandates of the past two decades. Improving countries' capacity to enhance the coverage, quality, and frequency of collection of sex-disaggregated data remains a priority, however.

The development of new statistical series requires a lengthy process of discussion between producers and users of statistics, pilot work and testing, and review of this experience. Country statistical agencies need an infusion of resources to strengthen their capacity and efforts to do all that is necessary to collect and prepare sex-disaggregated data. Work at the country level also requires technical support from key international statistical agencies to develop methodological guidelines and undertake new data collection efforts. Substantial funding is required to coordinate these activities within the appropriate international and regional organizations.

The world conferences on women—all of which recognized the importance of improving statistics on women—provided new momentum for gathering statistics on women, resulting in the highly regarded outputs, the Women's Indicators and Statistics Database (WISTAT) series, and *Trends in the World's*

Women, based on WISTAT. The task force recommends the continuation of WISTAT and *Trends in the World's Women*, which should continue to be published quinquennially.

From the early 1980s the UN Statistics Division included the post of focal point on statistics on women. Having a focal point in the UN statistical system to bring together the various gender indicators at the international level continues to be important, especially given the need to coordinate the development of statistics on gender that relate to each of the Millennium Development Goals, as well as to assist countries with the production of national reports.

Chapter 11

The financial costs of interventions to achieve gender equality

Because gender inequality is multidimensional and multisectoral, the financial costs of efforts to reduce it are difficult to calculate. Apart from a recent effort piloted by the UN Millennium Project, there have been few comprehensive attempts nationally or globally to estimate these costs. In the late 1990s many governments developed plans to implement the recommendations of the Beijing Program for Action, but few were backed by adequate resources. Yet knowing the resource requirements for implementing gender plans of action is critical. Recognizing this as a serious problem, women's organizations around the world called for tools and methodologies that can be used in discussions with governments and other agencies to identify the financing requirements for interventions to reduce gender bias and empower women.

This chapter reviews the evidence from previous attempts to estimate the cost of attaining gender equality in education and of interventions to achieve good reproductive health. It then describes the methodology developed by the UN Millennium Project to estimate the costs of gender-related interventions to achieve the strategic priorities described in this report and gender-related interventions within each of the other Millennium Development Goals.

Financing interventions to achieve gender equality in education and to provide reproductive health services

Several studies have estimated the financing requirements to achieve gender equality in education and health. The World Bank (2001a), for instance, estimates that achieving gender equality in primary education through universal enrollment would require an increase of slightly more than 3 percent a year in public spending on primary education in South Asia and the Middle East and North Africa, but as much as 30 percent a year in Sub-Saharan Africa.[1] The costs to achieve universal primary enrollment for girls only would be 2 percent

Implementing the strategic priorities requires significant financial, infrastructure, and human resources

in South Asia and the Middle East and North Africa and 20 percent in Sub-Saharan Africa. The World Bank report notes that ensuring equity in secondary education would add to these costs, but the total would still be affordable for the majority of countries that are currently off-track for achieving that target.

From a review of estimates of the financing necessary to achieve universal access to sexual and reproductive health services, the Alan Guttmacher Institute (AGI) and United Nations Population Fund (UNFPA) developed a new methodology for estimating the costs of providing family planning services. They estimated these costs at $11 billion a year (in 2003 dollars)—$7.1 billion to provide modern contraceptive services to current users and $3.9 billion to address unmet need. These estimates are higher than some others because they include labor, overhead and capital, as well as contraceptive supplies (AGI/UNFPA 2004).

The UN Millennium Project needs assessment

Implementing the strategic priorities outlined in this report will require substantial investments at national and subnational levels. Many countries have found that, although gender-responsive legislation and policies are an important first step, implementing these policies requires significant financial, infrastructure, and human resources. National planning exercises rarely estimate these resource needs.

Such estimates are important for several reasons:

- Translating the Millennium Development Goal on gender equality and women's empowerment into operational targets for planning and programming. Millennium Development Goal needs assessments provide a framework for deriving operational targets and linking them to intermediate objectives. By including a detailed needs assessment, governments commit themselves to specific targets and outcomes, which are relatively easy to track.
- Strengthening coherence between planning and budget processes. Estimates of the resources needed to meet the gender Goal can be included in any national poverty reduction strategy, ensuring the allocation of sufficient resources for gender-related priorities. Today, most poverty reduction strategies discuss at least a few gender issues, but budget funds are rarely allocated for implementation. Tracking performance and holding governments accountable for implementing gender strategies and plans are therefore difficult. Government strategies need to fully incorporate gender targets and goals, and adequate budget funds need to be allocated to meet them.
- Supporting the national policy dialogue and negotiations with development partners. By quantifying the needs, governments can estimate the type and scale of investments required to meet the Goal. Such resource

**A gender needs
assessment can
enable countries
to identify
constraints
and plan
systematically
to remove them**

estimates are a powerful advocacy tool for women's groups and other civil society organizations in national-level dialogue on specific actions needed to achieve gender equality. Gender-sensitive policies and laws often fail to be implemented because of lack of information and dialogue on the resources needed to implement them. A comprehensive and transparent assessment of the necessary resources will make national dialogue possible.

- Improving understanding of absorptive capacity and of how low-income countries can increase this capacity. Limited human resources, managerial skills, monitoring and evaluation systems, and infrastructure may constrain a country's ability to implement gender plans. These constraints can be substantially relaxed through investments in human resources, management systems, administrative capacity, and infrastructure. A gender needs assessment can enable countries to identify such constraints and plan systematically to remove them.

Detailed investment models derived from a Millennium Development Goals needs assessment provide clear targets that can form the basis for a monitoring and accountability framework for tracking country progress toward the gender Goal.

Needs assessment methodology and caveats

The UN Millennium Project has developed a detailed methodology for quantifying the human, financial, and infrastructure resources needed to meet the Millennium Development Goals (box 11.1). In collaboration with the UN Millennium Project Secretariat, Task Force 3 on Education and Gender Equality adapted this general needs assessment methodology for estimating the financing requirements for the gender-related interventions recommended in this report.

There are several important caveats about this methodology. First, the needs assessment includes only some of the actions necessary to meet the Goal of gender equality and empowerment of women. Adequate resources alone will not achieve gender equality. Most strategies require a mix of investments and changes in legislation, political and administrative rules, social attitudes, and norms. The needs assessment, therefore, should be seen as a minimal but necessary set of actions to meet the Goal of gender equality.

Second, a gender needs assessment is possible only at the country level and meaningful only as part of a national poverty reduction strategy in which all stakeholders participate. The interventions to be costed need to be locally identified, based on nationally determined targets.

Third, gender needs assessments should be carried out in conjunction with similar exercises for related areas such as education, health, transport and energy infrastructure, water and sanitation, agriculture, nutrition, urban development, and environment. Such simultaneous estimation of needs is

Box 11.1

The five steps of the UN Millennium Project needs assessment methodology

Source: Sachs and others 2004.

The needs assessment methodology developed by the UN Millennium Project for quantifying the resources needed to achieve the Millennium Development Goals consists of five basic steps:

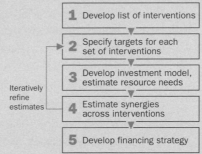

1. *Develop a list of interventions.* A set of basic interventions based on best available evidence or identified through country consultations is developed for each area of analysis.

2. *Specify targets for each set of interventions.* Concrete targets are identified for each set of interventions. These can be based on the Millennium Development Goals and on other internationally or nationally agreed-on targets. Where there is no consensus on targets, targets and key parameters should be obtained through consultative processes within the country or derived analytically.

3. *Develop an investment model and estimate resource requirements.* Using the country-specific intervention lists and targets, countries project the gradual scaling up of investments and resources required to meet the Millennium Development Goals by 2015.

4. *Estimate synergies across interventions.* Potential cost savings resulting from synergies across interventions are calculated.

5. *Develop a financing strategy.* A national financing strategy is developed, with the source of funds identified (household out of pocket expenditures, domestic government resources, and external finance).

important to ensure that the total resource estimates capture all gender-related interventions and strategies.

Finally, any assessment of needs has to be an iterative process that is refined on the basis of experience. To be credible, the analysis needs the inputs of all key stakeholders, including government officials at national, regional, and local levels, members of women's and other civil society organizations, and donors.

The UN Millennium Project approach to assessing the needs for gender-related interventions considers gender-related interventions to meet the Millennium Development Goals other than Goal 3 and specific interventions to meet Goal 3. Each track is discussed below.

Gender interventions for Millennium Development Goals other than Goal 3
Gender-specific interventions in agriculture, education, health, nutrition, rural development, urban development, water and sanitation, environment, trade, and science and technology are needed to reduce gender inequality and

empower women. For example, in agriculture a special effort is needed to recruit and train women extension workers to ensure that national extension services reach female farmers as well as they do male farmers. In education, enrolling and retaining girls in school may require subsidies and special facilities such as separate toilets for girls. In urban development, land or housing titling projects to improve the lives of male and female slum dwellers would need to ensure that women have equal access to secure tenure. In rural development poverty reduction interventions should include the provision of clean cooking fuels, electricity, and water and sanitation supply within the household or nearby to reduce the time women and girls spend on firewood and water collection.

The needs assessment for specific sectors include actions to address three of the seven strategic priorities for achieving gender equality and empowering women. Postprimary education for girls is costed within the education needs assessment methodology, the provision of sexual and reproductive health services is costed within the health sector needs assessment methodology, and infrastructure to reduce women's time burdens is costed within the infrastructure needs assessment methodology.

Additional specific interventions to meet Goal 3

The second track involves estimating the resources for additional specific interventions to meet Goal 3 because additional actions are needed that are not restricted to any particular sector. Examples of specific interventions for Goal 3 that are not costed in any other Millennium Development Goals needs assessment methodology include:

Strategic priority 2: guarantee sexual and reproductive health and rights [2]
- Providing education for increased awareness of sexual and reproductive health and rights through mass media and community-based programs.
- Providing comprehensive sexuality education in schools and community programs.

Strategic priority 5: reduce gender inequality in employment
- Promoting access to work through vocational training programs and school-to-work transition programs for adolescent girls.
- Providing care services (for children, the elderly, the disabled, and the sick) to allow women to work.

Strategic priority 6: increase women's political representation
- Providing training to women candidates in elections at the local, regional, and national level.
- Providing training to female elected representatives at the local, regional, and national level.

Strategic priority 7: combat violence against women
- Preventing violence against women through education, media campaigns, hotlines, and neighborhood support groups.

- Protecting women from violence through police training and provide medical services, counseling, and emergency housing or short-term shelters to victims of violence.
- Providing legal redress to ensure that perpetrators of violence against women are punished.

Systemic issues

- Strengthening the capacity of governments to deliver the interventions identified above.
- Strengthening national women's machineries through increased budgetary allocations and staffing of ministries of women's affairs and gender focal points in other ministries.
- Instituting sensitization programs to train judges, bureaucrats, land registration officers, and police officers.
- Investing in legal aid services to help women claim their rights and access the interventions identified above.
- Improving registration systems for issuing identification documents to women in settings where that is applicable.
- Investing in data collection and monitoring activities to track gender outcomes.

This list is not exhaustive, and the details will vary by country depending on the specific context and needs. It can be used by women's groups and governments as a starting point to identify actions to achieve the strategic priorities not costed in the other Millennium Development Goals needs assessments.

An illustrative national needs assessment

What resources are needed to implement a comprehensive gender strategy in a low-income country? Tajikistan's UN Millennium Development Goals Needs Assessment Team, in collaboration with the government's Working Group on Gender and with support from the UN Millennium Project, is conducting a gender needs assessment for Tajikistan.[3] The preliminary results will be reviewed and revised through several rounds of consultation with local stakeholders before being finalized and adopted by the government in its long-term Millennium Development Goals plan and short-term Poverty Reduction Strategy Paper (PRSP).

The gender needs assessment was undertaken in conjunction with needs assessments for universal primary and expanded secondary education, universal primary health care coverage and treatment of major diseases, and water and sanitation services.[4] The strategic priorities for promoting postprimary education for girls, guaranteeing sexual and reproductive health and rights, and investing in infrastructure to reduce time burdens of women and girls are partially embedded in each of these needs assessments. Preliminary estimates suggest that the costs for 2005–15 of universal primary and expanded secondary education in Tajikistan would be roughly $20 per capita annually. The costs of setting up a primary health care system (for child health and maternal health, major infectious diseases, and sexual and reproductive health) would average roughly $29 per capita annually.[5] The costs of water and sanitation provision would average roughly $9.50 per capita annually.

For the additional specific interventions to meet Goal 3, the analysis covers most of the interventions discussed above.[6] Coverage targets were set by the UN Millennium Development Goals Needs Assessment Team, in consultation with the government, based on available data and experience in the country.[7] Preliminary results suggest that the cost of gender-specific interventions (training and awareness campaigns, interventions to combat violence against women, and systematic interventions to improve the women's ministry capacities) will average $1.30 per capita annually for 2005–15 (table 11.1), with costs peaking at $2.00 per capita in 2015.[8] Most of these costs will be for programs to combat violence against women; these represent 76 percent of the costs of the gender-specific interventions in table 11.2.

Table 11.1

Estimated summary costs for promoting gender equality in Tajikistan, 2005–15

Source: UN Millennium Project 2004c.

Item	2005	2010	2015	2005–15
Total cost (US$ millions)	5.2	10.0	16.5	112.1
Capital costs	3.4	3.4	4.6	38.3
Recurrent costs	1.3	4.8	8.6	53.6
Share of GDP (percent)				*Average*
Total cost	.003	.001	.004	.003
Capital costs	.002	.001	.001	.001
Recurrent costs	.001	.002	.002	.002
Per capita (US$)				*Average*
Total cost	0.80	1.30	2.00	1.30
Capital costs	0.50	0.40	0.50	0.50
Recurrent costs	0.20	0.60	1.00	0.60

Table 11.2

Estimated costs for promoting gender equality in Tajikistan by main activities, 2005–15

US$ millions

Source: UN Millennium Project 2004c.

Item	2005	2010	2015	2005–15
Total cost	5.20	10.00	16.50	112.10
Increasing awareness of sexual and reproductive health issues	0.39	1.44	2.70	16.28
Helping the transition of girls to work	0.15	0.39	0.42	3.81
Encouraging political participation	0.05	0.07	0.12	0.48
Ending violence against women	4.17	7.44	12.25	84.31
Resolving systemic issues	0.18	0.16	0.25	1.87
General administrative costs	0.25	0.47	0.79	5.34

The in-country consultative process is critical for identifying appropriate interventions

In absolute numbers the cost of selected additional interventions to meet Goal 3 in Tajikistan is $10.56 million each year, for a total of $112 million for 2005–15. This amounts to approximately 0.003 percent of GDP over this period. To put this amount into context, debt-servicing payments alone in Tajikistan accounted for about 4 percent of GDP in 2001. It is important, though, to note again that this number is not the total cost of achieving gender equality and women's empowerment but only the cost of additional specific interventions to meet Goal 3. For a complete estimate of the costs to meet Goal 3, these specific costs must be combined with the costs of appropriate interventions to reach women and girls in each of the other Millennium Development Goals.

The Tajikistan gender needs assessment exercise shows how such an analysis can take place at the country level, in consultation with local stakeholders, to understand the resource requirements for addressing the challenge of gender equality. It demonstrates the resources that are needed to achieve gender equality. But more important, the in-country consultative process is critical for identifying appropriate interventions and validating the assumptions of the model. In the end, it is only through such a process that resources can be appropriately mobilized for gender equality interventions.

Conclusion

This chapter has shown that it is possible to estimate the resources needed for investments in gender equality. The estimates need to cover strong investments in building the capacity of women's ministries, data collection and monitoring, and training and sensitization programs. Estimates represent an illustrative set of actions that complement gender interventions in education, health, infrastructure, and other sectors. Such resource estimates, which must be done at the country level, can form the foundation for gender-responsive poverty reduction processes as well as financing mechanisms such as the medium-term expenditure framework and annual national budgets.

Chapter 12

Making it happen

Although no country has successfully addressed all seven strategic priorities, some countries have shown that significant progress can be made to empower women and reduce gender disadvantage. This chapter reflects on what it takes to achieve significant progress. It identifies the ingredients necessary for large-scale transformation, assesses the experience of five countries that are attempting significant institutional reform, and closes with recommendations for addressing gender inequality in MDG-based country poverty reduction processes.

This report has described seven strategic priorities and a series of practical actions for each to bring about gender equality and empower women. Various countries, communities, and institutions have implemented different combinations of these actions and shown good results. The problem is not a lack of practical ways to address gender inequality but rather a lack of change on a large and deep enough scale to bring about a transformation in the way societies conceive of and organize men's and women's roles, responsibilities, and control over resources. Essential for that kind of transformation are:

- Political commitment by and mobilization of a large group of change agents at different levels within countries and in international institutions.
- Technical capacity to implement change.
- Institutional structures and processes to support the transformation, including structures that enable women to successfully claim their rights.
- Adequate financial resources.
- Accountability and monitoring systems.

Commitment and mobilization of change agents

For transformation to occur within countries, there must be a critical mass of change agents committed to the vision of a gender-equitable society described

Gender mainstreaming is both a technical and political process requiring shifts in organizational culture

in chapter 1. These change agents include leaders at all levels of government who control critical levers for change—financial and technical resources—and set the priorities for actions affecting the lives of many. To be true to the vision, government leaders must work with civil society institutions, especially organizations that represent women's interests. Where progress has been made, as in South Africa, it has been with the strong and consistent support of government leaders who used the levers available to them to bring about necessary changes, along with the efforts of a vibrant and independent women's movement.

At the international level there must also be a critical mass of change agents in the institutions that provide support to national governments and civil society organizations for implementing the changes necessary for a gender-equitable society.

Technical capacity to implement change

Achieving gender equality and empowering women requires technical expertise and knowledge of how to mainstream gender concerns into development policies and programs. At the 1995 Fourth World Conference on Women the international community endorsed gender mainstreaming as a key institutional response for promoting gender equality and empowering women. Gender mainstreaming was defined by the UN Economic and Social Council in 1997 as:

> the process of assessing the implications for women and men of any planned action, including legislation, policies or programs, in all areas and at all levels. It is a strategy for making women's as well as men's concerns and experiences an integral dimension of the design, implementation, monitoring and evaluation of policies and programs in all political, economic and societal spheres so that women and men benefit equally and inequality is not perpetuated. The ultimate goal is to achieve gender equality (ECOSOC 1997).

This definition makes clear that gender mainstreaming is not an end in itself but a means to the goal of gender equality. It is both a technical and political process requiring shifts in organizational culture and ways of thinking and in the structures and resource allocations of organizations (Oxaal and Baden 1997). As a technical tool mainstreaming can be effective only if supported by a strong political and legal mandate. At the country level legal instruments such as the Convention on the Elimination of All Forms of Discrimination against Women (CEDAW) and others provide such a mandate. All UN agencies have a mandate from the General Assembly, the Security Council, the Economic and Social Council, and the Commission on the Status of Women to promote gender equality in their own policies and programs and to support governments in doing the same.

Gender mainstreaming is often compromised by a lack of conceptual clarity about the meaning of gender. As noted in chapter 2, gender is a social construct

Gender analysis involves gathering and examining information on what women and men do and how they relate to each other

that defines and differentiates the roles, rights, responsibilities, and obligations of women and men in a context of unequal power relationships. Yet, the term *gender* is often still equated with *women* and gender mainstreaming is seen solely as increasing the focus on women. Because of this confusion, managers often misinterpret gender mainstreaming to mean creating a balanced male-female representation in an institution's staff or in program beneficiaries.

Gender is also often equated with sex and thus seen as a biological rather than a social attribute. For instance, biological differences make the transmission of HIV much more likely from an infected man to a woman than from an infected woman to a man. Only recently, however, has it been understood that gender norms and differences, and the power imbalance they create between women and men, contribute to both women's and men's vulnerability to infection (box 12.1).

Another conceptual confusion is the assumption that certain policy areas, such as infrastructure development or macroeconomic policy, are gender neutral. This makes efforts to incorporate gender perspectives into these areas very difficult. As chapter 5 shows, infrastructure investments are not gender neutral. And a growing body of evidence shows that gender inequality affects macroeconomic outcomes, including growth, and that macroeconomic policy has gender-differentiated impacts (Çağatay and Ozler 1995; Grown, Elson, and Çağatay 2000).

The different types of conceptual confusion described above can be clarified through gender analysis and gender training. Gender analysis involves gathering and examining information on what women and men do and how they relate to each other. There is a large body of literature on gender analysis that can be applied to diagnose and rectify inequalities within societal institutions. Gender training builds capacity to use the information from gender analysis in policies and program development and implementation. To be effective, training must be tailored to different sectors and to the types of work

Box 12.1

Gender norms contribute to vulnerability to HIV/AIDS

Source: Rao Gupta 2000.

Women's economic vulnerability makes it more likely that they will be forced to sell sex for economic survival, less likely that they will be able to negotiate protection against sexually transmitted infections with a male sexual partner, and less likely that they will be able to leave a relationship that they perceive to be risky—all of which combine with biological vulnerability to increase rates of HIV/AIDS among women worldwide. Similarly, gender norms for masculinity that expect men to be sexually adventurous and to dominate women increase men's, particularly young men's, vulnerability to HIV infection by pressuring them to engage in risky and sometimes violent sex with multiple partners. Thus, gender norms also affect men's vulnerability to infection but in very different ways from those affecting women. Understanding these differences in vulnerability and the underlying gender-related reasons for them is critical in addressing the root causes of ill health and disease and to successfully intervene to mitigate negative impacts.

**Wmen's
organizations
are key agents
in bringing about
institutional
transformation**

done by different groups of professionals in the units of government or international agencies that set policies and allocate resources.

An unfortunate consequence of training a broad range of professionals is the elimination or downgrading of specialized gender units and professionals. Because mainstreaming requires a shift of responsibility for promoting gender equality to all personnel, especially managers, gender specialists are considered redundant. In fact, the reverse is true: the need for specialist support often increases with gender mainstreaming. A former gender equality director in Canada offered the following metaphor to counteract the argument that since her agency had mainstreamed gender equality it needed fewer gender advisors:

> We need to liken the need for gender equality expertise to the need for technical expertise in information technology. Twenty years ago, every department in our organization might have one computer for 20 people. At that time, there would be one technical person for the whole organization that would attend to any computer glitches. Now, twenty years later, everyone has a computer on their desks. Computers have been "mainstreamed." Does that mean we no longer need the one or two technical people who were there before? Just the opposite! We now need technical departments with different types of expertise. We need those who can attend to immediate problems and those who are doing the long-range, strategic thinking about the path that technology will take and what kinds of skills and policies the organization will need to maximize use. So it should be for gender equality expertise (Rivington 2004).

Institutional structures and processes

Institutional transformation—fundamental change in the rules that specify how resources are allocated and how tasks, responsibilities, and values are assigned in society—is the third ingredient essential for achieving gender equality and women's empowerment on a large scale (Kabeer and Subrahmanian 1996; Kelleher 2002). Women's organizations are key agents in bringing about institutional transformation nationally and internationally because they articulate women's priorities and organize and advocate for change. In India women's organizations transformed political institutions at the local level, successfully lobbying for two constitutional amendments in 1992 that required that at least a third of the seats in *panchayats* (local governing councils) be reserved for women. In Brazil civil society networks led the transformation of state and municipal health institutions to prioritize cervical cancer prevention, establish abortion services, and implement other aspects of the International Conference of Population and Development's Programme of Action.

At the international level global and regional women's movements actively mobilized throughout the 1990s to put gender equality and women's empowerment on the agendas of major UN conferences, transforming international

Through legislation, regulatory reform, and the expansion and strengthening of public services, governments can rectify the deep-seated gender biases inherent in their own institutions

norms on women's roles and rights. The international women's movement succeeded in having women's rights fully recognized as human rights in the Vienna Declaration and Programme of Action that resulted from the 1993 Second UN Conference on Human Rights.

Government agencies also play key roles in institutional transformation to create an enabling national environment for gender equality. Through legislation, regulatory reform, and the expansion and strengthening of public services, governments can rectify the deep-seated gender biases inherent in their own institutions and establish structures and processes that enable women to claim their rights, such as women-friendly law enforcement systems. To advance such institutional change, a central unit or ministry needs a mandate to ensure that gender equality and women's empowerment are addressed across all ministries and departments.

At the 1995 Fourth World Conference on Women in Beijing governments agreed that national women's machineries should be the institutional entity to support and build capacity to mainstream gender equality across all development planning and implementation processes. They are defined by the UN as "a single body or complex organized system of bodies, often under different authorities, but recognized by the government as the institution dealing with the promotion of the status of women." In most countries, the national women's machineries typically include a ministry of women's affairs and gender units or focal points in other line ministries, as well as task forces or high level advisory groups.

The location, structure, and size of national women's machineries and gender units influence their ability to promote gender equality in policies and programs. Although there is no one blueprint for the structure and placement of a gender unit or focal point, several generic requirements must be met. The unit should be structurally and functionally located in finance and planning ministries so that it can influence resource allocation decisions.[1] In addition, the primary responsibility of staff in the central gender unit should be to advise and support the efforts of others, who in turn must be mandated to incorporate gender into their work. If the national women's machinery is to promote gender equality across several other ministries, it needs to be appropriately staffed and have a policy rather than an operational mandate. Crucially, as Goetz (1995) points out, staff need to have financial skills to ensure that policy commitments are followed through in national and ministerial budgets.

To remain relevant, national women's machineries must have legitimacy and credibility with women's organizations and NGOs representing women's interests. They must create structures for consulting with and responding to the concerns of women's organizations, ranging from informal discussions or public hearings to seats for NGO representatives on government committees. A system of formal representation is likely to exclude small and lesser known organizations. Therefore, in settings where women's organizations are diverse,

Adequate finan-cial resources need to be allocated to enable direct interventions by governmental and nongovern-mental organ-izations, build capacity, collect data, and evalu-ate outcomes

public hearings combined with informal consultations may be more effective. Such direct links between national women's machineries and their constituency, women's organizations, can also help to maintain accountability.

International agencies require similar changes to those of national governments to bring about institutional transformation. This is particularly important given the interdependency between donors and low-income country governments. International institutions often set the parameters for the resource envelope and policy change that are possible at the country level.

Adequate financial resources

Even if all the other ingredients described here are in place, they cannot be effective without adequate resources. Adequate financial resources need to be allocated to enable direct interventions by governmental and nongovernmental organizations, build capacity, collect data, and evaluate outcomes. Rarely are sufficient funds allocated for these purposes.

Efforts to promote gender equality may be underfunded because separating the costs of gender interventions from the overall costs of a sectoral intervention is challenging. However, as seen in chapter 11, methodologies have been developed for estimating such costs. Another reason for underfunding is that the expenditures are perceived to be additional to the core investment and to achieve only a marginal return when in fact they are essential for maximizing the return on the core investment. In resource-constrained settings this perception is particularly wasteful. A third reason is that gender equality is viewed as a cross-cutting issue. Because cross-cutting issues are supposed to be everyone's business, they tend to become no one's responsibility and so typically receive lower priority in budgetary allocations than sector-specific issues.

What can be done to ensure that the required resources will be available and committed? To increase the availability of resources, changes are needed in the international system, including debt cancellation for highly indebted poor countries, dramatically scaled up and better quality development assistance, and trade reform that levels the playing field for developing countries. Domestic resource mobilization is also important for generating the resources to achieve gender equality.

Accountability and monitoring systems

Accountability and monitoring systems are needed nationally and internationally to ensure that fundamental change is broad-based and lasting. At the country level the needed systems include a strong legal framework and enforcement mechanisms within and outside government and a strong women's movement and open processes that enable women's groups to inform and influence government policies and resource allocations.[2]

The Convention on the Elimination of All Forms of Discrimination against Women (CEDAW) provides a powerful legal mechanism for stakeholders at

The reporting
obligation
established in
CEDAW creates
the conditions
for enabling
women to
fully enjoy
their rights

the country level to hold their governments accountable for meeting Goal 3. The reporting obligation established in the convention, supported by the work of the Committee on the Elimination of Discrimination against Women (the body of 23 experts that monitors implementation of the convention) and of civil society organizations, creates the conditions for enabling women to fully enjoy their rights. Frequently, this reporting process has created partnerships among government, NGOs, and UN agencies to work together to achieve the goals of the convention.

Good practices exist in many countries for reporting on actions to eliminate discrimination against women and for following up on CEDAW reports and their recommendations. In the Netherlands the government is required to report to Parliament every four years on implementation of the convention before the state party's report is submitted to the Committee on the Elimination of Discrimination against Women, and the concluding comments of the committee are also presented to the Parliament. Uruguay's Parliament organizes a session to follow up on the committee's recommendations and calls on members of the government to discuss them. Mexico and Sweden convene seminars or special meetings to discuss the committee's concluding comments. Many state parties publish their reports, together with the committee's comments, to give wide publicity to the convention and its implementation.

With the entry into force of the Optional Protocol to the Convention in December 2000, the mandate of the committee was expanded to complaints by or on behalf of individuals or groups of individuals who claim that their rights under the convention have been violated. As of November 2004, 76 states were signatories to the Optional Protocol. The Optional Protocol is the most visible means for women to seek redress at the international level when domestic judicial systems are faulty and discriminatory laws against women still exist. The Optional Protocol strengthens national mechanisms for ensuring women's full enjoyment of their rights by providing a path to relief for individual grievances and by improving understanding of the obligations imposed by the convention.

The convention has had a positive impact in countries throughout the world. It has led to the strengthening of constitutional provisions in many countries guaranteeing equality between women and men and providing a constitutional basis for the protection of women's human rights. The revised Brazilian Constitution includes extensive guarantees reflecting the convention, and the South African Constitution contains strong provisions guaranteeing women's equality.

National courts have also used the convention as a basis for decisionmaking. The Botswana Court of Appeal drew on international treaties, including the convention, to uphold a challenge to the nationality law which prevented Botswanan women married to non-Botswanan nationals to pass on their nationality to their children. The Supreme Court of Nepal referenced the convention in ordering the government to introduce a bill to remedy discriminatory

Women's and civil society organizations have taken the lead in holding governments and international agencies accountable for implementing commitments to gender equality

inheritance laws, which entitled a son to a share of his father's property at birth, but entitled a daughter to a share only when she reached the age of 35 and was unmarried. The Supreme Court of Canada also drew on the convention and the committee's general recommendation 19 on violence against women in a case of alleged sexual assault.

Women's organizations and civil society organizations have taken the lead in holding governments and international agencies accountable for implementing their commitments to gender equality and women's empowerment. Indeed, much of the progress made to date has resulted from the political efforts and the mobilization of such organizations. To do this work well, they need data, resources, and mechanisms for regular consultations. Gender audits are a monitoring tool that can help government agencies and NGOs assess what is being done within institutions to promote gender equality and identify the gaps and challenges that need to be addressed.

In interactions with countries the international system needs to support these components of a well functioning country-level accountability and monitoring system. Simultaneously, the United Nations and other international institutions, including the World Bank, International Monetary Fund, and regional development banks, must ensure that mechanisms are in place for holding themselves accountable for implementing international mandates and commitments to gender equality, and that external watchdog agencies, particularly international women's organizations, have sufficient input in policy formulation, implementation, and resource allocation.

Country case studies

The experience of several countries illustrates the complicated process involved in promoting gender equality and women's empowerment. This section describes the efforts of Cambodia, Chile, Rwanda, and South Africa to improve women's status and reduce gender inequality (boxes 12.2–12.5). These countries are attempting significant institutional reform, catalyzed by strong and dynamic advocacy by women's organizations and other actors such as donors and other civil society movements.[3] These countries have made varying progress on the seven strategic priorities identified by the task force although it is difficult to attribute changes to specific government actions.

Each of the four countries has been affected in its recent past by significant internal turmoil and conflict. In each case women's organizations and other powerful change agents in government have seized the opportunity to remedy societal inequalities. Although peace-building and postconflict periods by definition provide new opportunities for societal restructuring, such restructuring can occur in nonconflict settings if some combination of the five elements described at the beginning of this chapter (change agents with a vision, institutional structures and processes, technical capacity, financial resources, and accountability mechanisms) are in place.

Box 12.2

Cambodia: the changing role of the Ministry of Women's Affairs

Source: UNIFEM and others 2004.

More than 30 years of war and civil violence have left a devastating mark on Cambodia's women and men. War widows and other women head more than a quarter of Cambodian households, which are among the poorest in the country.

The 1993 Constitution guarantees gender equality in marriage, family, employment, and political life. Laws promoting women's empowerment have also been passed. The 1997 Labor Code eliminates discrimination against women and the exploitation of women in the work place. The Marriage and Family Law allows divorce and provides for equal property rights in marriage. The government modified a restrictive national law on abortion, making it legal through the first trimester.

The government implements its gender policies mainly through the Ministry of Women's and Veteran's Affairs. Initially the ministry used a direct project implementation approach, but over the past few years its role has evolved into a facilitator for mobilizing political and financial support for a broader range of policies addressing the needs of women. Following the elections in July 2004 the veterans' portfolio was removed from the ministry, and it was restructured to focus only on women's affairs. It has since developed a new Five-Year Strategic Plan and made organizational changes to implement it. In 2004 the ministry had 183 staff at the central level and 735 in provincial and communal departments. That makes it two-thirds the size of the only other cross-sectoral ministry in the government, the Ministry of Environment.

The government recently established a Technical Working Group on Gender, chaired by the minister of women's affairs with members from other line ministries, donors, and NGOs. Members of the working group also serve as gender focal points on other sectoral technical working groups, creating a potentially powerful mechanism for gender mainstreaming.

Gender equality indicators for Cambodia, 1990 and 2000

Indicator	1990	2000
Education		
Girls' to boys' gross enrollment ratio, primary	—	0.88
Girls' to boys' completion rate, primary	—	0.80
Girls' to boys' gross enrollment ratio, secondary	0.43	0.57
Sexual and reproductive rights and health		
Maternal mortality ratio (per 100,000 live births)	900	450
Fertility rate	5.56	3.8
Women as a share of those living with HIV/AIDS[a] (percent)	50	30
Political and economic opportunity		
Share of women-held seats in national parliament (percent)	—	11.45[b]
Share of women in nonagricultural wage employment (percent)	40.6	53.2[c]

— Not available.
a. Data are for 1997 and 2003.
b. Data are for 2003.
c. Data are for 2002.
Source: UNESCO 2004; UN 2004a, 2004b; World Bank 2004f; UNAIDS 2004; IPU 2004.

Women's share of nonagricultural employment is among the highest in the region. Cambodia's health indicators are improving. Maternal mortality and fertility rates have dropped significantly (see table). Cambodia, with the highest HIV/AIDS prevalence rate in Asia, has succeeded in reducing the national prevalence rate among adults from 3.9 percent in 1997 to 2.8 percent in 2004. The share of women among those infected with HIV/AIDS has dropped noticeably since 1997.

Box 12.2

Cambodia: the changing role of the Ministry of Women's Affairs

(continued)

There has been a reported increase in gender-based violence and in the number of women and children being trafficked into neighboring countries. Law enforcement in these areas is extremely weak. In response to this, Cambodia has added an additional target to Millennium Development Goal 3, to eliminate all forms of violence against women.

Women's participation in Parliament is low. Although a quota of 30 percent of seats for women was proposed prior to the 2002 election of commune councils, it was rejected, and women constituted only 8.5 percent of elected councilors.

Before the war women and men had equal access to land through inheritance and acquisition. In the postwar period, despite a new land law guaranteeing joint titling, women have become more vulnerable to market forces, debt, and landlessness.

Box 12.3

Chile: the influence of women's organizations

Source: Baldez 1997; UN 1979; JICA 1999; GTZ 2004.

Following the end of military rule in Chile in 1990, many women's organizations expressed disappointment that the transition to democracy was not accompanied by a radical change in state policy toward women. In response, the new government established the National Office for Women's Affairs (SERNAM) in 1991 as a branch of the National Planning and Cooperation Ministry. SERNAM's mission is to advance equality of opportunity between men and women. The head of SERNAM has ministerial rank, and today SERNAM is among the largest women's agencies in Latin America.

During the 1990s SERNAM organized efforts for legislative and legal reform aimed at improving women's status in labor markets, alleviating female poverty, and enhancing women's health and education. In 1994 SERNAM developed and implemented the National Plan for Equal Opportunities for Women, which acknowledged the role of government institutions in sustaining women's subordination. Since then, a series of laws on domestic violence, women's rights at work, and sexual abuse have been passed. SERNAM also introduced nationwide programs targeting low-income female-headed households to improve their access to employment; a program targeting parents, teachers, and adolescents in secondary school to reduce teenage pregnancy; and a program providing childcare during the harvest season for female seasonal workers in the agro-export sector. In May 2004, after a long struggle, the government passed a law legalizing civil divorce.

Despite these efforts, women in Chile are still disadvantaged in many ways. Women's representation in political office remains low. Unsafe abortion is the second leading cause of maternal mortality, and the law prohibits abortion under any circumstances. Women lack property rights in marriage. Despite two laws that toughened the punishment for domestic violence and sexual abuse, and extensive information campaigns, violence against women continues to be a major problem in Chile.

In 2001 SERNAM introduced gender impact analysis of public policies in the budget process. Working with the Finance Ministry, SERNAM has helped establish new administrative rules for analyzing programs for the impact on women and men and on girls and boys. Gender is one of six areas on which all ministries and public services report annually to the Budget Department.

Chile has a long history of political action by women's organizations. Women's organizations have had enormous impact on SERNAM's policy objectives and program priorities at critical junctures and were instrumental in shaping the National Plan for Equal Opportunities as well as Chile's platform at the Beijing Conference on Women in 1995.

Box 12.3

Chile: the influence of women's organizations

(continued)

Gender equality indicators for Chile, 1990 and 2000

Indicator	1990	2000
Education		
Girls' to boys' gross enrollment ratio, primary	0.98	0.98
Girls' to boys' completion rate, primary	1.05	1.02
Girls' to boys' gross enrollment ratio, secondary	1.08	1.02
Sexual and reproductive rights and health		
Maternal mortality ratio (per 100,000 live births)	65	31
Adolescent fertility rate	66	66[a]
Fertility rate	2.8	2.2
Women as a share of those living with HIV/AIDS[b] (percent)	18	33.5
Political and economic opportunity		
Share of women-held seats in national parliament (percent)	—	8.3[c]
Share of women-held seats at local level—mayors (percent)		12.7
Share of women in nonagricultural wage employment (percent)	36.2	36.5[d]

— Not available
a. Data are for 1996.
b. Data are for 1997 and 2003.
c. Data are for 2003.
d. Data are for 2002.
Source: UNESCO 2004; UN 2004a, 2004b; WISTAT 1999; World Bank 2004e, 2004f; UNAIDS 2004; IPU 2004; United Cities and Local Governments 2004.

In 1990 Chile had already achieved parity in both primary and secondary enrollments (see table). From 1990 to 2000 maternal mortality fell from 65 to 31 per 100,000 births and the fertility rate declined from 2.8 to 2.2. However, in the late 1990s the share of women among those infected with HIV/AIDS nearly doubled, from 18 percent in 1997 to 33.5 percent in 2003.

Box 12.4

Rwanda: a national commitment to gender equality

Source: Zuckerman 2001, 2002a; Zuckerman and Garrett 2003; Diop-Tine 2002.

The genocide and civil war in Rwanda in 1994 caused major trauma to the country's economy and social fabric. During the conflict women were systematically raped, murdered, and disfigured. Today, women constitute 54 percent of the Rwandan population, and 34 percent of households are headed by women.

Since the genocide the country as a whole has committed itself to gender equality, and women have played a pivotal role in political and economic reconstruction. The country is in the process of restructuring its social, political, and economic institutions. It adopted a new Constitution, which guarantees equal rights for women. Parliament has begun to repeal laws that are biased against women, including legislation prohibiting women from inheriting property. Rape is now considered a first-degree crime in local courts (previously it was considered a third-degree crime) and was prosecuted as a genocidal act under the International Criminal Tribunal for Rwanda.

Rwandan women are also assuming roles as community leaders, entrepreneurs, and elected officials. In the multiparty presidential and parliamentary elections in 2003, women gained 49 percent of the seats in the lower house and 30 percent of the seats in the upper house, up from 17 percent in 1990. Rwanda has also created local women's councils elected by women only and a government ministry for women to ensure that policies are gender equitable.

Box 12.4

Rwanda: a national commitment to gender equality

(continued)

The Ministry for Gender and Women in Development and women's organizations actively participated to mainstream gender concerns in the country's Poverty Reduction Strategy Paper. External evaluations note that Rwanda's Poverty Reduction Strategy is one of the best on gender equality issues. Budgetary expenditures prioritize activities that address gender inequalities, and all sector expenditures incorporate Ministry of Gender inputs.

Women's organizations have been critical in creating an enabling environment for promoting women's empowerment and gender mainstreaming in the aftermath of the genocide. Through organizing, networking, and lobbying together, women's organizations have helped to bring about the changes described above. At the national level, Collectif ProFemmes/Twese Hamwe brings together more than 40 women's organizations that promote a culture of peace and remembrance, protect widows and the displaced, promote the legal rights of widows and children, and fight violence against women and girls. At the local level, with the support of national and international development partners, women's organizations are implementing a range of economic development activities.

Gender equality indicators for Rwanda, 1990 and 2000

Indicator	1990	2000
Education		
Girls' to boys' gross enrollment ratio, primary	0.98	0.99
Girls' to boys' completion rate, primary	1.07	0.92
Girls' to boys' gross enrollment ratio, secondary	0.76	0.98
Sexual and reproductive rights and health		
Maternal mortality ratio (per 100,000 live births)	1,300	950[a]
Unmet need for contraception	38.8	35.6
Fertility rate	7.1	5.7
Women as a share of those living with HIV/AIDS[b] (percent)	48.6	56.5
Births attended by skilled health staff	25.8	31.3[c]
Political and economic opportunity		
Share of women-held seats in national parliament (percent)	17	39.4[a]
Share of women in labor force (percent)	49	49[a]

a. Data are for 2003.
b. Data are for 1997 and 2003.
c. Data are for 2001.
Source: UNESCO 2004; UN 2004a; World Bank 2004b, 2004f; UNAIDS 2004; ORC-Macro 2004; IPU 2004.

Despite enormous economic development challenges, Rwanda's gender indicators are above regional averages (see table). Although the absolute rates of secondary education are very low for both boys and girls, the gender gap at this level has closed rapidly between 1990 and 2000, and the country is on its way to achieve gender parity in both primary and secondary education in 2005.

The country's fertility rate has been declining steadily. Births attended by skilled health staff have increased, and the unmet need for contraception has declined for both adolescents and adult women.

Box 12.5
South Africa: mainstreaming gender concerns

Source: Baden 1999; Khan 2003; Unterhalter and others 2004; GTZ 2004.

The postapartheid government of South Africa made gender equality one of the priorities of the reconstruction process. South Africa's constitution now guarantees equality between women and men and provides for affirmative action to address gender inequalities in public life. The Constitution takes precedence over customary law when the equality clause and customary law conflict.

Several new laws have been introduced and existing laws revised to make them more gender-sensitive. The Public Service Act of 1994 and the Labor Relations Act of 1995 removed discriminatory practices in public services and labor markets. Abortion was legalized in 1996. The government also passed a law in 1993 criminalizing rape within marriage.

Gender concerns are fully mainstreamed into the government apparatus. South Africa does not have a separate ministry of women's affairs, but the Commission on Gender Equality, provided for in the Constitution, monitors and evaluates government and the private sector on gender, informs the public, and makes recommendations on laws and policies. The Office on the Status of Women is responsible for developing national gender policy, promoting affirmative action in government, supporting government bodies to integrate gender in all policies and programs, and organizing gender training. Its power, however, is limited because it is not directly involved in national policy, and many departments see gender equality only in terms of personnel and internal workings.

In 1995 South Africa was one of the first countries to pioneer analysis of the national budget from a gender perspective. The Women's Budget Initiative was a collaborative venture of women parliamentarians and women's organizations to make the case for reallocating expenditures and revenues to more adequately respond to the needs of women. Of the many tools used for monitoring gender mainstreaming, this one has caught the imagination of women's movements worldwide.

Women's organizations were very active in the antiapartheid movement and that activism helped to bring about a number of the constitutional and legal changes described above. Women's organizations lobbied strongly for legalizing abortion and protecting women against violence. They have also fought for women's land rights and for prevention and treatment of HIV/AIDS. However, the migration of many women's activists into government after 1994 weakened women's organizations, particularly in rural areas, limiting their ability to maximize the opportunities created by the national gender machinery.

Cambodia, Rwanda, and South Africa have all made significant progress in the last decade in closing gender gaps in primary and secondary education and improving key aspects of women's sexual and reproductive rights and health. However, despite improvements in maternal mortality and decreases in unmet need for contraception, women in South Africa, Rwanda, and Cambodia have been hit hard by the HIV/AIDS epidemic. Among the four countries Chile stands alone in opposing women's reproductive rights. On women's political participation Rwanda and South Africa have achieved high levels of representation of women at the national and local levels. Chile and Rwanda have taken strong legal measures to address violence against women, and Cambodia has added elimination of violence against women as an additional Millennium Development target.

Box 12.5

South Africa: mainstreaming gender concerns

(continued)

Gender equality indicators for South Africa, 1990 and 2000

Indicator	1990	2000
Education		
Girls' to boys' gross enrollment ratio, primary	0.98	0.95
Girls' to boys' completion rate, primary	1.12	1.02
Girls' to boys' gross enrollment ratio, secondary	1.16	1.09
Sexual and reproductive rights and health		
Maternal mortality ratio (per 100,000 live births)	340[a]	230
Unmet need for contraception		15
Fertility rate	3.3	2.8
Women as a share of those living with HIV/AIDS[b] (percent)	50	56.9
Political and economic opportunity		
Share of women-held seats in national parliament (percent)	2.8	30.7[c]
Share of women in labor force (percent)	37	38[c]

a. Data are for 1995.
b. Data are for 1997 and 2003.
c. Data are for 2003.
Source: UNESCO 2004; UN 2004a, 2004b; World Bank 2004c, 2004f; UNAIDS 2004; IPU 2004; ORC-Macro 2004.

Over the last decade, South Africa has made significant progress toward closing gender gaps in some sectors. Women now constitute 31 percent of parliamentarians (see table). Maternal mortality has been reduced, and the fertility rate has declined. However, HIV/AIDS is a major health problem for South African women. In 2003 women constituted more than half of those infected with HIV/AIDS, and the majority of new infections occur among adolescent girls.

Although the official indicators for primary and secondary education have not registered much improvement over 10 years, the government has taken steps to improve the quality of education. The Gender Equity Task Team has revised the curricula with attention to gender issues and has prepared a guide to educate teachers on gender issues. The incidence of sexual violence in schools remains a problem, however.

No country has adequately addressed women's poverty and economic opportunity—their participation in labor markets or asset ownership and control—although Cambodia and Rwanda have made commitments to securing women's rights to land and housing, Chile has implemented a poverty alleviation program targeting low-income female-headed households to improve their access to employment, although the results have been mixed, and Cambodia has reformed its labor code to eliminate discrimination against women.

In each of the four countries the conditions have been created for fostering large-scale societal transformation. Each country has a critical mass of change agents within government and civil society with a vision of gender equality and women's empowerment. In Rwanda and South Africa government leaders have worked in alliance with civil society leaders, while in Chile

Poverty
reduction
strategies in
low-income
countries are
the mechanism
for influencing
development
policies and
plans

the pressure of an independent women's movement forced change within government.

Institutional structures and processes are being transformed through constitutional change, legal reform, and the formation of new governmental organizations. Cambodia, Rwanda, and South Africa have all made commitments to gender equality a key component of their constitutions. All four countries have implemented major legal and legislative reforms to advance equality between women and men. And in all four countries a national women's machinery has been put in place, supported by political leaders, with strong mandates for achieving gender equality. South Africa also established a Gender Equality Commission, which serves as a monitoring mechanism and reports to the president's office.

It is difficult to establish whether adequate technical resources exist in these countries for implementing their commitments to gender equality. However, as the four case studies show, the multilayered responses (legislative, policy, and project) to gender inequality suggest that technical capacity is not lacking.

Similarly, it is hard to know whether the gender equality machinery has adequate financial resources to do its work, an area where information is sorely lacking. The limited information from Cambodia suggests that gender equality is underresourced relative to the other cross-sectoral ministry. Yet, the advent of gender-budget initiatives, especially in Chile, Rwanda, and South Africa holds the promise of such information becoming available and useful to gender equality advocates within and outside government.

Finally, in terms of monitoring and accountability, each country has women's movements that can hold governments to their promises. Gender budget initiatives are an important monitoring and accountability mechanism. Each country is a signatory to the Convention on the Elimination of All Forms of Discrimination against Women, but it is not clear whether the associated monitoring mechanism truly serves to hold governments accountable for bringing about the changes required to meet the convention's provisions.[4]

Gender mainstreaming in MDG-based country policy processes

Poverty reduction strategies in low-income countries are the mechanism for influencing development policies and plans and ensuring that actions to address the Millennium Development Goals are implemented. Thus, a critical entry-point for promoting gender equality and women's empowerment at the country level is the poverty reduction strategy process.

Gender has been mainstreamed unevenly across donor-initiated Poverty Reduction Strategy Papers (Zuckerman and Garrett 2003). Whitehead's (2003) review in four countries found that gender issues appear in fragmented fashion—addressed very little or not at all in policy sections of the documents. Despite guidelines in the World Bank Poverty Reduction Strategy Paper Sourcebook to treat gender as a cross-cutting issue, two of the four cases

A gender-aware public spending plan must include sex-disaggregated and gender-sensitive measures for inputs, outputs, and outcomes

Whitehead reviews do not do so. Perhaps partly in response to the Millennium Development Goals, the most consistently mentioned policy areas for women are health and education.

A core recommendation of the UN Millennium Project's (2005a) *Investing in Development: A Practical Plan to Achieve the Millennium Development Goals* is that every developing country restructure its short-term poverty reduction strategy in the context of a 10-year Millennium Development Goals (MDG) framework. This offers the opportunity to apply the lessons from past poverty reduction strategy processes so that the new MDG-based poverty reduction strategies succeed in fully mainstreaming gender and empowering women.

The UN Millennium Project suggests a five-step approach to designing an MDG-based poverty reduction strategy (UN Millennium Project 2005a). Gender considerations should be an integral component of each step.

First, as noted in chapter 10, the data that countries use to diagnose the nature and dynamics of poverty must be disaggregated by sex. Surveys will need to collect individual as well as household-level data to understand the gender-differentiated causes, dynamics, and consequences of poverty. Large-scale survey efforts already under way (such as the World Bank's Living Standards Measurement Study and ORC-Macro's Demographic and Health Surveys) provide an opportunity to collect information on sources and uses of income by different household members, to incorporate time allocation modules, and to use more participatory poverty appraisals. This will help to remedy one of the most glaring deficiencies in data on women's lives—the lack of information on female poverty—and will increase the efficiency of investments and programs to reduce poverty by ensuring that they are appropriately designed and targeted.

Second, in undertaking a systematic needs assessment to evaluate policies, governance structures, and public investments, countries should use the tools and methodologies described earlier in this chapter. Gender analysis will ensure that the needs assessment reflects the differentiated needs of male and female citizens, but that must occur through a consultative process that allows for the full participation of women's organizations. Moreover, the gender needs assessment described in chapter 11 will indicate the level of financial resources necessary to meet those needs.

Third, in converting the needs assessment into a detailed three-year MDG-based poverty reduction strategy in the context of a medium-term expenditure framework, both the plan for public spending and services and the financing strategy should be based on a gender analysis of public expenditure and revenue. As the case studies illustrate, gender budget analysis initiatives can illuminate the costs of public services and monitor the allocation of expenditure differentially for women and men. A gender-aware public spending plan must include sex-disaggregated and gender-sensitive measures for inputs, outputs, and outcomes. It must also make gender equality an explicit indicator of performance.

**The next 10
years provide a
new window of
opportunity to
take action on a
global scale to
achieve gender
equality and
empower women**

And it must incorporate into the budget framework new dimensions of costs and expenditures that are not typically included, such as the unpaid care of children, the elderly and sick, provided by women (Sharp 2003).

Finally, the public sector management strategy for implementation of the three-year poverty reduction strategy and the 10-year framework, with its focus on transparency, accountability, and results-based management, should include processes that allow stakeholders committed to gender equality to participate in meaningful ways. For example, women's organizations and other civil society groups that promote gender equality must be given full information and be able to participate in formal feedback mechanisms through which accountability can be exercised.

Conclusion

Much of what has been covered in this chapter has been known for several decades. But it has been difficult to translate this knowledge into development policy and practice at the scale required to bring about a fundamental transformation in the distribution of power, opportunity, and outcomes for both women and men. The next 10 years provide a new window of opportunity to take action on a global scale to achieve gender equality and empower women as part of meeting all the Millennium Development Goals. Governments and international organizations can provide an enabling environment to make this possible. Women's organizations need the space and resources to bring about the societal transformations that remove the constraints, fulfill the potential, and guarantee the rights of women in all countries. The recommendations in this chapter can pave the way toward that future.

Education projections and country level education data

The education indicators proposed by the United Nations for Millennium Development Goal 3 are:

- The ratio of girls to boys in primary and secondary education.
- The ratio of literate females to males among 15- to 24-year-olds.

This appendix reports projection results for primary and secondary enrollment for the target years of 2005 and 2015 and tertiary enrollment and the ratio of literate females to males for the target year 2015.

As discussed in chapter 10, each indicator has its limitations. The ratio of girls to boys in school does not provide a reference point to assess actual enrollment relative to the population of the age group that should be enrolled at that level. Net enrollment rates, which take into consideration the appropriate age for each grade, are a good indicator of access to education, but they are not available for many countries. Gross enrollment rates are more widely available, but they include repeat students in the calculation and so will be higher than net enrollment rates. Moreover, even though enrollment is a good indicator of the input side of education, it does not provide insights into student learning outcomes.

The literacy indicator, which can be interpreted as an indicator of learning outcomes, is also problematic. The quality of data is suspect in many countries. Some countries collect literacy information using sophisticated and comprehensive techniques while others are not able to provide even the most basic information. In addition, because literacy is not a simple concept with a single universally accepted meaning, different countries measure literacy differently. The UNESCO definition (people are considered literate if they have completed five or more years of schooling) has been widely criticized, because it assumes that people can be easily categorized as "literate" or "illiterate" and because adults with five or more years of schooling may still be functionally illiterate, while those with less than four years of schooling may have acquired literacy skills by nonformal means.[1]

In reviewing trends and projections for the target years, this report uses the ratio of female to male gross enrollment rates in primary, secondary, and tertiary education as well as the ratio of the female literacy rate to the male literacy rate. The ratio of rates is used in order to analyze whether reductions in gender disparity are being achieved through increases in the enrollment of girls or through decreases in the enrollment of boys. This methodology is also used by Abu-Ghaida and Klasen (2002) and UNIFEM (2003). The country level data for these indicators can be found in tables A1.7–A1.10.

Methodology for projections

The predictions below are computed following a methodology similar to the UNDP methodology described in Technical Note 2 of *Human Development Report 2002* (UNDP 2002).

The following formulas were used for primary, secondary, and tertiary enrollment to predict values in 2005 and 2015:

For 2005: {[(Value in 2000 − value in 1990)/10] × 5} + value in 2000

For 2015: {[(Value in 2000 − value in 1990)/10] × 15} + value in 2000

The methodology used here differs somewhat from UNDP (2002). First, it does not assume that a country that has achieved the target in 2000 will also achieve the target in 2005 or 2015. Moreover, the countries that have values between 0.9 and 0.99 in 2000 are not considered to be "on track" because their rate of change between 1990 and 2000 may be such that they are trending away from parity rather than toward parity.

This report uses slightly different terminology than UNDP (2002), which uses "achieved," "on track," "lagging," "far behind," and "slipping back." The categories used here are: "reverse gap," "parity," "on track," "falling behind," and "off track":

- Reverse gap: A ratio of 1 or greater
- Parity: A ratio of 1
- On track: 0.90 to 0.99
- Falling behind: 0.70 to 0.89
- Off track: A ratio less than 0.70

It is important to note a number of concerns about the methodology. The most important is the assumption used to calculate the rate of change. To assume that this rate is linear, independent of a range of social, economic, and political factors, is overly simple. A better approach would be to simulate the effect of different contextual conditions based on data for each country. The absence of such a simulation model, and the lack of data on women to use for such a model, however, limits us to this simpler approach. A second problem with the linear predictions for gross enrollment rates is that any increase over 100 signals a problem rather than an achievement because it means that students (boys or girls) are repeating grades.

Despite these limitations, results stemming from the projections of gender parity in enrollment rates provide valuable clues on countries' progress. These predictions also help pin down the countries and regions that are faring the worst and hence can provide guidance on where efforts and resources should be directed in the hard work to achieve gender parity in education.

Projection results

Most of the results are reported at the regional level using the UNDP (2002) country classification[2] (box A1.1) and supplemented by country-level statistics. The classification includes 188 countries.

Country prospects for meeting the primary education target

As discussed in chapter 3, gender gaps in primary gross enrollment ratios closed rapidly during 1990–2000. In all regions except South Asia and Sub-Saharan Africa the gender parity ratio for primary enrollment exceeded 0.90. The gap also narrowed in South Asia, moving from 0.77 to 0.89, and in Sub-Saharan Africa, moving from 0.80 to 0.86.

In Sub-Saharan Africa in 35 of 40 countries with data for 2000, the gross enrollment ratio of girls' to boys' enrollment rates was below 1.0. Of these 35 countries 19 had gender parity ratios below 0.90 (Angola, Benin, Burkina Faso, Burundi, Cameroon, Central African Republic, Chad, Comoros, Côte d'Ivoire, Eritrea, Ethiopia, Guinea, Guinea-Bissau, Liberia, Mali, Mozambique, Niger, Senegal, and Togo). In South Asia four of six countries had gender parity ratios below 1.0 (India, Islamic Republic of Iran, Nepal, and Pakistan).

If present trends continue, 46 of 133 countries with available data are expected to achieve gender parity or a reverse gender gap by 2005 (table A1.1). Sixty-eight countries are in the 0.90–0.99 interval. No countries are in the off-track category. Nineteen countries have a projected gender parity ratio of 0.70–0.89, which indicates that they are falling behind. Four of these countries are in the Middle East and North Africa (Djibouti, Iraq, Sudan, Yemen), 14 are in Sub-Saharan Africa (Benin, Burkina Faso, Burundi, Cameroon, Central African Republic, Chad, Côte d'Ivoire, Eritrea, Ethiopia, Guinea, Mali, Mozambique, Niger, Togo) and one is in South Asia (India).

Convergence toward parity can be achieved in several ways: declines in male enrollment rates with female rates remaining constant, declines in both female and male rates with male rates declining faster, or increases in both female and male rates, with female rates increasing faster. Parity is only meaningful if it is attained through genuine increases in female enrollment rates.

Box A1.1
Regional classifications

Developed countries

Australia, Austria, Belgium, Canada, Denmark, Finland, France, Germany, Greece, Iceland, Ireland, Italy, Japan, Luxembourg, Netherlands, New Zealand, Norway, Portugal, Spain, Sweden, Switzerland, United Kingdom, United States

East Asia and Pacific

Brunei Darussalam, Cambodia, China, Democratic People's Republic of Korea, Fiji, Hong Kong (China), Indonesia, Kiribati, Lao People's Democratic Republic, Malaysia, Marshall Islands, Federated States of Micronesia, Mongolia, Myanmar, Nauru, Palau, Papua New Guinea, Philippines, Republic of Korea, Samoa, Singapore, Solomon Islands, Thailand, Timor-Leste, Tonga, Tuvalu, Vanuatu, Viet Nam

Europe and Central Asia

Albania, Armenia, Azerbaijan, Belarus, Bosnia and Herzegovina, Bulgaria, Croatia, Cyprus, Czech Republic, Estonia, Georgia, Hungary, Kazakhstan, Kyrgyzstan, Latvia, Lithuania, Poland, Republic of Moldova, Romania, Russian Federation, Serbia and Montenegro, Slovakia, Slovenia, Macedonia TFYR, Tajikistan, Turkey, Turkmenistan, Ukraine, Uzbekistan

Latin America and the Caribbean

Antigua and Barbuda, Argentina, Bahamas, Barbados, Belize, Bolivia, Brazil, Chile, Colombia, Costa Rica, Cuba, Dominica, Dominican Republic, Ecuador, El Salvador, Grenada, Guatemala, Guyana, Haiti, Honduras, Jamaica, Mexico, Nicaragua, Panama, Paraguay, Peru, Saint Kitts and Nevis, Saint Lucia, Saint Vincent and the Grenadines, Suriname, Trinidad and Tobago, Uruguay, Venezuela

Middle East and North Africa

Algeria, Bahrain, Djibouti, Egypt, Iraq, Israel, Jordan, Kuwait, Lebanon, Libyan Arab Jamahiriya, Morocco, Oman, Palestinian Autonomous Territories, Qatar, Saudi Arabia, Sudan, Syrian Arab Republic, Tunisia, United Arab Emirates, Yemen

South Asia

Afghanistan, Bangladesh, Bhutan, India, Islamic Republic of Iran, Maldives, Nepal, Pakistan, Sri Lanka

Sub-Saharan Africa

Angola, Benin, Botswana, Burkina Faso, Burundi, Cameroon, Cape Verde, Central African Republic, Chad, Comoros, Congo, Côte d'Ivoire, Democratic Rep. of the Congo, Equatorial Guinea, Eritrea, Ethiopia, Gabon, Gambia, Ghana, Guinea, Guinea-Bissau, Kenya, Lesotho Liberia, Madagascar, Malawi, Mali, Mauritania, Mauritius, Mozambique, Namibia, Niger, Nigeria, Rwanda, São Tomé and Principe, Senegal, Seychelles, Sierra Leone, Somalia, South Africa, Swaziland, United Republic of Tanzania, Togo, Uganda, Zambia, Zimbabwe

Of the 14 countries that have not yet achieved but are projected to achieve gender parity or a reverse gender gap in primary enrollments by 2005, only 12 will do so through increases in female enrollment rates: Bolivia, Gambia, Kenya, Kuwait, Lithuania, Malawi, Mauritania, Mexico, Peru, Portugal, Rwanda, and Vanuatu.[3] Another two countries are expected to achieve a ratio of one or greater because of declines in both female and male rates, with male enrollment rates declining faster: Myanmar and Saudi Arabia.

Table A1.1

Country predictions by region for female to male gross primary enrollment ratios, 2005

Number of countries

Source: UNESCO 2004.

Region	Reverse gap (more than 1.0)	Parity (1.0)	On track (0.90–0.99)	Falling behind (0.70–0.89)	Off track (less than 0.70)	Total
Developed countries	4	8	10	0	0	22
East Asia Pacific	4	3	7	0	0	14
Europe and Central Asia	3	4	13	0	0	20
Latin America and the Caribbean	1	5	16	0	0	22
Middle East and North Africa	2	4	8	4	0	18
South Asia	1	0	2	1	0	4
Sub-Saharan Africa	5	2	12	14	0	33
Total	20	26	68	19	0	133

Table A1.2

Country predictions by region for female to male gross primary enrollment ratios, 2015

Number of countries

Source: UNESCO 2004.

Region	Reverse gap (more than 1.0)	Parity (1.0)	On track (0.90–0.99)	Falling behind (0.70–0.89)	Off track (less than 0.70)	Total
Developed countries	9	3	9	1	0	22
East Asia and Pacific	5	2	5	2	0	14
Europe and Central Asia	3	4	11	2	0	20
Latin America and the Caribbean	2	3	15	2	0	22
Middle East and North Africa	9	1	6	2	0	18
South Asia	3	0	1	0	0	4
Sub-Saharan Africa	11	2	8	11	1	33
Total	42	15	55	20	1	133

Projections for 2015 show a decisive improvement in gender parity (table A1.2). The exception is Eritrea, the only country that is predicted to drop below 0.70. If current trends continue, 57 of the 133 countries are expected to achieve gender parity or a reverse gender gap by the year 2015. Another 55 countries are on track, and 41 of them are close to achieving parity with ratios between 0.95 and 0.99. Of the 20 countries that are falling behind, 11 are in Sub-Saharan Africa (Botswana, Burkina Faso, Burundi, Cameroon, Central African Republic, Côte d'Ivoire, Ethiopia, Lesotho, Mozambique, Namibia, and Niger).[4] This result suggests that Sub-Saharan Africa requires a significant amount of extra attention in order to achieve the gender parity target by 2015.

Country prospects for meeting the secondary education target

Across the world there is greater variation in enrollment rates at the secondary level than at primary level. In 2000 both South Asia and Sub-Saharan Africa had female to male gross enrollment ratios below 0.90. In Sub-Saharan Africa, 30 of 36 countries with data had gender parity ratios below 1.0. In South Asia 4 of 6 and in East Asia and Pacific 9 of 18 countries had ratios below 1.0. In 2000, 78 of 149 countries had gender parity or a reverse gender gap.

Table A1.3

Country predictions by region for female to male gross secondary enrollment ratios, 2005

Number of countries

Source: UNESCO 2004.

Region	Reverse gap (more than 1.0)	Parity (1.0)	On track (0.90–0.99)	Falling behind (0.70–0.89)	Off track (less than 0.70)	Total
Developed countries	12	3	7	0	0	22
East Asia and Pacific	7	0	2	4	1	14
Europe and Central Asia	9	2	7	1	0	19
Latin America and the Caribbean	14	0	2	0	0	16
Middle East and North Africa	8	1	3	1	2	15
South Africa	2	0	1	2	0	5
Sub-Saharan Africa	7	1	6	6	7	27
Total	59	7	28	14	10	118

Table A1.4

Country predictions by region for female to male gross secondary enrollment ratios, 2015

Number of countries

Source: UNESCO 2004.

Region	Reverse gap (more than 1.0)	Parity (1.0)	On track (0.90–0.99)	Falling behind (0.70–0.89)	Off track (less than 0.70)	Total
Developed countries	11	3	8	0	0	22
East Asia and Pacific	6	0	3	5	0	14
Europe and Central Asia	8	1	5	5	0	19
Latin America and the Caribbean	10	0	4	2	0	16
Middle East and North Africa	10	0	2	1	2	15
South Asia	3	0	1	1	0	5
Sub-Saharan Africa	11	1	4	6	5	27
Total	59	5	27	20	7	118

If current trends continue, 7 of 118 countries would achieve a ratio of 1.0 in gross secondary enrollment by 2005 and 59 would have a reverse gap (table A1.3). Of the 28 countries that are on track with a gender parity ratio of 0.90–0.99, 15 are trending downward to ratios that are lower than they had in 2000.[5]

Twenty-four countries are expected to fall behind or be off track in 2005. In Sub-Saharan Africa six countries are falling behind (Burkina Faso, Burundi, Niger, Senegal, Tanzania, and Zimbabwe) and seven are off track (Benin, Chad, Côte d'Ivoire, Ethiopia, Mozambique, Toga, and Uganda). In Europe and Central Asia one country (Turkey) is falling behind. In East Asia and Pacific four countries (China, Lao PDR, Papua New Guinea, and Vanuatu) are falling behind and one is off track (Cambodia). In the Middle East and North Africa one country (Morocco) is falling behind and two are off track (Djibouti and Iraq). In South Asia two countries are falling behind (India and Pakistan).

Projections for 2015 reflect no evidence of an overall closure in the gender gap at the secondary level, with 27 countries projected to fall behind or be off track (table A1.4).[6]

Table A1.5

**Country predictions
by region for female
to male gross
tertiary enrollment
ratios, 2015**

Number of countries

Source: UNESCO 2004.

Region	Reverse gap (more than 1.0)	Parity (1.0)	On track (0.90–0.99)	Falling behind (0.70–0.89)	Off track (less than 0.70)	Total
Developed countries	20	0	0	0	0	20
East Asia and Pacific	2	0	0	1	1	4
Europe and Central Asia	16	0	0	1	1	18
Latin America and the Caribbean	8	0	0	1	0	9
Middle East and North Africa	7	0	0	0	0	7
South Asia	2	0	0	1	1	4
Sub-Saharan Africa	4	0	1	3	8	16
Total	59	0	1	7	11	78

Table A1.6

**Country predictions
by region for ratio
of literate females
to males, aged
15–24, 2015**

Number of countries

Source: UN 2004a.

Region	Reverse gap (more than 1.0)	Parity (1.0)	On track (0.90–0.99)	Falling behind (0.70–0.89)	Off track (less than 0.70)	Total
East Asia and Pacific	7	7	3	0	0	17
Europe and Central Asia	2	18	0	0	0	20
Latin America and the Caribbean	13	11	1	1	0	26
Middle East and North Africa	12	2	3	1	1	19
South Asia	2	1	1	3	0	7
Sub-Saharan Africa	19	3	4	10	3	39
Total	55	42	12	15	4	128

Country prospects for meeting the tertiary education target

If current trends persist, 59 of 78 countries with data will achieve a reverse gender gap by 2015 (table A1.5). One country is on track to achieve parity (Botswana). Seven countries are falling behind: three in Sub-Saharan Africa (Equatorial Guinea, Madagascar, and Uganda), one in East Asia and Pacific (Republic of Korea), one in Europe and Central Asia (Georgia), one in Latin America and the Caribbean (Cuba), and one in South Asia (India). Finally, 11 countries are off track, the majority in Sub-Saharan Africa (Benin, Burundi, Central African Republic, Congo, Ethiopia, Ghana, Mauritania, and Togo). Of the remaining three, one is in East Asia and Pacific (China), one in Europe and Central Asia (Tajikistan), and one in South Asia (Nepal).

Country prospects for meeting the literacy target

Eighty-five percent of 128 developing countries are projected to have female to male literacy ratios of 0.90 or greater by 2015 (table A1.6). Thirteen of the 39 countries in Sub-Saharan Africa with data are either falling behind or off track. In South Asia three of seven countries are predicted to fall behind. In contrast, only one country in Latin America and the Caribbean (Guatemala) is likely to fall behind, while two countries in the Middle East and North Africa are likely to fall behind (Yemen) and be off track (Iraq). Of the 62 countries that achieved gender parity in literacy by 2003, 59 have rates of female and male literacy of 90 percent or greater. However, three countries with female to male ratios of one or greater in 2003 also have relatively low literacy rates for both men and women (Haiti at 66 percent for men and 67 percent for women, Nicaragua at 72 percent for men and 73 for women, and Honduras at 85 percent for men and 88 percent for women).

Table A1.7

Female and male gross primary enrollment rates and ratios, 1990 and 2000, and projections for 2005 and 2015

— Not available.

a. Rank is defined as follows: 1 = ratio greater than 1 (reverse gap), 2 = ratio equal to 1 (parity), 3 = 0.90–0.99 (on track), 4 = 0.70–0.89 (falling behind), 5 = 0–0.69 (off track).

Source: UNESCO 2004.

Region/country	1990			2000			2005		2015	
	Female rate	Male rate	Female to male ratio	Female rate	Male rate	Female to male ratio	Projected female to male ratio	Rank[a]	Projected female to male ratio	Rank[a]
Developed countries										
Australia	107.4	108	0.99	102.1	102.1	1	1	2	1.02	1
Austria	100.6	100.7	1	103.2	104.2	0.99	0.99	3	0.98	3
Belgium	100.6	99.2	1.01	104.5	105.4	0.99	0.98	3	0.96	3
Canada	103	104.6	0.98	100	99.7	1	1.01	1	1.03	1
Denmark	98.3	98.2	1	101.9	102	1	1	2	1	2
Finland	98.5	99.1	0.99	101.4	101.8	1	1	2	1.02	1
France	107.6	109.2	0.99	104.2	105.5	0.99	0.99	3	0.99	3
Germany	—	—	—	103.7	103.9	1	—	—	—	—
Greece	98.1	98.7	0.99	99.2	99.4	1	1	2	1.02	1
Iceland	101	101.7	0.99	102.2	102.4	1	1	2	1.02	1
Ireland	102.7	102.2	1	119	119.8	0.99	0.99	3	0.98	3
Italy	103.5	103.8	1	100.5	101.3	0.99	0.99	3	0.98	3
Japan	99.9	99.6	1	100.8	100.8	1	1	2	1	2
Luxembourg	94.2	86.9	1.08	100.9	100.9	1	0.96	3	0.88	4
Netherlands	104.1	100.8	1.03	106.4	108.6	0.98	0.96	3	0.9	3
New Zealand	104.7	106.4	0.98	99.9	100	1	1.01	1	1.03	1
Norway	100.4	100.5	1	101.5	101.3	1	1	2	1	2
Portugal	120	125.9	0.95	120.3	122.1	0.98	1	2	1.02	1
Spain	108	109.1	0.99	104.8	105.3	0.99	0.99	3	0.99	3
Sweden	99.9	99.7	1	111.3	108.6	1.02	1.03	1	1.05	1
Switzerland	90.9	89.7	1.01	106.8	107.8	0.99	0.98	3	0.96	3
United Kingdom	105.5	102.9	1.03	98.9	98.9	1	0.99	3	0.96	3
United States	101.1	102.9	0.98	100.8	101.1	1	1.01	1	1.03	1
East Asia and Pacific										
Brunei Darussalam	111.8	118.7	0.94	102	106.2	0.96	0.97	3	0.99	3
Cambodia	—	—	—	103.3	116.8	0.88	—	—	—	—
China	120.3	129.6	0.93	113.8	113.8	1	1.03	1	1.11	1
Fiji	—	—	—	108	109.7	0.98	—	—	—	—
Hong Kong, China	—	—	—	—	—	—	—	—	—	—
Indonesia	112.9	115.7	0.98	108.8	111.2	0.98	0.98	3	0.98	3
Kiribati	—	—	—	129.1	126.7	1.02	—	—	—	—
Korea, DPR	—	—	—	—	—	—	—	—	—	—
Korea, Rep. of	105.3	104.6	1.01	101.5	100.7	1.01	1.01	1	1.01	1
Lao PDR	90.9	115.5	0.79	104.4	121.5	0.86	0.9	3	0.96	3
Malaysia	93.6	93.8	1	98.7	98.3	1	1	2	1	2
Marshall Islands	—	—	—	—	—	—	—	—	—	—
Micronesia, Fed. States	—	—	—	—	—	—	—	—	—	—
Mongolia	98.3	96.1	1.02	100.6	97	1.04	1.05	1	1.07	1
Myanmar	106.2	111.3	0.95	88.7	89.3	0.99	1.01	1	1.05	1
Nauru	—	—	—	—	—	—	—	—	—	—

Table A1.7

Female and male gross primary enrollment rates and ratios, 1990 and 2000, and projections for 2005 and 2015

(continued)

Region/country	1990 Female rate	1990 Male rate	1990 Female to male ratio	2000 Female rate	2000 Male rate	2000 Female to male ratio	2005 Projected female to male ratio	2005 Rank[a]	2015 Projected female to male ratio	2015 Rank[a]
Palau	—	—	—	109.3	112.7	0.97	—	—	—	—
Papua New Guinea	66.3	70.6	0.94	79.7	87.5	0.91	0.9	3	0.87	4
Philippines	109.3	110.3	0.99	112.5	112.7	1	1	2	1.02	1
Samoa	127.5	116.7	1.09	101.1	104.6	0.97	0.91	3	0.79	4
Singapore	102.3	105.1	0.97	—	—	—	—	—	—	—
Solomon Islands	79.2	91.9	0.86	—	—	—	—	—	—	—
Thailand	95.9	100.4	0.95	92.7	96.9	0.96	0.97	3	0.98	3
Timor-Leste	—	—	—	—	—	—	—	—	—	—
Tonga	—	—	—	111.8	113.5	0.99	—	—	—	—
Tuvalu	—	—	—	—	—	—	—	—	—	—
Vanuatu	95.3	96.9	0.98	107.7	109.2	0.99	1	2	1	2
Viet Nam	102.9	110.8	0.93	102.2	109	0.94	0.94	3	0.95	3
Europe and Central Asia										
Albania	100.4	100.1	1	107.1	107	1	1	2	1	2
Armenia	—	—	—	—	—	—	—	—	—	—
Azerbaijan	113	114	0.99	99.8	100.6	0.99	0.99	3	0.99	3
Belarus	—	—	—	107.8	109.3	0.99	—	—	—	—
Bosnia and Herzegovina	—	—	—	—	—	—	—	—	—	—
Bulgaria	96.3	98.8	0.97	101.7	104.6	0.97	0.97	3	0.97	3
Croatia	84.4	85	0.99	87.6	88.6	0.99	0.99	3	0.99	3
Cyprus	89.9	90.3	1	96.7	96.5	1	1	2	1	2
Czech Republic	96.5	96.2	1	103.8	104.8	0.99	0.99	3	0.98	3
Estonia	109.2	112.3	0.97	100.8	105.1	0.96	0.96	3	0.95	3
Georgia	97.2	97.4	1	95.6	95.3	1	1	2	1	2
Hungary	94.5	94.6	1	101.3	102.8	0.99	0.99	3	0.98	3
Kazakhstan	—	—	—	98.2	99.3	0.99	—	—	—	.
Kyrgyzstan	92.6	93	1	99.5	103.2	0.96	0.94	3	0.9	3
Latvia	94.4	95	0.99	99.6	100.9	0.99	0.99	3	0.99	3
Lithuania	88.8	93.2	0.95	100.7	101.9	0.99	1.01	1	1.05	1
Macedonia TFYR	98.5	100.1	0.98	98.8	98.9	1	1.01	1	1.03	1
Moldova, Rep. of	93.1	93	1	83.7	83.9	1	1	2	1	2
Poland	97.9	98.8	0.99	99	100.1	0.99	0.99	3	0.99	3
Romania	91.4	91.2	1	97.7	99.8	0.98	0.97	3	0.95	3
Russian Federation	109.1	109.2	1	108.5	109.2	0.99	0.99	3	0.98	3
Serbia and Montenegro	72.7	71.4	1.02	66.9	65.6	1.02	1.02	1	1.02	1
Slovakia	—	—	—	102.6	103.3	0.99	—	—	—	—
Slovenia	—	—	—	99.9	100.5	0.99	—	—	—	—
Tajikistan	90	91.9	0.98	100.2	108.2	0.93	0.91	3	0.86	4
Turkey	96	102	0.94	96.3	104.7	0.92	0.91	3	0.89	4
Turkmenistan	—	—	—	—	—	—	—	—	—	—
Ukraine	88.7	88.9	1	—	—	—	—	—	—	—
Uzbekistan	80.7	82.2	0.98	—	—	—	—	—	—	—
Latin America and the Caribbean										
Antigua and Barbuda	—	—	—	—	—	—	—	—	—	—
Argentina	—	—	—	119.8	120.4	1	—	—	—	—
Bahamas	—	—	—	89	92.1	0.97	—	—	—	—
Barbados	93.2	93	1	109.9	110.2	1	1	2	1	2
Belize	110.7	112.5	0.98	126.4	129.9	0.97	0.97	3	0.96	3
Bolivia	90.4	99	0.91	115.1	116.7	0.99	1.03	1	1.11	1
Brazil	—	—	—	149.9	159.1	0.94	—	—	—	—
Chile	99.1	100.6	0.98	101.4	103.9	0.98	0.98	3	0.98	3

Table A1.7

Female and male
gross primary
enrollment rates
and ratios, 1990 and
2000, and projections
for 2005 and 2015
(continued)

Region/country	1990			2000			2005		2015	
	Female rate	Male rate	Female to male ratio	Female rate	Male rate	Female to male ratio	Projected female to male ratio	Rank[a]	Projected female to male ratio	Rank[a]
Colombia	109.4	95.3	1.15	112.1	112.7	1	0.93	3	0.78	4
Costa Rica	100.1	101.4	0.99	105.3	108.3	0.97	0.96	3	0.94	3
Cuba	96.2	99.1	0.97	99.8	103.9	0.96	0.96	3	0.95	3
Dominica	—	—	—	—	—	—	—	—	—	—
Dominican Republic	—	—	—	122.2	125.7	0.97	—	—	—	—
Ecuador	—	—	—	114.9	115.1	1	—	—	—	—
El Salvador	81.5	80.7	1.01	106.9	111.6	0.96	0.94	3	0.88	4
Grenada	—	—	—	—	—	—	—	—	—	—
Guatemala	72.4	82.6	0.88	97.7	106.5	0.92	0.94	3	0.98	3
Guyana	92.9	94.2	0.99	117.7	121.6	0.97	0.96	3	0.94	3
Haiti	46.4	49.1	0.94	—	—	—	—	—	—	—
Honduras	111.5	106.1	1.05	107.1	105	1.02	1	2	0.98	3
Jamaica	100.9	101.7	0.99	99.1	100.1	0.99	0.99	3	0.99	3
Mexico	112.4	115.2	0.98	112.7	113.6	0.99	1	2	1	2
Nicaragua	96.5	90.7	1.06	104.1	103	1.01	0.99	3	0.94	3
Panama	104.1	108.3	0.96	110.1	113.1	0.97	0.98	3	0.99	3
Paraguay	103.5	107.2	0.97	111	115.2	0.96	0.96	3	0.95	3
Peru	116.8	120.1	0.97	126.4	127.5	0.99	1	2	1.02	1
St. Kitts and Nevis	—	—	—	—	—	—	—	—	—	—
St. Lucia	134.9	142.5	0.95	109.2	115.4	0.95	0.95	3	0.95	3
St. Vincent and the Grenadines	—	—	—	—	—	—	—	—	—	—
Suriname	100.1	100.4	1	126.5	126.8	1	1	2	1	2
Trinidad and Tobago	96.4	97	0.99	99.4	101.4	0.98	0.98	3	0.97	3
Uruguay	107.9	109.2	0.99	108.5	110.2	0.98	0.98	3	0.97	3
Venezuela	97.2	94.3	1.03	101	102.8	0.98	0.96	3	0.9	3
Middle East and North Africa										
Algeria	92.1	108.8	0.85	107.4	116.4	0.92	0.96	3	1.03	1
Bahrain	110.2	110	1	103.1	103.3	1	1	2	1	2
Djibouti	33.5	46.8	0.71	34.7	45.9	0.76	0.79	4	0.84	4
Egypt	85.9	101.5	0.85	96.1	102.9	0.93	0.97	3	1.05	1
Iraq	106.6	126	0.85	91.3	111.4	0.82	0.81	4	0.77	4
Israel	99.5	96.4	1.03	113.6	114.1	1	0.99	3	0.96	3
Jordan	101	100.3	1.01	101	100.6	1	1	2	0.99	3
Kuwait	58.7	61.7	0.95	93.3	94.8	0.98	1	2	1.02	1
Lebanon	—	—	—	97.2	100.6	0.97	—	—	—	—
Libyan Arab Jamahiriya	101.4	108.1	0.94	116.6	114.6	1.02	1.06	1	1.14	1
Morocco	53	77.1	0.69	87.7	100.8	0.87	0.96	3	1.14	1
Oman	81.9	90.3	0.91	70.8	73.7	0.96	0.98	3	1.03	1
Palestinian Autonomous Territories	—	—	—	108.5	107.3	1.01	—	—	—	—
Qatar	97.2	104.1	0.93	104.5	104.8	1	1.03	1	1.11	1
Saudi Arabia	71.6	81.9	0.87	66.2	68.7	0.96	1	2	1.1	1
Sudan	45.7	59.4	0.77	54	63.5	0.85	0.89	4	0.97	3
Syrian Arab Republic	102.3	114.2	0.9	105.1	113	0.93	0.95	3	0.98	3
Tunisia	106.6	119.5	0.89	114.7	119.8	0.96	0.99	3	1.07	1
United Arab Emirates	104	100.7	1.03	98.9	99.2	1	0.99	3	0.96	3
Yemen	32.7	82.7	0.45	61	96.5	0.63	0.72	4	0.9	3
South Asia										
Afghanistan	20.6	37.2	0.55	—	—	—	—	—	—	—
Bangladesh	73.6	85.2	0.86	100.9	99.7	1.01	1.09	1	1.24	1
Bhutan	—	—	—	—	—	—	—	—	—	—
India	84.5	111.2	0.76	91.7	110.8	0.83	0.87	4	0.93	3

Table A1.7

Female and male gross primary enrollment rates and ratios, 1990 and 2000, and projections for 2005 and 2015

(continued)

Region/country	1990 Female rate	1990 Male rate	1990 Female to male ratio	2000 Female rate	2000 Male rate	2000 Female to male ratio	2005 Projected female to male ratio	Rank[a]	2015 Projected female to male ratio	Rank[a]
Iran, Islamic Rep.	102.2	114.7	0.89	84.7	88	0.96	0.99	3	1.07	1
Maldives	—	—	—	131.2	131.1	1	—	—	—	—
Nepal	88.3	144.9	0.61	108	127.7	0.85	0.97	3	1.21	1
Pakistan	—	—	—	63.1	85.2	0.74	—	—	—	—
Sri Lanka	107.8	112	0.96	—	—	—	—	—	—	—
Sub-Saharan Africa										
Angola	—	—	—	69.1	78.1	0.88	—	—	—	—
Benin	38.7	78	0.5	77.6	113.4	0.68	0.77	4	0.95	3
Botswana	117.9	110.3	1.07	108.3	108.3	1	0.97	3	0.89	4
Burkina Faso	24.5	39.3	0.62	36.8	51.7	0.71	0.75	4	0.85	4
Burundi	65.1	77.7	0.84	57.9	72.5	0.8	0.78	4	0.74	4
Cameroon	91.7	106.7	0.86	100.2	115.4	0.87	0.88	4	0.89	4
Cape Verde	—	—	—	137.4	140.2	0.98	—	—	—	—
Central African Republic	50.1	78.8	0.63	61.2	88.9	0.69	0.72	4	0.78	4
Chad	33.6	75.2	0.45	56.7	89.6	0.63	0.72	4	0.9	3
Comoros	63.1	87	0.73	80.1	91.7	0.87	0.94	3	1.08	1
Congo, Dem. Rep	60.6	81.4	0.74	—	—	—	—	—	—	—
Congo, Rep.	124.6	141.1	0.88	92.8	101	0.92	0.94	3	0.98	3
Côte d'Ivoire	52.8	74.4	0.71	68.3	89.3	0.76	0.79	4	0.84	4
Equatorial Guinea	—	—	—	114.7	126	0.91	—	—	—	—
Eritrea	21.8	23.1	0.94	53.6	65.3	0.82	0.76	4	0.64	5
Ethiopia	26.4	40.1	0.66	52.4	76.4	0.69	0.7	4	0.73	4
Gabon	—	—	—	143.2	144.4	0.99	—	—	—	—
Gambia	51.3	75.7	0.68	78.3	86.3	0.91	1.02	1	1.25	1
Ghana	66.3	79.7	0.83	76.5	83.8	0.91	0.95	3	1.03	1
Guinea	21.7	45.9	0.47	55.8	77.9	0.72	0.85	4	1.1	1
Guinea-Bissau	—	—	—	66.3	99.1	0.67	—	—	—	—
Kenya	91.9	96.6	0.95	93.4	94.6	0.99	1.01	1	1.05	1
Lesotho	128.2	104.7	1.22	117.7	112.4	1.05	0.97	3	0.8	4
Liberia	—	—	—	99.3	136.7	0.73			—	—
Madagascar	92.5	94.7	0.98	101.1	105.1	0.96	0.95	3	0.93	3
Malawi	61	72.8	0.84	135.3	138.6	0.98	1.05	1	1.19	1
Mali	20.5	34.9	0.59	51.2	71.2	0.72	0.78	4	0.92	3
Mauritania	42.2	57.1	0.74	80.2	85.8	0.93	1.03	1	1.22	1
Mauritius	109.5	109	1	108.4	108.9	1	1	2	1	2
Mozambique	59.4	78.7	0.75	79.2	103.9	0.76	0.77	4	0.78	4
Namibia	134.1	122.9	1.09	112.9	111.5	1.01	0.97	3	0.89	4
Niger	20.3	34.7	0.58	28.6	42.2	0.68	0.73	4	0.83	4
Nigeria	80.4	102.5	0.78	—	—	—	—	—	—	—
Rwanda	70	71.5	0.98	118.3	119	0.99	1	2	1	2
São Tomé and Principe	—	—	—	—	—	—	—	—	—	—
Senegal	49.9	67.9	0.73	70.3	79.3	0.89	0.97	3	1.13	1
Seychelles	—	—	—	—	—	—	—	—	—	—
Sierra Leone	40.9	59	0.69	—	—	—	—	—	—	—
Somalia	—	—	—	—	—	—	—	—	—	—
South Africa	107.5	109.4	0.98	108.3	114.5	0.95	0.94	3	0.9	3
Swaziland	111.8	114	0.98	121.2	128	0.95	0.94	3	0.9	3
Tanzania, United Rep.	66.4	67.5	0.98	63.2	62.9	1	1.01	1	1.03	1
Togo	86.7	132.3	0.66	110.3	137.9	0.8	0.87	4	1.01	1
Uganda	61.3	76.4	0.8	128.9	142.6	0.9	0.95	3	1.05	1
Zambia	—	—	—	76	80.3	0.95	—	—	—	—
Zimbabwe	107.3	108.3	0.99	93.4	96.5	0.97	0.96	3	0.94	3

Table A1.8

Female and male gross secondary enrollment rates and ratios, 1990 and 2000, and projections for 2005 and 2015

— Not available.

a. Rank is defined as follows: 1 = ratio greater than 1 (reverse gap), 2 = ratio equal to 1 (parity), 3 = 0.90–0.99 (on track), 4 = 0.70–0.89 (falling behind), 5 = 0–0.69 (off track).

Source: UNESCO 2004.

Region/Country	1990			2000			2005		2015	
	Female rate	Male rate	Female to male ratio	Female rate	Male rate	Female to male ratio	Projected female to male ratio	Rank[a]	Projected female to male ratio	Rank[a]
Developed countries										
Australia	83.4	80.1	1.04	161.3	160.2	1.01	1	2	0.97	3
Austria	98.1	105.4	0.93	97	101	0.96	0.97	3	1	2
Belgium	102.2	101.4	1.01	104.5	105.4	0.99	0.98	3	0.96	3
Canada	101	100.5	1	106	106.7	0.99	0.99	3	0.98	3
Denmark	109.8	108.6	1.01	131.3	125.3	1.05	1.07	1	1.11	1
Finland	127	106.3	1.19	132.6	119.7	1.11	1.07	1	0.99	3
France	101.1	95.9	1.05	108.1	107.4	1.01	0.99	3	0.95	3
Germany	96.9	99.5	0.97	99	99.9	0.99	1	2	1.02	1
Greece	92.9	94.7	0.98	99.4	97.5	1.02	1.04	1	1.08	1
Iceland	98	101.4	0.97	112.6	105.1	1.07	1.12	1	1.22	1
Ireland	104.7	95.9	1.09	127.4	119	1.07	1.06	1	1.04	1
Italy	83	83.4	1	94.5	97.3	0.97	0.96	3	0.93	3
Japan	98	96.3	1.02	103	102	1.01	1	2	1	2
Luxembourg	—	—	—	97.3	91.7	1.06	—	—	—	—
Netherlands	114.7	124.1	0.92	122.4	126.4	0.97	0.99	3	1.05	1
New Zealand	89.8	88.3	1.02	115.9	109	1.06	1.08	1	1.12	1
Norway	104.6	101.4	1.03	115.9	113.4	1.02	1.02	1	1	2
Portugal	72.2	62.3	1.16	116.9	110.5	1.06	1.01	1	0.91	3
Spain	107.5	100.9	1.07	118.7	112.7	1.05	1.04	1	1.02	1
Sweden	92.3	88.2	1.05	166.5	132	1.26	1.37	1	1.58	1
Switzerland	96.4	101.7	0.95	96.4	102.7	0.94	0.94	3	0.93	3
United Kingdom	88.1	83	1.06	169.1	144.3	1.17	1.22	1	1.33	1
United States	93.5	92.3	1.01	95.6	94.7	1.01	1.01	1	1.01	1
East Asia and Pacific										
Brunei Darussalam	71.4	66.4	1.07	84.6	80.3	1.05	1.04	1	1.02	1
Cambodia	17.4	40.2	0.43	13.5	23.7	0.57	0.64	5	0.78	4
China	41.7	55.3	0.75	58.4	77.2	0.76	0.77	4	0.78	4
Fiji	—	—	—	83.4	76.7	1.09	—	—	—	—
Hong Kong, China	—	—	—	—	—	—	—	—	—	—
Indonesia	41.1	49.7	0.83	56.4	57.6	0.98	1.06	1	1.21	1
Kiribati	—	—	—	—	—	—	—	—	—	—
Korea, DPR	—	—	—	—	—	—	—	—	—	—
Korea, Rep. of	88.5	91.1	0.97	94.1	94.1	1	1.02	1	1.05	1
Lao, PDR	18.6	30	0.62	31.3	43.6	0.72	0.77	4	0.87	4
Malaysia	58.2	54.5	1.07	74	66.9	1.11	1.13	1	1.17	1
Marshall Islands	—	—	—	—	—	—	—	—	—	—
Micronesia, Fed. States	—	—	—	—	—	—	—	—	—	—
Mongolia	87.7	77.2	1.14	77	63.3	1.22	1.26	1	1.34	1
Myanmar	22.2	22.7	0.98	37.5	39.6	0.95	0.94	3	0.9	3
Nauru	—	—	—	—	—	—	—	—	—	—
Palau	—	—	—	85.8	83	1.03	—	—	—	—
Papua New Guinea	10.6	14.7	0.72	18.2	23.7	0.77	0.8	4	0.85	4
Philippines	72.4	69.7	1.04	80.9	73.8	1.1	1.13	1	1.19	1
Samoa	39.9	32.7	1.22	78.7	72.6	1.08	1.01	1	0.87	4
Singapore	65.6	70.5	0.93	—	—	—	—	—	—	—
Solomon Islands	10.7	16.9	0.64	—	—	—	—	—	—	—
Thailand	29.9	32.2	0.93	79.9	84	0.95	0.96	3	0.98	3
Timor-Leste	—	—	—	—	—	—	—	—	—	—
Tonga	—	—	—	102.9	96.6	1.07	—	—	—	—
Tuvalu	—	—	—	—	—	—	—	—	—	—

Table A1.8

Female and male gross secondary enrollment rates and ratios, 1990 and 2000, and projections for 2005 and 2015

(continued)

Region/Country	1990 Female rate	1990 Male rate	1990 Female to male ratio	2000 Female rate	2000 Male rate	2000 Female to male ratio	2005 Projected female to male ratio	2005 Rank[a]	2015 Projected female to male ratio	2015 Rank[a]
Vanuatu	14.8	18.6	0.79	25.7	30.7	0.84	0.87	4	0.91	3
Viet Nam	—	—	—	—	—	—	—	—	—	—
Europe and Central Asia										
Albania	72.2	84	0.86	79.6	77.2	1.03	1.12	1	1.29	1
Armenia	—	—	—	—	—	—	—	—	—	—
Azerbaijan	89.7	89.7	1	84	86.3	0.97	0.96	3	0.93	3
Belarus	—	—	—	85.8	83.1	1.03	—	—	—	—
Bosnia and Herzegovina	—	—	—	—	—	—	—	—	—	—
Bulgaria	76.8	73.7	1.04	93.1	95.3	0.98	0.95	3	0.89	4
Croatia	79.9	72.7	1.1	84.6	81.7	1.04	1.01	1	0.95	3
Cyprus	72.8	71.4	1.02	93.9	93	1.01	1	2	1	2
Czech Republic	89.7	92.5	0.97	96.1	93.3	1.03	1.06	1	1.12	1
Estonia	106.6	97.6	1.09	92.3	91.1	1.01	0.97	3	0.89	4
Georgia	93.5	96.1	0.97	78.3	77.1	1.02	1.05	1	1.1	1
Hungary	78.9	78.2	1.01	99	98.2	1.01	1.01	1	1.01	1
Kazakhstan	99.4	96.7	1.03	87.1	89.8	0.97	0.94	3	0.88	4
Kyrgyzstan	101.3	98.8	1.02	85.8	85.5	1	0.99	3	0.97	3
Latvia	93.3	93.1	1	91.5	90.3	1.01	1.02	1	1.02	1
Lithuania	—	—	—	94.8	95.6	0.99	—	—	—	—
Macedonia TFYR	55.5	56	0.99	82.9	85.4	0.97	0.96	3	0.94	3
Moldova, Rep.	83.4	76.7	1.09	72.1	70.2	1.03	1	2	0.94	3
Poland	83.5	79.6	1.05	100	102.6	0.97	0.93	3	0.85	4
Romania	91.5	92.5	0.99	82.9	81.8	1.01	1.02	1	1.04	1
Russian Federation	96.1	90.6	1.06	86.3	80.4	1.07	1.08	1	1.09	1
Serbia and Montenegro	64.5	62.4	1.03	60.8	58.2	1.04	1.05	1	1.06	1
Slovakia	—	—	—	87.9	86.7	1.01	—	—	—	—
Slovenia	—	—	—	107.5	105.3	1.02	—	—	—	—
Tajikistan	—	—	—	71.2	85.7	0.83	—	—	—	—
Turkey	36.6	57.5	0.64	47.7	67.3	0.71	0.74	4	0.82	4
Turkmenistan	—	—	—	—	—	—	—	—	—	—
Ukraine	—	—	—	—	—	—	—	—	—	—
Uzbekistan	94.9	103.8	0.91	—	—	—	—	—	—	—
Latin America and the Caribbean										
Antigua and Barbuda	—	—	—	—	—	—	—	—	—	—
Argentina	—	—	—	99.9	93.5	1.07	—	—	—	—
Bahamas	—	—	—	126.1	130.8	0.96	—	—	—	—
Barbados	—	—	—	102	101.3	1.01	—	—	—	—
Belize	47.1	40.9	1.15	77	71.2	1.08	1.05	1	0.98	3
Bolivia	33.6	39.5	0.85	77.9	81.3	0.96	1.01	1	1.13	1
Brazil	—	—	—	113.8	103.3	1.1	—	—	—	—
Chile	76.5	70.5	1.08	86.5	84.5	1.02	0.99	3	0.93	3
Colombia	52.8	46.8	1.13	73.2	66.6	1.1	1.09	1	1.06	1
Costa Rica	42.6	40.5	1.05	62.8	57.7	1.09	1.11	1	1.15	1
Cuba	95	83	1.14	86.6	82.6	1.05	1.01	1	0.92	3
Dominica	—	—	—	—	—	—	—	—	—	—
Dominican Republic	—	—	—	66.5	52.7	1.26	—	—	—	—
Ecuador	—	—	—	58	56.9	1.02	—	—	—	—
El Salvador	27.2	25.6	1.06	—	—	—	—	—	—	—
Grenada	—	—	—	—	—	—	—	—	—	—
Guatemala	—	—	—	35.4	38.5	0.92	—	—	—	—
Guyana	81.1	76.2	1.06	115.5	116.8	0.99	0.96	3	0.88	4

Table A1.8

Female and male
gross secondary
enrollment rates
and ratios, 1990 and
2000, and projections
for 2005 and 2015

(continued)

	1990			2000			2005		2015	
Region/Country	Female rate	Male rate	Female to male ratio	Female rate	Male rate	Female to male ratio	Projected female to male ratio	Rank[a]	Projected female to male ratio	Rank[a]
Haiti	20.2	21.1	0.96	—	—	—	—	—	—	—
Honduras	—	—	—	—	—	—	—	—	—	—
Jamaica	67.1	63.6	1.06	84.8	81.9	1.04	1.03	1	1.01	1
Mexico	53.5	53	1.01	77.3	73.4	1.05	1.07	1	1.11	1
Nicaragua	46.7	34	1.37	58.4	49.7	1.18	1.09	1	0.89	4
Panama	64.7	60.5	1.07	71.1	67.3	1.06	1.06	1	1.05	1
Paraguay	31.6	30.3	1.04	60.8	58.8	1.03	1.02	1	1.02	1
Peru	—	—	—	82.4	88.7	0.93	—	—	—	—
St. Kitts and Nevis	—	—	—	—	—	—	—	—	—	—
St. Lucia	62.8	43.3	1.45	100.4	76.9	1.31	1.24	1	1.1	1
St. Vincent and the Grenadines	—	—	—	—	—	—	—	—	—	—
Suriname	55.8	48.5	1.15	94.3	80	1.18	1.19	1	1.23	1
Trinidad and Tobago	82.4	78.5	1.05	83.6	78.1	1.07	1.08	1	1.1	1
Uruguay	—	—	—	104.5	91.8	1.14	—	—	—	—
Venezuela	40.3	29.2	1.38	64.8	54.1	1.2	1.11	1	0.93	3
Middle East and North Africa										
Algeria	54.3	67.4	0.81	73.4	68.2	1.08	1.22	1	1.49	1
Bahrain	101.4	98.1	1.03	105.1	97.8	1.07	1.09	1	1.13	1
Djibouti	10.7	16.7	0.64	14.4	23.3	0.62	0.61	5	0.59	5
Egypt	68.2	83.9	0.81	83.1	88.2	0.94	1	2	1.13	1
Iraq	38.1	59.8	0.64	29.1	47.1	0.62	0.61	5	0.59	5
Israel	91.5	84.9	1.08	93	93.5	0.99	0.95	3	0.85	4
Jordan	64.8	62.1	1.04	89	86.4	1.03	1.02	1	1.02	1
Kuwait	42.5	43.3	0.98	56.9	55	1.04	1.07	1	1.13	1
Lebanon	—	—	—	79.4	72	1.1	—	—	—	—
Libyan Arab Jamahiriya	—	—	—	—	—	—	—	—	—	—
Morocco	29.9	40.9	0.73	35	43.6	0.8	0.84	4	0.91	3
Oman	40.2	51.2	0.78	67.5	68.9	0.98	1.08	1	1.28	1
Palestinian Autonomous Territory	—	—	—	85.7	79.6	1.08	—	—	—	—
Qatar	85.6	78.8	1.09	91.7	86.4	1.06	1.05	1	1.02	1
Saudi Arabia	41.5	51.7	0.8	64.3	71.2	0.9	0.95	3	1.05	1
Sudan	19.1	24.2	0.79	—	—	—	—	—	—	—
Syrian Arab Republic	43.7	59.8	0.73	40.8	45.7	0.89	0.97	3	1.13	1
Tunisia	39.5	50	0.79	80.4	76.3	1.05	1.18	1	1.44	1
United Arab Emirates	72.3	57.9	1.25	79.7	71.1	1.12	1.06	1	0.93	3
Yemen	—	—	—	—	—	—	—	—	—	—
South Asia										
Afghanistan	—	—	—	—	—	—	—	—	—	—
Bangladesh	13.6	26	0.52	46.9	44.6	1.05	1.32	1	1.85	1
Bhutan	—	—	—	—	—	—	—	—	—	—
India	32.7	54.8	0.6	40.1	56.7	0.71	0.76	4	0.88	4
Iran, Islamic Rep.	50	66.9	0.75	75.4	80.7	0.93	1.02	1	1.2	1
Maldives	—	—	—	57.2	53.4	1.07	—	—	—	—
Nepal	20.7	46.7	0.44	43.2	57.5	0.75	0.91	3	1.21	1
Pakistan	16.2	33.7	0.48	19.7	29.1	0.68	0.78	4	0.98	3
Sri Lanka	78.5	72.4	1.09	—	—	—	—	—	—	—
Sub-Saharan Africa										
Angola	—	—	—	16	19.3	0.83	—	—	—	—
Benin	6.8	16.6	0.41	13.5	30.1	0.45	0.47	5	0.51	5
Botswana	45	40.8	1.1	81.5	76.8	1.06	1.04	1	1	2

		1990			2000			2005		2015	
Table A1.8 Female and male gross secondary enrollment rates and ratios, 1990 and 2000, and projections for 2005 and 2015 *(continued)*	Region/Country	Female rate	Male rate	Female to male ratio	Female rate	Male rate	Female to male ratio	Projected female to male ratio	Rank[a]	Projected female to male ratio	Rank[a]
	Burkina Faso	4.6	8.8	0.52	8	12.4	0.64	0.7	4	0.82	4
	Burundi	4	6.9	0.58	9	11.6	0.77	0.87	4	1.06	1
	Cameroon	22.9	32.2	0.71	—	—	—	—	—	—	—
	Cape Verde	—	—	—	76.7	75	1.02	—	—	—	—
	Central African Republic	6.7	17	0.39	—	—	—	—	—	—	—
	Chad	2.3	11.8	0.2	5.1	17.9	0.28	0.32	5	0.4	5
	Comoros	13.8	21.2	0.65	18.5	22.6	0.82	0.9	3	1.07	1
	Congo, Dem. Rep.	—	—	—	—	—	—	—	—	—	—
	Congo, Rep.	43.3	61.5	0.7	38.1	45.8	0.83	0.9	3	1.02	1
	Côte d'Ivoire	13.7	28.4	0.48	16.5	29.9	0.55	0.59	5	0.66	5
	Equatorial Guinea	—	—	—	18.6	43.4	0.43	—	—	—	—
	Eritrea	—	—	—	23.5	33.1	0.71	—	—	—	—
	Ethiopia	12	16	0.75	14.3	21.7	0.66	0.62	5	0.53	5
	Gabon	—	—	—	57.7	61.4	0.94	—	—	—	—
	Gambia	—	—	—	30.7	44.1	0.7	—	—	—	—
	Ghana	27.1	42.9	0.63	32.5	39.9	0.81	0.9	3	1.08	1
	Guinea	4.7	14.2	0.33	—	—	—	—	—	—	—
	Guinea-Bissau	—	—	—	14.4	26.4	0.54	—	—	—	—
	Kenya	20.2	27.4	0.74	29.2	32.1	0.91	1	2	1.17	1
	Lesotho	31.5	21.2	1.49	35.8	29.8	1.2	1.06	1	0.76	4
	Liberia	—	—	—	18.4	26.6	0.69	—	—	—	—
	Madagascar	17.4	17.9	0.97	—	—	—	—	—	—	—
	Malawi	4.8	10.3	0.46	30.8	40.5	0.76	0.91	3	1.21	1
	Mali	4.6	9.2	0.5	—	—	—	—	—	—	—
	Mauritania	8.8	18.9	0.47	19.6	22.3	0.88	1.09	1	1.5	1
	Mauritius	53.1	52.7	1.01	74.7	79.4	0.94	0.9	3	0.83	4
	Mozambique	5.5	9.5	0.57	9.3	14.5	0.64	0.68	5	0.75	4
	Namibia	45.1	35.9	1.26	65.5	58	1.13	1.07	1	0.93	3
	Niger	3.8	8.9	0.43	5.1	7.7	0.66	0.78	4	1.01	1
	Nigeria	21.5	27.9	0.77	—	—	—	—	—	—	—
	Rwanda	6.9	9.2	0.76	14	14.2	0.98	1.09	1	1.31	1
	São Tomé and Principe	—	—	—	—	—	—	—	—	—	—
	Senegal	11.2	21.2	0.53	14.2	21.4	0.66	0.73	4	0.86	4
	Seychelles	—	—	—	—	—	—	—	—	—	—
	Sierra Leone	12.1	21.1	0.57	23.8	29.1	0.82	0.95	3	1.19	1
	Somalia	—	—	—	—	—	—	—	—	—	—
	South Africa	71.8	61.9	1.16	91.2	83.4	1.09	1.06	1	0.99	3
	Swaziland	44.9	46.5	0.97	59.8	60	1	1.02	1	1.05	1
	Tanzania, United Rep.	3.9	5.6	0.7	5.2	6.4	0.81	0.87	4	0.98	3
	Togo	11.5	33.9	0.34	24.4	53.8	0.45	0.51	5	0.62	5
	Uganda	9	15.9	0.56	11.9	18.5	0.64	0.68	5	0.76	4
	Zambia	—	—	—	21.1	25.9	0.81	—	—	—	—
	Zimbabwe	45	51.5	0.87	41.6	47.3	0.88	0.89	4	0.9	3

Table A1.9

Female and male gross tertiary enrollment rates and ratios, 1990 and 2000, and projections for 2005 and 2015

— Not available.

a. For some countries, 1999 data were used when 2000 data were unavailable.

b. Rank is defined as follows: 1 = ratio greater than 1 (reverse gap), 2 = ratio equal to 1 (parity), 3 = 0.90–0.99 (on track), 4 = 0.70–0.89 (falling behind), 5 = 0–0.69 (off track).

Source: UNESCO 2004.

Region/Country	1990			2000[a]			2005		2015	
	Female rate	Male rate	Female to male ratio	Female rate	Male rate	Female to male ratio	Projected female to male ratio	Rank[b]	Projected female to male ratio	Rank[b]
Developed countries										
Australia	38.6	33.2	1.16	70.3	57	1.20	1.28	1	1.36	1
Austria	30.4	34.7	0.88	61.7	54	1.10	1.27	1	1.53	1
Belgium	37.9	39	0.97	62.4	54	1.20	1.25	1	1.44	1
Canada	102.9	83.7	1.23	68	51	1.30	1.4	1	1.51	1
Denmark	38.6	33.8	1.14	67.8	50	1.40	1.46	1	1.67	1
Finland	50.6	44.6	1.13	—	—	—	—	—	—	—
France	42.8	36.7	1.17	59.2	48	1.20	1.26	1	1.32	1
Germany	—	—	—	—	—	—	—	—	—	—
Greece	35.6	36.5	0.98	65.8	60	1.10	1.16	1	1.28	1
Iceland	28.9	20.8	1.39	62	36	1.70	1.92	1	2.27	1
Ireland	29.1	32.3	0.9	53.3	42	1.30	1.46	1	1.83	1
Italy	31	33.1	0.94	56.9	43	1.30	1.51	1	1.89	1
Japan	24.1	37	0.65	43.9	51	0.90	0.95	3	1.15	1
Luxembourg	—	—	—	10.1	9	1.20	—	—	—	—
Netherlands	35	42.2	0.83	56.8	53	1.10	1.19	1	1.43	1
New Zealand	42.2	38.5	1.1	84	55	1.50	1.73	1	2.15	1
Norway	45.9	38.7	1.19	84.8	56	1.50	1.69	1	2.02	1
Portugal	26.7	20.7	1.29	58.1	43	1.40	1.41	1	1.49	1
Spain	38.6	35.5	1.09	63.7	55	1.20	1.18	1	1.24	1
Sweden	35	28.6	1.22	84.8	56	1.50	1.67	1	1.97	1
Switzerland	17.8	31.3	0.57	36.8	47	0.80	0.89	4	1.1	1
United Kingdom	28.3	30.3	0.93	66.8	53	1.30	1.44	1	1.78	1
United States	81.7	65.4	1.25	82.8	63	1.30	1.36	1	1.43	1
East Asia and Pacific										
Brunei Darussalam	—	—	—	20.4	10	2.00	—	—	—	—
Cambodia	—	—	—	1.6	4	0.40	—	—	—	—
China	2	3.8	0.52	6.5	12	0.50	0.52	5	0.52	5
Fiji	—	—	—	—	—	—	—	—	—	—
Hong Kong, China	—	—	—	—	—	—	—	—	—	—
Indonesia	—	—	—	12.7	16	0.80	—	—	—	—
Korea, DPR	—	—	—	—	—	—	—	—	—	—
Korea, Rep.	25.4	52	0.49	57	97	0.60	0.64	5	0.74	4
Kiribati	—	—	—	—	—	—	—	—	—	—
Lao, PDR	—	—	—	2.5	4	0.60	—	—	—	—
Malaysia	7	7.9	0.89	29.3	27	1.10	1.18	1	1.37	1
Marshall Islands	—	—	—	—	—	—	—	—	—	—
Micronesia, Fed. States of	—	—	—	—	—	—	—	—	—	—
Mongolia	18.8	10	1.88	41.6	24	1.70	1.67	1	1.53	1
Myanmar	—	—	—	14.7	8	1.80	—	—	—	—
Nauru	—	—	—	—	—	—	—	—	—	—
Palau	—	—	—	40.1	22	1.80	—	—	—	—
Papua New Guinea	—	—	—	—	—	—	—	—	—	—
Philippines	32.7	23	1.42	—	—	—	—	—	—	—
Samoa	—	—	—	11.2	11	1.10	—	—	—	—
Singapore	14.6	21.4	0.68	—	—	—	—	—	—	—
Solomon Islands	—	—	—	—	—	—	—	—	—	—
Thailand	—	—	—	37.1	34	1.10	—	—	—	—
Timor-Leste	—	—	—	—	—	—	—	—	—	—
Tonga	—	—	—	4.3	3	1.30	—	—	—	—
Tuvalu	—	—	—	—	—	—	—	—	—	—

Table A1.9
Female and male gross tertiary enrollment rates and ratios, 1990 and 2000, and projections for 2005 and 2015
(continued)

Region/Country	1990 Female rate	1990 Male rate	1990 Female to male ratio	2000[a] Female rate	2000[a] Male rate	2000[a] Female to male ratio	2005 Projected female to male ratio	2005 Rank[b]	2015 Projected female to male ratio	2015 Rank[b]
Vanuatu	—	—	—	—	—	—	—	—	—	—
Viet Nam	—	—	—	8.2	11	0.70	—	—	—	—
Europe and Central Asia										
Albania	7.4	6.5	1.13	19.1	11	1.70	1.97	1	2.53	1
Armenia	—	—	—	—	—	—	—	—	—	—
Azerbaijan	19.3	28.5	0.68	22.4	23	1.00	1.15	1	1.45	1
Belarus	50.9	46.3	1.1	63.2	49	1.30	1.39	1	1.58	1
Bosnia and Herzegovina	—	—	—	—	—	—	—	—	—	—
Bulgaria	33.3	30.2	1.1	47.1	35	1.40	1.48	1	1.73	1
Croatia	—	—	—	34.8	30	1.10	—	—	—	—
Cyprus	13.3	12	1.1	25.5	19	1.40	1.48	1	1.73	1
Czech Republic	14.9	18.4	0.81	30.5	29	1.10	1.17	1	1.41	1
Estonia	27.1	25.2	1.07	70.2	45	1.60	1.79	1	2.27	1
Georgia	39.9	34.3	1.17	34.3	35	1.00	0.9	3	0.72	4
Hungary	14.8	14	1.06	44.9	35	1.30	1.38	1	1.59	1
Kazakhstan	—	—	—	33.6	28	1.20			—	—
Kyrgyzstan	—	—	—	42	40	1.00	—	—	—	—
Latvia	28.1	21.9	1.29	78.9	48	1.70	1.83	1	2.19	1
Lithuania	37.8	29.5	1.28	63.3	42	1.50	1.63	1	1.86	1
Macedonia TFYR	17.6	16	1.11	27.9	21	1.30	1.43	1	1.64	1
Moldova, Rep.	—	—	—	31.4	25	1.30	—	—	—	—
Poland	25.4	19	1.34	65.7	46	1.40	1.49	1	1.59	1
Romania	9.2	9.9	0.93	29.9	25	1.20	1.34	1	1.6	1
Russian Federation	59.9	47	1.27	72.3	56	1.30	1.3	1	1.32	1
Serbia and Montenegro	—	—	—	29.1	23	1.20	—	—	—	—
Slovakia	—	—	—	31.7	29	1.10	—	—	—	—
Slovenia	27.7	21.5	1.29	69.8	52	1.40	1.38	1	1.44	1
Tajikistan	17.3	28.4	0.61	6.8	21	0.30	0.18	5	−0.11	5
Turkey	9.4	18	0.52	19.9	27	0.70	0.84	4	1.05	1
Turkmenistan	—	—	—	—	—	—	—	—	—	—
Ukraine	48.7	47.5	1.03	—	—	—	—	—	—	—
Uzbekistan	—	—	—	—	—	—	—	—	—	—
Latin America and the Caribbean										
Antigua and Barbuda	—	—	—	—	—	—	—	—	—	—
Argentina	—	—	—	59.7	36	1.60	—	—	—	—
Bahamas	—	—	—	—	—	—	—	—	—	—
Barbados	30.9	24.4	1.27	—	—	—	—	—	—	—
Belize	—	—	—	—	—	—	—	—	—	—
Bolivia	—	—	—	—	—	—	—	—	—	—
Brazil	11.7	11	1.06	18.6	14	1.30	1.41	1	1.64	1
Chile	—	—	—	35.9	39	0.90	—	—	—	—
Colombia	13.8	12.9	1.07	24.3	22	1.10	1.1	1	1.12	1
Costa Rica	—	—	—	17.6	15	1.20	—	—	—	—
Cuba	24.6	17.4	1.41	26.4	23	1.10	1	2	0.73	4
Dominica	—	—	—	—	—	—	—	—	—	—
Dominican Republic	—	—	—	—	—	—	—	—	—	—
Ecuador	—	—	—	—	—	—	—	—	—	—
El Salvador	14.1	19.8	0.71	19.4	16	1.20	1.51	1	2.04	1
Grenada	—	—	—	—	—	—	—	—	—	—
Guatemala	—	—	—	—	—	—	—	—	—	—
Guyana	—	—	—	—	—	—	—	—	—	—

Table A1.9
Female and male gross tertiary enrollment rates and ratios, 1990 and 2000, and projections for 2005 and 2015
(continued)

	1990			2000ᵃ			2005		2015	
Region/Country	Female rate	Male rate	Female to male ratio	Female rate	Male rate	Female to male ratio	Projected female to male ratio	Rankᵇ	Projected female to male ratio	Rankᵇ
Haiti	—	—	—	—	—	—	—	—	—	—
Honduras	8	10.3	0.77	16.8	13	1.30	1.58	1	2.12	1
Jamaica	5.9	8.1	0.73	21.5	11	1.90	2.47	1	3.63	1
Mexico	13	17.5	0.74	20.3	21	1.00	1.07	1	1.29	1
Nicaragua	8.7	8.2	1.06	—	—	—	—	—	—	—
Panama	—	—	—	43.8	26	1.70	—	—	—	—
Paraguay	7.9	9	0.88	19.1	14	1.40	1.6	1	2.08	1
Peru	—	—	—	—	—	—	—	—	—	—
St. Kitts and Nevis	—	—	—	—	—	—	—	—	—	—
St. Lucia	5.8	4.2	1.38	—	—	—	—	—	—	—
St. Vincent and the Grenadines	—	—	—	—	—	—	—	—	—	—
Suriname	—	—	—	—	—	—	—	—	—	—
Trinidad and Tobago	6	7.6	0.79	7.8	5	1.50	1.9	1	2.64	1
Uruguay	—	—	—	47	26	1.80	—	—	—	—
Venezuela	—	—	—	34.6	24	1.50	—	—	—	—
Middle East and North Africa										
Algeria	—	—	—	—	—	—	—	—	—	—
Bahrain	19.9	13.8	1.44	—	—	—	—	—	—	—
Djibouti	—	—	—	0.7	1	0.70	—	—	—	—
Egypt	11.5	20.2	0.57	—	—	—	—	—	—	—
Iraq	—	—	—	9.5	18	0.50	—	—	—	—
Israel	36	35.5	1.01	61.6	44	1.40	1.58	1	1.96	1
Jordan	25.5	22.7	1.12	30.6	27	1.10	1.15	1	1.17	1
Kuwait	—	—	—	—	—	—	—	—	—	—
Lebanon	—	—	—	44.2	41	1.10	—	—	—	—
Libyan Arab Jamahiriya	—	—	—	47.9	50	1.00	—	—	—	—
Morocco	8.1	13.6	0.59	9.2	11	0.80	0.91	3	1.12	1
Oman	3.9	4.5	0.87	9.9	7	1.40	1.66	1	2.19	1
Palestinian Autonomous Territory	—	—	—	27.9	29	1.00	—	—	—	—
Qatar	43.8	14.9	2.94	37.6	13	3.00	2.99	1	3.02	1
Saudi Arabia	11.7	14.3	0.82	25.3	20	1.30	1.53	1	2	1
Sudan	2.7	3.1	0.88	—	—	—	—	—	—	—
Syrian Arab Republic	14.9	22.3	0.67	—	—	—	—	—	—	—
Tunisia	6.9	10.5	0.65	21.4	22	1.00	1.13	1	1.45	1
United Arab Emirates	—	—	—	—	—	—	—	—	—	—
Yemen	—	—	—	—	—	—	—	—	—	—
South Asia										
Afghanistan	1.3	2.7	0.48	—	—	—	—	—	—	—
Bangladesh	1.3	6.5	0.2	4.6	9	0.60	0.73	4	1.08	1
Bhutan	—	—	—	—	—	—	—	—	—	—
India	4.3	7.9	0.54	8.3	13	0.70	0.72	4	0.84	4
Iran, Islamic Rep.	6.5	13.4	0.48	9.5	10	0.90	1.16	1	1.61	1
Maldives	—	—	—	—	—	—	—	—	—	—
Nepal	2.6	7.9	0.32	1.9	7	0.30	0.25	5	0.2	5
Pakistan	2.6	4.4	0.59	—	—	—	—	—	—	—
Sri Lanka	3.8	5.6	0.68	—	—	—	—	—	—	—
Sub-Saharan Africa										
Angola	—	—	—	0.5	1	0.60	—	—	—	—
Benin	0.7	5	0.14	1.4	6	0.20	0.29	5	0.39	5
Botswana	3	3.6	0.83	4.4	5	0.90	0.92	3	0.98	3

Table A1.9

Female and male gross tertiary enrollment rates and ratios, 1990 and 2000, and projections for 2005 and 2015

(continued)

| Region/Country | 1990 | | | 2000[a] | | | 2005 | | 2015 | |
	Female rate	Male rate	Female to male ratio	Female rate	Male rate	Female to male ratio	Projected female to male ratio	Rank[b]	Projected female to male ratio	Rank[b]
Burkina Faso	0.3	1.1	0.28	—	—	—	—	—	—	—
Burundi	0.4	1.1	0.36	0.7	2	0.40	0.36	5	0.36	5
Cameroon	—	—	—	—	—	—	—	—	—	—
Cape Verde	—	—	—	—	—	—	—	—	—	—
Central African Republic	0.4	2.9	0.14	0.6	3	0.20	0.22	5	0.27	5
Chad	—	—	—	0.3	2	0.20	—	—	—	—
Comoros	—	—	—	0.9	1	0.70	—	—	—	—
Congo, Dem. Rep.	—	—	—	—	—	—	—	—	—	—
Congo, Rep.	1.9	9.3	0.21	1.2	9	0.10	0.09	5	0.01	5
Côte d'Ivoire	—	—	—	—	—	—	—	—	—	—
Equatorial Guinea	0.5	3.3	0.14	1.6	4	0.40	0.57	5	0.87	4
Eritrea	—	—	—	0.4	3	0.20	—	—	—	—
Ethiopia	0.3	1.3	0.22	0.7	3	0.30	0.3	5	0.35	5
Gabon	—	—	—	—	—	—	—	—	—	—
Gambia	—	—	—	—	—	—	—	—	—	—
Ghana	0.5	1.6	0.29	1.9	5	0.40	0.46	5	0.57	5
Guinea	0.1	1.9	0.07	—	—	—	—	—	—	—
Guinea-Bissau	—	—	—	0.1	1	0.20	—	—	—	—
Kenya	0.9	2.4	0.38	2.5	3	0.80	0.97	3	1.36	1
Lesotho	1.6	1.1	1.37	3.3	2	1.80	1.96	1	2.34	1
Liberia	—	—	—	—	—	—	—	—	—	—
Madagascar	3	3.6	0.82	2	2	0.80	0.85	4	0.87	4
Malawi	0.3	0.9	0.34	—	—	—	—	—	—	—
Mali	0.2	1.1	0.16	—	—	—	—	—	—	—
Mauritania	0.8	5.1	0.17	1.2	6	0.20	0.22	5	0.25	5
Mauritius	2.6	4.3	0.6	13.1	10	1.40	1.74	—	2.5	—
Mozambique	—	—	—	0.5	1	0.80	—	—	—	—
Namibia	—	—	—	6.6	5	1.20	—	—	—	—
Niger	10.1	13.4	—	0.7	2	0.30	—	—	—	—
Nigeria	—	—	—	—	—	—	—	—	—	—
Rwanda	—	—	—	1.1	2	0.50	—	—	—	—
São Tomé and Principe	—	—	—	—	—	—	—	—	—	—
Senegal	—	—	—	—	—	—	—	—	—	—
Seychelles	—	—	—	—	—	—	—	—	—	—
Sierra Leone	—	—	—	1.2	3	0.40	—	—	—	—
Somalia	—	—	—	—	—	—	—	—	—	—
South Africa	10.4	13.2	0.79	16.8	14	1.20	1.45	1	1.89	1
Swaziland	3.8	5.2	0.73	4.8	6	0.90	0.94	3	1.08	1
Tanzania, United Rep.	—	—	—	—	—	—	—	—	—	—
Togo	0.8	5.2	0.16	1.3	6	0.20	0.22	5	0.26	5
Uganda	0.7	1.7	0.39	2	4	0.50	0.59	5	0.72	4
Zambia	—	—	—	1.6	3	0.50	—	—	—	—
Zimbabwe	—	—	—	3	5	0.60	—	—	—	—

Table A1.10

Adult female and male ages 15–24 literacy rates and ratios, 1990 and 2003, and projections for 2015

— Not available.

a. Rank is defined as follows: 1 = ratio greater than 1 (reverse gap), 2 = ratio equal to 1 (parity), 3 = 0.90–0.99 (on track), 4 = 0.70–0.89 (falling behind), 5 = 0–0.69 (off track).

Source: UN 2004a.

Region/Country	1990			2003			2015	
	Female rate	Male rate	Female to male ratio	Female rate	Male rate	Female to male ratio	Projected female to male ratio	Rank[a]
East Asia and Pacific								
Brunei Darussalam	98.1	97.6	1.01	99.8	99.3	1.01	1	2
Cambodia	65.6	81.5	0.8	76.7	84.8	0.9	1	2
China	93.1	97.5	0.95	97.4	99.1	0.98	1.01	1
Fiji	97.6	98.1	0.99	99.3	99.3	1	1	2
Hong Kong, China	97.9	98.5	0.99	99.8	99.1	1.01	1.02	1
Indonesia	93.4	96.6	0.97	97.8	98.6	0.99	1.01	1
Kiribati	—	—	—	—	—	—	—	—
Korea, DPR	—	—	—	—	—	—	—	—
Korea, Rep. of	99.8	99.8	1	99.8	99.8	1	1	2
Lao, PDR	60.6	79.5	0.76	73.6	86.3	0.85	0.94	3
Malaysia	94.2	95.3	0.99	98.2	97.8	1	1.02	1
Marshall Islands	—	—	—	—	—	—	—	—
Micronesia, Fed. States	—	—	—	—	—	—	—	—
Mongolia	99.1	98.7	1	99.5	98.8	1.01	1.01	1
Myanmar	86.2	90.1	0.96	91.5	91.7	1	1.04	1
Nauru	—	—	—	—	—	—	—	—
Palau	—	—	—	—	—	—	—	—
Papua New Guinea	62.4	74.4	0.84	73.7	81.3	0.91	0.97	3
Philippines	97.4	97.1	1	99.2	98.8	1	1	2
Samoa	98.9	99.1	1	99.5	99.4	1	1	2
Singapore	99.2	98.8	1	99.8	99.8	1	1	2
Solomon Islands	—	—	—	—	—	—	—	—
Thailand	97.6	98.6	0.99	98.5	99.6	0.99	0.99	3
Timor-Leste	—	—	—	—	—	—	—	—
Tonga	—	—	—	—	—	—	—	—
Tuvalu	—	—	—	—	—	—	—	—
Vanuatu	—	—	—	—	—	—	—	—
Viet Nam	93.6	94.5	0.99	96	95.3	1.01	1.02	1
Europe and Central Asia								
Albania	91.9	97.4	0.94	97.2	99.4	0.98	1.01	1
Armenia	99.4	99.7	1	99.8	99.8	1	1	2
Azerbaijan	—	—	—	—	—	—	—	—
Belarus	99.8	99.8	1	99.8	99.8	1	1	2
Bosnia and Herzegovina	—	—	—	—	—	—	—	—
Bulgaria	99.3	99.5	1	99.6	99.8	1	1	2
Croatia	99.6	99.7	1	99.8	99.8	1	1	2
Cyprus	99.8	99.5	1	99.8	99.8	1	1	2
Czech Republic	—	—	—	—	—	—	—	—
Estonia	99.8	99.7	1	99.8	99.7	1	1	2
Georgia	—	—	—	—	—	—	—	—
Hungary	99.7	99.8	1	99.8	99.8	1	1	2
Kazakhstan	99.8	99.8	1	99.8	99.8	1	1	2
Kyrgyzstan	—	—	—	—	—	—	—	—
Latvia	99.8	99.8	1	99.8	99.8	1	1	2
Lithuania	99.8	99.8	1	99.8	99.8	1	1	2
Macedonia TFYR	—	—	—	—	—	—	—	—
Moldova, Rep. of	99.8	99.8	1	99.8	99.8	1	1	2
Poland	99.8	99.8	1	99.8	99.8	1	1	2
Romania	99.2	99.3	1	99.8	99.6	1	1	2
Russian Federation	99.8	99.8	1	99.8	99.8	1	1	2
Serbia and Montenegro	—	—	—	—	—	—	—	—

Table A1.10

Adult female and male ages 15–24 literacy rates and ratios, 1990 and 2003, and projections for 2015

(continued)

Region/Country	1990			2003			2015	
	Female rate	Male rate	Female to male ratio	Female rate	Male rate	Female to male ratio	Projected female to male ratio	Rank[a]
Slovakia	—	—	—	—	—	—	—	—
Slovenia	99.8	99.7	1	99.8	99.8	1	1	2
Tajikistan	99.8	99.8	1	99.8	99.8	1	1	2
Turkey	88.3	97.1	0.91	95.1	99.1	0.96	1.01	1
Turkmenistan	—	—	—	—	—	—	—	—
Ukraine	99.9	99.8	1	99.9	99.9	1	1	2
Uzbekistan	99.6	99.7	1	99.6	99.7	1	1	2
Latin America and the Caribbean								
Antigua and Barbuda	—	—	—	—	—	—	—	—
Argentina	98.4	98	1	98.9	98.4	1.01	1.01	1
Bahamas	97.5	95.4	1.02	98.4	96.5	1.02	1.02	1
Barbados	99.8	99.8	1	99.8	99.8	1	1	2
Belize	96.7	95.4	1.01	99.1	97.7	1.01	1.01	1
Bolivia	89	96.2	0.93	94.7	98.4	0.96	1	2
Brazil	93.1	90.5	1.03	97.2	94.4	1.03	1.03	1
Chile	98.3	97.9	1	99.2	98.9	1	1	2
Colombia	95.5	94.3	1.01	98	96.7	1.01	1.01	1
Costa Rica	97.7	97.1	1.01	98.8	98.2	1.01	1.01	1
Cuba	99.2	99.3	1	99.8	99.8	1	1	2
Dominica	—	—	—	—	—	—	—	—
Dominican Republic	88.2	86.8	1.02	92.7	91.2	1.02	1.02	1
Ecuador	94.9	96	0.99	97.4	97.9	0.99	1	2
El Salvador	82.6	85.1	0.97	88.6	90	0.98	1	2
Grenada	—	—	—	—	—	—	—	—
Guatemala	66.2	80.5	0.82	74.4	86.7	0.86	0.89	4
Guyana	99.8	99.8	1	99.8	99.8	1	1	2
Haiti	53.8	55.8	0.96	67.5	66.6	1.01	1.06	1
Honduras	80.8	78.5	1.03	88	84.8	1.04	1.05	1
Jamaica	95.2	87.1	1.09	97.9	91.6	1.07	1.05	1
Mexico	94.4	95.9	0.98	97.1	97.8	0.99	1	2
Nicaragua	68.7	67.7	1.01	73.3	71.9	1.02	1.02	1
Panama	94.8	95.7	0.99	96.7	97.5	0.99	0.99	3
Paraguay	95.2	95.9	0.99	97.4	97.4	1	1.01	1
Peru	92.1	96.9	0.95	96	98.5	0.97	1	2
St. Kitts and Nevis	—	—	—	—	—	—	—	—
St. Lucia	—	—	—	—	—	—	—	—
St. Vincent and the Grenadines	—	—	—	—	—	—	—	—
Suriname	—	—	—	—	—	—	—	—
Trinidad and Tobago	99.6	99.7	1	99.8	99.8	1	1	2
Uruguay	99.1	98.3	1.01	99.5	98.9	1.01	1	2
Venezuela	96.6	95.4	1.01	99.1	97.7	1.01	1.02	1
Middle East and North Africa								
Algeria	68.1	86.1	0.79	86.7	94.4	0.92	1.04	1
Bahrain	95	96.2	0.99	99	98.5	1.01	1.02	1
Djibouti	64.2	82.2	0.78	82.8	90.1	0.92	1.05	1
Egypt	51	70.9	0.72	65.8	77.8	0.85	0.96	3
Iraq	24.9	56.4	0.44	30.5	60.3	0.51	0.57	5
Israel	98.4	99	0.99	99.5	99.7	1	1	2
Jordan	95.3	97.9	0.97	99.6	99.3	1	1.03	1
Kuwait	87.2	87.9	0.99	94.3	92.5	1.02	1.04	1
Lebanon	88.6	95.5	0.93	94	97.6	0.96	1	2
Libyan Arab Jamahiriya	82.7	98.9	0.84	94.5	99.8	0.95	1.05	1

Appendix 1

Table A1.10

Adult female and male ages 15–24 literacy rates and ratios, 1990 and 2003, and projections for 2015

(continued)

Region/Country	1990			2003			2015	
	Female rate	Male rate	Female to male ratio	Female rate	Male rate	Female to male ratio	Projected female to male ratio	Rank[a]
Morocco	42	68	0.62	62.9	78.1	0.81	0.98	3
Oman	75.4	95.4	0.79	97.9	99.7	0.98	1.16	1
Palestinian Autonomous Territory	—	—	—	—	—	—	—	—
Qatar	93	88.3	1.05	97.7	93.5	1.04	1.04	1
Saudi Arabia	78.6	91.2	0.86	92.3	95.6	0.97	1.06	1
Sudan	54	75.6	0.71	75.5	84.4	0.89	1.06	1
Syrian Arab Republic	66.9	92.2	0.73	81.5	96	0.85	0.96	3
Tunisia	75.2	92.8	0.81	91.3	98.1	0.93	1.04	1
United Arab Emirates	88.6	81.7	1.08	95.3	88.6	1.08	1.07	1
Yemen	25	73.5	0.34	53.2	85	0.63	0.89	4
South Asia								
Afghanistan	—	—	—	—	—	—	—	—
Bangladesh	33.2	50.7	0.65	41.7	58.3	0.72	0.77	4
Bhutan	—	—	—	—	—	—	—	—
India	54.2	73.4	0.74	67.8	81.3	0.83	0.92	3
Iran, Islamic Rep.	80.8	91.7	0.88	93.1	97	0.96	1.03	1
Maldives	98.1	98.1	1	99.3	99.2	1	1	2
Nepal	27.3	67	0.41	47.5	78.7	0.6	0.78	4
Pakistan	30.6	62.5	0.49	45.4	73.1	0.62	0.74	4
Sri Lanka	94.2	95.9	0.98	97.1	97.3	1	1.01	1
Sub-Saharan Africa								
Angola	—	—	—	—	—	—	—	—
Benin	24.7	56.6	0.44	39.7	73.9	0.54	0.63	5
Botswana	87.2	79.3	1.1	93.2	86	1.08	1.07	1
Burkina Faso	14	35.7	0.39	26.9	48.9	0.55	0.7	4
Burundi	44.8	58.4	0.77	66.6	67.9	0.98	1.18	1
Cameroon	75.9	86.4	0.88	90.2	93.1	0.97	1.05	1
Cape Verde	76.2	87.1	0.87	87	92.3	0.94	1.01	1
Central African Republic	39.4	65.6	0.6	64.4	78.5	0.82	1.02	1
Chad	37.7	58.4	0.65	65.9	77	0.86	1.05	1
Comoros	49.6	63.8	0.78	52.4	65.8	0.8	0.81	4
Cote d'Ivoire	40.3	64.9	0.62	56.1	72.7	0.77	0.91	3
Congo, Dem. Rep.	57.6	80.3	0.72	79	90.2	0.88	1.02	1
Congo, Rep.	90.3	94.9	0.95	97.5	98.6	0.99	1.02	1
Equatorial Guinea	88.8	96.6	0.92	96.4	98.8	0.98	1.03	1
Eritrea	49.3	72.5	0.68	63.6	82.1	0.77	0.86	4
Ethiopia	34.1	51.5	0.66	53.3	63.9	0.83	0.99	3
Gabon	—	—	—	—	—	—	—	—
Gambia	34.1	50.5	0.68	54	69.2	0.78	0.88	4
Ghana	75.4	88.2	0.85	90.9	94.5	0.96	1.06	1
Guinea	—	—	—	—	—	—	—	—
Guinea-Bissau	26.5	62.2	0.43	49.2	75.4	0.65	0.86	4
Kenya	86.7	92.9	0.93	95.5	96.6	0.99	1.04	1
Lesotho	97.1	77.2	1.26	98.8	84.2	1.17	1.1	1
Liberia	38.6	75.4	0.51	56.9	87	0.65	0.79	4
Madagascar	66.6	77.8	0.86	79.1	85.1	0.93	1	2
Malawi	51.2	75.7	0.68	63.8	82.3	0.78	0.87	4
Mali	17.1	38.3	0.45	27.9	50	0.56	0.66	5
Mauritania	36.1	55.5	0.65	42.3	57.6	0.73	0.81	4
Mauritius	91.1	91.2	1	95.1	93.9	1.01	1.03	1
Mozambique	31.7	66.1	0.48	50.7	77.3	0.66	0.82	4
Namibia	89	85.9	1.04	94.3	90.9	1.04	1.04	1

Table A1.10

Adult female and male ages 15–24 literacy rates and ratios, 1990 and 2003, and projections for 2015

(continued)

Region/Country	1990			2003			2015	
	Female rate	Male rate	Female to male ratio	Female rate	Male rate	Female to male ratio	Projected female to male ratio	Rank[a]
Niger	9.3	24.9	0.37	15.7	34.8	0.45	0.52	5
Nigeria	66.5	80.8	0.82	87.5	91.3	0.96	1.08	1
Rwanda	67.4	78	0.86	84.6	86.8	0.97	1.08	1
São Tomé and Principe	—	—	—	—	—	—	—	—
Senegal	30.2	50	0.6	45.7	62.2	0.73	0.86	4
Seychelles	—	—	—	—	—	—	—	—
Sierra Leone	—	—	—	—	—	—	—	—
Somalia	—	—	—	—	—	—	—	—
South Africa	88.4	88.6	1	92	92	1	1	2
Swaziland	85.5	84.7	1.01	92.5	90.8	1.02	1.03	1
Tanzania, United Rep.	77.2	89.2	0.87	90.1	94.1	0.96	1.04	1
Togo	47.7	79.4	0.6	68	88.9	0.76	0.92	3
Uganda	60.5	79.8	0.76	75	86.8	0.86	0.96	3
Zambia	76.2	86.4	0.88	87.5	91.8	0.95	1.02	1
Zimbabwe	91.3	96.6	0.95	96.5	99	0.97	1	2

Reproductive health statistics

| Region and country (survey period) | Need for family planning | | | |
| | Early survey period (1990–95) | | Late survey period (1996–2001) | |
	Ages 15–19	All age groups	Ages 15–19	All age groups
East Asia and the Pacific				
Cambodia (2000)	—	—	29.5	29.7
Indonesia (1994, 1997)	13.7	10.6	9.1	9.2
Philippines (1993, 1998)	31.1	25.9	30.7	18.8
Viet Nam (1997)			9.7	6.9
Europe and Central Asia				
Armenia (2000)	—	—	17.7	11.8
Kazakhstan (1995, 1999)	20.0	15.7	13.0	8.7
Kyrgyzstan (1997)	—	—	11.5	11.6
Turkey (1993, 1998)	20.2	11.2	20.0	10.1
Turkmenistan (2000)	—	—	14.3	10.1
Uzbekistan (1996)	—	—	15.7	13.7
Latin America and the Caribbean				
Bolivia (1994, 1998)	29.4	23.2	33.9	26.1
Brazil[a] (1991, 1996)	26.2	18.3	19.1	7.3
Colombia (1990, 2000)	22.7	11.1	17.5	6.2
Dominican Republic (1991, 1999)	36.6	17.2	24.6	11.9
Guatemala (1995, 1998/1999)	28.8	24.3	25.4	23.1
Haiti (1994/1995, 2000)	61.6	44.5	58.4	39.8
Nicaragua (1997/1998)	—	—	27.4	14.7
Paraguay (1990)	19.4	15.0	—	—
Peru (1992, 2000)	32.7	15.5	23.6	10.2
Middle East and North Africa				
Egypt (1992, 2000)	23.8	19.8	9.8	10.7
Jordan (1990, 1997)	23.0	22.2	18.3	14.2
Morocco (1992)	16.6	19.7	—	—
Yemen (1997)	—	—	32.3	38.6
South Asia				
Bangladesh (1993/1994, 1999/2000)	21.9	18.1	20.0	15.3
India (1992/1993, 1998/1999)	27.2	16.5	27.1	15.8
Nepal (1996, 2001)	40.5	31.4	35.6	27.8
Pakistan (1990/1991)	33.6	31.8	—	—

Table A2.1

Unmet need for family planning, 1990–95 and 1996–2001

(continued)

amenorrheic women whose last child was unwanted, and fecund women who are neither pregnant nor amenorrheic and who are not using any method of family planning and who want no more children. Excluded are pregnant and amenorrheic women who became pregnant while using a contraceptive method (these women are in need of a better method of contraception).

Using for spacing is defined as women who are using some method of family planning and say they want to have another child or are undecided whether to have another.

Using for limiting Is defined as women who are using and who want no more children. Note that the specific methods used are not taken into account here.

Nonusers who are pregnant or amenorrheic and women whose pregnancy was the result of a contraceptive failure are not included in the category of unmet need, but are included in total demand for contraception (since they would have been using had their method not failed).

a. Data are for the Northeast region.

Source: ORC-Macro 2004.

Region and country (survey period)	Need for family planning			
	Early survey period (1990–95)		Late survey period (1996–2001)	
	Ages 15–19	All age groups	Ages 15–19	All age groups
Sub-Saharan Africa				
Benin (1996, 2001)	27.6	25.7	27.8	27.2
Burkina Faso (1992/1993, 1998/1999)	25.8	24.5	18.7	25.8
Cameroon (1991, 1998)	21.1	21.7	21.4	19.7
Central African Republic (1994/1995)	14.9	16.2	—	—
Chad (1996/1997)	—	—	7.6	9.7
Comoros (1996)	—	—	51.2	34.6
Cote d'Ivoire (1994, 1998/99)	27.9	27.1	22.4	27.7
Eritrea (1995)	34.8	27.5	—	—
Ethiopia (2000)	—	—	40.4	35.8
Gabon (2000)	—	—	29.1	28.0
Ghana (1993, 1998)	47.8	36.5	26.7	23.0
Guinea (1999)	—	—	19.9	24.2
Kenya (1993, 1998)	41.9	35.5	26.7	23.9
Madagascar (1992, 1997)	24.2	32.4	21.8	25.6
Malawi (1992, 2000)	33.2	35.7	28.8	29.7
Mali (1995/1996, 2001)	30.0	25.7	31.5	28.5
Mauritania (2000/2001)	—	—	34.9	31.6
Mozambique (1997)	—	—	24.1	22.5
Namibia (1992)	31.9	21.9	—	—
Niger (1992, 1998)	17.4	18.7	17.3	16.6
Nigeria (1990, 1999)	23.0	20.5	14.8	17.4
Rwanda (1992, 2000)	29.6	38.8	22.2	35.6
Senegal (1992/1993, 1997)	28.0	29.3	32.3	34.8
South Africa (1998)	—	—	26.1	15.0
Tanzania (1992, 1999)	21.5	27.9	15.1	21.8
Togo (1998)	—	—	38.9	32.3
Uganda (1995, 2000/2001)	24.9	29.0	25.6	34.6
Zambia (1992, 2001/2002)	27.0	30.7	22.8	27.4
Zimbabwe (1994, 1999)	19.9	14.9	12.4	12.9

Employment statistics

Table A3.1

Youth ages 15–24 unemployment rates, by sex, 1990 and 2000

Percent

Source: ILO 2003a.

Region and country	1990		2000	
	Men	Women	Men	Women
Developed countries				
Australia	13.9	12.4	13.3	12
Austria	3.8	3.8	5.4	5.5
Belgium	10.1	19.2	14.3	16.6
Canada	13.6	11	14.5	11
Denmark	11.4	11.6	7.3	9.3
Ecuador	11.1	17.3	10.6	20.4
Finland	10.4	8.3	19.6	20.2
France	15.3	23.9	16.2	21.8
Greece	15.1	32.6	21	35.7
Iceland	0.9	1.3	5.4	4.3
Ireland	19	16.1	6.4	5.8
Italy	26.2	37.8	23.2	32.2
Japan	4.5	4.1	10.7	8.7
Luxembourg	2.7	4.7	7.8	5.4
Netherlands	10	12.3	5.5	6.1
New Zealand	14.9	13.2	12.1	11.5
Norway	12.4	11	10.6	10.3
Portugal	7.1	12.8	7.2	11.9
Spain	23.2	39.7	16.1	27
Sweden	4.5	4.4	12.7	10.8
United Kingdom	11.1	9	12	8.7
United States	11.6	10.7	11.4	9.7
East Asia and the Pacific				
Hong Kong, China	3.6	3.3	13.5	9.2
Korea, Rep. of	9.5	5.5	12.2	8.2
Philippines	13.1	19.2	16.6	22.9
Thailand	4.3	4.2	7	6
Europe and Central Asia				
Estonia	1.8	1.8	19.1	26.4
Turkey	16.6	15	20.7	18.3
Latin America and the Caribbean				
Argentina	11.5	15.6	31.2	32.7

Table A3.1

Youth ages 15–24 unemployment rates, by sex, 1990 and 2000

(continued)

Region and country	1990		2000	
	Men	**Women**	**Men**	**Women**
Barbados	21.8	40.5	20.8	26.2
Bolivia	3.1	8.7	7	10.4
Brazil	6.7	6.8	14.6	22.4
Chile	13.4	12.4	17.1	22.1
Colombia	23.4	31.4	31.9	40.7
Costa Rica	7.6	10	11.9	16.4
Nicaragua	8.6	16.7	20.3	19.7
Paraguay	15	16.5	11.7	17.3
Venezuela	20	17.9	19.6	27.7
Middle East and North Africa				
Israel	21	23.4	18.6	18.3
Morocco	30.9	31.6	15.8	14.6
South Asia				
Pakistan	5.7	1.3	11.1	29.2

Table A3.2

Maternity leave benefits as of 1998

— Not available.

a. Up to a ceiling.
b. 10 more weeks may be taken up by either parent.
c. The Family and Medical Leave Act (FMLA) of 1993 provided a total of 12 work weeks of unpaid leave during any 12-month period for the birth of a child and the care of the newborn. FMLA applies only to workers in companies with 50 or more workers.

Source: ILO 1998, 2003c.

Region and country	Length of maternity leave	Share of wages paid in covered period (percent)	Provider of coverage
Developed countries			
Australia	1 year	0	—
Austria	16 weeks	100	Social Security
Belarus	126 days	100	Social Security
Belgium	15 weeks	82% for 30 days, 75% thereafter[a]	Social Security
Bulgaria	120–180 days	100	Social Security
Canada	17–18 weeks	57 for 15 weeks	Unemployment insurance
Croatia	6 months plus 4 weeks	—	—
Czech Republic	28 weeks	—	—
Denmark	18 weeks[b]	100[a]	Social Security
Estonia	18 weeks	—	—
Finland	105 days	80	Social Security
France	16–26 weeks	100	Social Security
Germany	14 weeks	100	Social Security to ceiling; employer pays difference
Greece	16 weeks	75	Social Security
Hungary	24 weeks	100	Social Security
Iceland	2 months	Flat rate	Social Security
Ireland	14 weeks	70% or fixed rate[a]	Social Security
Italy	5 months	80	Social Security
Japan	14 weeks	60	Health insurance/ Social Security
Liechtenstein	8 weeks	80	Social Security
Luxembourg	16 weeks	100	Social Security
Malta	13 weeks	100	Social Security
Netherlands	16 weeks	100	Social Security
New Zealand	14 weeks	0	—
Norway	38–48 weeks	100, and 26 extra paid weeks by either parent	Social Security
Poland	16-18 weeks	100	Social Security

Region and country	Length of maternity leave	Share of wages paid in covered period (percent)	Provider of coverage
Portugal	14 weeks	100	Social Security
Romania	112 days	50–94	Social Security
Russian Federation	140 days	100	Social Security
Spain	16 weeks	100	Social Security
Sweden	14 weeks	450 days paid parental leave: 360 days at 75% and 90 days at flat rate	Social Security
Switzerland	8 weeks	100	Employer
Ukraine	126 days	100	Social Security
United Kingdom	14–18 weeks	90 for 6 weeks, flat rate after	Social Security
United States	Federal: 12 weeks[c] States: varies	0	—
Africa			
Algeria	14 weeks	100	Social Security
Angola	90 days	100	Employer
Benin	14 weeks	100	Social Security
Botswana	12 weeks	25	Employer
Burkina Faso	14 weeks	100	Social Security
Burundi	12 weeks	50	Employer
Cameroon	14 weeks	100	Social Security
Central African Rep.	14 weeks	50	Social Security
Chad	13 weeks	50	Social Security
Comoros	14 weeks	100	Employer
Congo, Dem. Rep.	14 weeks	67	Employer
Congo, Rep.	15 weeks	100	Half employer/ half Social Security
Côte d'Ivoire	14 weeks	100	Half employer/ half Social Security
Djibouti	14 weeks	50	25% employer/ 25% Social Security
Egypt	50 days	100	Social Security/ Employer
Equatorial Guinea	12 weeks	75	Social Security
Eritrea	60 days	—	—
Ethiopia	90 days	100	Employer
Gabon	14 weeks	100	Social Security
Gambia	12 weeks	100	Employer
Ghana	12 weeks	50	Employer
Guinea	14 weeks	100	Half employer/ half Social Security
Guinea-Bissau	60 days	100	Employer/Social Security
Kenya	2 months	100	Employer
Lesotho	12 weeks	0	—
Libyan Arab Jamahiriya	50 days	50	Employer
Madagascar	14 weeks	50	Social Security
Mali	14 weeks	100	Social Security
Mauritania	14 weeks	100	Social Security
Mauritius	12 weeks	100	Employer
Morocco	12 weeks	100	Social Security
Mozambique	60 days	100	Employer

Table A3.2
Maternity leave benefits as of 1998
(continued)

Region and country	Length of maternity leave	Share of wages paid in covered period (percent)	Provider of coverage
Namibia	12 weeks	as prescribed	Social Security
Niger	14 weeks	50	Social Security
Nigeria	12 weeks	50	Employer
Rwanda	12 weeks	67	Employer
São Tomé and Principe	70 days	100	Social Security
Senegal	14 weeks	100	Social Security
Seychelles	14 weeks	flat monthly allowance	Social Security
Somalia	14 weeks	50	Employer
South Africa	12 weeks	45	Unemployment Insurance
Sudan	8 weeks	100	Employer
Swaziland	12 weeks	0	—
Tanzania, United Rep.	12 weeks	100	Employer
Togo	14 weeks	100	Half employer/ half Social Security
Tunisia	30 days	67	Social Security
Uganda	8 weeks	100 for one month	Employer
Zaire	14 weeks	67	Employer
Zambia	12 weeks	100	Employer
Zimbabwe	90 days	60/75	Employer
Latin America and the Caribbean			
Antigua and Barbuda	13 weeks	60	Social Security
Argentina	90 days	100	Social Security
Bahamas	8 weeks	100	40% employer/ 60% Social Security
Barbados	12 weeks	100	Social Security
Belize	12 weeks	80	Social Security
Bolivia	60 days	100% of national minimum wage plus 70% of wages above minimum wage	Social Security
Brazil	120 days	100	Social Security
Chile	18 weeks	100	Social Security
Colombia	12 weeks	100	Social Security
Costa Rica	16 weeks	100	Half employer/half Social Security
Cuba	18 weeks	100	Social Security
Dominica	12 weeks	60	Social Security
Dominican Republic	12 weeks	100	Half employer/ half Social Security
Ecuador	12 weeks	100	25% employer/ 75% Social Security
El Salvador	12 weeks	75	Social Security
Grenada	13 weeks	60 for 12 weeks	Social Security
Guatemala	12 weeks	100	33% employer/ 67% Social Security
Guyana	13 weeks	70	Social Security
Haiti	12 weeks	100 for 6 weeks	Employer
Honduras	10 weeks	100	33% employer/ 67% Social Security
Jamaica	12 weeks	100 for 8 weeks	Employer
Mexico	12 weeks	100	Social Security
Nicaragua	12 weeks	60	Social Security
Panama	14 weeks	100	Social Security
Paraguay	12 weeks	50 for 9 weeks	Social Security
Peru	90 days	100	Social Security

Region and country	Length of maternity leave	Share of wages paid in covered period (percent)	Provider of coverage
Saint Lucia	13 weeks	65	Social Security
Trinidad and Tobago	13 weeks	60[a]	Social Security
Uruguay	12 weeks	100	Social Security
Venezuela	18 weeks	100	Social Security
Asia			
Afghanistan	90 days	100	Employer
Azerbaijan	18 weeks	—	—
Bahrain	45 days	100	Employer
Bangladesh	12 weeks	100	Employer
Cambodia	90 days	100	Employer
China	90 days	100	Employer
Cyprus	16 weeks	75	Social Security
Hong Kong, China	12 weeks	66.7	Employer
India	12 weeks	100	Social Security
Indonesia	13 weeks	100	Employer
Iran	90 days	66.7	Social Security
Iraq	60 days	100	Social Security
Israel	12 weeks	75[a]	Social Security
Jordan	10 weeks	90	Employer
Korea, Rep.	60 days	100	Employer
Kuwait	70 days	100	Employer
Lao PDR	90 days	100	Social Security
Lebanon	40 days	100	Employer
Malaysia	60 days	100	Employer
Mongolia	101 days	—	—
Myanmar	12 weeks	66.7	Social Security
Nepal	52 days	100	Employer
Pakistan	12 weeks	100	Employer
Philippines	60 days	100	Social Security
Qatar	40-60 days	100% for civil servants	Agency concerned
Saudi Arabia	10 weeks	50 or 100	Employer
Singapore	8 weeks	100	Employer
Sri Lanka	12 weeks	100	Employer
Syrian Arab Republic	75 days	70	Employer
Thailand	90 days	100 for 45 days then 50% for 60 days	Employer for 45 days, then Social Security
Turkey	12 weeks	66.7	Social Security
United Arab Emirates	45 days	100	Employer
Viet Nam	4–7 months	100	Social Security
Yemen	60 days	100[a]	Employer
Oceania			
Fiji	84 days	Flat rate	Employer
Papua New Guinea	6 weeks	0	—
Solomon Islands	12 weeks	25	Employer

Table A3.3

Women's wage employment in nonagricultural sector as a share of total nonagricultural employment, 1990 and 2002

Percent

— Not available.

Source: UN 2004a.

Region and country	1990	2002
Developed countries		
Australia	44.6	48.9
Austria	40.1	44.1
Belgium	39.9	45.2
Canada	46.9	48.7
Denmark	47.1	49.0
Finland	50.6	50.7
France	43.9	47.0
Germany	40.7	45.9
Greece	34.7	40.5
Iceland	52.9	53.0
Ireland	41.7	47.6
Italy	34.3	40.9
Japan	38.0	40.6
Luxembourg	34.6	37.5
Netherlands	37.7	45.0
New Zealand	47.8	50.6
Norway	47.1	48.9
Portugal	44.4	46.5
Spain	32.6	39.9
Sweden	50.5	50.9
Switzerland	42.8	47.2
United Kingdom	47.8	50.4
United States	47.4	48.6
East Asia and the Pacific		
Brunei Darussalam	39.5	—
Cambodia	40.6	53.2
China	37.7	39.3
Korea, DPR	49.6	—
Fiji	29.9	34.8
Hong Kong, China	41.2	45.9
Indonesia	29.2	29.7
Kiribati	—	—
Korea, Rep.	38.1	39.7
Lao PDR	42.1	—
Malaysia	37.8	34.6
Marshall Islands	—	—
Micronesia, Fed. States of	—	—
Mongolia	48.6	47.4
Myanmar	35.2	—
Nauru	—	—
Palau	—	—
Papua New Guinea	24.1	—
Philippines	40.4	40.7
Samoa	—	—
Singapore	42.5	46.7
Solomon Islands	33.3	—
Thailand	45.3	46.1
Timor-Leste	27.9	—
Tonga	—	—
Tuvalu	—	—
Vanuatu	—	—
Viet Nam	52.9	—

Table A3.3

Women's wage
employment in
nonagricultural
sector as a share of
total nonagricultural
employment,
1990 and 2002

(continued)

Region and country	1990	2002
Europe and Central Asia		
Albania	39.6	40.2
Armenia	—	—
Azerbaijan	41.2	48.4
Belarus	55.7	55.8
Bosnia and Herzegovina	43.4	—
Bulgaria	54.2	51.3
Croatia	44.2	45.7
Cyprus	36.4	42.4
Czech Republic	46.0	46.7
Estonia	52.3	51.5
Georgia	44.5	46.5
Hungary	46.2	46.7
Kazakhstan	59.9	48.1
Kyrgyzstan	46.4	45.4
Latvia	52.3	53.4
Lithuania	57.8	50.3
Macedonia, TFYR	38.3	41.8
Moldova	52.9	53.7
Poland	47.2	47.5
Romania	42.7	45.2
Russian Federation	49.9	49.6
Serbia and Montenegro	46.4	—
Slovakia	48.2	52.0
Slovenia	48.9	47.9
Tajikistan	40.1	50.4
Turkey	15.2	20.6
Turkmenistan	—	—
Ukraine	50.6	53.2
Uzbekistan	46.2	41.8
Latin America and the Caribbean		
Antigua and Barbuda		
Argentina	36.6	45.9
Bahamas	49.0	48.5
Barbados	45.5	48.5
Belize	37.6	41.0
Bolivia	35.6	37.3
Brazil	40.2	46.6
Chile	36.2	36.5
Colombia	42.4	49.2
Costa Rica	37.2	39.6
Cuba	36.9	37.7
Dominica	—	—
Dominican Republic	35.2	34.9
Ecuador	37.3	40.0
El Salvador	32.3	31.1
Grenada	—	—
Guatemala	36.8	39.2
Guyana	44.8	—
Haiti	39.5	—
Honduras	48.1	50.2
Jamaica	50.9	47.2
Mexico	35.4	37.1
Nicaragua	49.0	—

Table A3.3

Women's wage
employment in
nonagricultural
sector as a share of
total nonagricultural
employment,
1990 and 2002

(continued)

Region and country	1990	2002
Panama	44.1	43.5
Paraguay	40.5	40.5
Peru	29.9	35.0
St. Kitts and Nevis	—	—
St. Lucia	—	—
St. Vincent and the Grenadines	—	—
Suriname	39.1	33.2
Trinidad and Tobago	35.6	40.8
Uruguay	41.9	45.8
Venezuela	35.2	41.8
Middle East and North Africa		
Algeria	8.0	—
Bahrain	7.3	12.5
Djibouti	—	—
Egypt	20.5	20.3
Iraq	12.7	—
Israel	43.0	48.7
Jordan	23.1	21.9
Kuwait	30.3	19.7
Lebanon	29.3	—
Libyan Arab Jamahiriya	18.9	—
Morocco	26.2	25.8
Oman	18.7	25.2
Palestinian Autonomous Territories	13.0	17.0
Qatar	17.2	13.8
Saudi Arabia	16.1	14.0
Sudan	22.2	14.7
Syrian Arab Republic	14.2	18.4
Tunisia	19.7	—
United Arab Emirates	16.0	12.7
Yemen	8.9	5.8
South Asia		
Afghanistan	4.7	—
Bangladesh	17.6	25.0
Bhutan	11.9	—
India	12.7	17.5
Iran, Islamic Rep.	18.0	—
Maldives	21.2	39.6
Nepal	11.7	—
Pakistan	6.6	8.2
Sri Lanka	39.1	44.6
Sub-Saharan Africa		
Angola	34.6	—
Benin	51.5	—
Botswana	48.2	44.8
Burkina Faso	12.5	14.0
Burundi	9.9	—
Cameroon	24.3	—
Cape Verde	50.0	—
Central African Republic	36.1	—
Chad	3.8	—
Comoros	16.1	—
Congo, Dem. Rep.	32.2	—
Congo, Rep.	32.5	—

Table A3.3

Women's wage employment in nonagricultural sector as a share of total nonagricultural employment, 1990 and 2002

(continued)

Region and country	1990	2002
Côte d'Ivoire	22.9	19.6
Equatorial Guinea	13.3	—
Eritrea	—	—
Ethiopia	—	—
Gabon	43.2	—
Gambia	24.0	—
Ghana	56.6	—
Guinea	30.1	—
Guinea-Bissau	10.5	—
Kenya	21.4	37.6
Lesotho	40.4	—
Liberia	28.3	—
Madagascar	26.0	—
Malawi	10.5	12.2
Mali	35.6	—
Mauritania	43.3	—
Mauritius	36.7	38.2
Mozambique	15.2	—
Namibia	39.1	50.0
Niger	—	—
Nigeria	36.4	—
Rwanda	16.7	—
São Tomé and Principe	—	—
Senegal	28.1	—
Seychelles	—	—
Sierra Leone	32.1	—
Somalia	27.6	—
South Africa	—	—
Swaziland	36.8	29.3
Tanzania, United Rep.	33.1	—
Togo	46.6	—
Uganda	43.2	—
Zambia	36.1	—
Zimbabwe	15.4	20.6

Statistics on women's political participation

Region and country	Female share of mayors	Female share of councilors
World (59 countries)	4.5	15
Europe		21
Andorra		
Austria		13
Belgium		22
Denmark		28
Finland		31
France		22
Germany		24
Greece		4
Ireland		15
Italy		18
Luxembourg		12
Netherlands		22
Portugal		12
Sweden		42
United Kingdom		27
East Asia and the Pacific	10.3	18.1
Australia	15	26
Bangladesh		25
India		38
Japan		5
Malaysia	1	9
Nepal		19
New Zealand	26	32
Pakistan	1	25
Philippines	18	14
Sri Lanka		2
Thailand	1	6
Viet Nam		16
Central America	8.1	30
Costa Rica	9	73
Dominican Republic	7	28

Table A4.1

Share of women in local decisionmaking bodies, latest available data

(continued)

Region and country	Female share of mayors	Female share of councilors
El Salvador	7	25
Guatemala	2	25
Honduras	10	22
Mexico	4	16
Nicaragua	10	34
Panama	16	13
South America	6.2	27.9
Argentina	7	
Bolivia	11	34
Brazil	5	12
Chile	13	48
Colombia	3	30
Ecuador	3	25
Paraguay	5	19
Peru	3	25
Venezuela	6	30
Middle East and Mediterranean	1.3	6.6
Bahrain		
Egypt, Arab Rep.		2
Iran, Islamic Rep.		1
Jordan	1	19
Lebanon		2
Morocco		1
Palestine		
Syria		7
Tunisia	2	20
Turkey	1	1
United Arab Emirates		
Africa	9.3	30.7
Ghana	11	30
Seychelles		
South Africa	15	29
Uganda	2	33

Table A4.2

Countries with gender quotas or reservations in legislative bodies, latest available data

a. Information on the number of reserved seats was not available.
b. Kosovo is a province of Serbia administered by the United Nations.
c. Twenty percent of seats in the lower house of congress are reserved for "marginalized sectors" of society, including women.

Source: Htun 2003b; International IDEA and Stockholm University 2004.

Country	Policy
Afghanistan	Reserved seats, 25.6% of lower house, 17% of upper house
Argentina	30% of candidates
Armenia	5% of party lists for proportional representation elections
Bangladesh	13% of seats at national level, reserved seats at local level[a]
Belgium	1/3 of candidates
Bolivia	35% of candidates for Chamber; 30% for Senate
Bosnia and Herzegovina	1/3 of candidates
Brazil	30% of candidates
China	Around 30% seats reserved
Costa Rica	40% of candidates
Djibouti	10% of parliamentary seats reserved
Dominican Republic	33% of candidates
Ecuador	30% of candidates for Chamber of Deputies
France	50% of candidates
Guyana	33% of candidates
Indonesia	30% of candidates
Kenya	6 of 12 parliamentary seats nominated by president
Kosovo[b]	33% of candidates
Macedonia	30% of candidates
Mexico	30% of candidates
Morocco	30 of 325 parliamentary seats reserved
Nepal	5% of candidates for lower house; 20% of local seats reserved
Korea, DPR	20% of parliamentary seats reserved
Pakistan	17% of seats reserved in national assembly; 33% at local level
Panama	30% of candidates for Chamber of Deputies
Paraguay	20% of candidates
Peru	30% of candidates
Philippines	Some parliamentary seats reserved[c]; 1 seat reserved per council
Rwanda	24 lower house seats and 30% of senate seats
Serbia and Montenegro	30% of candidates in Serbia
Sudan	10% of national assembly seats reserved
Taiwan Province of China	10% of legislative seats reserved at all levels
Tanzania	15% of parliamentary seats reserved; 25% of local councils
Uganda	56 parliamentary seats reserved; 33% of local councils
Local level only	
Greece	33% of candidates
India	33% of seats reserved
Namibia	33% of candidates

Table A4.3

Results of quotas in legislative bodies, latest available data

Percent

Note: All percentages have been rounded off.

Source: Htun 2003; IPU 2004; International IDEA and Stockholm University 2004.

Country	Size of quota or reservation	Share of women in lower house or unicameral chamber	Share of women in upper house
Argentina	30	31	33
Armenia	5	5	
Bangladesh	13	2	
Belgium	33	35	33
Bolivia	35/30	19	15
Bosnia and Herzegovina	33	17	0
Brazil	30	9	12
China	around 30	20	
Costa Rica	40	35	
Djibouti	10	11	
Dominican Republic	33	17	6
Ecuador	30	16	
France	50	12	11
Guyana	33	20	
Indonesia	30	8	
Kenya	3	7	
Korea, DPR	20	20	
Kosovo	33	28	
Macedonia	30	23	
Mexico	30	16	19
Morocco	10	11	1 woman of 270
Nepal	5	6	8
Pakistan	17	22	18
Panama	30	10	
Paraguay	20	10	9
Peru	30	18	
Philippines	some	18	13
Rwanda	24 seats and 30	49	30
Serbia and Montenegro	30		
Sudan	10	10	
Taiwan Province of China	10	22	
Tanzania	15	21	
Uganda	18	25	

Table A4.4

Share of women-held seats in national parliaments, 1990 and 2003

Percent

Source: IPU 2004.

Region and country	1990	2003
Developed countries		
Australia	6.1	27.1
Austria	11.5	27.5
Belgium	8.5	33.2
Canada	13.3	26.5
Denmark	30.7	38.0
Finland	31.5	37.5
France	6.9	11.6
Germany	15.4	28.4
Greece	6.7	
Iceland	20.6	30.2
Ireland	7.8	15.0
Italy	12.9	9.8
Japan	1.4	11.3
Luxembourg	13.3	16.7
Netherlands	21.3	34.4
New Zealand	14.4	28.3
Norway	35.8	36.4
Portugal	7.6	19.1
Spain	14.6	29.6
Sweden	38.4	45.3
Switzerland	14.0	24.5
United Kingdom	6.3	17.3
United States	6.6	13.6
East Asia and the Pacific		
Brunei Darussalam		
Cambodia		11.5
China	21.3	20.2
Fiji		6.0
Hong Kong, China		
Indonesia	12.4	8.0
Kiribati	0.0	4.8
Korea, DPR	21.1	
Korea, Rep.	2.0	5.5
Lao, PDR	6.3	22.9
Malaysia	5.1	
Marshall Islands		3.0
Micronesia, Fed. States		0.0
Mongolia	24.9	10.5
Myanmar		
Nauru	5.6	0.0
Palau		0.0
Papua New Guinea	0.0	0.9
Philippines	9.1	15.2
Samoa	0.0	6.1
Singapore	4.9	16.0
Solomon Islands	0.0	0.0
Thailand	2.8	9.9
Timor-Leste		
Tonga	0.0	0.0
Tuvalu	7.7	0.0
Vanuatu	4.3	1.9
Viet Nam	17.7	27.3

Table A4.4

Share of women-held seats in national parliaments, 1990 and 2003

(continued)

Region and country	1990	2003
Europe and Central Asia		
Albania	28.8	5.7
Armenia	35.6	4.6
Azerbaijan		10.5
Belarus		20.7
Bosnia and Herzegovina		8.4
Bulgaria	21.0	26.2
Croatia		17.8
Cyprus	1.8	10.7
Czech Republic		14.7
Estonia		18.8
Georgia		
Hungary	20.7	9.8
Kazakhstan		7.8
Kyrgyzstan		6.1
Latvia		21.0
Lithuania		10.6
Macedonia, TFYR		18.3
Moldova		12.9
Poland	13.5	21.6
Romania	34.4	8.2
Russian Federation		6.6
Serbia		7.9
Slovakia		19.3
Slovenia		12.2
Tajikistan		12.3
Turkey	1.3	4.4
Turkmenistan	26.0	26.0
Ukraine		5.3
Uzbekistan		7.2
Latin America and the Caribbean		
Antigua and Barbuda	0.0	8.6
Argentina	6.3	32.0
Bahamas	4.1	31.9
Barbados	3.7	18.6
Belize	0.0	13.2
Bolivia	9.2	16.7
Brazil	5.3	10.5
Chile		8.3
Colombia	4.5	10.4
Costa Rica	10.5	35.1
Cuba	33.9	36.0
Dominica	10.0	18.8
Dominican Republic	7.5	11.8
Ecuador	4.5	16.0
El Salvador	11.7	10.7
Grenada		28.8
Guatemala	7.0	8.2
Guyana	36.9	20.0
Haiti		14.8
Honduras	10.2	5.5
Jamaica	5.0	15.4

Table A4.4

Share of women-held seats in national parliaments, 1990 and 2003

(continued)

Region and country	1990	2003
Mexico	12.0	19.1
Nicaragua	14.8	20.7
Panama	7.5	9.9
Paraguay	5.6	9.5
Peru	5.6	18.3
St. Kitts and Nevis	6.7	13.3
St. Lucia	0.0	23.8
St. Vincent and the Grenadines	9.5	22.7
Suriname	7.8	17.6
Trinidad and Tobago	16.7	25.9
Uruguay	6.1	10.9
Venezuela	10.0	9.7
Middle East and North Africa		
Algeria	2.4	6.2
Bahrain		7.5
Djibouti	0.0	10.8
Egypt, Arab Rep.	3.9	4.1
Iraq	10.8	
Israel	6.7	15.0
Jordan	0.0	9.1
Kuwait		0.0
Lebanon	0.0	2.3
Libyan Arab Jamahiriya		
Morocco	0.0	10.8
Oman		
Palestinian Autonomous Territories		
Qatar		
Saudi Arabia		0.0
Sudan		9.7
Syrian Arab Republic	9.2	12.0
Tunisia	4.3	11.5
United Arab Emirates	0.0	0.0
Yemen	4.1	0.3
South Asia		
Afghanistan	3.7	
Bangladesh	10.3	2.0
Bhutan	2.0	9.3
India	5.0	9.6
Iran, Islamic Rep.	1.5	
Maldives	6.3	6.0
Nepal	6.1	7.1
Pakistan	10.1	19.8
Sri Lanka	4.9	4.4
Sub-Saharan Africa		
Angola	14.5	15.5
Benin	2.9	7.2
Botswana	5.0	17.0
Burkina Faso		11.7
Burundi		18.7
Cameroon	14.4	8.9
Cape Verde	12.0	11.1
Central African Republic	3.8	
Chad		5.8

Table A4.4

Share of women-held seats in national parliaments, 1990 and 2003

(continued)

Region and country	1990	2003
Comoros	0.0	
Congo, Dem. Rep.	5.4	7.3
Congo, Rep.	14.3	11.8
Côte d'Ivoire	5.7	8.5
Equatorial Guinea	13.3	5.0
Eritrea		22.0
Ethiopia		8.0
Gabon	13.3	11.2
Gambia	7.8	13.2
Ghana		9.0
Guinea		19.3
Guinea-Bissau	20.0	
Kenya	1.1	7.1
Lesotho		24.1
Liberia		
Madagascar	6.5	7.4
Malawi	9.8	9.3
Mali		10.2
Mauritania		4.6
Mauritius	7.1	5.7
Mozambique	15.7	30.0
Namibia	6.9	17.1
Niger	5.4	1.2
Nigeria		4.5
Rwanda	17.1	39.4
São Tomé and Principe	11.8	9.1
Senegal	12.5	19.2
Seychelles	16.0	29.4
Sierra Leone		14.5
Somalia	4.0	
South Africa	2.8	30.7
Swaziland	3.6	20.4
Tanzania		21.4
Togo	5.2	7.4
Uganda	12.2	24.7
Zambia	6.6	12.0
Zimbabwe	11.0	10.0

Employment indicators

Table A5.1

Share of women in employment by type

a No further subdivision, as most agricultural employment is self-employment and informal.
b. Current Goal indicator.
c. Employees holding informal jobs in formal sector enterprises, informal sector enterprises, or as paid domestic workers employed by households. Direct measurement (through Labor Force Survey data) or use of residual method.
d. Own-account workers, employers, contributing family workers, and where relevant members of producer cooperatives.
e. Contributing family workers and informal sector entrepreneurs (including members of informal producer cooperatives). Data on informal sector entrepreneurs currently not available for all countries. Missing data may be estimated using the share of informal sector entrepreneurs in total nonagricultural self-employment (own-account workers, employers, members of producer cooperatives) of countries in the same region or subregion.

Source: ILO 2004c.

Employment by type	Women as share of total employment (percent)
Total employment (all types)	X
1. Agricultural employment[a]	X
2. Nonagricultural wage employment[b]	X
2.1 Informal wage employment[c]	X
3. Nonagricultural self-employment[d]	X
3.1 Informal self employment[e]	X

Summary of e-discussion facilitated by ActionAid International, United Kingdom

The UN Millennium Project Task Force on Education and Gender Equality has written interim reports on achieving the Millennium Development Goals of universal primary education and gender equality and women's empowerment.[1] From June 14 to July 5, 2004, an electronic forum was created to discuss and provide feedback on the interim gender equality report.

ActionAid International partnered with the Commonwealth Education Fund, the Global Campaign on Education, and One World South Asia to launch the e-discussion.[2] As the lead partner, ActionAid International hired a moderator for the discussion and provided managerial support. The Commonwealth Education Fund provided managerial support and reached out to its large constituency of staff worldwide. One World South Asia provided the discussion platform, training for the moderator, and technical support for the website.

The moderator began the online dialogue each week by launching discussion questions on specific sections of the report. A one-page summary of the report was provided for the discussion group, and participants were also encouraged to read the executive summary and full report. Reactions to the overall framing of the gender equality Goal were collected in the first week of the e-dialogue. Discussions in the second week focused on the six strategic priorities outlined in the report. The third and final week focused on the "making it work" section.

Response volume and participant profiles

The discussion group attracted more than 1,200 participants, although not all contributed to the e-discussion. Response volume was "manageable" in that the group was not flooded with responses, and, for the most part, what was received was valuable. The discussion took about a week to gain momentum (only eight responses were received in the first week), but once it did, the discussion averaged five responses a day.

Response volume
A total of 1,538 people were subscribed to the discussion group at the beginning of the dialogue. On July 5, at the end of the three-week discussion, 1,272 members belonged to the group. The decrease is primarily the result of incorrect email addresses, although 33 people unsubscribed.

Approximately 1,100 subscribers were members of the Education Rights2Realities discussion group hosted by Global Campaign on Education over the past year. Some 538 new names were automatically subscribed from the list compiled by ActionAid International and Commonwealth Education Secretariat. An additional 261 people voluntarily subscribed to the group.

Participant profiles
There were 69 responses from 25 different countries over the three-week period. Accounting for multiple messages sent by any one participant, a total of 47 people participated—28 women and 19 men. They represented international NGOs, local civil society organizations, academia, and donor agencies. A regional breakdown of the 47 responses is provided below:
- Europe (Italy, Netherlands, Romania, Sweden, United Kingdom).
- Asia (Cambodia, India, Nepal, Pakistan, Philippines).
- Latin America (Argentina).
- Africa (Ghana, Kenya, Liberia, Malawi, Nigeria, Senegal, South Africa, Tanzania, Togo, Uganda, Zambia).
- Middle East (Yemen).
- North America (Canada, United States).

Week 1: opening the forum for discussion
This first week of the dialogue was intentionally left "unstructured" to monitor the areas participants felt were important to discuss. A few questions on how the report was framed as a whole were asked in order to catalyze discussions:
- Do you agree with the interpretation of the goals in the Millennium Development Goals report?
- Does the report miss the opportunity to highlight a failure and demand more immediate action to achieve the education target by 2005?
- Will this report succeed in galvanizing action on this Goal?
- What relevance do these goals have to your work?

Comments here related to the need to approach strategies from a gendered lens, transforming schools to be centers of learning, the report's capacity to pressure the international community on the unmet Millennium Development Target of gender parity in primary and secondary schools by 2005, recommendations for developing indicators to measure progress, and discussion on caveats to be considered when observing that a country is "making progress" toward a target or goal.

Preserving the gendered lens

Participants reminded the task force to stay true to *gendered* strategies (not just those focused on girls and women). As one participant pointed out, the strategic priorities target only women's groups. The interim report states, "The spirit of the goal—gender equality and the empowerment of women—requires fundamental transformation in opportunities and outcomes for both men and women" (p. 2). Understanding the influence men have over women's lives, and how they together can successfully negotiate better living situations for all, is an essential step toward gender equality. Issues of power must be clearly recognized in the report because in many cases, education, sexual, and economic initiatives that empower women to act independently are construed as taking power away from men. This perspective undermines progress achieved on gender equality. It was suggested that gender analyses take place in tandem with age- and area-specific analyses.

A gender lens also means looking at the disparities between boys' and girls' educational achievement. The report should therefore focus on regional specific trends in girls' and boys' educational rates. More research needs to be undertaken on the increasing trend of men and boys falling behind in education in some regions of the world, such as Latin America. Some participants noted that documentation indicates that the causes are linked to the structure and demands of the labor market as shaped by the globalized neoliberal economy, as well as in the interrelated changes in family composition and gender roles. This research shows that it may not be that the world's education systems have improved and gender inequalities have decreased, but rather that current problems such as conflict, HIV/AIDS, and poverty are skewing educational achievements for both sexes.

Transforming schools

There is a strong underlying assumption in the report that schools are positive environments. There is not enough about the potentially negative experience of schools—about violence and discrimination against girls in schools. More analysis on how schools can be transformational rather than reproducing prejudice and discrimination needs to be undertaken. How can schools be a microcosm of the society we want to create? Offering subjects of relevance to a community can increase girls' participation rates in school (box A6.1). If schools can be made into transformational environments, then they can play a more profound role in achieving gender equality.

Participants also expressed concern that the report downplays the importance of education (of high quality) in empowering girls and women. In fact, the majority of responses received during the three-week dialogue pertained to

Box A6.1 **The All China Women's Federation makes education relevant to learners** *Source:* L. Wright, United States.	Schools often serve as sites for the socialization of gender roles that contribute to inequality. Education needs to be relevant to its learners. The All China Women's Federation achieved high rates for rural girls in school by incorporating traditional classroom learning with skills for growing crops. Because agricultural skills are valued in the community, schooling became seen as an important resource, and women's status in the community was elevated. The positive influence of women teachers on girls' education was also cited, and appropriate support to recruit, train and support women entering the teaching force was suggested.

the way education was framed in the report. These responses will be detailed in the discussion's second week summary below. However, it should be noted that the volume and diversity of responses on education indicate that the report should more forcefully credit the role of education in empowering women and attaining gender equality.

Paying due attention to the Millennium Development Target of achieving gender parity in primary and secondary schools by 2005

Participants expressed the need to give substantial dedicated attention to the failure of so many countries to achieve this target. This is the only target set for 2005. Its failure could threaten the value of the other Goals. This report should be the one that builds a sense of urgency around this failure and should propose very real steps that will help ensure that this target is met. Participants also called on governments and donor agencies to keep their promises to ensure that primary education is free and compulsory. Some even suggested that education up to grade 12 should be free and compulsory.

The report's comprehensive review of the progress of the target in Goal 3 shows that "few countries will achieve a ratio of 1.0—or gender parity—either by 2005 or 2015. Many countries that are on track to meet the target will do so in ways that are not empowering to girls because they will not increase overall female enrollment rates." The report should better document the reasons that this target has failed. Comprehensively reviewing initiatives that have led to progress in some countries and the strategies that have failed would be very instructive. Illustration of radical actions required to achieving the target would be the next step. In short, the report has the potential to make a real difference—but fails to do so in its present form.

The following response summarizes the participant's recommendations:

The report should be re-balanced to have at least half of it linked strongly to the education target that is being missed and the other half opening up the agenda. The heart of the report must take clear and focused positions on what the global community should do to achieve gender equality in primary and secondary education. This is a unique political opportunity for us to demand action now (and particularly at the United Nations Heads of State Summit in Autumn 2005). Whilst action on this target alone will not change everything we could at least galvanize real global action on it—and this would be a great first step.

—D. Archer, United Kingdom.

Developing better indicators

The task force's proposal of expanding the indicators measuring educational attainment (by including completion rates) is noteworthy, as are the additional three indicators to measure women's empowerment and gender equality. Participants suggested the need for more instruments to monitor and evaluate the impact of international policy rhetoric at the village and NGO levels, the quality of development programs, and transparency and accountability at all levels. Participants suggested some tools that might be useful to this end, such as the recently developed gender empowerment measure in education.[3]

Another resource is a "scorecard" ranking the progress of Commonwealth countries in Africa on girls' education initiatives. Case studies on Kenya, South Africa, and Uganda illustrate how NGO coalitions, governments, and international agencies can develop a shared understanding of accountability and approach the task of assessing progress toward reaching the Goal.[4] The scorecard looks at access and retention in broader ways than the other existing measures. It looks at not only the number of girls who attend and remain in primary school but also whether those girls are able to translate that attendance and retention into future schooling at a secondary level and have healthy lives where they earn a reasonable income.

The report's overview of the nuanced differences between gender parity and gender equality was appreciated. Participants agreed that the target of the Millennium Development Goal should be interpreted through equality benchmarks, especially since achieving gender parity does not automatically translate to substantive positive change in girls' and young women's status and life options. In the Philippines, for example, it was pointed out that although national aggregated statistics show a near parity between girls' and boys' access to education, this has not led to a marked improvement in gender equality in society.

Lastly, one participant noted that gender inequality and poverty are complex phenomena. "We are obsessed with maintaining a narrow goal with narrow indicators because we assume that donor funds will not be increased to the level required to achieve the wider agenda. However it is the wider agenda that correctly addresses the complexity of poverty, which should be our framework for action. This wider agenda is not new as it has been set by numerous covenants, conferences, and programs of action (such as the 1994 International Conference on Population and Development Programme of Action, a 20-year program, covers many of the points we are discussing)" (M. Blackett, Uganda).

Defining "progress"

Participants reminded the task force that the devil is in the details, and aggregate figures mask vast regional and socioeconomic disparities. Progress has not been universal. Even in countries where there have been advances, pockets of poverty and inequality continue to exist and even widen.

While there has been progress in literacy levels and primary school enrollment in the past decade, aggregate figures hide low educational achievement in rural hamlets and urban slums. In addition, access and quality issues become far more pronounced as one goes down the social and economic pyramid. According to a report by one of the participants that was shared in the discussion, there are wide discrepancies between the percentage of boys and girls completing primary school in India. According to data, all enrolled children in Kerala and 82 percent in Maharashtra completed primary school, as compared to 28 percent in Bihar and 26 percent in West Bengal. For girls, socially disadvantaged groups, and those in rural areas, completion rates are even lower. Educational statistics further reveal that 59 million children in the 6–14 age group are still out of school, of whom 35 million, or 59 percent, are girls (V. Ramachandran, India).[5]

In countries and regions where progress on the target for Goal 3 was achieved, participants still cautioned that "access should be accompanied with quality because quality is the essence of equity" (V. Ramachandran, India). When the quality of education and the schooling experience remains troublesome and alarming (sexual violence against girls in Zambia), it is difficult to conclude that progress has been made. Drastic changes must take place to ensure children acquire reading, writing, and cognitive skills appropriate for each level of education. This necessitates a multipronged approach of changing curriculum, classroom teaching practices, teacher training, classroom environment, teacher attitudes, and school-community linkages.

Week 2: the task force's strategic priorities to achieve gender equality and women's empowerment

The report outlines six essential strategies for empowering women and meeting the gender equality Goal:

- Improving secondary education.
- Ensuring adequate reproductive health information and services.
- Investing in infrastructure designed to reduce women's and girls' time burdens.
- Guaranteeing inheritance and property rights for women.
- Adopting gender quotas and reservations to increase women's political participation.
- Combating violence against women.

Although comments on all six actions were welcomed, the task force expressed the desire for feedback and project examples on secondary education, investment in infrastructure designed to reduce time burden, and adoption of gender quotas and reservations for women's political participation. The discussion questions were framed around this request:

- Are the six strategic priorities outlined in the report the best way to achieve gender equality and empower women? Do you have comments on these priorities or can you suggest other actions?
- In particular, which level of education is likely to have the greatest payoff for women's empowerment: primary or secondary? What exactly do we mean by "the greatest payoff for women's empowerment"?
- Is affirmative action the most effective route to increase women's voices at the national and local levels? Do quotas and reservations address the fundamental issues that affect women and create the space necessary to look at the root causes of gender inequalities?
- Investment in infrastructure designed to reduce girls and women's time burden is good. But will this on its own lead to women's greater decision-making power and ability to negotiate their time and work burdens?
- Does a decrease in women's time burden necessarily lead to their increased participation in productive and fulfilling activities?
- Finally, please share examples from your projects that have contributed to empowering women and minimizing inequalities. Tell us about the successful strategies and obstacles!

Overall, there was consensus on the need to expand the understanding of gender equality beyond the education sphere to other areas (reproductive health, a society free of violence, and the like) because achieving gender equality in these other realms empowers women and builds on the gains made through the Beijing Declaration and the Convention on the Elimination of All Forms of Discrimination Against Women processes. There was considerable debate about the task force's emphasis on postprimary education for girls and the effectiveness of quotas for women's political participation.

Strategic priority 1: strengthen opportunities for secondary education for girls and eliminate gender gaps at that level

Don't downplay the importance of primary education and the missed 2005 gender parity target. Some participants urged the task force not to overlook the importance of primary education. "By shifting the agenda upward to secondary schooling and outwards to other gender equality issues, we risk losing or overstretching the powerful consensus that underpins the [Millennium Development Goals]" (D. Archer, United Kingdom). For example, in the Brong Ahafo Region in Ghana, enrollment rates decrease as children progress through the basic education cycle. In 1998/99 the dropout rate in class 2 was 20 percent. For grade 6 this figure climbed to 30.1 percent for boys and 36.5 percent for girls (J. Adu-Gyamfi, Ghana). The conflict-riddled northern region of Uganda provides another example where achieving gender parity in primary schooling is still a dream. "Shifting goals [targets] to secondary education would not make any sense to the nation or even to the girls themselves" (T. Muzoora, Uganda).

Participants applauded the task force for highlighting that the current returns to primary schooling at present are low. However, they asked that the report better document why more progress had not been achieved. Now is the time to overhaul or fundamentally reform primary schools.

The merits of secondary education. Participants agreed that children who finish primary school are better able to analyze problems and have more skills to obtain better jobs than those who have dropped out. There is little disagreement over the benefits of secondary education. Some participants even welcomed the task force's emphasis on post-primary education, citing that where they live (Latin America, areas in India and Cambodia, nomadic pastoral societies in Nigeria and Nepal), children need to have increased access to secondary education. In Cambodia, a dormitory for girls helps ensure their transfer from primary to lower secondary school (T. Seanlay, Cambodia). It was also pointed out that in some countries, such as India, investment in secondary education is higher than investments in primary education.

Interventions needed to improve enrollment and retention at primary and secondary levels are very different, as children and parents have different constraints and concerns at these stages. The reasons for girls' failure to attend school at the primary level, such as tending to household chores, could be very different from the reasons they do not advance to secondary school, such as early marriage and pregnancy (box A6.2).

Strategic priority 3: invest in gender-responsive infrastructure to reduce girls' and women's time poverty

Participants agreed with the need to invest in gender-responsive infrastructure to reduce women's and girls' poverty. The discussion, however, was brought back to the earlier point of gender equality. Investment in infrastructure alone

Box A6.2

Botswana's Diphalana initiative for keeping pregnant girls in school

Source: C. Challendar, United Kingdom.

The Diphalana initiative in Botswana is an example of how concerns across a range of social sectors—health, education and social welfare—can be integrated to provide an imaginative response to the issue of schoolgirl pregnancy. Pregnant schoolgirls at Pekenene School are allowed to return to school after giving birth, for as long as they wish (previously Botswanan law only allowed re-entry in certain circumstances, and girls had to wait a year). During maternity leave, schoolwork and other resources are sent to girls' homes, and the school has developed a curriculum with some distance education modules that can be followed at this time. When girls are certified fit to return to school by a doctor, they return with their babies. The school has crèche facilities, which can take babies as young as four months, and nappies and milk are provided. At break and lunchtimes the young mothers breastfeed their children. The Diphalana project requires that the father, if he is at school, share the responsibility of looking after the baby at break and lunch times.

does not lower women's time burden. Many other factors have to be favorable in order for women to access to resources and decisionmaking power.

For example, if appropriate infrastructure to reduce girls and women's time burden were to exist, would it necessarily enable them to engage in productive activities? Unless we address the root cause of gender inequality and powerlessness, which in most places is socially constructed, then investment in infrastructure will only uphold the status quo (C. Anywanyu, United Kingdom).

Strategic priority 5: increase women's representation in political bodies

While participants agree with reserving quotas for women in local management committees and governance structures at all levels, they recognize that these measures don't guarantee choice and control over decisionmaking processes. Nor do quotas provide the space to discuss the root causes of gender inequality, especially from the perspective of poor women. Participants noted that there are numerous examples of how women's participation has been symbolic more than meaningful. Reserving seats for women in school management committees, parent-teacher associations, and the like is now a common practice. However, women rarely participate in decisionmaking and their contribution (often cooking for meetings) is not remunerated. Other projects intentionally exclude women if they are not perceived to be proficient on the subject matter.

Participants urged the task force to provide examples of how greater participation of women in leadership roles can enable them to access information and take part in decisionmaking. Quotas and reservations are not an effective strategy unless women are well recognized and are involved in major decisionmaking processes. In short, quotas and reservations are a first step. The next step is to support women and men to make the most of these opportunities. Giving women choice in what to participate in is also very important.

Other suggested priorities

Participants recommended three additional priorities to include in the report: adult education, HIV/AIDS, and nonformal education.

Adult education. The link between women's educational achievement and girls' enrollment and completion has been well documented. In rural Yemen, for example, increased community demand for women's and adolescent's education occurred after some adult women in the community learned to read and write (N. Adra, Yemen). Social change and increase in girls' enrollment and community engagement is more likely to occur when women are given a voice. The report should support adult literacy programs for women and girls who have dropped out of school. Examples from ActionAid International's Reflect program and the Forum for African Women's Educationalists adult literacy initiative illustrate the importance of a well designed, intensive, and long-term initiative as opposed to short-term, project-linked literacy courses.

Participants were surprised about the absence of women's literacy or education in the report, especially since adult education is an essential component to women's empowerment. This could be tied to many of the issues raised in this report—a way of developing an integrated response to address awareness of rights, legal literacy, sexual and reproductive health, confidence, and so on. How else are we to achieve the transformation we desire if not by giving women themselves time and space to do their own analysis of issues and strengthen their communication skills? One suggestion was to include this as a central thread to the report.

Nonformal learning for girls and boys. Alternative approaches to provide lifelong learning opportunities for children and adults who have dropped out are incredibly important, especially given the large number of people who do not complete primary school, much less advancing to secondary. Rather than confine education within school walls, nonformal education will become more and more necessary if we are to reach the marginalized and achieve education for all. Pakistan, where the dropout rate for children is nearly 45 percent, is just one case in point. A large number of these children rely on nonformal education to gain a second chance to return to the educational system (S. Rahman, Pakistan).

Impact of HIV/AIDS on gender equality and women's empowerment. HIV/AIDS affects all areas of development and life. With infection and deaths increasing at alarming rates, understanding the impact of HIV/AIDS on gender equality and women's empowerment has to be a central strategy in achieving gender equality and women's empowerment (box A6.3).

Other strategies

Additional strategies suggested by participants include the following:

- Expand community-based preschools to promote girls' enrollment in grade 1.

Box A6.3

Zambian girls defy traditional barriers to stay in school

Source: P. Merckx, Belgium.

Zambia has the highest proportion of orphans in Southern Africa. One in five mothers is HIV-positive in Zambia. At least one third of all children have lost a parent. A staggering half a million children have lost both parents to AIDS. Three-quarters of Zambian families are caring for at least one orphan. Under conditions where most of the people do not have enough to live on, many children go uncared for and live on the streets. Orphanages run by the churches and NGOs are unable to cope and many were soon living out on the streets again.

Girls drop out of school at higher rates, as they are the first to care for their family, cook, and care for younger siblings. Zambian girls are defying traditional barriers, teenage pregnancy, and the risk of HIV infection to go back to school to finish their education. When you combine the high teenage pregnancies and HIV-infection rates, as well as the girls' fear of being sexually abused on their way to school or in school, you realize how great the odds are.

- Conduct public awareness campaigns for parents to send girls to school.
- Reduce the distance to school.
- Abolish public school fees.
- Reform curriculum to eliminate gender bias.
- Expand nonformal education opportunities for women.
- Develop teaching and learning strategies to increase girls' interest and performance in science and math, which are keys areas in fighting poverty.
- Pay more attention to the language of schooling, as indigenous and rural communities are often effectively excluded from the school system due to language barriers.
- Document the impact of conflict on education.
- Include other forms of violence, such as trafficking and exploitation of women.
- Provide appropriate training for women workers with the support of employers and the government.
- Encourage workers to form unions or associations.

Week 3: making it happen

In the final section of the report, the task force also recommends four key actions to achieve the six strategic priorities. Questions relating to these four actions were circulated to the discussion group:

- What can the international community do to make more rapid progress in achieving the 2005 gender parity target that will be missed? What kinds of efforts can be undertaken leading up to the G8 or UN Heads of State Summit that show that the international community is taking this target seriously?
- What kinds of changes need to take place in institutional structures (and in which ones) in order for each of the six priorities to be addressed effectively?
- The e-discussion highlighted that many groups—men and boys, nomadic and pastoral communities—need to be engaged in the discussion if transformation in gender relations is to take place. What successful examples and lessons learned do you have from past international campaigns (Education For All, Global Campaign on Education) and actions on the ground to make gender equality a reality?
- Participants raised questions about the feasibility of implementing the six strategic priorities and accountability. How can civil society organizations and communities take action and hold governments responsible for delivering on these? What kind of coordination needs to take place so international agencies feel the pressure to create systems and processes to galvanize action?

Involve civil society

Participants pointed out that NGOs, civil society organizations, and citizens are essential to reaching the Millennium Development Goals. They called for a global mobilization of civil society—poor people, women and girls, men and boys—to articulate the actions they think are necessary and feasible, and they called on governments, NGOs, and donor agencies to reject the strategies that do not serve the people. Worldwide mobilization for influencing policy and funding priorities at the upcoming G8 and UN Heads of State Summit should be undertaken immediately.

Another reason for involving civil society is that sociocultural practices remain an obstacle for women's empowerment and gender equality. While the example cited in the box above pertains to pastoralist societies, practices that undermine women's advancement are found in all walks of life.

Finally, participants highlighted that children should also be part of efforts to transform norms and influence policy. Initiatives such as the Girls' Education Movement in Africa involve girls as key actors in policy and program development on the issues that affect their education. Another youth-driven program in South Africa, the Gendering Adolescent AIDS Project, encourages and empowers young people to understand their own sexuality and to protect themselves against gender-based violence, HIV/AIDS, unwanted pregnancies, and sexually transmitted diseases (J. Kirk, Canada).

International commitment: the need for adequate financial and technical resources

The Millennium Development Goals can be valuable in that they represent a significant commitment from governments. But they also represent huge compromises in terms of who decides the target and funding priorities and what is feasible (especially politically) to expect from government leaders and UN agencies. To date, international commitments for increased resources for universal primary education (that is, Education For All and Fast Track Initiative) have not been met. The cumulative and interconnected nature of Goals 2 and 3 present an opportunity to demand an increase of resources for education with a special focus on girls. The other concern is the effectiveness and management of resources to implement programs. Participants agreed that it is not only about how much money is allocated, but how it is spent and who decides how to spend it.

Achieving gender equality: modifying institutional structures

Meeting the gender equity goal requires organizations to look at the composition of their own staff. The overwhelmingly male and U.S.-driven composition of the task force's co-coordinator group was highlighted. For example, there are 19 men and 7 women. The gender working group comprises three of these women—hardly a gender balance without a man. To a certain extent, this imbalance questions the objectivity of the task force's recommendations on gender equity.

At the same time, achieving changes at an institutional level does not necessarily translate into changes in the household. "Primary and secondary school encompass a period of time that is the most hectic time for girls in rural Africa. Girls are learning how to prepare meals, look after siblings and participate in all other chores at home. When do they have time to concentrate on education? How can we influence such values and release young girls of social responsibilities, or at least help them find a balance?" (D. Ruta, Uganda)

More work and time is also required to change people's attitudes, behaviors, and knowledge on equity and equality, especially in the face of strong cultural and religious practices. In most developing countries, girls will need support and motivation from their families and communities to help them attend and remain in school. Traditional norms (girls made to remain at home and help with housework and farming and attend traditional schools to prepare for marriage) and poverty (parents' poor economic status resulting in the lack of interest) are key factors underlying gender disparity in education in the developing world. However, it was also pointed out that not all aspects of tradition are detrimental to women's empowerment, and not all modernity is beneficial. A balance needs to be achieved.

Transforming gender relations: the role of women's and grassroots organizations

Women's organizations and movements contribute a great deal to achieving gender equality. These organizations can help define the type of education for girls that will best promote the broad empowerment of women. How can we connect women's organizations with other organizations to meet empowerment and equality goals?

Gender equality and empowerment, however, need the support of a wide array of organizations, and not only those that focus exclusively on women. Grassroots organizations in particular play an important role in transforming social norms. Appropriate financial and technical assistance should be provided for all organizations to constructively work on gender issues (G. Mitton, United States). This speaks to the earlier point on gender equality—men and boys need to be involved for a transformation in attitudes, norms, and behaviors to occur. Gender equality is not about women taking power away from men, but about women working alongside men in community development, and receiving their fair share of opportunities.

Accountability mechanisms

The issue of accountability applies at various levels, from not having sufficient legislation to support women's access to and control over resources, to delivering on policies. Leaders need to be accountable to citizens and not just the international community. Poor people and youth need to be mobilized to demand their rights and to question what resources are used and the allocation of donor monies.

Finally, what happens when the Millennium Development target of gender parity is not met by 2005? Who is held accountable? The consequence will be felt most by uneducated children and their parents—but what happens to the government and donor agencies that do not deliver on their promise?

Establish effective priorities. Participants pointed out the need to distinguish the immediate political opportunities presented by the Millennium Development target and the wider issue of how we might collectively work toward achieving gender equality and women's empowerment. Participants reiterated that the report should focus on the missed target.

Although worthwhile, some participants wondered if the task force's strategic priorities might negatively affect priority-setting. Is it possible that they might actually dilute priority-setting and not contribute to actual change? They cautioned that adding new strategic priorities may distract governments and donors, especially when these are more ambitious, complex, and expensive than the original targets that are neither being funded nor achieved. Next, how can actions whose priorities are set at international levels still address local needs (where the changes are likely to have the greatest impact)?

Analysis and recommendations

The purpose of this analysis is to discuss the impact of the e-dialogue and the diversity of subject matters and to recommend priority areas of action for the task force based on the greatest number of responses received.

Impact

As aforementioned, not all of the more than 1,200 subscribers to the e-discussion actively participated. Many noted that when they were in agreement with responses already sent, they preferred not to send a duplicate message. Rather, they contributed when they held a different perspective. Many people also shared that although they had not participated, they keenly followed the dialogue and the outcomes would have an impact on their future policy and program formulation. The small number of people who actually unsubscribed during the three weeks suggests that interest in the dialogue was high. Finally, this dialogue was organized in a relatively short period of time; more preparation time would have enhanced both the diversity and volume of responses.

Diversity of subjects discussed

The majority of responses focused on the report's coverage of educational issues. However, in the second week's debate on strategic priorities, participants also commented on gender-responsive infrastructure and quotas. This was primarily because discussion questions specifically focused on these issues (as requested by the International Center for Research on Women, questions on only three of the six matters were asked). One reason the dialogue favored education is that education specialists working on gender matters were more heavily represented on the list. Although the list of more than 300 names provided by the International Center for Research on Women was intended to balance this membership, more than a third of the email addresses were incorrect, and the onus was on the potential participants to subscribe to the discussion. This list was sent to the moderator two days into the dialogue. Past experience shows that people are likely to join and stay engaged if involved at the beginning of the dialogue rather than asked to join once it has begun. Finally, the International Center for Research on Women was not able to advertise the dialogue on their web page, which could have been an ideal opportunity to attract participants.

Recommendation 1: focus on why the target for Goal 3 has not been met, and galvanize action toward achieving the target by 2015

Participants requested that the task force call on the international community to redouble efforts to achieve the gender parity target by 2005 or as soon thereafter as possible. The report itself states that missing the target for Goal 3 is the first visible Millennium Development Goal failure. "But instead of serving as an opportunity to underscore the failures of the international community, 2005 should be used to issue a clarion call for re-energizing efforts so that the second deadline for the target—2015—is honored" (UN Millennium Project 2004d).

A strong report that exposes the failure to achieve this target and proposes radical action to achieve it (such as, a global movement to abolish all user fees in primary and secondary education) could make a real difference in ensuring the target is reached sooner rather than later.

Recommendation 2: do not emphasize secondary education to the exclusion of primary

There is a debate about which level of education (primary or secondary) is most beneficial to girls and women. Participants overwhelmingly agreed that more education is better, and applauded the task force for widening the definition of empowerment to include education at all levels, in different situations (such as nonformal education), as well as recognizing the importance of quality, and not just access. But they also reminded the task force that most children (the majority of them girls) drop out during primary school, in which case the question of promotion to secondary school is irrelevant. The report's "progress toward the goal" section clearly and comprehensively states this fact. This further confuses the reader—the facts say one thing, but the recommendation says another. As the above analysis explained, focus on getting one thing right first.

Recommendation 3: transform schools and other institutions to be more gender-sensitive

The Millennium Development Target for 2005 will be missed. This signals that we cannot continue implementing development programs using the same strategies as we have in the past few decades. Substantial efforts must be undertaken to challenge the status quo and overhaul the system, whether it be education, health, or trade. Supporting dysfunctional systems is not effective; let's change what doesn't work.

Recommendation 4: recognize the impact of HIV/AIDS, conflict, and globalization on women's empowerment—with strategies such as adult education and nonformal education

A number of key priorities emerging from today's global context have to be considered. Situations such as the increasing rate of HIV/AIDS infection and deaths, conflicts, and violence undermine development efforts, making it difficult to conduct "business as usual." In addition, greater emphasis needs to be placed on the importance of a high quality education, the intergenerational link between women's education (literacy) and children's educational and health outcomes, and the need for alternative learning modalities for AIDS orphans, street children, dropouts, indigenous people, and other marginalized groups.

Recommendation 5: Clarify how the Millennium Development Goals support other UN led policy initiatives and whether the Goals supersede previously agreed upon targets and policies

Discussants commented that the UN Millennium Project and corresponding development goals should be better linked to other UN-led initiatives, such as Education For All and the Fast Track Initiative. How does this report work in conjunction with Commission on the Status of Women and the recommendations issued from Beijing and the reviewing progress conferences? How can the task force ensure that efforts will not be duplicated?

Participants pointed out that the necessary frameworks, recommendations, and strategies are already there in detail. Concepts, ideas, and definitions were spelled out in Jomtien, Thailand, in 1990. The 2000 Dakar Framework for Action lays out concrete goals, strategies, and roles and responsibilities for governments, donors, and civil society organizations. More strategies and roles can be found in the guidelines for poverty reduction strategy papers, in the Fast Track Initiative, and so on.

Conclusions

The task force's desire to collect civil society feedback on the report is encouraging. The goal of this consultation was to elicit perspectives from civil society organizations on the content of the report. For their part, civil society organizations engaged in a lively three-week debate over the report. What is not clear is the extent to which key recommendations and other responses will be integrated into the final report. The potential of civil society influence on this report would have been greater if consultations had taken place earlier, when the report's main tenets were being formulated and throughout the process of revisions. This is troubling not only because it questions the genuine space created for participation, but also because participants challenged and disagreed with two of the report's key strategic objectives.

Albeit these limitations, there is space for the task force to integrate the main recommendations of this consultation as they undertake final revisions. Examples provided by participants could also substantiate, strengthen, and diversify those currently presented in the report. Finally, this summary could be attached as an appendix to the report. ActionAid International welcomes the task force's feedback—both directly to the agency and for the e-discussion group—on how this kind of dialogue can be more influential and valuable to the UN Millennium Project.

Finally, the unavailability of the task force papers in different languages limits regional representation. The executive summary of the report is available in Spanish, but there is no document in French or Portuguese.

In order to make this consultation globally representative, ActionAid International facilitated a Spanish language consultation. The Regional Program for Training in Gender and Public Policy in Argentina also moderated a Spanish-language discussion on the gender equality Millennium Development Goal in August. In addition, ActionAid International translated the executive summary of the task force report into French and launched a discussion in this language. Feedback from these two dialogues was forwarded to the task force.

Notes

Chapter 1

1. One hundred and seventy-eight states are parties to the convention, the most recent being Timor-Leste and the Syrian Arab Republic, in early 2003 (Hannan 2003a).

2. Other important conferences of the 1990s with a focus on gender equality include the World Conference on Human Rights in Vienna in 1993 and the World Summit on Social Development in Copenhagen in 1995.

3. At each of the major UN international conferences of the past two decades governments agreed to a number of time-bound targets, with 1990 as the base year, to serve as benchmarks of progress (Grown, Rao Gupta, and Khan 2003). While most of these targets focus on education and health, the Beijing Platform for Action includes a target for increasing the representation of women in positions of power and decisionmaking. Targets for decreasing women's poverty or increasing women's economic equality are notable by their absence. Although poverty and women's economic rights were key themes at both the Copenhagen and Beijing conferences, governments' commitments to addressing these issues did not result.

4. This vision is similar to that put forth by Development Alternatives with Women for a New Era (DAWN) (Sen and Grown 1987, p. 80).

Chapter 2

1. The task force recognizes that there are cases where interventions must target boys, for example, in countries with reverse gender gaps in secondary education.

Chapter 3

1. The supply of teachers, even for primary education, depends on investments in secondary and tertiary education, and this is another reason for focusing on the education system.

2. This chapter draws from the companion report on achieving universal primary education, also prepared by the Task Force on Education and Gender Equality (UN Millennium Project 2005c).

3. Increases in women's education are associated with declines in fertility around the globe. But how much education is needed for fertility to decline? A review of 59 studies

from many different countries found that the level of women's education associated with a 10 percent decline in the fertility rate varied with the degree of gender stratification (Jejeebhoy 1996). In the most nonegalitarian settings (in Sub-Saharan Africa and South Asia), a 10 percent decline in fertility was attained only among women with some secondary education—or not at all—in 73 percent of the studies. In moderately egalitarian settings a 10 percent decline was attained by women with some primary schooling in half the studies. And in the most egalitarian settings—in Latin America—a 10 percent decline was attained by women with some primary school in 57 percent of the studies.

4. For lower levels of education the existence of a positive effect varies by type of outcome: primary education tends to affect the use of prenatal services more than the use of delivery or postnatal services (Elo 1992; Bhatia and Cleland 1995).

5. This confirms an earlier study in India which found that higher levels of education among women are associated with a lower lifetime incidence of violence against women (Duvvury and Allendorf 2001).

6. Although researchers attempted to control for underlying differences between participants and nonparticipants, this remains a methodological challenge and should be taken into consideration in interpreting the results.

7. UNESCO (2004) puts the figure at 54 percent, while UNICEF (2003b) estimates it at 57 percent.

8. Convergence toward parity can be attained through several types of change: declines in male rates with female rates remaining constant, declines in both female and male rates with male rates declining faster, or increases in both female and male rates with female rates increasing faster. Parity is desirable only if it is attained through increases in female rates.

9. These countries are Botswana, Burkina Faso, Burundi, Cameroon, Central African Republic, Côte d'Ivoire, Eritrea, Ethiopia, Lesotho, Mozambique, Namibia, and Niger.

10. UNESCO defines the *completion rate* as "the total number of students successfully completing, or graduating from, the last year of school in a given year, expressed as a proportion of the total number of children of official graduation age in the population." Since national-level completion or graduation data are hard to compile and are not suitable for cross-country comparisons, UNESCO uses as a proxy completion rate: first time enrollment to the final grade of a school cycle as a proportion of the total number of children of official graduation age in the population.

11. In a recent analysis of Demographic and Health Survey data from 24 Sub-Saharan African countries, Hewett and Lloyd (2004) provide a somewhat more optimistic estimate than that based on the World Bank data used in this chapter. They note that girls' primary completion rates have risen from 48 percent to 53 percent over the 1990s in these 24 countries.

12. These countries are Cambodia, China, Lao PDR, Papua New Guinea, and Samoa; Bulgaria, Estonia, Kazakhstan, and Poland; Turkey; Guyana and Nicaragua; Djibouti, Iraq, and Israel; India; Benin, Burkina Faso, Chad, Côte d'Ivoire, Ethiopia, Lesotho, Mauritius, Mozambique, Senegal, Togo, and Uganda.

13. Lloyd and Hewett (2003) also note that gender inequalities in primary school completion are magnified among the poor.

14. The reason for a female advantage in education among poorer households in these countries is unclear and could be a result of the underlying data collection methodology.

15. For a discussion of more equitable and efficient financing sources, see Sachs and others (2004).

Chapter 4

1. Reproductive health is a state of physical, mental, and social well-being in all matters relating to the reproductive system at all stages of life. Reproductive health implies

that people are able to have a satisfying and safe sex life and that they have the capability to reproduce and the freedom to decide if, when, and how often to do so. Implicit are the rights of men and women to be informed and to have access to safe, effective, affordable, and acceptable methods of family planning of their choice and the right to appropriate health-care services that enable women to safely go through pregnancy and childbirth (WHO 1998b).

2. This section draws on Barroso and Girard (2003), a background paper commissioned by the task force.

3. The definition of unmet need for contraception includes women at risk of pregnancy who do not want another child (limiting desires) or want to postpone their next birth at least two years (spacing desires) but who are not currently using a method of birth control. Data on unmet need for contraception are available through Demographic and Health Surveys conducted in a large number of developing countries by ORC-Macro.

4. The body mass index is calculated as weight in kilograms divided by squared height in meters.

5. DALYs represent the sum of two components: the cumulative number of years lost as a result of premature death and the cumulative number of healthy years of life lost to disability. They are further adjusted for age and stage of life in which the disease or disability emerges.

6. Interventions to improve nutrition go well beyond the health sector; these are discussed at length in the report of the Task Force on Hunger (UN Millennium Project 2005d).

Chapter 5

1. These women also spend somewhat more time engaged in housework and other miscellaneous activities.

2. Ellis and Hine (1998) find that for journeys as long as 30 kilometers, transport charges are up to 2.5 times more expensive in Africa than in Asia.

3. When projects have addressed women's needs, it has sometimes been for incorporating domestic water uses in the design of irrigation systems, most obviously for washing and bathing (Zwarteveen 1997). Although this recognition is important, planners have ignored women's need for water for productive purposes. Zwarteveen (1997), for instance, cites a 1990 study of an irrigation project in Burkina Faso where 3,00 women farmers, organized into groups of 40, received water rights in only 1 percent of the total command area.

4. Khandker, Lavy, and Filmer (1994) report that in the absence of a paved road, just 21 percent of rural girls ever attended school, whereas 58 percent of rural boys do. With paved roads, enrollment rates would have increased to 48 percent for girls and 76 percent for boys.

Chapter 6

1. Productive assets refer to forms of property—land, house, livestock—that can be used to generate income and additional wealth.

2. See Tinker and Summerfield (1999) for additional information on the gender distribution of property rights in parts of China, Lao PDR, and Viet Nam.

3. Matrilineal inheritance can be found in northern and central Kerala, in south India and Meghalaya, in the northeast (Agarwal 1994, 1995), and in parts of Sri Lanka.

4. The Hindu Succession Act of 1956 made sons, daughters, and widows equal claimants in a man's separate property and in his share in the joint family property and gave women full control over the land they inherited. The Muslim Personal Law Shariat Application Act of 1937 also enhanced Muslim women's property rights compared with those prevailing under custom (Agarwal 2002).

5. A condition of such ownership was that women would contribute labor to cocoa farming (Quisumbing, Estudillo, and Otsuka 2004).

6. Land tenure systems in Sub-Saharan Africa are too complex and diverse to summarize here and are changing due to economic and social processes; see Lastarria-Cornhiel (1997) and Platteau (1997) for detailed treatment of the topic.

7. In countries like Ghana and South Africa there are concerns about the decision-making power vested in "traditional" authorities and chiefs in rural local government, where "traditionalism" is deeply inimical to the interests of women and young men.

8. It is important to distinguish between formal market transactions, where titled land is bought and sold, and other kinds of informal transactions, including loans, leases, sharecropping contracts, and pledges, which form the bulk of land transfers (Whitehead and Tsikata 2003).

9. However, land titling is feasible only when land rights are sufficiently individualized and in areas of high market and property rights development. The privatization and individualization of land is hotly debated in many countries. Concerns have been raised about poor people who lose the security provided by customary tenure while being unable to complete the bureaucratic process of registration. In both urban and rural areas titling programs have seen tenants and other vulnerable land users displaced.

10. Some argue for local-level customary institutions to allocate land and manage disputes; see Whitehead and Tsikata (2003) for a discussion of the debates in Sub-Saharan Africa.

11. Women in cohabiting or polygamous unions may fall outside the laws, and new legislation often needs to be put in place to give them rights to land.

12. One of the most interesting examples of this is the Deccan Development Society (DDS), an NGO working with poor women's collectives in some 75 villages in Medak district, a drought-prone tract of Andhra Pradesh in southern India. DDS has helped women from landless families establish claims on land, through purchase and lease, using various government schemes (Menon 1996; Satheesh 1997; Agarwal 2002).

13. Under one of DDS's programs, women in Andhra Pradesh lease land from private owners. Initiated in 1989 the program is now reported to cover 623 acres in 52 villages. Under another of DDS's efforts women's groups have used loan money available from a government poverty alleviation scheme, Development of Women and Children in Rural Areas, to lease land. Committees of women examine the lease proposals, assess land quality, keep records of each woman's work input, and ensure equitable distribution of wages and produce (Agarwal 2002).

14. Agarwal (2002) notes that women would be stakeholders in a land trust. Each woman in the group would have use rights but not the right to alienate the land. The daughters-in-law and daughters of such households who reside in the village would share these use rights. Daughters leaving the village on marriage would lose such rights but could reestablish them by rejoining the production efforts, should they return as a result of divorce or widowhood. Thus, land access would be linked formally with residence and working on the land, as was the case under some traditional systems when land was held collectively by a clan (Agarwal 2002).

Chapter 7

1. There are three types of unpaid work. Reproductive work consists of managing a household, cooking, cleaning, gathering fuel and hauling water, maintaining the home in good condition, and caring for family members, friends, and neighbors. These are all vital services for the paid economy. In many developing countries unpaid work also includes subsistence production—production for home use of goods and services that in principle could be marketed—such as food, clothing, and other items. Finally, unpaid

work includes unpaid community work, for instance, soup kitchens organized by women in poor neighborhoods; groups of mothers organizing care of children, the elderly, and those who are sick or disabled; and (unpaid) work for local or national nonprofit charitable organizations.

2. Informal employment is part of the market economy. It comprises self-employment in informal enterprises (small or unregistered), formal enterprises, households, and for no fixed employer, and wage employment in informal jobs (without secure contracts, worker benefits, or social protection). It includes domestic workers, casual or day laborers, industrial outworkers (such as homeworkers and own-account operators), and unpaid family workers in informal enterprises. In all developing regions self-employment constitutes a greater share of informal nonagricultural employment than wage employment: 70 percent of informal employment in Sub-Saharan Africa, 62 percent in North Africa, 60 percent in Latin America, and 59 percent in Asia (WIEGO 2002).

3. The results of these studies must be viewed cautiously because the data refer to participation in formal sector work.

4. Glick and Sahn (1997) find that more education reduces the likelihood of being self-employed and strongly increases the likelihood of working in the public sector. In India and Thailand Mammen and Paxson (2000) find that more educated women are more likely to work in nonmanual, white-collar jobs than in production or agricultural jobs. In Mexico Anderson and Dimon (1999) find that as years of schooling increase, the probability of working in the formal sector increases at a high rate for a largely agricultural base in Torrean, but at a low rate for a largely manufacturing base in Tijuana. Years of schooling is more important for women in non-export-oriented contexts and for married women. Similarly, Birdsall and Behrman (1991) conclude that in Brazil the more schooling women have, the less likely they are to work in the informal and domestic sectors. Assaad and El-Hamidi (2001) note that in both rural and urban areas of Egypt women with low levels of education are virtually shut out of regular wage work.

5. Women's choice of teaching as a career is linked to the fact that teachers' work hours overlap with children's school hours, enabling women to balance child-rearing responsibilities with career responsibilities.

6. Job ads often also specified age and appearance.

7. Neoclassical human capital theory argues that wage differentials result from individual differences in productivity arising from employees' different investments in education, training, tenure on the job, and other factors. However, human capital theorists have only been able to explain about 50 percent of the gender wage gap with human capital variables.

8. An alternative is that children are left at home without adult supervision while their mother goes to work, a particularly problematic arrangement for young children, in part because it often pulls older sisters out of school to provide childcare.

9. The work participation rate for females in rural Maharashtra are higher than participation rates in the Employment Guarantee Scheme.

10. Social protection comprises health insurance, work-related disability insurance, unemployment insurance, child maintenance, social security, and old age pensions.

11. In some microcredit schemes women do not control the use of the loan; see Goetz and Sengupta 1996.

12. In common law countries the judiciary has played an important role in developing antidiscrimination law. In India, for instance, a Supreme Court ruling included guidelines prohibiting sexual harassment in the workplace. In Zimbabwe a Labor Court supported a claim of sexual harassment despite the lack of relevant legal provisions (ILO 2003d).

13. Voluntary actions by firms to change pay grading structures seem to have little impact (Rubery and others 2002).

14. The pension is paid out of general government revenues and accounts for 1.4 percent of GDP (Burns, Keswell, and Leibbrandt forthcoming).

15. Barrientos (1998) also finds that the availability of personal pension plans would not increase the pension gender gap (which is almost nonexistent in Chile) and might close it.

Chapter 8

1. This chapter is based on the paper written by Mala Htun (2003b) commissioned by the task force.

2. A study by Kaufmann, Kraay, and Zoido-Lobatón (1999) found a strong, negative, and statistically significant relationship between the proportion of women in a country's legislature and the level of corruption as measured by the *International Country Risk Guide* corruption index. For a large cross-section of countries Dollar, Fisman, and Gatti (2001) found that the level of corruption fell as women's representation in parliament increased. Another study using several datasets shows that corruption is less severe where women constitute a larger share of the labor force and hold a larger share of parliamentary seats (Swamy and others 2001).

3. Regional and country breakdowns for women's representation in national parliaments are based on data provided by the Inter-Parliamentary Union.

4. These countries are: Australia, Austria, Belarus, Bulgaria, Canada, China, Eritrea, Germany, Grenada, Guyana, Lao People's Democratic Republic, Latvia, Lesotho, New Zealand, Nicaragua, Poland, Saint Lucia, Saint Vincent and the Grenadines, Seychelles, Spain, Swaziland, Switzerland, Tanzania, Trinidad and Tobago, Turkmenistan, Uganda, and Viet Nam.

5. The countries are: Albania, Armenia, Bangladesh, Cameroon, Cape Verde, China, Congo, El Salvador, Equatorial Guinea, Gabon, Guyana, Honduras, Hungary, Indonesia, Malawi, Maldives, Mauritius, Mongolia, Nauru, Niger, Romania, São Tomé and Principe, Sri Lanka, Tuvalu, Vanuatu, Venezuela, Yemen, and Zimbabwe.

6. Though the text of the Mexican law suggests that the quota applies to both the proportional representation and the plurality elections, sanctions for noncompliance are administered only for proportional representation elections.

Chapter 9

1. This section draws heavily on Moser and Moser (2003). The task force is grateful to Caroline Moser and Annalise Moser for permission to draw on several sections of their work.

2. For comprehensive overviews of debates identifying such issues, see Pickup, Williams, and Sweetman (2001); WHO (2002b); Buvinic, Morrison, and Shifter in Morrison and Biehl (1999); Spindel, Levy, and Connor (2000).

3. The most common reasons for underreporting include fear of retaliation by the attacker, cultural stigma, and the belief that such violence is justified as a legitimate aspect of a woman's role (Pickup, Williams, and Sweetman 2001; UNICEF 2000). Underrecording often occurs where gender-based violence is not considered a crime.

4. Most systematic studies have been carried out in industrial countries. Those undertaken in developing countries are generally very localized.

5. Gender-based violence is not inevitable. An ethnographic study of 90 societies around the world identified societies in which gender-based violence seems not to exist (Levinson 1989).

6. In an extreme case in 1991 at a school in Meru, Kenya, after 71 teenage girls were raped by their classmates and 19 others were killed, the school's principal stated, "The boys never meant any harm against the girls. They just wanted to rape" (Green 1999).

7. Figures on rape are likely to be conservative. In Chile, for example, around 615 cases of rape are reported to the police each year, but the estimated number of rapes is closer to 20,000 (Seager 2003).

8. See Leslie (2001); WHO (2002b); Seager (2003); Brunet and Rousseau (1998); and Kumar (2001).

9. The discussion of the four kinds of costs is adapted from Buvinic, Morrison, and Shifter in Morrison and Biehl (1999).

10. Many countries have developed national plans for the elimination of violence against women and are required to report on measures they have taken to implement their plans on a biennial basis at the General Assembly. Regrettably, these plans have often proved more valuable as symbols of commitment than as instigators of change.

11. November 10 commemorates the date that the three Mirabel sisters were murdered in the Dominican Republic for opposing the rule of dictator Rafael Trujillo. It is now celebrated as the International Day to End Violence against Women.

Chapter 10

1. See millenniumindicators.un.org for more information on the statistical work being undertaken by the UN system to support international and country-level monitoring of the Millennium Development Goals and others.

2. For a longer discussion of the technical limitations of each indicator, see Grown, Rao Gupta, and Kahn 2003.

3. Although aggregate indicators of women's empowerment, such as gender wage differentials, literacy, secondary school enrollment, and political participation are well represented in the recommendations, there are few indicators of empowerment at the individual and household level that are part of the task force recommendations. Two examples of individual empowerment indicators are land ownership by sex and hours per day (or year) women and men spend fetching water and collecting fuel.

4. Net enrollment rates, which take into consideration the appropriate age for each grade, are a preferable indicator of access to education, but they are not available for a large number of countries. Gross enrollment rates are more widely available, but they include repeat students, and so results will be higher than with net enrollment rates.

5. In 2000 UNESCO had primary completion rates for 128 countries, 125 of them sex disaggregated. The World Bank had data for 116 countries, of which 99 were sex disaggregated.

6. The OECD and UNESCO maintain a World Economic Indicators program that tracks sex-disaggregated secondary school completion rates, mostly for OECD countries.

7. Unmet need for family planning captures the proportion of women who are not using family planning but who wish to space their next birth at least two years or avoid another birth (Bernstein 2004). Contraceptive prevalence is the proportion of married women (including women in consensual unions) ages 15–49 currently using any method of modern contraception: male and female sterilization, IUD, the pill, injectables, hormonal implants, condoms, and female barrier methods.

8. The adolescent fertility rate, as reported by countries, is available for 1970, 1980, 1990, and most recent year. In some countries data on the adolescent fertility rate have been collected separately for urban and rural areas.

9. The adolescent fertility rate counts only live births; stillbirths, and spontaneous or induced abortions are not reflected in the calculations (UNFPA 2003b).

10. The ILO has sex-disaggregated earnings data for the manufacturing sector for only 43 countries, most in the OECD (ILO 2003a).

11. The countries are Bangladesh, Brazil, Japan, Namibia, Peru, Tanzania, Thailand, and Samoa. The research has been replicated in six other countries: Chile, China, Ethiopia, Indonesia, New Zealand, Serbia, and Viet Nam.

Chapter 11

1. Using data on GNP, share of GNP spent on education, and the share of primary education in public education, the study first computes initial public spending on primary education. Then it calculates the necessary increase in public spending to achieve universal primary education. The calculation takes into account the price elasticity of demand for education for girls and boys and the price cut needed to increase demand and factors in the estimated decline in private spending due to reduced prices. Finally, it includes a 9 percent increase in program costs.

2. The interventions related to sexual and reproductive health that fall within the health system are costed under the health sector needs assessment. The interventions here are not costed in either the health or education sector needs assessments.

3. The government's Working Group on Gender comprises focal points from each ministry, the State Statistical Committee, the Committee on Women's Affairs under the Presidential Office, international agencies, and local women's NGOs.

4. The overall sector needs assessments include the costs of reaching both men and women.

5. These costs are primarily for setting up a functioning health system (doctor and nurse recruitment, training and salaries, construction of hospitals, clinics and health posts, purchase of supplies and drugs). The health system created under this plan would be expected to provide the major interventions needed to achieve the child health and maternal health Goal—interventions like family planning services, supervised delivery, and emergency obstetric care.

6. The interventions that are not costed are: child and elderly care services, police and medical services to address violence against women, legal redress, legal aid services, registration systems, and data collection and monitoring systems.

7. Interventions related to community-based awareness campaigns for sexual and reproductive health are assumed to reach 50 percent of the adult population by 2015. Also, mass media campaigns are assumed to run one time each year to spread awareness about sexual and reproductive rights as well as other economic and legal rights to end violence against women. Finally, vocational training is targeted to reach 30 percent of the adolescent female population out of school by 2015. School to work programs target 20 percent of graduating female students. Support for women candidates will target 100 percent of women candidates in national elections by 2015. In 2004, 50 percent of women were estimated to be potential victims of domestic violence. Given this high degree of prevalence, a reasonable assumption is that approximately 20 percent of potential victims will need the full range of shelter services by 2015. Also by 2015, sensitization and training campaigns will be targeted to 100 percent of judges, 10 percent of civil servants, and 20 percent of the entire police force (UN Millennium Project 2004c). Finally, by 2015, each of the 18 ministries is targeted to have one gender focal point.

8. This analysis assumes a linear scaling up of costs from 2005 to 2015. The analysis focuses on financial costing and calculates total costs as opposed to incremental costs. It uses average unit costs and calculates both capital and recurrent costs for the 11-year period. For more details, see Sachs and others 2004.

Chapter 12

1. For instance, one review of national women's machineries suggested that those placed within the president's or prime minister's office (such as in the Philippines and Tonga), the planning ministry (such as in Chile), or the ministry of finance (such as in Zambia) were most effective (Obang 1993).

2. Many countries have a strong legal framework, but few have adequate enforcement mechanisms.

3. The assessment of progress on a majority of the seven strategic priorities was made on the basis of existing data. As noted in chapter 10, no country has data on the distribution of land or housing ownership by sex, and few countries have data on the impact of infrastructure investments on women's time use or on the prevalence of violence against women. In the absence of such data, we analyzed other country literature to deduce the progress made in these areas.

4. The first impact study of the Convention on the Elimination of All Forms of Discrimination against Women, which included South Africa, does not answer this question (McPhedran and others 2000).

Appendix 1

1. Additional problems include the fact that censuses are usually conducted only once every 10 years. In some cases countries report data from only one to three censuses. Trends are therefore difficult to detect. And more than 30 countries have never published any kind of literacy data. Also, UN agencies do not have the same data points for all countries.

2. A few changes were made to the original UNDP (2002) grouping of countries: Southern European countries Turkey and Cyprus were merged in Europe and Central Asia. Somalia was moved from Middle East and North Africa to Sub-Saharan Africa, and Israel was moved from "Other UN member countries" to Middle East and North Africa.

3. Table A1.1 shows that 26 countries will have a ratio of 1 in 2005, and 20 countries will have a ratio greater than 1. Of these, 32 countries had already achieved parity or a reverse gap in 2000. The remaining 14 countries had ratios less than 1.

4. The other countries are Luxembourg, Papua New Guinea, and Samoa in East Asia and Pacific; Tajikistan and Turkey in Europe and Central Asia; Colombia and El Salvador in Latin America and the Caribbean; and Djibouti and Iraq in Middle East and North Africa.

5. The countries are Belgium, France, Italy; Myanmar; Azerbaijan, Bulgaria, Estonia, Kazakhstan, Kyrgyzstan, Macedonia TFYR, Poland; Chile, Guyana; Israel; and Mauritius.

6. The countries are Cambodia, China, Lao People's Democratic Republic, Papua New Guinea, Samoa, Bulgaria, Estonia, Kazakhstan, Poland, Turkey, Guyana, Nicaragua, Djibouti, Iraq, Israel, India, Benin, Burkina Faso, Chad, Côte d'Ivoire, Ethiopia, Lesotho, Mauritius, Mozambique, Senegal, Togo, and Uganda.

Appendix 6

1. This report was prepared by the moderator of the e-discussions, Akanksha A. Marphatia. These comments are based on an earlier version of the report, and the current version reflects many of the comments.

2. Contacts for these organizations are as follows: David Archer (ActionAid International), Chike Anywanyu (Commonwealth Education Fund), Anne Jellema (Global Campaign for Education), and Geeta Sharma, Kedar Dash, and Atanu Gurai (One World South Asia).

3. The full report can be obtained from Elaine Unterhalter with the Beyond Access Project: e.unterhalter@oie.ac.uk.

4. The paper is available at http://k1.ioe.ac.uk/schools/efps/GenderEducDev/Where%20are%20we%20scaling%20up%20from%20FINAL%20FINAL.pdf.

5. Full article can be found at www.india-seminar.com, April 2004 issue.

References

Aboim, M. 2002. "Brazil: Domestic Violence and the Women's Movement." Family Violence Prevention Fund, San Francisco, Calif. [http://endabuse.org/programs/display.php3?DocID=96].

Abu-Ghaida, D., and S. Klasen. 2002. *The Costs of Missing the Millennium Development Goal on Gender Equity.* University of Munich, Department of Economics, Discussion Paper in Economics 2.

ACC/SCN (United Nations Administrative Committee on Coordination Subcommittee on Nutrition). 2000. *Nutrition throughout the Life Cycle: Fourth Report on the World Nutrition Situation.* Geneva: ACC/SCN in collaboration with the International Food Policy Research Institute.

ADB (Asian Development Bank). 2000. *Gender Checklist: Water Supply and Sanitation.* Manila.

Agarwal, B. 1994. "Gender and Command over Property: A Critical Gap in Economic Analysis and Policy in South Asia." *World Development* 22 (10): 1455–78.

———. 1995. "Women's Legal Rights in Agricultural Land in India." *Economic and Political Weekly* 30 (12): A39–56.

———. 2002. *Are We Not Peasants Too? Land Rights and Women's Claims in India.* SEEDS Number 21. Population Council, New York.

———. 2003. "Women's Land Rights and the Trap of Neo-Conservatism: A Response to Jackson." *Journal of Agrarian Change* 3 (4): 571–85.

Aggio, C. 2001. "Lady Leaders: The Case of Quotas for Women's Representation in Argentina." Sustainable Development Department, Inter-American Development Bank, Washington, D.C.

AGI (Alan Guttmacher Institute). 1998. *Into a New World: Young Women's Sexual and Reproductive Lives.* New York.

AGI/UNFPA (Alan Guttmacher Institute/United Nations Fund for Population Activities). 2004. *Adding It Up: The Benefits of Investing in Sexual and Reproductive Health Care.* New York.

Ainsworth, M., K. Beegle, and A. Nyamete. 1996. "The Impact of Women's Schooling on Fertility and Contraceptive Use: A Study of Fourteen Sub-Saharan African Countries." *World Bank Economic Review* 10 (1): 85–122.

Akerkar, S. 2001. *Gender and Participation.* Brighton, UK: BRIDGE Gender and Development and Institute of Development Studies.

Akpalu, E. A., E. Ofei-Aboagye, and H. Derbyshire. 1999. *Gender Mainstreaming: Emerging Lessons from Ghana.* London: Department for International Development.

Alaka and Chetna. 1987. "When Women Get Land—A Report from Bodhgaya." *Manushi* 40: 25–26.

Alderman, H., and E. M. King. 1998. "Gender Differences in Parental Investment in Education." *Structural Change and Economic Dynamics* 9 (4): 453–68.

Allély, D., and O. Drevet-Dabbou. 2002. *Water, Gender and Sustainable Development: Lessons Learnt from French Co-Operation in Sub-Saharan Africa.* Paris: Drevet-Dabbous Groupe de recherche et d'échanges technologique.

Allen, L., and S. Gillespie. 2001. *What Works? A Review of the Efficacy and Effectiveness of Nutrition Interventions.* ACC/SCN (UN Administrative Committee on Coordination/Sub-Committee on Nutrition) Nutrition Policy Paper 19. Geneva.

Alva, S. 1999. "Women's Employment in North Vietnam: Understanding Choices Made in Rural Households." Paper presented at Annual Meetings of the Population Association of America, March 25–27, New York.

Amin, S. 1997 "Transition to Adulthood of Female Factory Workers: Some Evidence from Bangladesh." Policy Research Division Working Papers 102. Population Council, New York.

Amin, S., and C. B. Lloyd. 1998. "Women's Lives and Rapid Fertility Decline: Some Lessons from Bangladesh and Egypt." Policy Research Division Working Paper 117. Population Council, New York.

Amin, S., J. Cleland, J. F. Phillips, and G. M. Kamal. 1995. "Socioeconomic Change and the Demand for Children in Rural Bangladesh." Policy Research Division Working Papers 70. Population Council, New York.

Amin, S., I. Diamond, R. T. Naved, and M. Newby. 1998. "Transition to Adulthood of Female Garment-factory Workers in Bangladesh." *Studies in Family Planning* 29(2): 185–200.

Amnesty International USA. 2004. "Sudan: Darfur in Crisis—Speaking Out On Violence against Women in Darfur." New York. [Retrieved July 17, 2004 from www.amnestyusa.org/countries/sudan/index.do].

Ampofo, A. 1993. "Controlling and Punishing Women in Ghana." *Review of African Political Economy* 20 (56): 102–11.

Anderson, J., and D. Dimon. 1999. "Formal Sector Job Growth and Women's Labor Sector Participation: The Case of Mexico." *Quarterly Review of Economics and Finance* 39 (2): 169–91.

Anker, R. 1998. *Gender and Jobs: Sex Segregation of Occupations in the World.* Geneva: International Labour Office.

Anker, R., I. Chernyshev, P. Egger, F. Mehran, and J. Ritter. 2002. "Measuring Decent Work with Statistical Indicators." Policy Integration Paper 1. International Labour Office, Geneva.

Anker, R., and C. Hein. 1985. "Why Third World Urban Employers Usually Prefer Men." *International Labour Review.* 124 (1): 73–90.

Appleton, S., J. Hoddinott, and P. Krishnan. 1996. "The Gender Wage Gap in Three African Countries." Centre for the Study of the African Economies Working Paper 96–7. University of Oxford, Oxford, U.K.

Armstrong, A. 1990. *Women and Rape in Zimbabwe.* Lesotho: Human People's Rights Promotion Project.

Aromolaran, A. 2002. *Private Wage Returns to Schooling in Nigeria: 1996–1999.* New Haven, Conn.: Yale University Press.

Arriagada, I., and L. Godoy. 2000. "Prevention or Repression? The False Dilemma of Citizen Security." *CEPAL Review* 70:111–36.

Artecona, R., and W. Cunningham. 2002. "Effects of Trade Liberalization on the Gender Wage Gap in Mexico." World Bank Policy Research Report Working Paper 21. Washington, D.C.

Assaad, R., and F. El-Hamidi. 2001. "Is All Work the Same? A Comparison of the Determinants of Female Participation and Hours of Work in Various Employment States in Egypt." In M. Cinar, ed., *The Economics of Women and Work in the Middle East and North Africa, Research in the Middle East Economies*, vol. 4. Greenwich, Conn.: JAI Press.

Assaad, R., and S. Zouari. 2003. "Estimating the Impact of Marriage and Fertility on the Female Labor Force Participation When Decisions Are Interrelated: Evidence from Urban Morocco." *Topics in Middle Eastern and North African Economics. Electronic Journal* 5 (September).

Astill, J., and R. Guest. 2003. "Civil Wars: The Global Menace of Local Strife." *The Economist.* May 24–30.

AusAID. 2000. "Gender Guidelines: Water Supply and Sanitation." Supplement of *AusAID Guide to Gender and Development.* Canberra

Baden, S., ed. 1995. "Raising Gender Awareness among Policy-Makers and Practitioners. Issue 2: Poverty Reduction Strategies." Development and Gender Quarterly Update from BRIDGE. University of Sussex, Institute of Development Studies, Brighton, U.K.

———. 1999. "Country Gender Profile: South Africa." Women'sNet, Pretoria, South Africa. [Retrieved August 10, 2004 from http://womesnet.org.za/links/genderpr.htm].

Balakrishnan, R. 2002. *The Hidden Assembly Line: Gender Dynamics of Subcontracted Work in a Global Economy.* Bloomfield, Conn.: Kumarian Press.

Baldez, L. 1997. "Democratic Institutions and Feminist Outcomes: Chilean Policy toward Women in the 1990s." Working Paper 340. Washington University, Department of Political Science, St. Louis, Mo.

———. 2003. "Elected Bodies: The Adoption of Gender Quotas for Legislative Candidates in Mexico." Paper presented at the 2003 Meeting of the American Political Science Association, August 28–31, Philadelphia, Penn.

Bamberger, M. 1999. "Designing Travel and Transport Projects which Respond to the Needs of Both Women and Men." Paper presented at RTTP (Rural Travel and Transport Program), December 1–3, Pretoria.

Bardhan, P., and D. Mookherjee. 2003. "Decentralization and Accountability in Infrastructure Delivery in Developing Countries." Boston University Economics Department Working Paper. Boston, Mass.

Bari, A. W. 2002. *Struggling for a Political Voice: Women Contesting the System in Pakistan.* Washington, D.C.: Association of Asian Studies.

Barnes, D., and M. Sen. 2003. "The Impact of Energy on Women's Lives in Rural India." ESMAP (World Bank Energy Sector Management Assistance Programme) Formal Report 276/04, Washington, D.C.

Barrientos, A. 1998. "Pension Reform, Personal Pensions and Gender Differences in Pension Coverage." *World Development* 26 (1): 125–37.

Barrientos, S. 2001. "Gender, Flexibility, and Global Value Chains." *IDS Bulletin* 32 (3): 83–93.

Barrientos, A., and S. Barrientos. 2002. *Extending Social Protection to Informal Workers in the Horticulture Global Value Chain.* World Bank Social Protection Discussion Paper Series 0216. Washington, D.C.

Barroso, C., and F. Girard. 2003. "Reproductive Health and Gender Equality." Paper commissioned by the UN Millennium Project Task Force on Education and Gender Equality. UN Millennium Project, New York.

Barwell, I. 1998. *Transport and the Village.* World Bank Discussion Paper 344. Washington, D.C.

Basu, K. 2003. "Empowerment and the Triad." Paper presented at the workshop Measuring Empowerment: Cross-Disciplinary Perspectives, World Bank, February 4–5, Washington, D.C.

Beck, S. A. 2001. "Acting as Women: The Effects and Limitations of Gender in Local Governance." In S. J. Carroll, ed., *The Impact of Women in Public Life.* Bloomington, Ind.: Indiana University Press.

Behrman, J. R., and Z. Zhang. 1995. "Gender Issues and Employment." *Asian Development Review* 13 (2): 1–49.

Bejar, R. 1998. "El Salvador de postguerra: Formas de violencia en la transición." In United Nations Development Programme, ed., *Violencia en una sociedad en transición.* San Salvador.

Belem do Para. 1994. "The Inter-American Convention to Prevent, Punish, and Eradicate Violence against Women." Acclamation presented at the 24th Regular Session of the General Assembly of the Organization of American States, June 9.

Bell, E. 2003. "Gender and PRSPs: With Experiences from Tanzania, Bolivia, Viet Nam and Mozambique." BRIDGE Development and Gender Report 76. University of Sussex, Institute of Development Studies, Brighton, U.K.

Bell, E., B. Byrne, J. K. Laier, S. Baden, and R. Marcus. 2002. "National Machineries for Women in Development: Experiences, Lessons, and Strategies." BRIDGE Development and Gender Report 66. University of Sussex, Institute of Development Studies, Brighton, U.K.

Beneria, L. 2001. "Changing Employment Patterns and the Informalization of Jobs: Gender Trends and Gender Dimensions." Paper presented at *Women at Work: A Challenge for Development*, March 17, Santiago, Chile.

———. 1999. "The Enduring Debate over Unpaid Labour." *International Labour Review* 139 (3): 287–309.

Benschop, M. 2002. "Rights and Reality: Are Women's Equal Rights to Land, Housing and Property Implemented in East Africa?" UN-HABITAT, Nairobi.

Bernstein, Stan. 2004. "A Proposal for Including a Measure of Unmet Need for Contraception and Adolescent Fertility or Early Marriage Levels as Indicators of the Reproductive Health Component of Gender Equality." Paper commissioned for the UN Millennium Project. New York.

Bettio, F., and P. Villa. 1996. "Trends and Prospects for Women's Employment in the 90s: Italy." EC Network on the Situation of Women in the Labour Market. University of Manchester Institute of Science and Technology, Manchester, U.K.

Bhalla, S. S., S. Saigal, and N. Basu. 2003. "Girls' Education Is *It*—Nothing Else Matters (Much)." Background paper for *World Development Report 2004: Making Services Work for Poor People.* Oxus Research and Investments, New Delhi, India. [http://econ.worldbank.org/wdr/wdr2004/library/doc?id=29789].

Bhatia, J. C., and J. Cleland. 1995. "Determinants of Maternal Care in a Region of South India." *Health Transition Review* 5 (2): 127–42.

Bid, P., R. Nanavaty, and N. Patel. 2002. "Women, Water and Transportation." In P. Fernando and G. Porter, eds., *Balancing the Load: Women, Gender, and Transport.* London: Zed Books.

Bird, K. 2002. *Who are the Women? Where are the Women? And What Difference Can They Make? The Effects of Gender Parity on French Municipal Elections.* Boston, Mass.: American Political Science Association.

Birdsall, N., and J. Behrman. 1991. "Why Do Males Earn More than Females in Urban Brazil: Earnings Discrimination or Job Discrimination?" In N. Birdsall and R. Sabot, eds., *Unfair Advantage: Labor Market Discrimination in Developing Countries.* Washington, D.C.: World Bank.

Birdsall, N., and L. M. Fox. 1985. "Why Males Earn More: Location and Training of Brazilian Schoolteachers." *Economic Development and Cultural Change* 33 (3): 55–72.

Black, D. A., J. Schumacher, A. Smith Slep, and R. Heyman. 1999. "Partner, Child Abuse Risk Factors Literature Review." National Network of Family Resiliency and National Network for Health, Iowa State Univeristy,

Blaxall, J. 2004. Paper presented at "Scaling Up Poverty Reduction: A Global Learning Process and Conference," May 25–27, Shanghai, China.

Boles, J. 2001. "Local Elected Women and Policy-Making: Movement Delegates or Feminist Trustees?" In S. J. Carroll, ed., *The Impact of Women in Public Office.* Bloomington, Ind.: Indiana University Press.

Bollen, S., L. Artz, L. Vetten, and L. Louw. 1999. "Violence against Women in Metropolitan South Africa: A Study on Impact and Service Delivery." Institute of Security Studies Monograph Series 41. Pretoria, South Africa.

Bongaarts, J., and J. Bruce. 1995. "The Causes of Unmet Need for Contraception and the Social Content of Services." *Studies in Family Planning* 26 (2): 57–73.

Booth, D., L. Hanmer, and E. Lowell. 2000. "Poverty and Transport." Report prepared for the World Bank in collaboration with the UK Department for International Development. [www.odi.org.uk/pppg/publications/papers_reports/dfid/issues/trans02.pdf].

Bradley, K. 1994. "Why Male Violence against Women Is a Development Issue: Reflections from Papua New Guinea." In M. Davies, ed., *Women and Violence: Realities and Responses Worldwide.* London: Zed Books.

———. 2000. "The Incorporation of Women in Higher Education: Paradoxical Outcomes." *Sociology of Education* 73 (1): 1–18.

Braveman, P. 1998. "Monitoring Equity in Health: A Policy-Oriented Approach in Low- and Middle-Income Countries." World Health Organization, Department of Health Systems, Equity Initiative Paper 3. WHO/CHC/HSS/98.1. Geneva.

Bridger, S., R. Kay, and K. Pinnick. 1996. *No More Heroines? Russia, Women and the Market.* London and New York: Routledge Press.

Brouwer, E., B. Harris, and S. Tanaka. 1998. *Gender Analysis in Papua New Guinea.* Washington, D.C.: World Bank.

Brown, D. 1998. "In Africa, Fear Makes HIV an Inheritance." *Washington Post.* June 30.

Bruce, J., and S. Clark. 2003. "Including Married Adolescents in Adolescent Reproductive Health and HIV/AIDS Policy." Paper presented at the meeting for Technical Consultation on Married Adolescents, December 9–12, Geneva.

Bruce, J., C. Lloyd, and A. Leonard. 1995. *Families in Focus.* New York: Population Council.

Brunet, A., and S. Rousseau. 1998. "Acknowledging Violations, Struggling against Impunity: Women's Rights, Human Rights." In I. L. Sajor, ed., *Common Grounds: Violence against Women in War and Armed Conflict Situations.* Quezon City, Philippines: Asian Center for Women's Human Rights.

Bruns, B., A. Mingat, and R. Rakotomalala. 2003. *Achieving Universal Primary Education by 2015: A Chance for Every Child.* Washington, D.C.: World Bank.

Bryceson, D. F., and J. Howe. 1993. "Rural Household Transport in Africa: Reducing the Burden on Women?" *World Development* 21 (11): 1715–28.

Bullock, L., and J. McFarlane. 1989. "The Battering Low Birth Weight Connection." *American Journal of Nursing* 89: 1153–55.

Bunch, C., R. Carrillo, and R. Shore. 1998. "Violence against Women." In N. Stromquist, ed., *Women in the Third World: An Encyclopedia of Contemporary Issues.* New York: Garland.

Burchfield, S. A. 1997. "An Analysis of the Impact of Literacy on Women's Empowerment in Nepal." Cambridge, Mass.: Harvard Institute for International Development.

Burchfield, S. A., H. Hua, T. Suxo Iturry, and V. Rocha. 2002. "A Longitudinal Study of the Effect of Integrated Literacy and Basic Education Programs on the Participation of Women in Social and Economic Development in Bolivia." [http://www.dec.org/pdf_docs/PNACR860.pdf].

Burns, J., M. Keswell, and M. Leibbrandt. Forthcoming. "Large Cash Transfers to the (Non) Elderly in South Africa." *Feminist Economics.*

Butalia, U. 2001. "Women and Communal Conflict: New Challenges for the Women's Movement in India." In C. Moser and F. Clark, eds., *Victims, Perpetrators or Actors? Gender, Armed Conflict and Political Violence.* London: Zed Books.

Buvinić, M., and A. Morrison. 2000. "Technical Notes on Violence Prevention." Economic and Social Consequences Technical Note 4. World Bank, Washington, D.C.

Byrne, B., J. K. Laier, S. Baden, and R. Marcus. 1996. "National Machineries for Women in Development: Experiences, Lessons and Strategies for Institutionalizing Gender in Development Policy and Planning." BRIDGE Development and Gender Report 36. University of Sussex, Institute of Development Studies, Brighton, U.K.

Cairoli, M. L. 1999. "Garment Factory Workers in the City of Fez." *The Middle East Journal* 53(1)Winter: 28–43.

Çağatay, N., D. Elson, and C. Grown. 1995. "Introduction: Gender, Adjustment, and Macroeconomics." *World Development* 23 (11): 1145–56.

Çağatay, N., and S. Ozler. 1995. "Feminization of the Labor Force: The Effects of Long-Term Development and Structural Adjustment." *World Development* 23 (11): 1883–94.

Cameron, L. A., M. J. Dowling, and C. Worsick. 2001. "Education and Labor Market Participation of Women in Asia: Evidence from Five Countries." *Economic Development and Cultural Change* 49 (3): 459–77.

Carney, D., ed. 1998. "Sustainable Rural Livelihoods: What Contributions Can We Make?" Paper presented at the DFID Natural Resource Advisers' Conference, UK Department for International Development, July, London.

Carr, M., and M. Chen. 2002. "Globalization and the Informal Economy: How Global Trade and Investment Impact on the Working Poor." Working paper on the Informal Economy. International Labour Office, Geneva.

Carr, M., M. Chen, and J. Tate. 2000. "Globalization and Home-Based Workers." *Feminist Economics* 6 (3): 123–42.

Carrillo, R. 1992. *Battered Dreams: Violence against Women as an Obstacle to Development.* New York: United Nations Development Fund for Women.

Carroll, R. 2003. "Vicious Circle Traps Starving Ethiopians." *Guardian.* May 31.

Carroll, S. J. 2001. "Representing Women: Women State Legislators as Agents of Policy-Related Change." In S. J. Carroll, ed., *The Impact of Women in Public Office.* Bloomington, Ind.: Indiana University Press.

Carton, A. 2001. "The General Elections in Belgium in June 1999: A Real Breakthrough for Women Politicians?" *European Journal of Women's Studies* 8 (1): 127–35.

Case, A., and A. Deaton. 1998. "Large Cash Transfers to the Elderly in South Africa." *The Economic Journal* 108 (450): 1330–61.

Caul, M. 2001. "Political Parties and the Adoption of Candidate Gender Quotas: A Cross-National Analysis." *Journal of Politics* 63 (4): 1214–29.

CAWP (Center for the American Woman and Politics). Website www.rci.rutgers.edu/~cawp/.

CDC (Center for Disease Control and Prevention). 2000. "Building Data Systems for Monitoring and Responding to Violence against Women: Recommendations from a Workshop." *Morbidity and Mortality Weekly Report* 49.

———. 2002. *Vital Statistics Report.* Atlanta, Ga.

CESCR (Committee on Economic, Social and Cultural Rights). 1991. "The Right to Adequate Housing." General Comment 7. Geneva. [www.unhchr.ch/tbs/doc.nsf/(Symbol)/469f4d91a9378221c12563ed0053547e?Opendocument].

Chadha, G. K. 1992. *Non-Farm Sector in India's Rural Economy: Policy, Performance and Growth Prospects.* Delhi, India: Jawaharlal Nehru University, Center for Regional Development.

Chambers, R., and G. Conway. 1992. *Sustainable Rural Livelihoods: Practical Concepts for the 21st Century.* Institute of Development Studies Discussion Paper 296. Brighton, U.K.: University of Sussex.

Chang, H., and Y. Kim. 1999. "A Study of the Roles and Difficulties of Working Housewives." *Women's Studies Forum* 15 (62).

Chang, M. L. 2004. "Cross-National Variation in Sex Segregation in Sixteen Developing Countries." *American Sociological Review* 69 (1): 114–7.

Charmes, J. 1999. "Gender and the Informal Sector." In *World's Women 2000: Trends and Statistics.* United Nations Statistics Division, New York.

———. 2000. "Informal Sector, Poverty and Gender: A Review of Empirical Evidence." Background paper for the *World Development Report 2001.* World Bank, Washington, D.C.

Chatterjee, M. and J. Macwan. 1992. "Taking Care of Our Children: The Experiences of SEWA Union." SEWA Academy Working Paper Series 1. Ahmedabad, India.

Chattopadhyay, R., and E. Duflo. 2004. "Women as Policy Makers: Evidence from a Randomized Policy Experiment in India." *Econometrica* 72 (5): 1409–43.

Chen, M., J. Sebstad, and L. O'Connell. 1999. "Counting the Invisible Workforce: The Case of Home-Based Workers." *World Development* 27 (3): 603–10.

Chen, M. A., J. Vanek, and M. Carr. 2004. *Mainstreaming Informal Employment and Gender in Poverty Reduction*: A *Handbook for Policy-Makers and Other Stakeholders.* London: Commonwealth Secretariat.

Chiarotti, S. 1998. "Violence against Women in the Private Sphere in the Latin American and Caribbean Region." Paper presented at the Oxfam International Workshop on Violence against Women, November, Sarajevo.

Christian, P. 2003. "Micronutrients and Reproductive Health Issues: An International Perspective." *Journal of Nutrition* 133 (12, suppl.): 1969S–73S.

Cleaver, F., and D. Elson. 1995. "Women and Water Resources: Continued Marginalization and New Policies." International Institute for Environment and Development Gatekeeper Series 49. London.

Coalition for Health and Education Rights. 2002. "User Fees: The Right to Education and Health Denied." Policy Brief. New York.

Cockburn, C. 1998. *The Space between Us: Negotiating Gender and National Identities in Conflict.* London: Zed Books.

————. 2001. "The Gendered Dynamics of Armed Conflict and Political Violence." In C. Moser and F. Clark, eds., *Victims, Perpetrators or Actors? Gender, Armed Conflict and Political Violence*. London: Zed Books.

COHRE (Centre on Housing Rights and Evictions). 2004. *Bringing Equality Home: Promoting and Protecting the Inheritance Rights of Women: A Survey of Law and Practice in Sub-Saharan Africa*. Geneva.

Connelly, R., D. S. DeGraff, and D. Levison. 1996. "Women's Employment and Child Care in Brazil." *Economic Development and Cultural Change* 44 (3): 619–56.

Coomaraswamy, R. 1994. "Violence against Women: Causes and Consequences." In UNICEF, ed., *Fire in the House: Determinants of Intra-Familial Violence and Strategies for Its Elimination*. Bangkok, Thailand: UNICEF East Asia and Pacific Regional Office.

————. 1998. "Report of the Special Rapporteur on Violence against Women, Its Causes and Consequences." Paper presented at the Commission on Human Rights, Fifty-fourth Session. March 30, Geneva.

Cornwell, A. 2000. "Missing Men? Reflections on Men, Masculinities and Gender in GAD." *IDS Bulletin* 31 (2): 18–27.

Correa, S. 1999. *Implementing ICPD: Moving Forward in the Eye of the Storm*. DAWN's Platform for Cairo +5. Suva, Fiji: Development Alternatives with Women for a New Era.

Council of Europe. 1997. "Final Report of the Group of Specialists for Combating Violence against Women, Including a Plan of Action for Combating Violence against Women." June 25 draft, EG-S-VL. Strasbourg, Austria.

CRLP (Center for Reproductive Law and Policy). 1998. "Women's Reproductive Rights in South Africa: A Shadow Report." Paper presented at the 19th Session of the CEDAW Committee, June 22–July 10, New York.

Crossette, B. 2002. "Population Estimates Fall as Poor Women Assert Control." *New York Times*. March 10.

Crowley, E. 2002. *Gender and Access to Land*. FAO Land Tenure Studies 4. Rome, Italy: Food and Agriculture Organization of the United Nations. [www.ifpri.org/2020/focus/focus06/focus06_02.htm].

Curry, M., N. Perrin, and E. Wall. 1998. "Effects of Abuse on Maternal Complications and Birth Weight in Adult and Adolescent Women." *Obstetrics and Gynecology* 92 (4): 530–34.

Davidson, L., V. King, J. Garcia, and S. Marchant. 2000. *Reducing Domestic Violence: What Works? Health Services*. Briefing Note for Crime Reduction Research Series. London: Policing and Crime Reduction Unit, Home Office.

Dawson, J., and A. Jeans. 1997. *Looking Beyond Credit: Business Development Services and the Promotion of Innovation Among Small Producers*. London, U.K.: Intermediate Technology Publications.

De Walque, D. 2002. *How Does Educational Attainment Affect the Risk of Being Infected by HIV/AIDS? Evidence from a General Population Cohort in Rural Uganda*. Chicago, Ill.: University of Chicago Press.

Dean, J. 1996. *Solidarity of Strangers, Feminism after Identity Politics*. Berkeley, Calif.: University of California Press.

Deere, C. D. 1990. *Household and Class Relations: Pheasants and Landlords in Northern Peru*. Berkeley, Calif.: University of California Press.

Deere, C. D., and M. Leon. 2000. "Mechanisms of Inclusion: Recent Advances in Women's Land Rights in Latin America." In *Securing Women's Rights to Land, Property, and Housing: Country Strategies*. Montreal: Rights and Democracy, International Centre for Human Rights and Democratic Development.

———. 2001. *Empowering Women: Land and Property Rights in Latin America*. Pittsburgh, Penn.: University of Pittsburgh Press.

———. 2003. "The Gender Asset Gap: Land in Latin America." *World Development* 31 (6): 925–47.

DeJaeghere, J. G. 2004. "Background Paper for Workshop 1: Quality Education and Gender Equality." Paper presented at the International Conference on Education, 47th Session, August 13, Geneva.

Deolalikar, A. 1994. "Gender Differences in the Returns to Schooling and in School Enrollment Rates in Indonesia." *Journal of Human Resources* 28 (Fall): 889–932.

Derbyshire, H. 2002. *Gender Manual: A Practical Guide for Development Policy Makers and Practitioners*. London: Department for International Development.

Deutsch, R. 1998. "How Early Childhood Interventions Can Reduce Inequality: An Overview of Recent Findings." IDB, Washington, D.C.

Deutsch, R., A. Morrison, C. Piras, and H. Nopo. 2002. "Working within Confines: Occupational Segregation by Gender for Three Latin American Countries." Sustainable Development Department Technical Papers Series. Inter-American Development Bank, Washington, D.C.

Diop-Tine, N. 2002. "Rwanda: Translating Government Commitments into Action." In D. Budlender and G. Hewitt, eds., *Gender Budgets Make Cents Vol. 2: Country Studies and Good Practices*. London: Commonwealth Secretariat.

Doan, R. M., and B. M. Popkin. 1993. "Women's Work and Infant Care in the Philippines." *Social Science and Medicine* 36 (3): 297–304.

D'Oliveira, A. F., S. G. Diniz, and L. B. Schraiber. 2002. "Violence against Women in Health-Care Institutions: An Emerging Problem." *Lancet* 359 (9318): 1681–85.

Dollar, D., R. Fisman, and R. Gatti. 2001. "Are Women Really the 'Fairer' Sex? Corruption and Women in the Government." World Bank Gender and Development Working Paper Series 1. Washington, D.C.

Doulaire, N. 2002. *Promises to Keep: The Toll of Unintended Pregnancies on Women's Lives in the Developing World*. Washington, D.C.: Global Health Council.

Drimie, S. 2002. *The Impact of HIV/AIDS on Rural Households and Land Issues in Southern and Eastern Africa*. Rome: Food and Agriculture Organization of the United Nations Sub-Regional Office for Southern and Eastern Africa.

Druschel, K., J. Quigley, and C. Sanchez. 2001. "The State of the Microcredit Summit Campaign 2001 Report."

Duflo, E. 2001. "Schooling and Labor Market Consequences of School Construction in Indonesia: Evidence from an Unusual Policy Experiment." *American Economic Review* 91 (4): 795–813.

Durrieu, M. 1999. *Se dice de nosotros*. Buenos Aires: Catálogas.

Duryea, S., A. Cox Edwards, and M. Ureta. 2001. "Women in the Latin American Labor Market: The Remarkable 1990s." Labor Markets Policy Briefs Series. Inter-American Development Bank, Sustainable Development Department, Social Development Division, Washington, D.C.

Duvvury, N., and K. Allendorf. 2001. "Domestic Violence in India: The Roles of Education and Employment." Paper presented at the Sixth Women's Policy Research Conference on the Status of Women: Facing the Facts, Forging the Future, June 8–9, Washington, D.C.

ECOSOC (Economic and Social Council). 1997. *1997 Resolutions of ECOSOC*. New York: United Nations. [Retrieved August 10, 2004, from www.un.org/esa/coordination/ecosoc/1997res.htm].

El Bushra, J., and E. Piza Lopez. 1993. "Gender-Related Violence: Its Scope and Relevance." *Focus on Gender* 1 (2): 1–9.

El-Gibaly, O., B. Ibrahim, B. S. Mensch, and W. H. Clark. 1999. "The Decline in Female Circumcision in Egypt: Evidence and Interpretation." Population Council Policy Research Division Working Paper. New York.

Ellis, S. D., and J. L. Hine. 1998. "The Provision of Rural Transport Services: Approach Paper." Sub-Saharan Africa Transport Policy Program Working Paper 37. World Bank, Washington, D.C.

Ellsberg, M., R. Peña, A. Herrera, J. Liljestrand, and A. Winkvist. 2000. "Candies in Hell: Women's Experience of Violence in Nicaragua." *Social Science and Medicine* 51 (11): 1595–610.

Elo, I. 1992. "Utilization of Maternal Health-Care Services in Peru: The Role of Women's Education." *Health Transition Review* 2 (1): 49–69.

Elson, D. 1999. "Labor Markets as Gendered Institutions: Equality, Efficiency and Empowerment Issues." *World Development* 27(3): 611–27.

Engkvist, R. 1995. "Poverty Alleviation and Rural Development through Public Works: The Case of the Employment Guarantee Scheme in Maharashtra." University of Lund, Department of Economics, Lund, Sweden.

Engle, P. L. 2000. *Urban Women: Balancing Work and Childcare.* 2020 Focus 3, Brief 9. Washington, D.C.: International Food Policy Research Institute.

Esim, S. 2001. "Why Women Earn Less? Gender-Based Factors Affecting the Earnings of Self-Employed Women in Turkey." In *The Economics of Women and Work in the Middle East and North Africa.* Greenwich, Conn.: Middle East Economic Association, JAI Press.

Evans, J. L. 1995. "Child Day Care in Developing Countries." Paper presented at the Community and International Child Health, American Academy of Pediatrics, April 11, Philadelphia, Penn.

Evans, J. L., and R. G. Myers. 1995. "Childbearing Practices: Creating Programs Where Traditions and Modern Practices Meet." In N. P. Stromquist, ed., *Encyclopedia of Third World Women.* New York: Garland Publishing.

Fajnzylber, P., D. Lederman, and N. Loayza. 1998. *Determinants of Crime Rates in Latin America and the World.* Washington, D.C.: World Bank.

Family Care International and the Safe Motherhood Inter-Agency Group. 1998. "The Safe Motherhood Initiative." Working paper on 1987 intiative. New York. [Retrieved March 11, 2004, from www.safemotherhood.org].

Family Health International. 1998. "Contraception Improves Employment Prospects." *Network Summer* 18 (4); 19–22.

Family Violence Prevention Fund. 1997. *News Flash.* November 24. [www.fvfp.org]

FAO (Food and Agriculture Organization of the United Nations). 2003. *HIV/AIDS and Agriculture: Impacts and Responses.* Rome, Italy.

Felitti, V. 1991. "Long-Term Medical Consequences of Incest, Rape, and Molestation." *Southern Medical Journal* 84 (3): 328–31.

Fernando, P., and G. Porter. 2002. "Introduction: Bridging the Gap between Gender and Transport." In P. Fernando and G. Porter, eds., *Balancing the Load: Women, Gender, and Transport.* London: Zed Books.

Filmer, D. 1999. "The Structure of Social Disparities in Education: Gender and Wealth." Background paper for the World Bank Policy Research Report on Gender and Development. Washington, D.C.

Filmer, D., and L. Pritchett. 1999. "The Effect of Household Wealth on Educational Attainment: Evidence from 35 Countries." *Population and Development Review* 25 (1): 85–120.

Filmer, D., B. Prouty, and C. Winter. 2002. *The Linkage between Poverty and Girls' Educational Opportunities.* Washington, D.C.: World Bank.

Floro, M. 1995. "Economic Restructuring, Gender and the Allocation of Time." *World Development* 23 (11): 1913–29.

Folbre, N. 1994. *Who Pays for the Kids? Gender and the Structure of Constraint.* London: Routledge Press.

Fong, M. S., W. Wakeman, and A. Bhushan. 1996. "Toolkit on Gender in Water and Sanitation." Gender Toolkit Series 2. World Bank, Washington, D.C.

Fontana, M., S. Joekes, and R. Masika. 1998. "Global Trade Expansion and Liberalization: Gender Issues and Impacts." Department for International Development, London.

Forum for African Women Educationalists. 2001. "Girls' Education and Poverty Eradication: FAWE's Response." Paper presented at the Third United Nations Conference on the Least Developed Countries, May 14–20, Brussels, Belgium.

Friedman, E. 2000. *Unfinished Transitions: Women and the Gendered Development of Democracy in Venezuela, 1936–1996.* University Park, Penn.: Pennsylvania State University Press.

Fultz, E., M. Ruck, and S. Steinhilber, eds. 2003. *The Gender Dimensions of Social Security Reform in Central and Eastern Europe: Case Studies of the Czech Republic, Hungary and Poland.* Budapest, Hungary: International Labour Office, Sub-Regional Office for Central and Eastern Europe.

Gallup Poll. 2000. "Latin American Women Leadership Study: A Look at Changing Attitudes of Latin Americans toward Gender and Women's Leadership Capabilities." Report for the Inter-American Development Bank, Washington, D.C.

Ganatra, B. R., K. J. Coyaji, and V. N. Rao. 1998. "Too Far, Too Little, Too Late: A Community-Based Case-Control Study of Maternal Mortality in Rural West Maharashtra, India." *Bulletin of the World Health Organization* 76: 591–98.

———. 1996. *Community cum Hospital Based Case-Control Study on Maternal Mortality: A Final Report.* Pune, India: KEM Hospital Research Centre.

Garcia-Moreno, C. 1999. "Violence against Women, Gender and Health Equity." Harvard Center for Population and Development Studies Working Paper Series 99.15. Cambridge, Mass.

Germain, A. 2000. "Population and Reproductive Health: Where Do We Go Next?" *American Journal of Public Health* 90 (12): 1845–47.

Gertler, P., and P. Glewwe. 1992. "The Willingness to Pay for Education for Daughters in Contrast to Sons: Evidence from Rural Peru." *The World Bank Economic Review* 6 (1): 17–188.

Gibson, M. A. 1990. *Equity for Female Teachers: A National Survey of Employment, Papua New Guinea (PNG).* Boroko, Papa New Guinea: PNG National Research Institute.

Gindling, T., and M. Crummet. 1977. *Maternity Leave Legislation and the Work and Pay of Women in Costa Rica.* Baltimore, Md.: University of Maryland.

Giovarelli, R., and S. Lastarria. 2004. "Gender Issues in Land Administration and Land Reform." Paper presented at the Gender and Rural Development and the Land Thematic group jointly sponsored brown bag lunch, April 29, World Bank, Washington, D.C.

Glick, P., and D. E. Sahn. 1997. "Gender and Education Impacts on Employment and Earnings in West Africa: Evidence from Guinea." *Economic Development and Cultural Change* 45 (4): 793–823.

Global Campaign for Education. 2004. *Learning to Survive: How Education for All Would Save Millions of Young People from HIV/AIDS.* Global Campaign for Education Briefing Paper. Brussels, Belgium.

Goetz, A. M. 1995. "The Politics of Integrating Gender into State Development Processes: Trends, Opportunities and Constraints in Bangladesh, Chile, Jamaica, Mali, Morocco and Uganda." UNRISD Occasional Paper 2. United Nations Research Institute for Social Development, Geneva, Switzerland.

Goetz, A. M., and R. Sengupta. 1996. "Who Takes the Credit? Gender, Power and Control over Loan Use in Rural Credit Programs in Bangladesh." *World Development* 24 (1): 45–63.

Goldin, C. 2002. "A Pollution Theory of Discrimination: Male and Female Earnings in Occupations and Industries." National Bureau of Economic Research Working Paper 4985. Cambridge, Mass.

Govindasamy, P. 2000. "Poverty, Women's Status, and Utilization of Health Services in Egypt." In B. Garcia, ed., *Women, Poverty, and Demographic Change.* Oxford, U.K.: Oxford University Press.

Greaves, L., O. Hankivsky, and J. Kingston-Riechers. 1995. *Selected Estimates of the Costs of Violence against Women.* London: Center for Research on Violence against Women and Children.

Green, D. 1999. *Gender Violence in Africa: African Women's Response.* New York: St. Martin's Press.

Greene, M. E., Z. Rasekh, and K. A. Amen. 2004. "Involving Men in Reproductive Health: Contributions to Development." Occasional paper commissioned for the UN Millennium Project. George Washington University, Washington, D.C.

Gross, B., C. van Wijk, and N. Mukherjee. 2001. "Linking Sustainability with Demand, Gender, and Poverty: A Study in Community Managed Water Supply Projects in Fifteen Countries." Water and Sanitation Program Report. International Water and Sanitation Centre, Delft, Netherlands.

Grown, C., D. Elson, and N. Çağatay. 2000. "Introduction: Special Issue on Growth, Trade, Finance, and Gender Equity." *World Development* 28 (7): 1145–156.

Grown, C., G. Rao Gupta, and Z. Khan. 2003. "Promises to Keep: Achieving Gender Equality and the Empowerment of Women." Background paper for the UN Millennium Project Task Force on Education and Gender Equality. ICRW (International Center for Research on Women), Washington, D.C.

Grunseit, A. 1997. *Impact of HIV and Sexual Health Education on the Sexual Behavior of Young People: A Review Update.* Geneva: UNAIDS.

Grupo Cultural Yuyachkani. 1992. *Documentos de teatro: Talleres 'Teatro Mujer.'* Lima: Edicion Grupo Cultural.

GTZ (Deutsche Gesellschaft für Technische Zusammenarbeit). 2004. [www.gtz.de.]

Guyer, J. 1988. "Dynamic Approaches to Domestic Budgeting: Cases and Methods from Africa." In D. Dwyer and J. Bruce, eds., *A Home Divided: Women and Income in the Third World.* Palo Alto, Calif.: Stanford University Press.

Haddad, L., J. Hoddinott, and H. Alderman. 1997. *Intrahousehold Resource Allocation in Developing Countries: Methods, Models and Policy.* Baltimore, Md.: Johns Hopkins University Press.

Hallman, K. 2000. "Mother-Father Resource Control, Marriage Payments, and Girl-Boy Health in Rural Bangladesh." Food Consumption and Nutrition Division Discussion Paper 93. International Food Policy Research Institute, Washington, D.C.

Hallman, K., A. Quisumbing, R. Agnes, M. T. Ruel, and B. de la Briere. 2003. "Childcare and Work: Joint Decisions among Women in Poor Neighborhoods of Guatemala City." Food Consumption and Nutrition Division Discussion Paper 151. International Food Policy Research Institute, Washington, D.C.

Hannan, C. 2003a. "Convention on the Elimination of All Forms of Discrimination against Women (CEDAW)." Paper commissioned by the UN Millennium Project Task Force on Education and Gender Equality. New York.

———. 2003b. "Gender Mainstreaming: Reflections on Implementation of the Strategy." Paper presented at the seminar Integrating Gender Equality into Development Co-operation: Drawing Lessons from Recent Evaluations, November 27–28, Brussels, Belgium.

Harding, S. 1996. "Gendered Ways of Knowing and the 'Epistemological Crisis' of the West." In N. R. Goldberger, J. M. Tarule, B. M. Clinchy, and M. F. Belenky, eds., *Knowledge, Difference, and Power: Essays Inspired by Women's Ways of Knowing*. New York: Basic Books.

Harrison, J., and S. Murphy. 1999. "A Care Package for Managing Female Sexual Assault in Genitourinary Medicine." *International Journal of Sexually Transmitted Disease and AIDS* 10 (5): 283–89.

Hayward, R. 2000. *Breaking the Earthenware Jar: Lessons from South Asia to End Violence against Women and Girls*. New York: UNICEF.

Heise, L. 1989. "International Dimensions of Violence against Women: Response to the Victimization of Women and Children." 12 (1): 3–11.

Heise, L., M. Ellsberg, and M. Gottemoeller. 1999. *Ending Violence against Women*. Baltimore, Md.: Johns Hopkins University School of Public Health, Center for Communications Programs, Population Information Program.

Heise, L., J. Pitanguy, and A. Germaine. 1994. *Violence against Women: The Hidden Health Burden*. World Bank Discussion Paper 225. Washington, D.C.

Helburn, S. 1999. "Childcare." In J. Peterson and M. Lewis, eds., *The Elgar Companion to Feminist Economics*. Cheltenham and Camberley, U.K.: Edward Elgar.

Hernandez Cajo, T. 1999. "Domestic Violence and Child Abuse: Causes and Responses." Presented at the workshop for Rising Violence and the Criminal Justice Response in Latin America: Towards an Agenda for Collaborative Research in the 21st Century, May 6–9, University of Texas, Austin, Tex.

Herz, B., and A. Measham. 1987. *Safe Motherhood: Proposals for Action*. World Bank Discussion Paper 9. Washington, D.C.

Herz, B., and G. B. Sperling. 2004. "What Works in Girls' Education: Evidence and Policies from the Developing World." Report for the Council on Foreign Relations, Washington, D.C.

Herz, B., K. Subbarao, M. Habib, and L. Raney. 1995. *Letting Girls Learn: Promising Approaches in Primary and Secondary Education*. World Bank Discussion Paper 133. Washington, D.C.

Hewett, P. C., and C. B. Lloyd. 2004. "Progress towards "Education for All:" Trends and Current Challenges for Sub-Saharan Africa." Population Council, New York.

Hijab, N., and C. F. El-Solh. 2003. "Laws, Regulations and Practices Impeding Women's Economic Participation in the MENA Region." Expanded report submitted to the World Bank. Washington, D.C.

Hill, M. A., and E. M. King. 1995. "Women's Education and Economic Well-Being." *Feminist Economics* 1 (2): 1–26.

Himes, J. R., C. Landers, and J. Leslie. 1992. "Women, Work and Child Care—Summary Report." Paper presented at the United Nations International Children's Emergency Fund Innocenti Global Seminar, Florence, Italy.

Hoffman, K. L., D. H. Demo, and J. N. Edwards. 1994. "Physical Wife Abuse in a Non-Western Society: An Integrated Theoretical Approach." *Journal of Marriage and the Family* 56: 131–46.

Hoffmann-Barthes, A. M., S. Nair, and D. Malpede. 1999. "Scientific, Technical, and Vocational Education of Girls in Africa." UNESCO Working Paper. United Nations Educational, Scientific, and Cultural Organization, Paris.

Htun, M. N. 2002. "Puzzles of Women's Rights in Brazil." *Social Research* 69 (3): 733–51.

———. 2003a. *Sex and the State: Abortion, Divorce, and the Family under Latin American Dictatorships and Democracies*. New York: Cambridge University Press.

————. 2003b. "Using Gender Quotas to Increase Women's Representation in Politics: Experiences and Challenges." Paper commissioned by the UN Millennium Project Task Force on Education and Gender Equality. UN Millennium Project, New York.

————. 2003c. "Women and Democracy." In J. Dominguez and M. Shifter, eds., *Constructing Democratic Governance in Latin America*. Baltimore, Md.: Johns Hopkins University Press.

Human Rights Watch. 1995. *Violence against Women in South Africa: State Response to Domestic Violence and Rape*. New York.

————. 1996. *Shattered Lives: Sexual Violence during the Rwandan Genocide and Its Aftermath*. New York.

————. 2000. *Seeking Protection: Addressing Sexual and Domestic Violence in Tanzania's Refugee Camps*. New York.

————. 2001. *Uzbekistan: Sacrificing Women to Save the Family? State Response to Violence against Women*. New York.

————. 2002. *Suffering in Silence: The Links between Human Rights Abuses and HIV Transmission to Girls in Zambia*. New York.

————. 2003. *Just Die Quietly: Domestic Violence and Women's Vulnerability to HIV in Uganda*. New York.

Hunt, J., and N. Kasynathan. 2001. "Pathways to Empowerment? Reflections on Microfinance and Transformation in Gender Relations in South Asia." In C. Sweetman, ed., *Gender, Development and Money*. Oxford, U.K.: Oxfam.

Huq, L., and S. Amin. 2001. "Dowry Negotiations and the Process of Union Formation in Bangladesh: Implications of Rising Education." Population Council, New York.

ICRW (International Center for Research on Women). 2000. *A Summary Report for a Multi-Site Household Survey*. Domestic Violence in India 3. Washington, D.C.

IDB (Inter-American Development Bank). 1998. *Colombia. Proposal for Financing in Support of Peaceful Coexistence and Citizen Security*. Washington, D.C.

————. 1999. *The Challenge of Mainstreaming: A Report to the Board of Executive Directors on Implementation of the WID Action Plan 1995 1997*. Sustainable Development Department Strategy and Policy Series. Washington, D.C.

————. 2000. "Boletin de la red de alcaldes contra la violencia." Program de Prevencion de la Violencia, División de Desarrollo Social 2. Washington, D.C.

————. 2001a. *Jamaica. Proposal for a Loan and Nonreimbursable Technical-Cooperation Funding for a Citizen Security and Justice Program*. Washington, D.C.

————. 2001b. "Women at Work: A Challenge for Development." Paper presented at the Women at Work Conference, March 17, Santiago, Chile.

————. 2002. *El Salvador. Proposal for a Project to Support the Social Peace Program*. Washington, D.C.

————. 2003. *Honduras: Proposal for a Loan for a Peace and Citizen Security Project for the Municipalities of the Sula Valley*. Washington, D.C.

Idrus, N., and L. R. Bennett. 2003. "Presumed Consent: Marital Violence in Bugis Society." In L. Manderson and L. R. Bennett, eds., *Violence against Women in Asian Societies*. London: Routledge Curzon.

IFPRI (International Food Policy Research Institute). 2001. "Food for Education: Feeding Minds Reduces Poverty." Issue Brief 4. Washington, D.C.

————. 2002. "Guatemala: The Community Day Care Centers Program." Issue Brief 9. Washington, D.C.

ILO (International Labour Organization). 1998. "More than 120 Nations Provide Paid Maternity Leave. Gap in Employment Treatment for Men and Women Still Exists." Press Release. February 10. Geneva.

———. 2000. "Decent Work for Women." Proposal to accelerate the implementation of the Beijing Platform for Action. Geneva.

———. 2001a. *Decent Work Development Index, 1990–2000.* Geneva.

———. 2001b. "ILO Convention on Home Work." Geneva. [www.homenetww.org.uk/conv.html].

———. 2002a. "Decent Work and the Informal Economy, Report VI." Paper presented at the International Labour Conference, 90th Session, Geneva.

———. 2002b. *Women and Men in the Informal Economy: A Statistical Picture.* Geneva.

———. 2002c. "Gender Equality in the World of Work." *ILO Electronic Newsletter* 2. Geneva.

———. 2003a. *Key Indicators of the Labour Market 2003*, 3rd ed. Geneva.

———. 2003b. "Database on Labour Statistics." LABORSTA Internet. ILO Bureau of Statistics, Geneva. [www.laborsta.ilo.org].

———. 2003c. "Maternity Protection." In *Work and Family: International Labour Standards.* Geneva. [Retrieved August 24, 2004, from www.ilo.org/public/english/protection/condtray/maternity/maternity_publ.htm].

———. 2003d. "Time for Equality at Work." Global report for the follow-up to the ILO Declaration on Fundamental Principles and Rights at Work. Geneva.

———. 2004a. *Global Employment Trends.* Geneva.

———. 2004b. *Improving Prospects for Young Women and Men in the World of Work: A Guide to Youth Employment.* Geneva.

———. 2004c. "Proposed Indicator on Employment: Share of Women in Employment by Type." ILO Bureau of Statistics, Geneva.

ILO/UNCTAD (United Nations Conference on Trade and Development) Advisory Group. 2001. "The Minimum Income for School Attendance (MISA) Initiative: Achieving International Development Goals in African Least Developed Countries." Report of the Advisory Group. Geneva.

India SAFE Steering Committee. 1999. *India SAFE Steering Committee Report.* Washington, D.C.: International Center for Research on Women.

Inter-American Dialogue. 2001. "Women and Power in the Americas: A Report Card." Program Report and Country Study. Washington, D.C.

International IDEA and Stockholm University. 2004. "Global Database of Quotas for Women." Stockholm, Sweden. [www.quotaproject.com].

International Institute of Population Sciences. 1995. *National Family Health Survey: India 1992–93.* Mumbai.

IPU (Inter-Parliamentary Union). 2004. "Women in National Parliaments Data Tables." [www.ipu.org/wmn-e/classif.htm].

IRC (International Water and Sanitation Centre). Website http://irc.nl.

IRNVAW (International Research Network on Violence against Women). 1998. "Summary Report." Paper presented at Third Annual Meeting of the IRNVAW, January, Washington, D.C.

Jackson, C. 2003. "Gender Analysis of Land: Beyond Land Rights for Women?" *Journal of Agrarian Change* 3 (4): 453–80.

Jacobson, R. 1993. "Domestic Violence as a Development Issue." In H. O'Connell, ed., *Women and Conflict.* Oxford, U.K.: Oxfam.

Jaffe, P., M. Sudermann, D. Reitzel, and S. M. Killip. 1992. "An Evaluation of a Secondary School Primary Intervention Program on Violence in Intimate Relationship." *Violence and Victims* 7 (2): 129–46.

Jain, S. 2003. "Gender Equality in Education: Community-Based Initiatives in India." Background paper for *EFA Global Monitoring Report 2003/4.* UNESCO, Paris.

Jarret, D. 1994. "The Health of Women." In J. Mati, B. T. Nasah, and J. Kasonde, eds., *Contemporary Issues in Maternal Health Care in Africa.* Luxembourg: Harwood Academic Publishers.

Jejeebhoy, S. 1996. "Women's Education, Autonomy, and Reproductive Behavior: Assessing What We Have Learned." East-West Center Occasional Paper, Honolulu, Hawaii.

Jewkes, R., C. Vundule, F. Maforah, and E. Jordaan. 2001. "Relationship Dynamics and Adolescent Pregnancy in South Africa." *Social Science and Medicine* 52 (2): 733–44.

Jha, J., and R. Subrahmanian. 2004. "Secondary Education in the Indian State of Uttar Pradesh: Gender Dimensions of State Policy and Practice." Paper for Gender and Social Policy Programme. United Nations Research Institute for Social Development, Geneva.

JICA (Japan International Cooperation Agency). 1999. "Country WID Profile: Chile." Tokyo.

Johns Hopkins School of Public Health. 1999a. "Why Family Planning Matters." *Population Reports* J (49).

———. 1999b. "Ending Violence against Women." *Population Reports* L (11).

Johnson-Welch, C. 1999. *Focusing on Women Works: Research on Improving Micronutrient Status through Food-Based Interventions.* Washington, D.C.: ICRW (International Center for Research on Women).

Johnson-Welch, C., P. Bonnard, A. Spring Ritchie, R. Strickland, and M. Sims. 2000. "They Can't Do It All: A Call for Expanded Investments in Childcare." Paper for the United Nations Children's Fund, Washington, D.C.

Jones, M. 1998. "Gender Quotas, Electoral Laws, and the Election of Women: Lessons from the Argentine Provinces." *Comparative Political Studies* 31 (1): 3–21.

Jones, M., and M. Htun. 2002. "Engendering the Right to Participate in Decision Making: Electoral Quotas and Women's Leadership in Latin America." In M. Molyneaux, ed., *Gender and the Politics of Rights and Democracy in Latin America.* London: Palgrave.

Jorgensen, S. R., V. Potts, and B. Camp. 1993. "Project Taking Charge: Six Month Follow-Up of a Pregnancy Prevention Program for Early Adolescents." *Family Relations* 42: 401–06.

Kabeer, N. 1994. *Reversed Realities: Gender Hierarchies in Development Thought.* London: Verso.

———. 1999. "The Conditions and Consequences of Choice: Reflections on the Measurement of Women's Empowerment." UNRISD Discussion Paper 108. United Nations Research Institute for Social Development, Geneva.

———2000. *The Power to Choose: Bangladeshi Women and Labour Market Decisions in London and Dhaka.* London: Verso.

Kabeer, N., and R. Subrahmanian. 1996. "Institutions, Relations, and Outcomes: Framework and Tools for Gender Aware Planning." Institute of Development Studies, Discussion Paper 35. University of Sussex, Brighton, U.K.

Kalichan, S., E. Williams, C. Cherry, L. Belcher, and D. Nachimson. 1998. "Sexual Coercion, Domestic Violence, and Negotiating Condom Use among Low-Income African American Women." *Journal of Women's Health* 7 (3): 371–78.

Kambhapati, U. S., and S. Pal. 2001. "Role of Parental Literacy in Explaining Gender Difference: Evidence from Child Schooling in India" *European Journal of Development Research* 13 (2): 97–119.

Kandiyoti, D. 1988. "Bargaining with Patriarchy." *Gender and Society* 2 (3): 274–90.

Kathlene, L. 2001. "Words That Matter: Women's Voice and Institutional Bias in Public Policy Formation." In S. J. Carroll, ed., *The Impact of Women in Public Office.* Bloomington, Ind.: Indiana University Press.

Kaufmann, D., A. Kraay, and P. Zoido-Lobatón. 1999. "Governance Matters." Policy Research Working Paper 2196. World Bank, Washington, D.C.

Kelleher, D. 2002. "Organizational Learning: A Borrowed Toolbox?" *Development in Practice* 12 (3–4).

Kelly, L., and J. Radford. 1998. "Sexual Violence against Women and Girls: An Approach to an International Overview." In R. E. Dobash and R. P. Dobash, eds., *Rethinking Violence against Women*. Thousand Oaks, Calif.: Sage Press.

Kerns, V. 1992. "Preventing Violence against Women: A Central American Case." In D. Counts, J. Brown, and J. Campbell, eds., *Sanctions and Sanctuary: Cultural Perspectives on Beating of Wives*. Boulder, Colo.: Westview Press.

Kessler, T. 2002. "Preconditions for Privatizing Essential Infrastructure Services: A Proposal for a Feasibility Study." CNES Policy Analysis Series Paper 2. Citizens' Network on Essential Services, Takoma Park, Md.

Kevane, M., and B. Wydick. 2001. "Microenterprise Lending to Female Entrepreneurs: Sacrificing Economic Growth for Poverty Alleviation?" *World Development* 29(7): 1225–36.

KfW (Kreditanstalt für Wiederaufbau) and City of Cape Town. 2002. "Violence Prevention through Urban Upgrading: Feasibility Study." Kreditanstalt für Wiederaufbau, Cape Town.

Khan, M., S. Ahmed, A. Bhuiya, and M. Chowdhury. 1998. "Domestic Violence against Women: Does Development Intervention Matter?" Unpublished paper of the BRAC-IICDDR Joint Research Project, Dhaka, Bangladesh.

Khan, Z. 2003. *Closing the Gap: Putting EU and UK Gender Policy into Practice: South Africa, Nicaragua and Bangladesh*. London: One World Action.

Khandker, S. R., V. Lavy, and D. Filmer. 1994. *Schooling and Cognitive Achievements of Children in Morocco*. World Bank Discussion Paper 264. Washington, D.C.

King, E., and R. Bellew. 1991. "Gains in the Education of Peruvian Women, 1940-1980." In B. Herz and S. R. Khandkher, eds., *Women's Work, Education and Family Welfare in Peru*. World Bank Discussion paper 116. Washington, D.C.

King, E., and L. A. Lillard. 1987. "Education Policy and Schooling Attainment in Malaysia and the Philippines." *Economics and Education Review* 6(2): 167-81.

King, J. 2003. "The Risk of Maternal Nutritional Depletion and Poor Outcomes Increases in Early or Closely Spaced Pregnancies." *Journal of Nutrition* 133(12): 1732S-6S.

Kirby, D., M. Korpi, R. P. Barth, and H. H. Cagampang. 1997. "The Impact of Postponing Sexual Involvement Curriculum among Youths in California." *Family Planning Perspectives* 29(3): 100-8.

Kishor, S. and K. Johnson. 2004. *Profiling Domestic Violence: A Multi-Country Study*. Measure *DHS+* project. Calverton, MD: ORC-Macro. [www.measuredhs.com].

Klasen, S. 2001. "In Search of the Holy Grail: How to Achieve Pro-Poor Growth." Growth and Equity Task Team of the Strategic Partnership with Africa (SPA). Deutsche Gesellschaft für Technische Zusammenarbeit (GTZ), Munich.

Knowles, S., P. K. Lorgelly, and P. D. Owen. 2002. "Are Educational Gender Gaps a Brake on Economic Development? Some Cross-country Empirical Evidence." *Oxford Economic Papers* 54(1): 118-49.

Konje, J. C., and O. A. Ladipo. 2000. "Nutrition and Obstructed Labor." *American Journal of Clinical Nutrition* 72(1): 291S–7S.

Korf, D. J., H. Meulenbeek, E. Mot, and T. van den Brandt. 1997. *Economic Costs of Domestic Violence against Women*. Utrecht, Netherlands: Dutch Foundation of Women's Shelters.

Koss, M. 1993. "The Impact of Crime Victimization of Women's Medical Use." *Journal of Women's Health* 2(1): 67-72.

Kudva, N. 2003. "Engineering Elections: The Experiences of Women in Panchayati Raj in Karnataka, India." *International Journal of Politics, Culture and Society* 16(3): 445–63.

Kula, O., and V. Lambert. 1994. *The Child Care Sub-sector in Volgograd, Russia.* GEMINI Technical Report 99. New York: Pact Publications.

Kumar, K. 2001. "Civil Wars, Women and Gender Relations: An Overview." In K. Kumar, ed. *Women and Civil War: Impact, Organizations and Action.* Boulder, Colo.: Lynne Rienner.

Kurz, K. and C. Johnson-Welch. 2000. *Enhancing Nutrition Results: A Women's Resources Approach.* International Center for Research on Women. Washington, D.C.

Laack, S. 1995. "Thoughts about Male Involvement." Paper presented at the Youth Sexuality Conference, August 13–18, Arusha, Tanzania.

Laack, S., H. Carlberg, and O. Berggren. 1997. "Report on the RFSU Young Men's Clinic." Swedish Association of Sex Education and Swedish Family Planning Association, Stockholm.

Landsberg-Lewis, I. 2002. *Bringing Equality Home: Implementing the Convention on the Elimination of All Forms of Discrimination against Women (CEDAW).* New York: United Nations Development Fund for Women. [http://unifem.undp.org/resources/cedaw/cedaw05.html].

LaPin, D. 1992. 1992. "Assessing Psychosocial Needs of Refugee Women and Children Using Rapid Field Techniques." Paper presented at 120th meeting of the American Public Health Association, November 8–12, Washington, D.C.

Larraín, S., J. Vega, and I. Delgado. 1997. *Relaciones familiares y maltrato infantil.* Santiago: UNICEF.

Lastarria-Cornhiel, S. 1997. "Impact of Privatization on Gender and Property Rights in Africa." *World Development* 25(8): 1317-33.

Laurence, L., and R. Spalter-Roth. 1996. *Measuring the Costs of Domestic Violence against Women and the Cost-Effectiveness of Interventions: An Initial Assessment and Proposals for Further Research.* Washington, D.C.: Institute for Women's Policy Research.

Lavy, V. 1996. "School Supply Constraints and Children's Educational Outcomes in Rural Ghana." *Journal of Development Economics* 51(2): 291–314.

Lentin, R., ed. 1997. *Gender and Catastrophe.* London: Zed Books.

Leonard, A., and C. Landers. 1991. *Child Care: Meeting the Needs of Working Mothers and Their Children.* SEEDS *number 13.* Population Council, New York.

Leslie, H. 2001. "Healing the Psychological Wounds of Gender-related Violence in Latin America: A Model for Gender-sensitive Work in Post-Conflict Settings." *Gender and Development* 9(3): 50–9.

Leye, E., A. Githaniga, and M. Temmerman. 1999. *Health Care Strategies for Combating Violence against Women in Developing Countries.* Ghent, Belgium: International Center for Reproductive Health.

Levinson, D. 1989. *Family Violence in Cross-Cultural Perspective.* Thousand Oaks, Calif.: Sage Publications.

Lillard, L. A., and R. J. Willis. 1994. "Intergenerational Education Mobility: Effects of Family and State in Malaysia." *Journal of Human Resources* 29(4): 1126–66.

Lloyd, C. B., and P. C. Hewett. 2003. "Primary Schooling in Sub-Saharan Africa: Recent Trends and Current Challenges." Population Council Policy Research Division Working Paper 176. Population Council, New York.

———. 2004. "Universal Primary Schooling in Sub-Saharan Africa: Is Gender Equity Enough?" Population Council, New York.

Lloyd, C. B., and B. S. Mensch. 1999. "Implications of Formal Schooling for Girls' Transitions to Adulthood in Developing Countries." In J. Casterline, C. Bledsoe, J. Johnson-Kuhn, and J. Haaga, eds., *Critical Perspectives on Schooling and Fertility in the Developing World*. Washington, D.C.: National Academy Press.

Lloyd, S., and N. Tulac. 1999. "The Effects of Male Violence on Female Employment." *Violence against Women* 5(4): 370–92.

Long, L., L. N. Hung, A. Truitt, L. T. P. Mai, and D. N. Anh. 2000. "Changing Gender Relations in Vietnam's Post Doi Moi Era." World Bank Policy Report Background Paper 14. Washington, D.C.

Louw, A., and M. Shaw. 1997. "Stolen Opportunities: The Impact of Crime on South Africa's Poor." Institute for Security Studies Monograph 14. Institute for Security Studies, Johannesburg.

Luke, N., and K. Kurz. 2002. *Cross-Generational and Transactional Sexual Relations in Sub-Saharan Africa: Prevalence of Behavior and Implications for Negotiating Safer Sexual Practices*. Washington, D.C.: ICRW.

Lukhumalani, V. 1998. "Women against Violence: A South Asian Perspective." *Network Newsletter* 15.

Lule, E., N. Oomman, D. Huntington, J. Epp, and J. Rosen. 2003. "Review of Determinants, Interventions, and Challenges for Achieving the Millennium Development Goal of Improving Maternal Health." World Bank Health, Nutrition and Population Working Paper Series. World Bank, Washington, D.C.

Lund, F., and J. Nicholson, eds. 2003. *Chains of Production, Ladders of Protection, Social Protection for Workers in the Informal Economy*. Durban, South Africa: University of Natal, School of Development Studies.

Lund, F., and S. Srinivas. 2000. *Learning from Experience: A gendered approach to social protection from workers in the informal economy*. Geneva and Cambridge, U.K.: International Labour Office and Women in Informal Employment Globalizing and Organizing.

Macdonald, M. 2003. "Gender Equality and Mainstreaming in the Policy and Practice of the UK Department for International Development (DFID): A Briefing from the U.K. Gender and Development Network." U.K. Gender and Development Network, London.

Maine, D. 1991. *Safe Motherhood Programs: Options and Issues*. New York: Center for Population and Family Health, Columbia University.

Maitse, T. 1998. "Political Change, Rape, and Pornography in Post-Apartheid South Africa." *Gender and Development* 6(3): 55–9.

Malhotra, A., R. Pande, and C. Grown. 2003. "Impact of Investments in Female Education on Gender Equality." International Center for Research on Women, Washington, D.C.

Malhotra, A., S. Schuler, and C. Boender. 2002. "Measuring Women's Empowerment as a Variable in International Development." World Bank Gender and Development Group Background paper. World Bank, Washington, D.C. [www.icrw.org/docs/MeasuringEmpowerment_workingpaper_802.doc.]

Malmberg Calvo, C. 1994. "Case Study on the Role of Women in Rural Transport: Access of Women to Domestic Facilities." Sub-Saharan Africa Transport Policy Program, World Bank and Economic Commission for Africa Working Paper 11. World Bank, Washington, D.C.

———. 1996. "Promoting Intermediate Means of Transport." Sub-Saharan Africa Transportation Policy Program Working Paper 20. World Bank, Washington, D.C.

Malmberg Calvo, C., and L. Pouliquen. 1999. "Empowerment and the Institutional Basis of Antipoverty Policies and Interventions: The Case of Rural Infrastructure." Villa Borsig Workshop Series. Deutsche Stiftung fur internationale Entwicklung (DSE), Bonn, Germany.

Maman, S., J. Campbell, M. Sweat, and A.C. Gielen. 2000. "The Intersection of HIV & Violence: Directions for Future Research and Interventions." *Social Science and Medicine* 50(4): 459–78.

Mammen, K., and C. Paxson. 2000. "Women's Work and Economic Development." *The Journal of Economic Perspectives* 14(4): 141–64.

Manimala. 1983. "Zameen kenkar? Jote onkar! Women's Participation in the Bodhgaya Land Struggle." *Manushi* 14: 2–16.

Mansbridge, J. 1999. "Should Blacks Represent Blacks and Women Represent Women? A Contingent 'Yes.'" *The Journal of Politics* 61(3): 628–57.

Marphatia, A. 2004. "Summary of E-discussion on Universal Primary Education MDG and Task Force Report." ActionAid International with the Commonwealth Education Fund (CEF), the Global Campaign on Education (GCE), and One World South Asia (OWSA), London.

Martin, S. L., A. O. Tsui, K. Maitra, and R. Marinshaw. 1999. "Domestic Violence in Northern India." *American Journal of Epidemiology* 150(4): 417–26.

Masika, R., and S. Baden. 1997. "Infrastructure and Poverty: A Gender Analysis." BRIDGE Development and Gender Report 51. University of Sussex, Institute of Development Studies, Brighton, U.K.

Mason, K. and H. Carlsson. 2004. "The Impact of Gender Equality in Land Rights on Development." Paper presented at the Human Rights and Development: Towards Mutual Reinforcement conference hosted by the New York University School of Law, March 1, New York.

Mathur, S., M. Greene, and A. Malhotra. 2003. *Too Young to Wed. The Lives, Rights, and Health of Young Married Girls.* Washington, D.C.: International Center for Research on Women.

Mattison, T. 2003. "Challenging Gender-based Violence across Genders." *Internet Relay Chat.* [www.irc.org].

McCann, B. 1998. "The Building Bridges: A Review of Infrastructure Services Projects Addressing Gender Integration." Women in Development and Gender Equity Division of the Canadian International Development Agency, Quebec.

McDonagh, E. 2002. "Political Citizenship and Democratization: The Gender Paradox." *American Political Science Review* 96(3): 535–52.

McGlen, N. E., and M. R. Sarkees. 1993. *Women in Foreign Policy: The Insiders.* New York: Routledge.

McPhedran, M., S. Bazilli, M. Erickson, and A. Byrnes. 2000. *The First CEDAW Impact Study. Final Report.* Toronto: York University, Centre for Feminist Research and the International Women's Rights Project.

Mehra, R., and S. Gammage. 1999. "Trends, Countertrends, and Gaps in Women's Employment." *World Development* 27(3): 533–50.

Menon, G. 1996. "Re-negotiating Gender: Enabling Women to Claim their Right to Land Resources." Paper presented at NGO Forum on the UN Conference on Human Settlements—HABITAT II, June 3–14, Istanbul.

Menon-Sen, K. 2003. *Millennium Development Goals Reports: A Quick Look through a Gender Lens.* BDP-PNUD. New York.

Mensch, B., J. Bruce, and M. Greene. 1998. *The Uncharted Passage: Girls' Adolescence in the Developing World.* New York: Population Council.

Mitra, N. 1998. "Best Practices among Responses to Domestic Violence: A Study of Government and Non-Government Responses in Madhya Pradesh and Maharashtra." International Center for Research on Women, Washington, D.C.

Mladjenvoic, L., and D. Matijasevic. 1996. "SOS Belgrade July 1993-1995: Dirty Streets." In C. Corrin, ed., *Women in a Violent World: Feminist Analysis and Resistance Across Europe*. Edinburgh: Edinburgh University Press.

Modi, V. 2004. "Energy and Transport for the Poor." Paper commissioned for the UN Millennium Project Task Force 1. Earth Institute and Columbia University Department of Mechanical Engineering, New York.

Morduch, J. 1999. "The Microfinance Promise." *Journal of Economic Literature* 37(4): 1569–614.

Morley, S., and D. Coady. 2003. *Targeted Education Subsidies in Developing Countries: A Review of Recent Experiences*. Washington, D.C.: Center for Global Development.

Morrison, A., and L. Biehl, eds. 1999. *Too Close to Home: Domestic Violence in Latin America*. Washington, D.C.: Inter-American Development Bank.

Moser, C. 1993. *Gender Planning and Development, Theory, Practice and Training*. London and New York: Routledge Press.

———. 1996. *Confronting Crisis: A Summary of Household Responses to Poverty Vulnerability in Four Poor Urban Communities*. Environmentally Sustainable Development Studies and Monograph Series 7. Washington, D.C.: World Bank.

———. 1998. "The Asset Vulnerability Framework: Reassessing Urban Poverty Reduction Strategies." *World Development* 26(1): 1–19.

———. 2001. "The Gendered Continuum of Violence and Conflict." In C. Moser and F. Clark, eds., *Victims, Perpetrators, or Actors? Gender Armed Conflict and Political Violence*. London: Zed Books.

Moser, C., and F. Clark. 2001. "The SIDA Seedcorn Fund: Capacity Building Initiatives to Strengthen Women's Participation in the Peace Process in Colombia." Swedish International Development Cooperation Authority and World Bank Trust Fund, Stockholm and World Bank, Sweden.

Moser, C., and C. McIlwaine. 2004. *Encounters with Daily Violence in Latin America*. London: Routlege Press.

Moser, C., and A. Moser. 2003. "Background Paper on Gender-Based Violence." Paper commissioned by the World Bank. Washington, D.C.

Mullender, A., and S. Burton. 2000. *Reducing Domestic Violence: What Works?* Perpetrator Programs Briefing ote. London: Policing and Crime Reduction Unit, Home Office.

Mulugeta, E., M. Kassaye, and Y. Berhane. 1998. "Prevalence and Outcomes of Sexual Violence among High School Students." *Ethiopia Medical Journal* 36: 164–74.

Murphy, C. C., B. Schei, T. L. Myhr, and J. DuMont. 2001. "Abuse: A Risk Factor for Low Birth Weight? A Systematic Review and Meta-Analysis." *Canadian Medical Association Journal* 164 (11): 1567–72.

Mwaniki, P. K., E. W. Kabiru, and G. G. Mbugua. 2002. "Utilisation of Antenatal and Maternity Services by Mothers Seeking Child Welfare Services in Mbeere District, Eastern Province, Kenya." *East African Medical Journal* 79 (4): 184–7.

Myers, R., and C. Indriso. 1986. "Women's Work and Child Care: Supporting the Interpretation of Women's Productive and Reproductive Roles in Resource-Poor Households in Developing Countries." Paper prepared for Rockefeller Foundation workshop on Issues Related to Gender, Technology, and Development. Rockefeller Foundation, February 26–27, New York.

Nam, J. L. 1991. "Income Inequality between the Sexes and the Role of the State: South Korea 1960–1990." Ph.D. dissertation, Indiana University, Department of Sociology.

Nanda, P. 2002. "Gender Dimensions of User Fees: Implications for Women's Utilization of Health Care." *Reproductive Health Matters* 10(20): 127–34.

Narayan, D. 1997. *Voices of the Poor: Poverty and Social Capital in Tanzania*. Washington, D.C.: World Bank.

Nduna, S., and L. Goodyear. 1997. *Pain Too Deep for Tears: Assessing the Prevalence of Sexual and Gender Violence among Burundian Refugees in Tanzania.* New York: International Rescue Committee.

New South Wales Domestic Violence Committee. 1991. "Costs of Domestic Violence." Premiers Department, Women's Correction Unit, Sydney.

Ngwira, N., A. Chiweza, E. Kayambazinthu, and N. Kanyogolo. 2002. "Upholding Women's Property and Inheritance Rights in Malawi: Changes Required to Meet the Challenges." Paper presented at the Eighth Women's World Congress, July 21–26, Kampala, Uganda.

Nilofer, S. 1998. "Reforming Rape Law in India." Paper presented at the Oxfam International Workshop on Violence against Women, November 30–December 4, Sarajevo.

Njovana, E. 1994. "Gender-based Violence and Sexual Assault." *African Women* 8: 17.

Norris, P. 2001. "Breaking the Barriers: Positive Discrimination Policies for Women." In J. Klaussen and C. Maier, eds., *Has Liberalism Failed Women? Assuring Equal Representation in Europe and the United States.* London: Palgrave, pp. 89–110.

North-South Institute. 1999. "Time for Work: Linkages between Paid and Unpaid Work in Human Resource Policy." Paper presented at Asia Pacific Economic Cooperation (APEC) Human Resource Development Working Group, Network on Economic Development Management conference, May 8, Hong Kong.

Nyblade, L., R. Pande, S. Mathur, K. MacQuarrie, R. Kidd, H. Banteyerga, A. Kidanu, G. Kilonzo, J. Mbwambo, and V. Bond. 2003. *Disentangling HIV and AIDS Stigma in Ethiopia, Tanzania and Zambia.* Washington, D.C.: International Center for Research on Women.

Obang, D. 1993. "Commonwealth Plan of Action: Appraisal of Progress." Paper presented at Women's Affairs Department, Fourth Meeting of Commonwealth Ministers Responsible for Women's Affairs, July 5–9, Nicosia, Cyprus.

OECD (Organisation for Economic Co-operation and Development) and UIS (UNESCO Institute for Statistics). 2003. World Education Indicators. Paris: OECD. [www.uis. unesco.org/].

OEF (Overseas Education Fund). 1979. "Childcare Needs of Low-income Mothers. Final Report: A Synthesis of Recommendations from an International Conference In-Country Workshops, and Research in Six Countries." League of Women Voters, Washington, D.C.

OHCHR (Office of the United Nations High Commissioner on Human Rights). 2003. "Women's Equal Ownership, Access to and Control over Land and the Equal Rights to Own Property and to Adequate Housing." *ST Resolution 2003/22.* [Retrieved September 20, 2004 from www.unhchr.ch/Huridocda/Huridoca.nsf/TestFrame/ 3c0cfbf78314b564c1256d1d0033bb23?Opendocument].

Omaar, R., and A. de Waal. 1994. "Crimes without Punishment: Sexual Harassment and Violence against Female Students in Schools and Universities in Africa." Discussion Paper 4. African Rights, London.

Omorodion, F. I., and O. Olusanya. 1998. "The Social Context of Reported Rape in Benin City, Nigeria." *African Journal of Reproductive Health* 2(2): 37–43.

Oostendorp, R. 2002. "Does Globalization Reduce the Gender Wage Gap?" Economic and Social Institute, Free University of Amsterdam, Amsterdam, Netherlands.

ORC-Macro. 2004. "Demographic and Health Surveys (DHS) Database." Data from various years. [Retrieved on November 30, 2004, from www.measuredhs.com].

Orlando, M. B. 2004. "Success Stories in Policy Interventions towards High Quality Universal Primary Education." United Nations Millennium Project, Task Force on Education and Gender Equality Background Paper. United Nations, New York.

Ostro, B. J., M. Sanchez, C. Aranda, and G. S. Eskeland. 1995. "Air Pollution and Mortality Results from Santiago, Chile." World Bank Policy Research Paper 1453. World Bank, Washington, D.C.

Oxaal, Z., and S. Baden. 1997. "Gender and Empowerment: Definitions, Approaches and Implications for Policy." BRIDGE Development and Gender Report 40. University of Sussex, Institute of Development Studies, Brighton, U.K.

Panda, P. 2002. "Rights-Based Strategies in the Prevention of Domestic Violence." ICRW Working Paper 344. International Center for Research on Women, Washington, D.C.

Parikh, J., and V. Laxmi. 2000. "Biofuels, Pollution and Health Linkages: A Survey of Rural Tamilnadu." *Economic and Political Weekly* 35(47): 4125–37.

Parker, S. W., and C. Pederzini. 2000. "Gender Differences in Education in Mexico." World Bank Departmental Working Paper 21023. Washington, D.C.

Paul-Majumder, P., and A. Begum. 2000. "The Gender Imbalances in the Export Oriented Garment Industry in Bangladesh." PRR Gender and Development Working Paper Series No. 12. World Bank: Washington, D.C.

Payne, L. 1998. *Re-Building Communities in a Refugee Settlement: A Casebook from Uganda.* Oxford, U.K.: Oxfam.

Pearce, J. 1998. "From Civil War to 'Civil Society': Has the end of the Cold War brought peace to Central America?" *International Affairs* 74(3): 587–615.

Pickup, F., S. Williams, and C. Sweetman. 2001. *Ending Violence against Women: A Challenge for Development and Humanitarian Work.* Oxford, U.K.: Oxfam.

Pitt, M. and S. R. Khandker. 1998. "The Impact of Group-based Credit Programs on Poor Households in Bangladesh: Does the Gender of Participants Matter?" *Journal of Political Economy* 106: 958–96.

Platteau, J. P. 1997. "Reforming Land Rights in Sub-Saharan Africa." *Journal for Entwicklungspolitik* 13(1): 57–98.

Population Council and ICRW (International Center for Research on Women). 2000. "Adolescent Girls' Livelihoods. Essential Questions, Essential Tools: A Report on a Workshop." Population Council and ICRW, New York and Washington, D.C.

Population Reference Bureau. 2000. "The World's Youth 2000." Population Reference Bureau, Washington, D.C.

———. 2001. "Abandoning Female Genital Cutting: Prevalence, Attitudes, and Efforts to End the Practice." Population Reference Bureau, Washington, D.C.

Prasad, S. 1996. "The Medico-Legal Response to Violence against Women in India: Implications for Women's Citizenship." Paper presented at the International Conference on Violence, Abuse and Women's Citizenship, November 10–15, Brighton, U.K.

Prosterman, R. L., and T. Hanstad. 2003. *Land Reform in the 21st Century: New Challenges, New Responses.* RDI Reports on Foreign Aid and Development 117. Rural Development Institute, Seattle

PROWID (Promoting Women in Development). 1999. *Elimination of Violence through Research and Education: Promoting Women's Human Rights in Bulgaria.* Report-in-Brief. Washington, D.C.: International Center for Research on Women and Center for Development and Population Activities.

Psacharopoulos, G., and H. A. Patrinos. 2002. "Returns to Investment in Education: A Further Update." Policy Research Working Paper 2881. World Bank, Washington, D.C.

Public Health Working Group of the Microbicide Initiative. 2002. *The Public Health Benefits of Microbicides in Lower-Income Countries.* New York: Rockefeller Foundation.

Pyne, H. H., M. Claeson, and M. Correia. 2002. *Gender Dimensions of Alcohol Consumption and Alcohol-Related Problems in Latin America and the Caribbean.* World Bank Discussion Paper 433. Washington, D.C.: World Bank.

Quimsumbing, A. 2003. "Resources at Marriage and Intrahousehold Allocation: Evidence from Bangladesh, Ethiopia, Indonesia, and South Africa." *Oxford Bulletin of Economics and Statistics* 65(3): 283–327.

Quimsumbing, A., and B. de la Briere. 2000. "Women's Assets and Intrahousehold Allocation in Bangladesh: Testing Measures of Bargaining Power." Food Consumption and Nutrition Division Discussion Paper 86. International Food Policy Research Institute, Washington, D.C.

Quimsumbing, A. R., and J. Maluccio. 2000. "Intrahousehold Allocation and Gender Relations: New Empirical Evidence from Four Developing Countries." FCND Discussion Paper 84. IFPRI, Washington, D.C.

Quimsumbing, A. R., J.P. Estudillo, and K. Otsuka. 2004. *Land and Schooling: Transferring Wealth across Generations.* Baltimore, Md.: The Johns Hopkins University Press and the International Food Policy Research Institute.

Quimsumbing, A. R., L. Haddad, and C. Peña. 2001. "Are Women Overrepresented among the Poor? An Analysis of Poverty in Ten Developing Countries." Food Consumption and Nutrition Division Discussion Paper 115. International Food Policy Research Institute, Washington, D.C.

Quimsumbing, A. R., K. Hallman, and M. T. Ruel. 2003. "Maquiladoras and Market Mamas: Women's Work and Childcare in Guatemala City and Accra." Food Consumption and Nutrition Division Discussion Paper 153. International Food Policy Research Institute, Washington, D.C.

Quisumbing, A. R., E. Payongayong, J. Aidoo, and K. Otsuka. 2001. "Women's Land Rights in the Transition to Individualized Ownership: Implications for the Management of Tree Resources in Western Ghana." *Economic Development and Cultural Change* 50(1): 157–82.

Raju, S., and A. Leonard, eds. 2000. *Men As Supportive Partners in Reproductive Health: Moving from Myth to Reality.* New Delhi, India: Population Council.

Rao Gupta, G. 2000. "Gender, Sexuality, and HIV/AIDS: The What, the Why, and the How." Plenary address at the 13th International AIDS Conference, Durban, South Africa.

Rao Gupta, G. and E. Weiss. 1994. *Bridging the Gap: Addressing Gender and Sexuality in HIV Prevention.* Washington, D.C.: International Center for Research on Women.

Ravallion, M., and D. van de Walle. 2004. "Land Allocation in Vietnam's Agrarian Transition Part 2: Introducing a Land Market." EWP 03/04. Institute for Fiscal Studies and Center for the Evaluation of Development Policies, London.

Razavi, S. 1997. "Fitting Gender into Development Institutions." *World Development* 25(7): 1111–25.

———. 2004. "Agrarian Change, Land Tenure Reform, and Gender Equality." mimeo. United Nations Research Institute for Social Development, Geneva.

Razavi, S., and C. Miller. 1995. "Gender Mainstreaming: A Study of Efforts by the UNDP, the World Bank, and the ILO to Institutionalize Gender Issues." Social Effects of Globalization paper 4. United Nations Research Institute for Social Development, Geneva.

Reed, H. E., M. A. Koblinsky, W. H. Mosley, Committee on Population, and the National Research Council. 2000. *The Consequences of Maternal Morbidity and Maternal Mortality: Report of a Workshop.* Washington, D.C.: National Academy Press.

Regmi, S.C., and B. Fawcett. 1999. "Integrating Gender Needs into Drinking-Water Projects in Nepal." *Gender and Development* 7(3): 62–72.

Rehn, E., and E. Johnson Sirleaf. 2002. *Women, War, Peace: The Independent Experts' Assessment on the Impact of Armed Conflict on Women and Women's Roles in Peace-Building.* New York: United Nations Development Fund for Women.

Reyna, C., and E. Toche. 1999. *La inseguridad en el Perú.* Serie Políticas Sociales 29. Santiago, Chile: Economic Commission for Latin American and the Caribbean.

Ridker, R., ed. 1997. *Determinant of Educational Achievement and Attainment in Africa: Findings form Nine Case Studies.* Sustainable Development Publication Series, Technical Paper 62. Washington, D.C.: USAID, Office of Sustainable Development, Bureau for Africa.

Rivington, D. 2004. Email correspondence on institutional efforts to mainstream gender equality. Development Counselor, Permanent Mission of Canada to the United Nations. September 29. New York.

Rodgers, K. 1994. "Wife Assault: The Findings of a National Survey." *Juristat Service Bulletin* 14(9): 1–21.

Rodgers, Y. 1999. "Protecting Women and Promoting Equality in the Labor Market: Theory and Evidence." Policy Research Report on Gender and Development Working Paper Series 6. World Bank, Washington, D.C.

Romkens, R. 1997. "Prevalence of Wife Abuse in the Netherlands: Combining Quantitative and Qualitative Methods in Survey Research." *Journal of Interpersonal Violence* 12: 99–125.

Rose, P., G. Yoseph, A. Berihum, and T. Nuresu. 1997. *Gender and Primary Schooling in Ethiopia.* Research Report 31. Brighton, U.K: University of Sussex, Institute of Development Studies.

Rosen, S., and J. R. Vincent. 1999. "Household Water Resources and Rural Productivity in Sub-Saharan Africa: A Review of the Evidence." Harvard Institute for International Development Paper DDP 673. Harvard University, Cambridge, Mass.

Rubery, J., D. Grimshaw, and H. Figuereido. 2002. "The Gender Pay Gap and Gender Mainstreaming Pay Policy in EU Member States." University of Manchester Institute of Science and Technology, School of Management, European Work and Employment Research Centre, Manchester, U.K.

Rugh, A. 2000. *Starting Now: Strategies for Helping Girls Complete Primary.* SAGE Project Technical Report 1. Academy for Educational Development. Washington, D.C.

Sachs, J., J. McArthur, G. Schmidt-Traub, C. Bahadur, M. Faye, and M. Kruk. 2004. "MDG Needs Assessment: Country Case Studies of Bangladesh, Cambodia, Ghana, Tanzania, and Uganda." January draft of UN Millennium Project Working paper. UN Millennium Project, New York.

Safa, H. 1995. *The Myth of the Male Breadwinner.* Boulder, Colo.: Westview Press.

Sancho-Liao, N. 1993. "Clutching a Knifeblade: Human Rights and Development from Asian Women's Perspective." In H. O'Connell, ed., *Women and Conflict.* Oxford, U.K.: Oxfam.

Sandler, J. 1997. "UNIFEM's Experiences in Mainstreaming for Gender Equality." Paper presented at UNICEF Meeting of Gender Focal Points, May 5-9.

———. 2003. "How Can the Millennium Development Goals Make Development Gender-responsive?" Presentation to the Interaction Conference session on Gender, Poverty and the Millennium Development Goals, May 19, Washington, D.C.

Sansone, R., M. Wiederman, and L. Sansone. 1997. "Health Care Utilization and History of Trauma among Women in a Primary Care Setting." *Violence and Victims* 12(2): 165–72.

Satheesh, P. V. 1997. "History in the Making: Women Design and Manage an Alternative Public Distribution System." *Forests, Trees and People Newsletter* (34): 1–4.

Schuler, S., S. Hashemi, and S. Badal. 1998. "Men's Violence against Women in Rural Bangladesh: Undermined or Exacerbated by Microcredit Programs?" *Development in Practice* 8(2): 148–57.

Schuler, S. R., S. Hashemi, and A. Riley. 1997. "The Influence of Women's Changing Roles and Status in Bangladesh's Fertility Transition: Evidence from a Study of Credit Programs and Contraceptive Use." *World Development* 25(4): 563–75.

Schuler, S., S. Hasemi, A. Riley, and S. Akhter. 1996. "Credit Programs, Patriarch and Men's Violence Against Women in Rural Bangladesh." *Social Science and Medicine* 42(12): 1729–42.

Schultz, T. P. 1993. "Returns to Women's Schooling." In E. King and M.A. Hill, eds., *Women's Education in Developing Countries: Barriers, Benefits, and Policy*. Baltimore Md.: Johns Hopkins University Press.

———. 2001. "Why Governments Should Invest More to Educate Girls." *World Development* 30(2): 207–25.

Seager, J. 2003. *The Penguin Atlas of Women in the World*, Third Edition. New York: Penguin Books.

Seguino, S. 1997. "Export-led Growth and the Persistence of Gender Inequality in the NICs." In J. Rives and M. Yousefi, eds., *Economic Dimensions of Gender Inequality: A Global Perspective*. Westport, Conn.: Greenwood Press.

———. 2000. "Accounting for Asian Economic Growth: Adding Gender to the Equation." *Feminist Economics* 6(3): 27–58.

———. 2003. "Is Economic Growth Good for Well-being?: Evidence on Gender Effects in Latin America and the Caribbean, 1970-2000." Background paper commissioned by the UN Millennium Project Task Force on Education and Gender Equality.

Seguino, S., and C. Grown. 2003. "Feminist-Kaleckian Macroeconomic Policy for Developing Countries." University of Vermont and International Center for Research on Women, Brattleboro, Vt. and Washington, D.C.

Seifert, R. 1995. "War and Rape: A Preliminary Analysis." In A. Stiglmayer, ed., *Mass Rape: The War against Women in Bosnia-Herzegovina*. Lincoln, Neb.: University of Nebraska Press.

Sen, A. 2000. *Development as Freedom*. New York: Anchor Books.

Sen, G., and C. Grown. 1987. *Development, Crises and Alternative Visions: Third World Women's Perspectives*. New York: Monthly Review Press.

Sen, P. 1998. "Development Practice and Violence against Women." *Gender and Development* 6(3): 7-16.

Sharp, R. 2003. *Budgeting for Equity: Gender Budget Initiatives within a Framework of Performance Oriented Budgeting*. UNIFEM. Harare, Zimbabwe.

Sipahimlani, V. 1999. "Education in the Rural Indian Household: The Impact of Household and School Characteristics on Gender Differences." Working Paper 68. National Council of Applied Economic Research, New Delhi, India.

Skoufias, E., and B. McClafferty. 2003. "Is PROGRESA Working? Summary of the Results of an Evaluation by IFPRI." In A. R. Quisumbing, ed., *Household Decisions, Gender and Development: A Synthesis of Recent Research*. Washington, D.C.: International Food Policy Research Institute.

Smith, K. R. 1987. *Biofuels, Air Pollution and Health: A Global Review*. New York: Plenum.

———. 1998. *Indoor Air Pollution in India: National Health Impacts and Cost Effectiveness Intervention*. Mumbai, India: Indira Gandhi Institute for Developmental Research.

Smith, K. R., and S. Mehta. 2000. "The Burden of Disease from Indoor Air Pollution in Developing Countries: Comparison of Estimates." Paper presented at USAID/WHO

Global Technical Consultation on the Health Impacts of Indoor Air Pollution and Household Energy in Developing Countries, May 3–4, Washington, D.C.

South Africa, Department of Social Development. 2002a. *National Report on the Status of Older Persons: Report to the Second World Assembly of Aging.* Discussion paper. Pretoria: Government Printer.

———. 2002b. *Report of the Committee of Inquiry into a Comprehensive System of Social Security for South Africa.* Consolidated report. Government of the Republic of South Africa. Pretoria: Government Printer.

Sowerine, J. 1999. "New Land Rights and Women's Access to Medicinal Plants in Northern Vietnam." In I. Tinker and G. Summerfield, eds., *Women's Rights to House and Land: China, Laos, and Vietnam.* Boulder, Colo.: Lynne Rienner.

Spindel, C., E. Levy, and M. Connor. 2000. *With an End in Sight: Strategies from the UNIFEM Trust Fund to Eliminate Violence against Women.* New York: United Nations Development Fund for Women.

Standing, G. 1989. "Global Feminization through Flexible Labor." *World Development* 17(7): 1077–95.

———. 1999. "Global Feminization Revisited." *World Development* 27(7): 583–602.

Stanley, C. 1992. "Domestic Violence: An Occupational Impact Study." Unpublished paper. Domestic Violence Intervention Services, Inc., Tulsa, OK.

Stark, E., A. Flitcraft, D. Zuckerman, A. Grey, J. Robison, and W. Frazier. 1981. *Wife Abuse in the Medical Setting: An Introduction for Health Personnel.* Domestic Violence Monograph 7. Rockville, Md.: National Clearinghouse on Domestic Violence.

Stewart, S. 1995. "Working with a Radical Agenda: the Musasa Project." *Gender and Development* 3(1): 30–5.

Strickland, R. 2004. *To Have and To Hold: Women's Property Rights in the Context of HIV/ AIDS in sub-Saharan Africa.* International Center for Research on Women Working Paper, June. Washington, D.C.

Subbarao, K., and L. Rainey. 1995. "Social Gains from Female Education." *Economic Development and Cultural Change* 44(1): 105–28.

Subrahmanian, R. 2002. "Gender and Education: A Review of Issues for Social Policy." Social Policy and Development Program Paper 9. United Nations Research Institute for Social Development, Geneva.

Swamy, A., S. Knack, Y. Lee, and O. Azfar. 2001. "Gender and Corruption." *Journal of Development Economics* 64(1): 25–55.

Sweetman, C. 1998. "Editorial." *Gender and Development* 6(3): 2-8.

Swera, M. 2002. *The Difference Women Make: The Policy Impact of Women in Congress.* Chicago, Ill.: University of Chicago Press.

Tadele, F. 1996. "Sustaining Urban Development through Participation: An Ethiopian Case Study." In C. Sweetman, ed., *Women and Urban Settlement.* Oxford, U.K.: Oxfam.

Tansel, A. 1994. "Wage Employment, Earnings, and Returns to Schooling for Men and Women in Turkey." *Economics of Education Review* 13(4): 305–20.

Taylor, C. 1994. *Multiculturalism.* Princeton, N.J.: Princeton University Press.

The Global Gag Rule Impact Project. 2003. *Access Denied: U.S. Restrictions on International Family Planning.* Executive Summary. The Global Gag Rule Impact Project. Population Action International, Planned Parenthood Federation of America, EngenderHealth, and Pathfinder International, New York.

The Inter-Agency Group for Safe Motherhood. 1997. *The Safe Motherhood Action Agenda: Priorities for the Next Decade.* New York: Family Care International.

The Lancet. 2004. "Towards Evidence to Secure Reproductive Rights." *The Lancet* 363(9402): 1–75.

Thomas, D. 1992. "The Distribution of Income and Expenditure within the Household." Paper presented at IFPRI–World Bank Conference, *Intrahousehold Resource Allocation: Policy Issues and Research Methods*, February 12–14, Washington, D.C.

Thomas, S. 1991. "The Impact of Women on State Legislative Policies." *The Journal of Politics* 50(4): 958–76.

Tinker, I. 2002."Quotas for Women in Elected Legislatures: Does this Really Empower Women?" Paper presented at WGGP Gender and Transnational Networks Symposium October 17–19, University of Illinois Champaign/Urbana.

Tinker, I., and G. Summerfield. 1999. *Women's Rights to House and Land: China, Laos, Vietnam*. Boulder, Colo. and London: Lynne Rienner Publishers.

Torres, R. 2002. "Lifelong Learning: A New Momentum and a New Opportunity for Adult Basic Learning and Education (Able) in the South." Department for Democracy and Social Development, New Education Division Document 14. Swedish International Development Cooperation Agency (SIDA), Buenos Aires, Argentina.

Traverso, M. T. 2001. *Shrouded in Silence: Domestic Violence in Uruguay*. Washington, D.C.: Inter-American Development Bank.

Turshen, M. 2001. "The Political Economy of Rape." In C. Moser and F. Clark, eds., *Victors, Perpetrators or Actors?: Gender, Armed Conflict and Political Violence*. London: Zed Books.

Tzannatos, Z. 1999. "Women and Labor Market Changes in the Global Economy: Growth Helps, Inequalities Hurt, and Public Policy Matters." *World Development* 27(3): 551–69.

UIS (UNESCO Institute for Statistics). 2000. *Education for All Year 2000 Assessment: A Statistical Document*. International Consultative Forum on Education for All and UNESCO. Paris.

Ulrich, J. 2000. "Confronting Gender-Based Violence with International Instruments: Is a Solution to the Pandemic within Reach?" *Indiana Journal of Global Legal Studies* 7(2): 629–54.

UN (United Nations). 1979. *Convention on the Elimination of All Forms of Discrimination against Women*. UN Document A/34/46. New York.

———. 1993. *Declaration on the Elimination of Violence against Women*. UN Document A/48/49. New York.

———. 1994. "Report from the International Conference on Population and Development." New York.

———. 1995. "Beijing Declaration and Platform for Action." The Fourth World Conference on Women, September 4–15, Beijing.

———. 1998. Rome Statute of the International Criminal Court. UN Document A/CONF 183/9*. New York.

———. 2000. *The World's Women 2000: Trends and Statistics*. United Nations Department of Economic and Social Affairs. New York.

———. 2002a. *Gender Mainstreaming: An Overview*. New York: UN Office of the Special Adviser on Gender Issues.

———. 2002b. "United Nations Millennium Development Goals Data and Trends, 2002." Report of the Inter-Agency Expert Group on MDG Indicators. Statistics Division, Department of Economic and Social Affairs. New York.

———. 2004a. "Goals, Targets and Indicators." UN Millennium Indicators Database. Washington, D.C. [Retrieved on December 1, 2004, from UN statistical database at http://millenniumindicators.un.org/unsd/mi/mi_goals.asp].

———. 2004b. "Statistical Division–Common Database." United Nations, New York. [Retrieved August 23, 2004, from http://unstats.un.org/unsd/cdb/etc/logon.asp?rpage=%2Funsd%2Fcdb%2Fcdb%5Fadvanced%5Fdata%5Fextract%2Easp%3F&type=4].

UNAIDS. 2003a. *Access to HIV Prevention: Closing the Gap.* Global HIV Prevention Working Group, Geneva.

———. 2003b. *Progress Report on the Global Response to the HIV/AIDS Epidemic, 2003.* Geneva.

———. 2004. *Report on the Global AIDS Epidemic.* Geneva.

UNAIDS (Joint United Nations Programme on HIV/AIDS) and WHO (World Health Organization). 2004. *The AIDS Epidemic Update.* Geneva: UNAIDS.

UNDAW (United Nations Division for the Advancement of Women). 1999. *1999 World Survey on the Role of Women in Development: Globalization, Gender, and Work.* New York.

———. 2003. "The Role of Men and Boys in Achieving Gender and Equality." Report of the Expert Group Meeting, October 21–24, Brasilia, Brazil.

———. 2004. "Implementing The Convention on the Elimination of All Forms of Discrimination against Women." October 2, Geneva.

UNDP (United Nations Development Programme). 1995. *Human Development Report 1995.* New York: Oxford University Press.

———. 2000. *Women's Political Participation and Good Governance: 21st Century Challenges.* New York.

———. 2002. *Human Development Report 2002: Human Rights and Human Developemnt.* New York: Oxford University Press.

———. 2003. *Transforming the Mainstream: Gender in UNDP.* New York.

UNESCO (United Nations Educational, Scientific and Cultural Organization). 1999. *UNESCO Statistical Yearbook.* Paris.

———. 2004. *EFA Global Monitoring Report 2003/4.* Paris.

UNESCO/NEPAD (United Nations Educational, Scientific and Cultural Organization and New Partnership for Africa's Development). 2003. "NEPAD Human Resource Development with Special Reference to Female Participation in Education." Paper presented at Expert Meeting, December 10–12, Geneva.

UNFPA (United Nations Fund for Population Activities). 2003a. "Securing Essential Supplies." New York. [www.unfpa.org/supplies/essentials/2a.htm].

———. 2003b. *Making 1 Billion Count: Investing in Adolescents' Reproductive Health and Rights. State of the World Population 2003.* New York: UNFPA.

UNFPA and EngenderHealth. 2003. *Obstetric Fistula Needs Assessment Report: Findings from Nine African Countries.* New York: UNFPA.

UN-HABITAT (United Nations Human Settlements Programme). 2001a. *Cities in a Globalizing World: Global Report on Human Settlements 2001.* London and Sterling, Va.: Earthscan Publications.

———. 2002. *Housing Rights Legislation: Review of International and National Legal Instruments.* UN Housing Rights Programme, Report 1. Nairobi.

———. 2004. "Global Campaign for Secure Tenure. Implementing the Habitat Agenda: Adequate Shelter for All." Nairobi. [www.un-habitat.org/campaigns/tenure/tenure.asp].

UNHCR (United Nations High Commission on Refugees). 1995. *Sexual Violence against Refugees: Guidelines on Prevention and Response.* Geneva.

———. 2003. *Sexual and Gender-Based Violence against Refugees, Returnees and Internally Displaced Persons: Guidelines for Prevention and Response.* Geneva.

UNHCR and SCF (United Nations High Commission on Refugees and Save the Children Fund). 2002. *Note for Implementing and Operational Partners on Sexual Violence and Exploitation: The Experience of Refugee Children in Guinea, Liberia and Sierra Leone.* Geneva: UNHCR.

UNICEF (United Nations Children's Fund). 1999. *The State of the World's Children 1999.* New York.

———. 1999. "Women in Transition." Regional Monitoring Report 6. UNICEF International Child Development Center (later renamed the Innocenti Research Center), Florence.

———. 2000. *Domestic Violence against Women and Girls.* Innocenti Digest, 6. Florence, Italy: Innocenti Research Center.

———. 2001. "Fourth Consolidated Report to the Government of Norway on the UNICEF African Girls' Education Initiative." New York: UNICEF Program Division/ Education Section.

———. 2002. "Case Studies on Girls' Education." New York.

———. 2003a. "Support for Water, Sanitation and Hygiene at Schools Accelerated Efforts towards Girls' Education." Draft paper for discussion. New York.

———. 2003b. *The State of the World's Children 2004.* New York: UNICEF.

———. 2004. "Quality Education and Gender Equality." Background paper for Workshop 1, International Conference on Education, 47th Session, September 8–11, Geneva.

UNIFEM (United Nations Development Fund for Women). 1999. "Women @ Work to End Violence: Voices in Cyberspace." Women, INK and UNIFEM, New York.

———. 2000. *Progress of the World's Women 2000.* New York: UNIFEM.

———. 2001. *Picturing a Life Free of Violence: Media and Communications Strategies to End Violence against Women.* New York.

———. 2003a. *Not a Minute More: Ending Violence against Women.* New York.

———. 2003b. *Progress of the World's Women 2002.* Volume 2. New York.

———. 2003c. "Women's Right to Land and Sustainable Livelihood in Kyrgyzstan." New York.

UNIFEM (United Nations Development Fund for Women), World Bank, ADB (Asian Development Bank), UNDP (United Nations Development Program), and DFID/ UK (Department for International Development, United Kingdom). 2004. *A Fair Share for Women: Cambodia Gender Assessment.* Phnom Penh, Cambodia.

UN Millennium Project. 2004a. Background paper on the Cases of Malaysia and Sri Lanka for the Task Force on Child Health and Maternal Health. New York.

———. 2004b. "Millennium Development Goals Needs Assessment." Background paper for *Ending Africa's Poverty Trap.* New York.

———. 2004c. "Millennium Development Goals Needs Assessment, Tajikistan." Dushanbe, Tajikistan: United Nations.

———. 2004d. "From Promises to Action: Interim Report on Gender Equality of the Task Force on Education and Gender Equality." New York.

———. 2005a. *Investing in Development: A Practical Plan to Achieve the Millennium Development Goals.* New York.

———. 2005b. *Who's Got the Power? Transforming Health Systems for Women and Children.* New York.

———. 2005c. *Toward Universal Primary Education: Investments, Incentives, and Institutions.* New York.

———. 2005d. *Halving Hunger: It Can Be Done.* New York.

United Cities and Local Governments. 2004. Database. Barcelona. [www.cities-localgovernments.org/uclg/].

United Nations General Assembly. 2003. "The Empowerment of Women and Integration of Gender Perspectives in the Promotion of Economic Growth, Poverty Eradication and Sustainable Development." Report of the Secretary-General (A/58/50/Rev.1 and Corr.1). New York.

United Nations Secretariat. 2004. "Gender Mainstreaming in Operational Work of the United Nations System." Substantive session of 2004 E/2004/CRP.1. New York.

United Nations Secretary-General. 2004. "Report of the Secretary-General on Review and Appraisal of the System-wide Implementation of the Economic and Social Council's Agreed Conclusions 1997/2 on Mainstreaming the Gender Perspective into All Policies and Programmes in the United Nations System." Substantive session of 2004 (E/2004/59). United Nations Economic and Social Council, New York.

Unterhalter, E., E. Kioko-Echessa, R. Pattman, R. Rajagopalan, and F. N'Jai. 2004. "Scaling Up Girls' Education: Towards a Scorecard on Girls' Education in the Commonwealth." A paper commissioned by the Commonwealth Secretariat from the Beyond Access Project. University of London, Institute of Education and Oxfam U.K., London.

van Ginneken, W. 1999. "Social Security for the Informal Sector: A New Challenge for the Developing Countries." *International Social Security Review* 52(January): 48–69.

van Koppen, B. 1990. "Women and the Design of Farmer Managed Irrigation Schemes: Experiences Provided by Two Projects in Burkina Faso." Paper presented at the International Workshop Design for Sustainable Farmer-Managed Irrigation Schemes in Sub-Saharan Africa, February, Wageningen Agricultural University, 5–8 February, Wageningen, Netherlands.

Vandermoortele, J. 2001. "Towards Gender-Responsive Budgeting: Are User Fees and Narrow Targeting Gender Neutral?" UNDP, New York.

Vandermoortele, J., and E. Delmonica. 2000. "Education 'Vaccine' against HIV/AIDS." *Current Issues in Comparative Education* 3(1).

Vanek, J. 2004. "Statistics and Gender Equality Indicators." Paper commissioned by the UN Millennium Project Task Force on Education and Gender Equality. United Nations Millennium Project, New York

ver Beek, K. A. 2001. "Maquiladoras: Exploitation or Emancipation? An Overview of the Situation of Maquiladora Workers in Honduras." *World Development* 29(9): 1553–67.

Villanueva, Z. 1997. "Legislative Reform and Legal Treatment of Domestic Violence: San Jose, Costa Rica." Paper presented at the Inter-American Development Bank conference, Domestic Violence in Latin America and the Caribbean: Costs, Programs and Policies, October 20–1, Washington, D.C.

Vyasulu, P., and V. Vyasulu. 2000. "Women in the Panchayati Raj: Grassroots Democracy in India." In United Nations Development Programme, *Women's Political Participation and Good Governance: 21st Century Challenges.* New York: UNDP.

Walker, C. 2003. "Piety in the Sky? Gender Policy and Land Reform in South Africa." *Journal of Agrarian Change* 3(1): 113–48.

Walker, E., A. Gelfand, W. J. Katon, M.P. Koss, M. Von Korff, D. Bernstein, and J. Russo. 1999. "Adult Health Status of Women with Histories of Childhood Abuse and Neglect." *American Journal of Medicine* 107: 332–9.

Walker, L., and S. Robinson, eds. 1996. "Report: A Costing Framework for the Protocol on Child Abuse and Neglect." IDASA. Institute for Child and Family Development, Cape Town.

Wallace, T. 1993. "Refugee Women: Their Perspectives and Our Responses." In H. O'Connell, ed., *Women and Conflict.* Oxford, U.K.: Oxfam.

Ward, J. 2002. "If Not Now, When? Addressing Gender-Based Violence in Refugee, Internally Displaced, and Post-Conflict Settings: A Global Overview." Paper presented at Reproductive Health for Refugees Consortium, April 30, New York.

Watts, C., and C. Zimmerman. 2002. "Violence against Women: Global Scope and Magnitude." *The Lancet* April 6.

Whitehead, A. 2003. "Failing Women, Sustaining Poverty: Gender in Poverty Reduction Strategy Papers." Report for the UK Gender and Development Network (GADN). GADN and Christian Aid, London.

Whitehead, A., and N. Kabeer. 2001. "Living with Uncertainty: Gender, Livelihoods and Pro-Poor Growth in Rural Sub-Saharan Africa." Institute of Development Studies Working Paper 134. University of Sussex, Institute of Development Studies, Brighton, U.K.

Whitehead, A., and D. Tsikata. 2003. "Discourses on Women's Land Rights in Sub-Saharan Africa: The Implications of the Re-turn to the Customary." *Journal of Agrarian Change* 3(1,2): 67–112.

WHO (World Health Organization). 1996. "Violence against Women. WHO Consultation." Geneva,.

———. 1997a. *Coverage of Maternity Care: A Listing of Available Information*. Document WIIO/RHT/MSM/96.28. Geneva.

———. 1997b. "Violence against Women: A Priority Issue Information Pack." Geneva. [Retrieved March 4, 2004 from www.who.int/gender/violence/vawpriority/en/].

———. 1997c. "Unsafe Abortion: Global and Regional Estimates of Incidence of and Mortality Due to Unsafe Abortion." WHO/RHT/MSM/97.16. Geneva.

———. 1998a. *Female Genital Mutilation: A Joint WHO/UNICEF/UNFPA Statement*. Geneva.

———. 1998b. "Progress in Reproductive Health Research #45." Newsletter published by HRP (the UNDP/UNFPA/WHO/World Bank Special Programme of Research, Development and Research Training in Human Reproduction). Geneva.

———. 1999a. "WHO Multi-Country Study of Women's Health and Domestic Violence: Core Protocol." WHO/EIP/GPE/99.3. Global Programme on Evidence for Health Policy, Geneva.

———. 2002a. "WHO Multi-Country Study on Women's Health and Domestic Violence against Women." Department of Gender and Women's Health, Geneva.

———. 2002b. "World Report on Violence and Health." Geneva. [www5.who.int/violence_injury_prevention/main.cfm?p=0000000117].

———. 2003. *Safe Abortion: Technical and Policy Guidance for Health Systems*. Geneva.

WHO/UNICEF/UNPFA. 2003. *Maternal Mortality in 2000: Estimates Developed by WHO, UNICEF, and UNFPA*. Geneva.

WIEGO (Women in Informal Employment Globalizing and Organizing). 2001. *Addressing Informality, Reducing Poverty: a Policy Response to the Informal Economy*. Cambridge, Mass.

———. 2002. "Fact Sheets on Informal Economy." [www.wiego.org].

Wisner, C. L., T. Gilmer, L. Saltzman, and T. Zink. 1999. "Intimate Partner Violence against Women: Do Victims Cost Health Plans More?" *The Journal of Family Practice* 48(6): 439–44.

WISTAT (Women's Indicators and Statistics). 1999. *Wistat 4*. New York. Database, Version 4. (United Nations Statistics Division, Department of Economics and Social Affairs CD-ROM).

Women's Commission for Refugee Women and Children. 2002. *UNHCR's Policy on Refugee Women and Guidelines on their Protection: An Assessment of Ten Years of Implementation*. New York.

World Bank. 1993. *World Development Report 1993: Investing in Health*. New York City: Oxford University Press.

———. 1996. "Implementing the World Bank's Gender Policies." Progress Report 1. Washington, D.C.

————. 1999. "Gender and Transport: A Rationale for Action." PREM Notes. Washington, D.C.

————. 2000. *World Development Report 2000/01: Attacking Poverty.* New York: Oxford University Press.

————. 2001a. *Engendering Development through Gender Equality in Rights, Resources and Voice.* Policy Research Report. New York: Oxford University Press.

————. 2001b. "Gender." In *Poverty Reduction Strategy Sourcebook.* Washington, D.C.

————. 2002a. "Caribbean Youth Development: Issues and Policy Directions." Washington, D.C.

————. 2002b. "Education for Dynamic Economies: Action Plan to Accelerate Progress towards Education for All." Washington, D.C.

————. 2002c. "Integrating Gender into the World Bank's Work: A Strategy for Action." Washington, D.C.

————. 2002d. "Land Use Rights and Gender Equality in Vietnam." Promising Approaches to Engendering Development Series #1. Washington, D.C.

————. 2003a. *Breaking the Conflict Trap: Civil War and Development Policy.* New York: Oxford University Press.

————. 2003b. "Empowerment through Mobilization of Poor Women on a Large Scale. Case Study on the Self Employed Women's Association (SEWA), India." Washington, D.C.

————. 2003c. *Gender Equality and the Millennium Development Goals.* Washington, D.C.

————. 2003d. "Implementation of the Gender Mainstreaming Strategy: FY'02." First Annual Monitoring Report. Washington, D.C.

————. 2003e. "The First Ghana Community Water and Sanitation Project: Poverty and Gender Issues." Africa Region Findings 232. Washington, D.C.

————. 2003f. *The Social Dimensions of Poverty Reduction: A World Bank Strategy for Social Development.* Washington, D.C.

————. 2004a. "Implementing the Bank's Gender Mainstreaming Strategy." Second Annual Monitoring Report. Washington, D.C.

————. 2004b. "Rwanda Summary Gender Profile." Washington, D.C. [Retrieved September 20, 2004, from www.worldbank.org/afr/gender/rwanda.pdf].

————. 2004c. "South Africa Summary Gender Profile." Washington, D.C. [Retrieved September 20, 2004, from www.worldbank.org/afr/gender/southafrica.pdf].

————. 2004d. "The Marrakech Action Plan for Statistics: Better Data for Better Results—An Action Plan for Improving Development Statistics." Paper presented at the Second International Roundtable on Managing for Development Results, February, Washington, D.C.

————. 2004e. "World Bank Chile Summary Gender Profile." GenderStats Database of Gender Statistics. Washington, D.C. [Retrieved September 20, 2004, from http://devdata.worldbank.org/genderstats/genderRpt.asp?rpt=profile&cty=CHL,Chile&hm=home].

————. 2004f. "World Development Indicators." Washington, D.C. [http://devdata.worldbank.org/dataonline/].

Zarkov, D. 2001. "The Body of the Other Man: Sexual Violence and the Construction of Masculinity, Sexuality and Ethnicity in the Croatian Media." In C. Moser and F. Clark, eds., *Victims, Perpetrators or Actors? Gender, Armed Conflict and Political Violence.* London: Zed Books.

Zuckerman, E. 2001. "Why Engendering PRSPs Reduce Poverty and the Case of Rwanda." Discussion Paper 2001/112. World Institute for Development Economics Research, Helsinki.

———. 2002a. *A Primer on Poverty Reduction Strategy Papers and Gender.* Washington, D.C.: Gender Action.

———. 2002b. "'Engendering Poverty Reduction Strategy Papers (PRSPs): The Issues and the Challenges." *Gender and Development, An Oxfam Journal* 10(3).

———. 2002c. "Evaluation of Gender Mainstreaming in Advocacy Work on Poverty Reduction Strategy Papers (PRSPs)." Synthesis Report. Oxfam, Oxford, U.K.

Zuckerman, E., and A. Garrett. 2003. "Do Poverty Reduction Strategy Papers (PRSPs) Address Gender? A Gender Audit of 2002 PRSPs." Washington, D.C.: Gender Action.

Zwarteveen, M. Z. 1997. "Water: From Basic Need to Commodity. A Discussion on Gender and Water Rights in the Context of Irrigation." *World Development* 25(8): 1335–50.